Strategic Level Spiritual Warfare: A Modern Mythology?

A detailed evaluation of the biblical, theological and historical bases of spiritual warfare in contemporary thought.

Michael S B Reid

xulon
PRESS

Strategic Level Spiritual Warfare: A Modern Mythology?

A detailed evaluation of the biblical, theological and historical bases of spiritual warfare in contemporary thought.

by Michael S B Reid

Printed in the United States of America

Library of Congress Control Number: 2002116120

ISBN 1-591604-58-3

Xulon Press
11350 Random Hills Road
Suite 800
Fairfax, VA 22030
(703) 279-6511
XulonPress.com

To order additional copies, call 1-866-909-BOOK (2665).

TO

The body of believers worldwide, who are lovers of, and seekers after, truth. As Jesus Himself said, "If ye continue in my word, *then* are ye my disciples indeed; And ye shall know the truth, and the truth shall make you free" (John 8:31, 32).

"Out of his mouth went a sharp two-edged sword."

The conquering power of the gospel is in Christ himself; it does not lie with his ministers. The power with which Christ contends for the mastery against all the powers of darkness resides not with his servants, but dwells with himself. The two-edged sword of the Lord is in the mouth of the Lord. We shine, dear friends, -- such little twinkling stars as any of us are, -- we shine, and God blesses the shining; but if ever there is a soul saved, we have not saved it; and if ever there is an enemy of Christ who is wounded and slain, the deed is not done by our sword. By ourselves, we have no power; the really effectual work is done by Christ himself, and by him alone. The sword that goes forth out of our mouth is a poor blunt instrument, which can accomplish nothing; it is the sword that goes out of Christ's mouth that does everything in the great battle for the right. Notice how the right hand of Christ has to be used even to hold up these stars; ministers are not his right hand, they are only as stars that he holds up with his right hand. They derive all their power from him; but even when they are held up by his right hand, they are not the real warriors, it is not their strength with which the battle is fought and won; the power is in Christ himself, it is out of his mouth that there goeth forth the sharp two-edged sword that wins the victory.

C. H. Spurgeon, January 3rd, 1897

Metropolitan Tabernacle Pulpit, vol. 43 of 63.

CONTENTS

This project has used English (British) spelling, with the
exception of direct quotations which have corresponded exactly
with the original spelling.

FOREWORD – TL Osborn

My dear and esteemed friend, Brother Michael,

I commend you on the remarkable job that you have accomplished in presenting this sound, helpful and urgently needed work to the Christian world today. Your literary work is a testament to the degree to which many church leaders have failed to teach people the gospel of the New Testament and the revelation of redemption. This dearth of truth has sadly resulted in the proliferation of the quasi-pagan concepts being fostered by proponents of SLSW, and this 'other gospel' must be confronted by believers of the New Testament gospel.

I am appalled by all the demonic phobia that currently possesses so many pseudo-charismatic leaders who 'sound off' like public witchdoctors, with absolutely no solidity or valid information to support them. This is a serious scourge that proliferates among innocent and unlearned Christians who imagine themselves delving into profound high-level spirituality, when in reality they are simply toying with witchcraft. Accordingly, I am so grateful to you for being willing to dedicate so much time, effort and energy to building a repertoire of sound information for people to draw from.

Over the past 56 years, I have travelled to the nations of our world, the poor nations. I have dealt with tens of thousands of victims of witchcraft. I yearn in my heart to give them some truth that will bring to them peace and tranquillity, and that will purge their minds of the nonsense about evil spirits and a God who may turn on them at any moment. I know what they need. You are making available the information that is needed and I have no doubt that it will be a stabilising influence among sincere Pentecostals and Charismatics.

In chapter 6, your conclusions are powerfully stated and represent my doctrinal position completely. They constitute the reason for our 56 years of unprecedented success in over 80 nations.

During this time, I have proclaimed the miracle gospel to multitudes of practically every major religion on earth, addressing audiences of 20,000 to 300,000 people. The SLSW hypotheses are unbiblical variations of paganism in modern dress that have been totally unknown to me, they are alien, unbiblical concepts and therefore have had no part in our global success of leading tens of millions of people to faith in Jesus Christ.

I am pleased with each quote that you used from my book. I am glad that you have publicised the fact of my position so indelibly and unmistakably. It has enhanced my commitment to continue focussing my remaining years to share the essentials of Truth that Bible believing Christians must comprehend and embrace in order to continue what Jesus began.

Your special friend and co-worker with Christ,

T.L. Osborn

OSFO International

January 2002

FOREWORD – Charles Green

This book surprised me! When I picked it up, I expected it to be the average, dull presentation characterized by many religious theses. Instead, I found a presentation of the Gospel of Jesus Christ that is powerful, articulate and challenging.

Michael Reid makes the Biblical record clear on the subject of 'Strategic Level Spiritual Warfare.' He defines the strategy of those who advocate this new-found philosophy. He quotes their own words to tell what they believe, what they are doing and what they want to achieve. He disagrees without being personally disagreeable.

In this book, Dr. Reid makes it clear that God has not and does not struggle to defeat the devil and overcome his activity. He also points out and gives Bible evidence and examples to prove it— Jesus has defeated our foe and has given to us the power of His name as our authority over the devil and his crowd. We don't have to struggle, plead or 'bind.' We can speak the Word of authority and obtain great victories.

The author reminds us over and over, the 'power is in the product.' And the 'product' is the Gospel of Jesus Christ. It—the Gospel—is the power of God unto the Salvation of the soul, the healing of the body and the deliverance from every satanic work. He agrees that human experience is wonderful in creating testimonies, but that our personal experiences must not be used to create a theology the Bible does not teach and will not support. Michael Reid's cry in this book—'Back to the Bible!'

Don't let the length of the book scare you away. Open it, read it for one uninterrupted hour—and you will be 'hooked.' Michael Reid is to be commended for producing such a definitive and excellent work on this important subject.

Charles Green
Founding Pastor-Faith Church, New Orleans, Louisiana
President, Harvest Ministries to the World

PREFACE

Over the last twenty to thirty years, there has been a radical change in the whole perception of spiritual warfare within the Christian world, and the emergence of what has come to be known as Strategic-Level Spiritual Warfare ("SLSW"). Protagonists of SLSW describe it as a vital methodology empowering believers to overcome satanic powers as a necessary prelude to the work of evangelisation; opponents claim that it is without solid biblical foundation and is apparently based on the evaluation of experience and anecdotal evidence.

So, between such opposing views, what is the truth? Fired by the conviction that the concepts and teaching of SLSW have drawn people away from the eternal truths of scripture, I began my investigation. This work is the result. It was originally written as a dissertation in partial fulfilment of the requirements for a Doctor of Ministry degree at Oral Roberts University, Tulsa, Oklahoma. I intended to re-edit and publish these findings in a format that would appeal to a wider readership but, due to the demand for the full thesis from many pastors and church leaders worldwide, decided to proceed with publication of the academic text.

The study includes an evaluation of the biblical, theological and historical bases for the current teaching on SLSW within the wider context of spiritual warfare per se, together with a review of contemporary literature on the subject. The theological reflections in the concluding chapter represent my understanding of the very heart of the gospel. It is my earnest hope that this work will promote dialogue on the whole comprehension of SLSW within the body of Christ, leading many to review their practices in order to bring them into line with the true biblical perspective of New Testament church life. The devil is a subtle foe; he comes not only with outright lies but with half-truths, his purpose always being to deflect the believer from the simplicity of the gospel. It is my prayer that as you, my readers, refocus your understanding on what the Bible actually teaches about spiritual warfare, you may be strengthened in your faith, and enabled to live and walk in the reality of Christ's total victory over the devil and all demonic powers at Calvary.

There are many people who have contributed to this project. I would like to thank my project committee, Dr. Tom Mathew, Dr. Ken Mayton, and Dr. Roy Hayden, who made what seemed like an insurmountable task, manageable. In addition, I benefited from the expertise of Dr. Chuck Lowe, Dr. T. L. Osborn, Dr. Bill Faupel, and Dr. Terry Law, who were a source of inspiration. I am also grateful to the congregation of Peniel Church who have listened to my reflections on the many issues raised by this project, and especially to Carolyn Linnecar and Sheila Graziano for their research and computing help.

Finally, I gratefully acknowledge the constant support and encouragement of my wife, Ruth.

To God be all the Glory!

Michael S B Reid

September 2002

CHAPTER 1

INTRODUCTION

The Problem

In the recent history of the church worldwide there has been a remarkable upsurgence of interest in the spirit world. This new emphasis has captured the public imagination and "Strategic Level Spiritual Warfare" (SLSW) has been widely promoted as a vital new tool in evangelism. There has been a proliferation of populist writing on the subject allied with teaching seminars and international conventions. However, any rigorous academic analysis remains very limited and much SLSW teaching is apparently based on the evaluation of anecdotal evidence.

The purpose of this research project was, therefore, to measure and assess the impact of teaching a course on "spiritual warfare" to a sample population of pastors and church leaders. This included an evaluation of the biblical, theological and historical bases for the current teaching on SLSW within the context of the broader scope of "spiritual warfare" per se, together with a review of contemporary literature on the subject.

Statement of the Problem

The traditional teaching on spiritual warfare in most evangelical churches until about twenty years ago was based on Ephesians 6.[1] It was taught as part of fundamental church doctrine and believers were enjoined to put on the whole armour of God in order to stand against the wiles of the devil.[2] However, since the early 1980s, the Christian world has seen a radical change in its understanding of the term "spiritual warfare," and this has brought about a vast increase in the scope and influence of the subject. What has come to be described as SLSW is now viewed as a vital new methodology empowering believers, both as individuals and corporately, to

---

[1] For a systematic exposition of this chapter please refer to D. Martyn Lloyd-Jones, *The Christian Warfare: An Exposition of Ephesians 6:10 to 13* (Edinburgh: The Banner of Truth Trust, 1976); and D. Martyn Lloyd-Jones, *The Christian Soldier: An Exposition of Ephesians 6:10 to 20* (Edinburgh: The Banner of Truth Trust, 1977).

[2] Lloyd-Jones, *The Christian Soldier*, 11-25.

overcome the enemy in order to gain territory for the kingdom of God.[3]

The search for a new and effective approach to evangelism can be traced back to the problems faced by some missionaries abroad during the mid-twentieth century, who felt helpless in the face of resistance to the progress of the gospel and church growth. Many missionaries testified to their own powerlessness and the fact that numerous heathen tribes seemed to have real authority in the spirit realm. It appeared that their sorcerers performed miracles and their exorcists drove out evil spirits; Hindus and Muslims spoke in "tongues"; psychics apparently undertook bodily surgery. While some missiologists clung to the belief that their failure to compete was due to cultural, historical and sociological differences, others increasingly believed that it could be attributed to demonic influence.[4]

Missiologists from North America, a culture that is highly oriented toward technique and pragmatics,[5] looked for the key to a breakthrough in these nations.[6] Every new method for evangelism lifted hope, only to dash it again when, with the passage of time, it proved ineffective.[7] Then, in the mid-1980s, a number of popular books appeared which put forward the concept of "power evangelism."[8] A power encounter, such as Paul demonstrated in his

---

[3] George Otis Jr., *Informed Intercession: Transforming Your Community Through Spiritual Mapping and Strategic Prayer* (Ventura, CA: Renew Books, 1999), 55-75.

[4] David J. Garrard, "Contemporary Issues in Mission," class lecture notes, M.A. in Missiology, Mattersey Hall, England, Spring 2001, p. 22.

[5] Chuck Lowe, "Prayer, Evangelization and Spiritual Warfare," paper presented at the Inaugural Billy Graham Center Evangelism Round Table, Billy Graham Center, Wheaton College, Wheaton, Illinois, 19 Jan. 2001.

[6] Wagner quotes Donald Miller, in this context: "If Christianity is going to survive, it must continually reinvent itself, adapting its message to the members of each generation, along with their culture and geographical setting." Donald Miller, *Reinventing American Protestantism* (Berkeley, CA: University of California Press, 1997), 18; quoted in C. Peter Wagner, *Churchquake* (Ventura, CA: Regal Books, 1999), 18.

[7] David Hesselgrave, *Scripture and Strategy: The Use of the Bible in Post-Modern Church and Mission*, Evangelical Missiological Society Series, no. 1 (Pasadena, CA: William Carey Library, 1994), 88-89.

[8] For example, John Wimber, *Power Evangelism* (San Francisco, CA: Harper and Row, 1986).

confrontation with Elymas the sorcerer (Acts 13:8-12), was acclaimed as the answer for converting a once resistant people.[9]

John Wimber was one of the leading proponents of this doctrine, and co-authored the *MC510 Signs and Wonders* course in association with C. Peter Wagner. This had a significant impact throughout the Christian world and was taken to every continent. As a result of his own experiences and research on the mission field worldwide, Wagner observed that there was a direct correlation between church growth and the demonstration of signs and wonders.[10] The investigation of this relationship led Wagner to conclusions that contributed to the development of SLSW, which was hailed by its protagonists as the panacea for many of the problems encountered by missionaries on the field. It was promoted as being the key for the fulfillment of the Great Commission in their lifetime.[11]

At about this time Frank Peretti published his novel *This Present Darkness*, the impact of which was phenomenal. "It introduced hundreds of thousands of Christian novel readers to an extreme theological position which only diehard students of prayer and spiritual warfare would be familiar with. There is evidence that many of the readers began to take the contents seriously in relation to their Christian lives . . . It was a watershed, a moment of critical mass, for the doctrine of spiritual warfare."[12] Even Wagner, one of the main proponents of, and certainly the most prolific writer about SLSW, recognises the impact of Peretti's books. He states, "I am grateful for Frank Peretti who, through his fiction, raised many important questions in the minds of Christians across the theological spectrum in the 1980s. I believe that God providentially used him to prepare

---

[9]Edward Rommen, Introduction to *Spiritual Power and Missions: Raising the Issues*, ed., Edward Rommen, Evangelical Missiological Society Series, no. 3 (Pasadena, CA: William Carey Library, 1995), 1-2. Rommen argues that the subject of a spiritual power encounter against opposition is not new and has been discussed by Church Councils and Medieval missionaries.

[10]C. Peter Wagner, "MC510: Genesis of a Concept," in C. Peter Wagner, ed., *Signs & Wonders Today* (Altamonte Springs, FL: Creation House, 1987), 39-49.

[11]C. Peter Wagner, *Warfare Prayer: Strategies for Combating the Rulers of Darkness* (Crowborough, England: Monarch Publications, 1997), 45, 65.

[12]Roland Howard, *Charismania: When Christian Fundamentalism Goes Wrong* (London: Mowbray, 1997), 30.

the way for the insights about strategic-level spiritual warfare that are now coming from such non-fiction authors as John Dawson, Cindy Jacobs, Francis Frangipane . . ."[13]

This focus on the spirit realm within Christendom replicates a very similar driving emphasis in the secular world. The second half of the twentieth century and early years of the twenty-first century have witnessed an unparalleled increase of interest in the spirit world.[14] J. R. R. Tolkien was one of the modern pioneers of this genre; his trilogy, *The Lord of the Rings*, was first published in 1954. A recent article in the Reader's Digest states, "He created a world so astonishingly true to life that he included more than 100 pages of appendices filled with maps, calendars, genealogies and cultural anthropology. In fact, *The Lord of the Rings* established many of the symbols and archetypes that fantasy books and films would adapt over the next half-century."[15] Much more recently J. K. Rowling has produced the phenomenally successful Harry Potter series.[16] Both of these authors have engendered in the world of fiction what is essentially a parallel reality. As Catherine Butcher states in an article for *Christianity and Renewal,* "in settings like . . . Hogwarts and Tolkien's Wilderland, wizards and magic are literary devices. They help us to enter another world where the impossible happens; where life has a supernatural dimension; where principalities and powers are at war."[17]

---

[13]C. Peter Wagner, *Confronting the Powers: How the New Testament Church Experienced the Power of Strategic-Level Spiritual Warfare* (Ventura, CA: Regal Books, 1996), 74.

[14]For example, in respect to the recently released film, *The Fellowship of the Ring,* when "New Line made a short preview available at its website (lordoftherings.net) in April 1999, 1.7 million eager fans viewed it on the first day. After the site was relaunched in January, it received more than 350 million visitors over the next three months." Scott Smith, "Middle Earth," *Reader's Digest,* Dec. 2001, 94.

[15]Smith, 96.

[16]J. K. Rowling, *Harry Potter and the Philosopher's Stone* (New York: Arthur A. Levine Books, 1997); also by same author and publisher, *Harry Potter and the Chamber of Secrets* (1998), *Harry Potter and the Prisoner of Azakaban* (1999) and *Harry Potter and the Goblet of Fire* (2000).

[17]Catherine Butcher and Mark Stibbe, "Harry Potter: Friend or Foe?" *Christianity and Renewal,* Dec. 2001, 19.

The problem is that for many readers the dividing line between fact and fantasy has become increasingly blurred;[18] it is all too easy to transpose the same dualism into the real spiritual world and assume that the devil poses an actual threat to the Almighty God.[19] For example, in *The Handbook for Spiritual Warfare*, Ed Murphy authoritatively declares: "The universe exists in a state of cosmic-earthly conflict or spiritual warfare. Cosmic dualism is a reality: spiritual warfare exists in heaven. Earthly dualism is a reality: spiritual warfare rages on earth . . . From a biblical perspective, however, this dualism is revealed to be an on-going conflict waged on two fronts: God and His angelic kingdom confront Satan and his demonic kingdom, while the children of God contend with the children of Satan."[20] In the author's opinion, such a statement challenges such basic Christian concepts as the sovereignty, omnipotence and transcendence of God Almighty, as well as betraying an apparent lack of understanding of Christ's full and final victory over the devil and all his host at Calvary.[21]

SLSW encourages Christians to throw off the confines of a "Western rational worldview" and offers a dynamic spiritual

---

[18]Ibid. "These books are gripping the hearts of children who have never heard the Gospel, but who long for something supernatural to be revealed, battles to fight and adventures to live in." In the author's opinion, this problem has been exacerbated by the recent adaptation of such fiction for the big screen. With the advance of technology, special effects have become capable of reproducing the magic of fantasy in a way which is both tangible and convincing. Thus what was once locked into the realm of the individual imagination has been effectively translated into a supposed reality.

[19]Ibid. Mark Stibbe warns that, "The world of Harry Potter is a typically post-modern one where no moral absolutes exist. It is not like pre-Christian myths (where there are many redemptive analogies); rather, this is a world that is subversive anti-Christian and has nothing obviously redemptive about it. Put simply, it is a world with a witch but no lion."

[20]Edward F. Murphy, *The Handbook for Spiritual Warfare* (Nashville, TN: Thomas Nelson Publishers, 1996), 13.

[21]Clinton Arnold states, "The testimony of scripture from beginning to end is that Yahweh is sovereign. He created everything in heaven and on earth. All of the spiritual powers derive their life from him. He holds them in the palm of his hand and can do with them just as he wills. In fact, he has already revealed the final outcome of the battle. Christians are on the winning side." Clinton E. Arnold, *Spiritual Warfare: What Does the Bible Really Teach?* (London: Marshall Pickering, 1997), 8.

methodology to defeat evil powers.[22] In line with the current postmodern emphasis on the existential, it promotes the adoption of a more mystical approach to the revelation of truth, which gives considerable weight to a person's subjective interpretation of experience.[23] Jonathan Edwards warned in the eighteenth century:

> One erroneous principle, which scarce any has proved more mischievous to the glorious work of God, is a notion that it is God's manner in these days, to guide his saints, at least some that are more eminent, by inspiration, or immediate revelation. They suppose he makes known to them what shall come to pass hereafter, or what is his will that they should do, by impressions made upon their minds, either with or without texts of Scripture; whereby something is made known to them, that is not taught in Scripture.[24]

SLSW is promoted as a "new way" of addressing spiritual problems.[25] It involves such practices as warfare prayer / strategic-level intercession, Prayer marches, all-night intercessory prayer, prolonged fasting, pulling down spirits over nations, taking cities, spiritual mapping, identificational repentance, and the aggressive use of tongues (glossolalia). The basic premise underlying such techniques is the belief that demons and cosmic powers have established strongholds in people and/or regions which must be brought down before the message of salvation can be preached effectively.[26] It is, therefore, the duty of the church to engage, and overcome these powers in a spiritual battle for the hearts and minds of unbelievers, in order to advance the kingdom of God and see real

---

[22]Murphy, 7-8.

[23]Ibid., xiii.

[24]Jonathan Edwards, "Some Thoughts on Revival Concerning the Present Revival of Religion in New England and the Way in Which It Ought to be Acknowledged and Promoted; Humbly Offered to the Public, in a Treatise on that Subject," in vol. 1 of 2, *The Works of Jonathan Edwards*, rev. and corrected by Edward Hickman (Edinburgh: The Banner of Truth Trust, 1974), 404.

[25] Chuck Lowe, *Territorial Spirits and World Evangelisation?: A Biblical, Historical and Missiological Critique of Strategic Level Spiritual Warfare* (Fearn and Kent: Mentor and OMF, 1998), 10.

[26]Wagner quotes Edgardo Silvoso, "Evangelists begin to pray over cities before proclaiming the gospel there. Only after they are sure that spiritual powers over the region have been bound will they begin to preach." Edgardo Silvoso, "Argentina: Battleground of the Spirit," *World Christian*, Oct. 1989, 16; quoted in Wagner, *Warfare Prayer*, 27.

church growth. Thus, warfare prayer (more recently called "strategic-level intercession") has dominated numerous conventions, with multitudes turning up to nights of prayer and fasting.[27]

SLSW is also seen as a method of promoting spirituality in individual Christians. In Nigeria, for example, some groups are fasting for 120 days and only eating after sundown, a practice with striking parallels to the Moslem observance of Ramadan. In some instances, in order to meet the criteria for ministry, pastors have been expected to fast for a minimum of forty days every year. These customs result from the belief that God has said they are vital to spiritual growth.[28]

However, it is not only missionaries to Third World nations who have adopted SLSW as a tool. In 1987, Robert Reynolds, of *Moody* magazine, reported Stewart Custer's comments on spiritual warfare in the US, "I would attribute [it] to the New Age Movement ... People are pulling spiritualistic influences into society, so there's going to be more attention to it. It used to be you could hardly find anyone involved in spiritism in this country. Now the whole thing is wide open; Ouija boards are sold as parlor games. Spiritual warfare is a reaction against this."[29] In his assessment of how spiritual warfare came into the United States, Jonas Clark writes: "The restoration of the truth about battling demonic principalities and powers came out of the intercessor's prayer closet and from those who were in the deliverance ministry . . . This wrestling, that began in the prayer closet came out when people got hold of the prayer of agreement and the understanding of their authority as believers (Lev. 26:8). Slowly a militancy and fervency began to be restored."[30]

---

[27]See, for example, George Otis Jr., *Transformations: A Documentary*, prod. Global Net Productions, 58 min., The Sentinel Group, 1999, videocassette. Otis promulgates the power of prayer and all-night prayer vigils as he answers the question, "Can you change the spiritual DNA of a community?" with examples from transformed communities in three continents.

[28]The author makes many overseas ministry trips, which include travels throughout much of the continents of Africa and South America, and bases these comments on personal observation over a period of thirty years.

[29]Robert Reynolds, "Is There Spiritual War?" *Moody*, July/Aug. 1997, 15-17.

[30]Jonas Clark, "Spiritual Warfare," *The Ambassador Journal Cyber Newsletter*, online posting, http://catchlife.org/spiritual_warfare.html; accessed 16 Dec. 2001. Wagner

Whilst most Christians would not deny that spiritual warfare is real, many are concerned with the emphases in today's teaching of SLSW,[31] and also with the new methodologies that are being propagated. To some, SLSW may appear as just another gimmick. David Hesselgrave writes enumerating a long list of evangelistic techniques, each of which initially purported to be "*the* best way to evangelise the world, proving itself to be *a* way of contributing to that goal, and thus yielding to another method elevated to *the* way."[32] The catalogue includes such strategies as Evangelism Explosion, Discipling a Whole Nation, the Church Growth Movement, Evangelism-in-Depth, and, the use of mass media.

Now, SLSW has captured the imagination of much of Christendom for the moment,[33] but no doubt will be deposed in due course.[34] However, the significance of SLSW is greater than its claim to be potentially, "a significant, relatively new spiritual technology

---

also ascribes his interest in the role of SLSW to the influence of Cindy Jacobs (co-founder of Generals of Intercession, "a missionary organization devoted to training in prayer and spiritual warfare") who introduced him to the concept in the early 1980s. C. Peter Wagner, "Practical Holiness," a sermon presented at Oral Roberts University Students' Chapel, Tulsa, Oklahoma. 16 Jan. 2001.

[31]This applies not only within the immediate context of SLSW practices. For example, some leaders in the SLSW movement take an extreme adversarial position in respect to certain aspects of the faith movement. In Murphy, 188, he states, "A repulsive new theology has developed in our day to justify a luxuriant lifestyle. Its emphasis is on this-world prosperity, an 'all this and heaven too' theology. 'Something good is going to happen to you.' 'Seed money.' 'Name it and claim it.' '. . . Speak the word of faith and it will be yours.' Such a prosperity doctrine is possible only in an advanced middle-class economy. I would like to see its advocates proclaim it among the starving Christians of Africa, Asia, Latin America and the thousands of true believers who are found among the homeless in the Western world." However, the truth is that the gospel lifts people from despair and failure in every aspect of their lives, as demonstrated, for example, in the ministry throughout the third world of Oral and Richard Roberts, T. L. Osborn, Benson Idahosa, Marilyn Hickey, and Terry Law.

[32]See Hesselgrave, 88-89 (original emphasis).

[33]As Rommen comments: "If tearing down strongholds is presented as a guarantee for evangelistic success, its popularity is no mystery." Rommen, 5.

[34]The author notes there are already signs that the influence of warfare prayer is waning; the restoration of apostolic authority and ministry and strategic-level intercessory prayer is the new order of the day.

God has given us to meet the greatest challenge to world missions since William Carey went to India more than 200 years ago."[35] Rather, as a new methodology, it is representative of a whole gamut of extra-biblical teaching which has infiltrated the church of Jesus Christ, in which experience-led opinions have taken the place of biblically-based convictions. It is for this reason that SLSW has been selected as the subject for this research project. As Sir Robert Anderson points out, "Opinions are our own, and should not be too firmly held. Truth is Divine and is worth living and dying for." He continues:

> Listening to the discordant voices that abound on every side, men are content to give heed only to the points on which the greater number appear to be agreed: and even these are held on sufferance until some new voice is raised to challenge them . . . How different from the spirit of the age is the language of the inspired Apostle! "Though WE or an ANGEL FROM HEAVEN preach any other gospel unto you than that which we have preached unto you, let him be accursed." Such warnings in Holy Writ are not the words of wild exaggeration. In the last days the new light which men seek for to dispel "the deepening gloom" will not be wanting: but it will prove a wrecker's fire, though seemingly accredited as the beacon light of truth.[36]

The Christian stands in truth; he dare not abandon the word of God as the only and all-sufficient basis for faith. As MacArthur comments:

> Whether our purpose is to lead men and women to saving faith in Jesus Christ, to teach God's word to believers, to refute error in the church, to correct and rebuild erring believers, or to train believers to live righteously, our supreme and sufficient resource is God's Word. It not only gives us the information to teach but shapes us into living examples of that truth . . . Through the convincing and convicting power of the Holy Spirit, Scripture is *God's own provision* for every spiritual truth and moral principle that men need to be saved, to be equipped to live righteously in this present life and to

---

[35]Wagner, *Confronting the Powers*, 89.

[36]Sir Robert Anderson, preface to *The Gospel and Its Ministry: A Handbook of Evangelical Truth*, 13th ed. (London: Pickering and Inglis, 1969), vi-vii.

hear one day in the life to come, "Well done good and faithful servant . . . enter into the joy of your Master" (Matthew 25:21).[37]

For the Jewish people, physical landmarks had a tremendous significance (Deut. 19:14), "on account of the close connection in which a man's possession as the means of his support stood to the life of the man himself, 'because property by which life is supported participates in the sacredness of the life itself.'"[38] The fundamentals of the faith have the same significance for the Christian, for they guard his life. "If the foundations be destroyed, what can the righteous do?" (Psa. 11:3). Arthur W. Pink states, "Christianity is based upon the impregnable rock of Holy Scripture. The starting point of all doctrinal discussion must be the Bible."[39] It is time to point the people of God back to the ancient landmarks (Prov. 22:28). It is time to return to a faith which is based solely on the word of God.

As Iain Murray concludes:

> We only reach sure ground when we remember that revivals are the work of the Spirit of truth bringing home to the mind and conscience of large numbers the teaching of the Word of God with efficacious power. If through the unfaithfulness or ignorance of men that teaching has its cutting edge smoothed down; if such truths as Christ's finished work at Calvary, together with the entire dependence of sinners upon him for salvation are not preached, and the reliability of God's word not fully declared, then hope that the Holy Spirit will do his work is a terrible mistake. If there is any lesson which ought to be beyond doubt it is that revivals come through the preaching of scriptural truth.[40]

---

[37]John MacArthur Jr., *2 Timothy*, in *MacArthur's New Testament Commentary* (Chicago, IL: Moody Bible Institute, 1995), in *QuickVerse* ver. 7 [CD-ROM] (Omaha, NE: Parsons Technology, 1997), (original emphasis).

[38]C. F. Keil, *The Pentateuch*, in vol. 1, *Commentary on the Old Testament* by C. F. Keil and Franz Delitzsch (Peabody, MA: Hendrickson Publishers, 1996), 938.

[39]Arthur W. Pink, *The Divine Inspiration of the Bible*, in *Books for the Ages*, ver. 1 [CD-ROM] (Albany, OR: Ages Software, 1997).

[40]Iain H. Murray, *The Puritan Hope: Revival and the Interpretation of Prophecy* (Edinburgh: The Banner of Truth Trust, 1971), 232-33. Murray also quotes Donald Maclean speaking of the men who initiated the commencement of missions from Scotland. They "grasped the fact that Paul's declarations of profound mysteries in his Epistle to the Romans were not the cold intellectual conclusions of an exclusive dogmatist, but flames from the soul of a Christian missionary consumed with zeal for the salvation of men." Donald MacLean,

In the course of the author's ministry both at home and abroad, he has encountered numerous pastors and church leaders, as well as individual Christians who are confused by the whole topic of SLSW. Over the last decade there has been an almost exponential expansion of literature on the subject; it has been heralded in the Christian press,[41] and the websites of various Christian ministries demonstrate the adoption of assorted aspects of the teaching on a fairly general basis. For example, the ministry mandate for John G. Lake Ministries cites as its first objective, the advancement of the kingdom of God by "Forcefully and aggressively attacking the ungodly spiritual forces of the areas in which we minister."[42] Similarly, Morris Cerullo's website has the sub-title, "Mobilising Christians onto the Frontlines of Intercession." It exhorts:

> Before the battle can be won you must penetrate the enemy's resistance through prayer. The type of prayer we are talking about, that is capable of piercing "enemy lines," is not the average five or ten minute prayer. It is not based upon a specific formula. It is a deeper dimension of prayer where you are travailing, agonizing and

---

"Scottish Calvinism and Foreign Missions," in *Records of the Scottish Church History Society*, vol. 6, pt. 1, 1936, 12; quoted in Murray, 233.

[41]For example: Art Moore, "Spiritual Mapping Gains Credibility Among Leaders," *Christianity Today,* Jan. 1998, 55, online posting, http://www.christianitytoday.com/ct/8t1/8t1/055.html; accessed 21 Aug. 2001. Chuck Lowe, "Do Demons Have Zip Codes?" *Christianity Today,* July 1998, 57, online posting, http://www.christianitytoday.com/ct/8t8/8t8057.html; accessed 21 Aug. 2001. Sandra Chambers, "Storming the Capital with Prayer," *Charisma*, May 2001, online posting, http://www.charismamag.com/online/ articledisplay.pl? ArticleID=1038; accessed 21 Aug. 2001. "Winning the Battle for Your Neighbourhood: How You Can Drive Away the Demon Forces Now Dominating the Streets Where You Live," and "Defeating Territorial Spirits: Battles against evil spiritual forces controlling our cities can be waged and won," *Charisma*, Apr. 1990, quoted in Valley Bible Church, *Spiritual Warfare*, online posting, http://www.valleybible.net/resources/PositionPapers/SpiritualWarfare.shtml; accessed 7 Jan. 2002. Andy Butcher, "Strange Encounters With Another World," *Charisma*, Apr. 2001, 52, online posting, http://www.alienresistance.org/ce4casefiles.htm; accessed 7 Jan. 2002.

[42]John G. Lake Ministries, "Statement of Faith, The Ministry Mandate of the International Apostolic Council," online posting, http://www.jglm.org/statement_of_faith.htm; accessed 17 Dec. 2001.

groaning before God. This type of prayer involves engaging the enemy in one-to-one combat . . . wrestling . . . battling the powers, principalities and evil spirits that are at work and not letting go until you have overcome their resistance and have broken their hold.[43]

This represents a gospel of works which places the ultimate responsibility for the success or failure of the evangelism process on the shoulders of the individual Christian. This is a burden which God never intended; it demeans the mighty gospel of Jesus Christ; it is a philosophy born of fear and engendering fear. As David Garrard states, "Fear has its origin in the work of Satan, and any concept or ideology, whether real or imaginary, which he is able to use to bind the mind of man to himself he uses with great effect to neutralize the positive effects of faith in God."[44] A. W. Pink expresses a similar warning, "Heresy is not so much the total denial of the truth as a perversion of it. That is why half a lie is always more dangerous than a complete repudiation. Hence, when the Father of Lies enters the pulpit it is not his custom to flatly deny the fundamental truths of Christianity, rather does he tacitly acknowledge them, and then proceed to give an erroneous interpretation and a false application."[45]

Today, SLSW is so firmly fixed on the Christian horizon that it has almost become an accepted part of the landscape. There remain many champions of the SLSW cause but few who have publicly raised their voices in remonstration.[46] As a bishop of the International Communion of Charismatic Churches, President of the Global Gospel Fellowship, an Associate Regent of Oral Roberts University, a Trustee of the International Charismatic Bible Ministries, President of Peniel College of Higher Education, Senior Pastor of Peniel Church, and having ministerial experience which spans thirty-five years, the author has encountered the devastation which false doctrine, of whatever type, wreaks in the lives of

---

[43]Global Prayer Covering, "Prayerwatch," online posting, http://www.prayerwatch .org/penetrating.html; accessed 17 Dec. 2001.

[44]Garrard, 36.

[45]Arthur W. Pink, "Another Gospel," online posting, http://users,aol.com/libcfl/ another.htm; accessed 18 Dec. 2001.

[46]Lowe, *Territorial Spirits,* and Mike R. Taylor, *Do Demons Rule Your Town?: An Examination of the 'Territorial Spirits' Theory* (London: Grace Publications Trust, 1993). Each has made a significant contribution to the debate on this subject by challenging the basis of SLSW on a scholarly and well-researched basis.

individuals. He has lived long enough to see that error re-emerges in a slightly different guise, on an almost cyclical basis. It is for this reason that he is compelled to raise his voice in the defence of truth, not merely as a theoretician but as a seasoned practitioner who has learned over the course of years that "there is no new thing under the sun" (Eccl. 1:9).

Research Questions and Hypothesis

Two questions have been addressed in this study; the first and most important concerned the issue of whether or not SLSW teaching and new methodologies are based on a sound biblical and theological foundation. Every minister of the gospel has a responsibility to ensure that he/she does not embrace teaching that is opposed to Scripture or not supported as truth within Scripture. In 1 Corinthians 4:6, Paul declares that the opinions of men never take precedence over the written word of God. The second question concerned examining whether or not SLSW teaching could be found as a positive influence throughout church history, and if so, to assess its validity. General acceptance of any doctrine can never be a measure of its biblical authenticity.

The author's hypothesis is that the exposition of biblical and theological truth, applied in both an historical and a modern context, with the opportunity for study, discussion and re-evaluation of relevant concepts, would ensure that the understanding and practice of spiritual warfare were brought into alignment with the word of God. This hypothesis was put to the test in the context of a group of church leaders from a variety of denominations and doctrinal backgrounds, men and women of integrity who hold to the principle that the Bible is the infallible word of God and, it was therefore assumed that as such, would be prepared to amend their own thinking and practice where it was shown to be unbiblical. The author's conviction was that the concepts and teaching of SLSW have drawn people away from the eternal truths of Scripture, but by refocusing their understanding on what the Bible actually teaches about spiritual warfare ("The Peniel Model." see appendix C), individuals would be enabled to live and walk in Christ's total victory over the devil and all demonic powers, conquered at Calvary. The gospel of Jesus Christ is "the power of God unto salvation to every one that believeth; to the Jew first, and also to the Greek" (Rom.

1:16). In his teaching, the author asserted, it is the preaching of the gospel alone, and not the best devised stratagems of SLSW, that brings people to salvation in Christ.

Setting of the Project

The setting of the project originated within the context of the author's own life and ministry. In November 1976, he founded what is today known as Peniel Church. From an initial membership of three, this has developed into a flourishing family church of some seven hundred members, with a strong emphasis on the word of God and on miracles, healing and faith. In the increasingly ungodly ambient of the UK, this represents a substantial congregation.

In January 1982, Peniel Academy (PA) was opened for the education of church children. It is a private, independent school catering for all ages (5 years to 18 years) and has received full accreditation from the Department for Education and Science. In a recent education survey in The Times,[47] PA was ranked third in the county of Essex in terms of the national examination results at ages 16 and 18. The vast majority of the pupils, who are drawn from a wide range of backgrounds, continue into tertiary education and the school is respected by various top-ranking British universities as providing students of a high calibre with a solid work ethic.

PA has also gained a reputation for considerable prowess in the field of sport. In 2001, teams from the school won all eight titles in the National Schools Table Tennis Competition, a feat which has never been achieved by any one school before. Pupils from PA have represented their country within the international arena, both as individuals and in a team context.

In August 2001, Peter Brierley, the Executive Director of UK Christian Research, was commissioned to carry out a survey of Congregational Attitudes and Beliefs at Peniel Church. On "Survey Sunday" in October 2001, 496 adult survey forms were completed by the main body of the church, together with 30 forms from eleven to fourteen year olds and 41 from children. The resultant independent survey draws the following conclusions:

---

[47]"Complete League Tables of GCSE and A-Level Results for England," *The Times School Report* (London), 22 Nov. 2001, p. 11.

1) *Mature believing young people.* The children and young people who attend Peniel are markedly different from the majority of such in other English churches, and would suggest that the policy of integration of children in the services and throughout the church is not only important for the church, but vitally important for their faith and well being.

2) *A church profile which matches the population.* The proportion of people at different ages, genders, and marital statuses is broadly as in the population at large, not just showing that Peniel is reaching people of all types but that its mix of people is "normal". This is far from the case for many churches in Britain. There was however an above average number of professional well educated people, something not associated with many churches.

3) *An important linkage between church and school.* Peniel Academy is closely linked with Peniel Church, and many church attenders had also attended the Academy. Many of the children and young people were currently attending. The re-enforcement of teaching between Church and School enables a firm belief system to develop, as shown in the higher percentages of credal belief between young people and adult churchgoers.

4) *Regularity and commitment are intertwined at Peniel.* Most of those attending Peniel come every week, and have a firm commitment to the church. This practice has been in place for many years, and results in a majority feeling a strong sense of belonging to the church. Half of the church is attending as much as it did 5 years ago, and most of the rest more frequently.

5) *Personal relationships seem the key for growing the congregation.* Most have started attending Peniel through a personal invitation from a friend or relative. There is also a high level of willingness to bring people to a service. Three-quarters have their closest friends in the congregation.

6) *The teaching at Peniel is of vital importance.* The Sunday worship and sermons are regarded as a key factor for a person's growth in faith, whether they are adult or young person. Virtually everyone finds the preaching always or mostly inspiring and informative. Seminars are also important for many.

7) *Private faith secure.* Most of those attending Peniel are willing to talk about their faith, and believe that they exert a positive witness for Christ. Their beliefs are strong, and the majority read the Bible privately at least once a week. They acknowledge this influences both their belief and their behaviour. Most would say they are born again, and charismatic. A majority have experienced the Holy Spirit. Virtually all have had water baptism.

8) *High level of satisfaction.* A majority of respondents felt that the church should keep going as it is. There was little desire for change. Some people would like to be involved more in decision making, and/or to have the opportunity to use their gifts to a greater extent. The level of pastoral care received was exceptionally high, as the senior leadership was seen to be almost always available. The ideal pastor was seen to be an educator, evangelist and visionary, who inspires others to action but who also takes charge as necessary.[48]

It can only be concluded that the history of the Peniel congregation is a testimony to the faithfulness of Jesus Christ, who promised, "I will build my church; and the gates of hell shall not prevail against it" (Matt. 16:18).

In his attitude to education, the author identifies strongly with the understanding of the Puritans who viewed it as a vital part of the church's ministry. Knowledge of the word is essential for every age group. Alexander Duff once wrote, "Spurning the notion of a present day's success and a present year's wonder, we direct our views not merely to the present, but to future generations. While you engage in directly separating as many precious atoms from the mass as the stubborn resistance to ordinary appliances can admit, we shall, with the blessing of God, devote our time and strength to the preparing of a mine and the setting of a train which shall one day explode and tear up the whole from its lowest depths."[49] It is the commitment to education which has been the motivating force for the establishment

---

[48]Peter Brierley, "Peniel Pentecostal Church Congregational Attitudes and Beliefs Survey" *Christian Research Report* (n.p., Nov. 2001), 40-41.

[49]Alexander Duff, *The British and Foreign Evangelical Review* 30 (1881): 73; quoted in Iain H. Murray, 181.

of Peniel College of Higher Education (PCHE) in 1997. PCHE has full affiliate status with Oral Roberts University (Tulsa, Oklahoma) and offers fully accredited degrees (Bachelor and Masters in Theology and Masters in Education) through this affiliation. Pastors and church leaders from outside the Peniel congregation form a substantial part of the student body.

Similarly, it was the desire to share the truths of God within the Body of Christ worldwide which resulted in the setting up of the Global Gospel Fellowship (GGF) in August 2000. This is an international, interdenominational fellowship of miracle ministries which aims to "reach out to every continent and nation to create a forum for leaders of Christian churches and fellowships to share teaching and ongoing education; receive the wisdom of fathers in the faith; obtain encouragement from fellow ministers; achieve ordination and fulfil the challenge of spreading the Gospel of Jesus Christ to all people throughout the world."[50]

The establishment of GGF was the formal recognition of an existing network of ministers that had already developed out of the worldwide ministry of the author over a period of approximately 20 years. Its vision is to foster Christian fellowship on an international basis and this vision is shared with T. L. Osborn,[51] one of the spiritual fathers of the movement.

The research for this project was conducted within the auspices of GGF (South East England) regional pastors' meetings, held at Peniel Church headquarters.[52] The group numbers approximately one hundred and twenty pastors and church leaders from a range of denominational and ethnic backgrounds, of whom about fifteen to twenty are women. The monthly lunchtime meetings are geared to fellowship, teaching and discussion. Several pastors travel from mainland Europe in order to attend these sessions, and often visitors come from Africa, Venezuela and North America.

---

[50]Global Gospel Fellowship Handbook (n.p., 2001), 5.

[51]T. L. Osborn is best known for his international mass-miracle ministry. With his late associate-minister wife, Daisy, he has proclaimed the gospel to millions in 78 nations. Dr. Osborn has authored many books, including, *Healing the Sick: A Living Classic* (Tulsa, OK: Harrison House, 1992). This has over one million copies in print and is now in its 43d printing.

[52]Peniel Church, 49 Coxtie Green Road, Brentwood, Essex, CM14 5PS, England.

In view of his personal experience both at home and abroad, of the confusion caused by SLSW methodology, the author felt it was necessary to devise a seminar course based on sound biblical teaching and evidence from church history, and to review the mass of literature and teaching that has sprung up concerning SLSW. His aim was to bring the pastors to examine such teaching on the basis of scripture alone, much in the same way as the Jews of Berea applied the measure of the word of God in their evaluation of the gospel (Acts 17:10-11). It is clear that much of what is taught today in the context of SLSW is assumed to be authentic because it is presented in a way which "seemeth right" (Prov. 14:12). As Pink writes concerning error in general, "By virtue of the fact that it appropriates to itself religious terminology, sometimes appeals to the Bible for its support (whenever this suits its purpose), holds up before men lofty ideals, and is proclaimed by those who have graduated from our theological institutions, countless multitudes are decoyed and deceived by it."[53] It is therefore vital that any "new" teaching is demonstrated to be within the biblical pattern.

Background and Significance

There are many strands in the tapestry of a life, especially one in which God has sovereignly chosen to intervene. It is not possible to enumerate all of these strands, but the following excerpt provides a synopsis of the author's spiritual background and the major influences in his life:

> I believe in miracles. To me they are as natural as breathing. When Jesus was on this earth He went about doing miracles – the cripples walked, deaf ears were opened, the blind received their sight, lives were transformed. He hasn't changed – He is eternally the same. I have a saying – *No miracles, no Jesus* – because the miracles which were the hallmark of His earthly ministry from the beginning, still operate today. I know, for with my own eyes I've witnessed what only God can do. I've seen Him reach out to those in hopeless situations and bring life and healing in the place of death and despair. If you need a miracle, you need Him – because where He is that supernatural power will always flow.
>
> This . . . is written for those who are tired of struggling to believe, tired of the false faith emphasis which condemns and discourages. It is written for those who are prepared to realign their thinking on the

---

[53]Pink, "Another Gospel."

Biblical basis for faith, which is *Christ in you, the hope of glory* (Colossians 1:27). When He comes in truth, all things are possible.

My theological background is very broad based. I was led to the Lord and received the baptism of the Holy Spirit under the ministry of Demos and Rose Shakarian; greatly influenced by the first generation Quaker writings of George Fox, William Penn, James Naylor, Robert Barclay and Isaac Pennington; enriched by the Wesley brothers, George Whitefield and other Puritan writers; blessed by the books of Finney, Spurgeon, Count Zinzendorf and the Moravians; and inspired by the works of the Marechale, Smith Wigglesworth, Maria Woodworth-Etter, Aimee Semple Macpherson and Kathryn Kuhlman.

I enjoyed many years of rich fellowship and ministry with the late Archbishop Benson Idahosa, who was truly an outstanding apostle of faith of the twentieth century, a man who believed God and did exploits.

My life has been challenged by the work and writings of both Oral and Richard Roberts and I am honoured to count Dr T L Osborn as a friend and father in the faith.

I am grateful to Dr Judson Cornwall, for his wisdom, encouragement and friendship over many years. He also has been part of my shaping in God.

Now from such a varied spiritual background, I want to offer you, my readers, a new insight into the life of faith. Perhaps you will find the message . . . a little controversial. I make no apology – it is my intention to shake your preconceived ideas and cherished idols so that *those things which cannot be shaken may remain* (Hebrews 12:27). However, my purpose is always and only to lift up Jesus, the *author and finisher of our faith* (Hebrews 12:2), and to magnify His name; . . .

The only basis of true ministry is to do His will. We need to stop trying to coerce God into doing what we want and re-establish the heart cry, *Thy will be done on earth as it is in heaven* (Matthew 6:10). When we align ourselves with what God is doing, miracles happen; when He is the source, it's so, so easy![54]

From the moment of his new birth, God gave the author a real hunger for the knowledge of Himself. As a result, he avidly studied the Bible as well as many books written by men inspired of God. Looking back, it is this more than anything else, which could be

---

[54]Michael S. B. Reid, preface to *Faith: It's God Given* (Brentwood, England: Alive UK, 2000), 9-11 (original emphasis).

described as the most significant influence on his spiritual insight and development. It has provided the framework for the evaluation of truth and error. At times in the history of the Peniel family, it has seemed that the enemy would come in like a flood, but always God has faithfully raised up His standard (Isa. 59:19). In His divine mercy and grace, He has intervened to point the way back to simple faith in the gospel, saying. "This is the way, walk ye in it" (Isa. 30:21). SLSW is not even part of the equation, nor has it ever been.

Archbishop Benson Idahosa proved the power of the gospel in his native country of Nigeria. In the course of his lifetime he built a work, founded on the truths of the Scriptures, of some six thousand churches and seven million precious people. His living faith in the word of God ignited that same faith in many of his nation and transformed lives worldwide. That which he planted in his life of ministry and devotion to God continues to bear fruit after his death.[55]

Similarly, T. L. Osborn, a faithful contender for the faith over a period of almost sixty years has proved in his international ministry that the gospel "is the power of God unto salvation" (Rom. 1:16). He has produced a twenty-four volume publication,[56] cataloguing details of numerous evangelistic campaigns where tens of thousands have been converted, healed and delivered by the simple proclamation of the gospel. [57]

This evaluation of SLSW is not written to bring condemnation but comes from a heart of compassion. It is written in an attempt to bring back the biblical perspective that in Christ Jesus the victory is already won and redemption is a finished work. It is written to promote dialogue within the body of Christ. The author has always acknowledged there is a spiritual warfare and it is very real; it is the battle for the old, old truths of the gospel, first proclaimed by Peter on the day of Pentecost. SLSW debases God's sovereign plan of

---

[55]For further details of Benson Idahosa's life and ministry please refer to Ruthanne Garlock, *Fire in his Bones: The Story of Benson Idahosa* (Tulsa, OK: Praise Books, 1971).

[56]T. L. Osborn and Daisy Osborn, *Faith Library in 23 Volumes* (Tulsa, OK: OSFO International, n.d.).

[57]T. L. Osborn gives a beautiful account of the message of the gospel which he has proclaimed worldwide in *The Message that Works* (Tulsa, OK: OSFO Publishers, 1997).

salvation by suggesting that it is dependent on the intervention of man.[58] It is clear that men throughout the ages have been used of God to proclaim His gospel, but the application of that truth which sweeps away all opposition and births the life of God within a human heart is the work of the Holy Spirit. To quote the words of Martyn Lloyd-Jones: "There is only one way whereby anyone can receive the gospel, and that is that he be enlightened by the Holy Spirit. 'For by grace are ye saved through faith; and that not of yourselves: it is the gift of God' (Eph. 2:8). We need a spiritual understanding, and this gospel offers us a new birth . . . It is only as the result of this that we are able to see, believe, and receive the truth – and so the glory goes entirely to God."[59]

Definition of Terms

Third Wave of the Holy Spirit[60]

The term "third wave" was created whilst Peter Wagner was being interviewed by *Pastoral Renewal* magazine. It refers to three distinct moves of the Holy Spirit: the first wave being the Pentecostal movement at the beginning of last century; the second, the Charismatic movement in the middle of last century; and the third, the Spiritual Warfare movement at the close of last century.

Territorial Spirits

The belief in a hierarchy of demons includes powers that "have been assigned to specific geographical areas."[61]

Strategic-Level Spiritual Warfare

According to C. Peter Wagner, this is a "specific type of intercession." He says, "Ground-level spiritual warfare refers to the casting out of demons from people, occult-level spiritual warfare deals with shamans, New Age channelers, occult practitioners,

---

[58]See, for example, in respect to strategic-level intercession in this context, Dutch Sheets, *Intercessory Prayer: How God Can Use Your Prayers to Move Heaven and Earth* (Ventura, CA: Regal Books, 1996), 209.

[59]D. Martyn Lloyd-Jones, *Knowing the Times: Addresses Delivered on Various Occasions 1942-1977* (Edinburgh: The Banner of Truth Trust, 1989), 296.

[60]C. Peter Wagner, *The Third Wave of the Holy Spirit: Encountering the Power of Signs and Wonders* (Ann Arbor, MI: Vine Books, 1988).

[61]Mike Wakely, "A Critical Look at a New 'Key' to Evangelisation," *Evangelical Missions Quarterly* 31, no. 2 (Apr. 1995): 152.

witches and warlocks, Satanist priests, fortune-tellers and the like, and strategic-level spiritual warfare contends with 'an even more ominous concentration of demonic power: territorial spirits.'"[62]

Warfare Prayer

This form of prayer is used in SLSW. It is seen as the chief weapon for engaging the enemy in battle and aims to overcome the resistance of the evil powers to God's will. It generally involves a high volume, high energy, prolonged challenge to taunt the spirits until they manifest in one way or another. Then the power of Jesus Christ over the demonic forces can be displayed.[63]

Spiritual Mapping

This technique is a key component in SLSW prayer strategy. It involves research and spiritual discernment, where warriors target geographical locations and "attempt to see a city or nation or the world … as it really is, not as it appears to be."[64] This includes discovering the location of demons, their activities, their names and their power.[65]

Identificational Repentance

The term was originally coined by John Dawson,[66] and the technique is claimed to give Christians the power to heal the past. It involves the recognition that nations and/or cities can and do sin corporately and if such sin is not remitted the iniquity can become worse in each succeeding generation. This cycle can be stopped by corporate or identificational repentance which effectively removes the foothold Satan has used to hold populations in spiritual darkness and social misery. It is claimed that this will open the way for the revival of churches and an unprecedented harvest of souls.[67]

---

[62]Wagner, *Warfare Prayer*, 17, 18, 151, 153.

[63]Wagner, *Warfare Prayer*, 27.

[64]Otis, *Informed Intercession*, 85; hailed as an exploration of spiritual mapping for intercessors.

[65]Wagner, *Warfare Prayer*, 151-53.

[66]Arnold, 167.

[67]C. Peter Wagner, "The Power to Heal the Past," online posting, http://www.pastornet.net.au/renewal/journal8/8d-wagner.html; accessed 11 Oct. 2001.

Naming of Spirits

This is based on the heathen practice of naming spirits (for example, "Infertility" or "Lust"). Accordingly, SLSW encourages Christians to discover the name of demons in their territory (city or country) and bind them in the name of Christ.

The 10/40 Window (and 40/70 Window)

The 10/40 Window refers to an imaginary frame encompassing "some 95 percent of the world's unreached people"[68] which Satan holds in his bonds. In geographical terms it is located "between the latitudes of 10 and 40 degrees north" of the equator.[69] "The Garden of Eden," "Iran and Iraq," are "situated at the epicentre of the Window."[70] The SLSW focus has now shifted to the 40/70 Window.[71]

Postmodernist Thinking

In the late twentieth century, society faced a radical revolution in thinking, which is widely described as "Postmodernism."[72] The effect of this shift of thought has been the abolition of Absolute Truth. Postmodernists advance the concept that each individual thinks differently and will therefore have his/her own individual model of truth, which applies to him/her alone.

Limitations of Study

Due to the proliferation of writing on the subject, SLSW presents an extremely wide field of study. This project, however, has been narrowly focussed on the writings of mainstream SLSW leaders in terms of their primary beliefs and practices in this context. Many associated issues have not been addressed (for example, the influence

---

[68]George Otis, Jr., *The Last of the Giants: Lifting the Veil on Islam and the End Times* (Grand Rapids, MI: Chosen Books, 1991), 97.

[69]Ibid.

[70]Ibid., 97-99.

[71]Global Harvest Ministries, "The 40/70 Window Prayer Initiative," online posting, http://www.globalharvestministries.org/home.qry?ID=204; accessed 27 Sept. 2001.

[72]Dennis McCallum, *Death of Truth: Responding to Multiculturalism, the Rejection of Reason and the new Postmodern Diversity* (Minneapolis, MN: Bethany House Publishers, 1996), for an excellent critique on postmodernism and how it is impacting our culture.

of eschatological beliefs in the emergence of SLSW) and must remain the subject of subsequent research.

In the interests of both integrity and truth, the author has taken considerable care not to misrepresent or exaggerate the views expressed in publications examined in the course of this study.

In this project, reference has been made to a wide range of authors from an extensive spectrum of theological opinion. This in no way implies that the author endorses every facet of their teaching.

Assumptions

It is assumed that the original text of the Bible is inerrant.

It is assumed that the Bible is the only touchstone of truth and that the scriptures are all-sufficient for doctrinal understanding.

It is accepted that the term "spiritual warfare" is not specifically mentioned in the Bible but that the concept is validated by teaching in both the Old and New Testaments.

CHAPTER 2

BIBLICAL, THEOLOGICAL & HISTORICAL BASES

Biblical Foundations of the Project

Any teaching for which biblical authority is claimed, must of necessity find its origin and substantiation throughout the word of God. Accordingly, it must be in harmony with the whole canon of Scripture, the only touchstone of truth. A doctrine may, therefore, be defined as the teaching of the entire Bible in respect to a particular topic.[1]

The purpose of this section is to examine the biblical basis for spiritual warfare. Strictly speaking, the term is not a scriptural one and so it is of prime importance to distinguish clearly what the Bible actually teaches in this context. As C. H. Spurgeon said: "Men go after novel and false doctrines because they do not really know the truth; for if the truth had gotten into them and filled them, they would not have room for these day-dreams."[2]

Old Testament Basis

Genesis has often been described as the "book of beginnings,"[3] or "origins."[4] This is the introductory section to the entire body of Hebrew sacred literature and of revealed truth in general. In the early chapters, it narrates those events which form the basis for the great history of human redemption: namely, the Creation, the nature of sin and the Fall, and the promise of the coming Redeemer.

The stage is set in the Garden of Eden where mankind, the pinnacle of all God's creation, becomes the target for Satan's attack. The devil presents himself as a serpent,[5] and is described as being

---

[1]Wayne Grudem, *Systematic Theology: An Introduction to Biblical Doctrine* (Leicester: InterVarsity Press, 1994), 25.

[2]Charles H. Spurgeon, *Sermons Preached and Revised by C. H. Spurgeon, During the Year 1883*, vol. 29 of 63, *The Metropolitan Tabernacle Pulpit* (Pasadena, TX: Pilgrim Publications, 1973), 215.

[3]For example, *The Illustrated Bible Dictionary*, pt. 1, s.v. "Genesis" (Leicester: InterVarsity Press, 1980).

[4]For example, Merrill F. Unger, *Unger's Bible Dictionary*, s.v. "Genesis" (Chicago, IL: Moody Press, 1960).

[5]Sydney H. T. Page, *Powers of Evil: A Biblical Study of Satan and Demons* (Grand Rapids, MI: Baker Books, 1995), 15. Page compares Gen. 3:15 with Rom. 16:20, making it clear that the serpent was, in fact, Satan.

"more subtle than any beast of the field which the Lord God had made" (Gen. 3:1). However, it is clear that man's supremacy over the animal world was God-given in its origin and comprehensive in its scope (Gen. 1:26). The First Adam had dominion over the serpent as long as he remained in obedience to the commandment of God.

God gave one commandment to man. He said, "But of the tree of the knowledge of good and evil, thou shalt not eat of it: for in the day that thou eatest thereof thou shalt surely die" (Gen. 2:17). The serpent introduced an opposing thought. He said, "Ye shall not surely die: For God doth know that in the day ye eat thereof, then your eyes shall be opened, and ye shall be as gods, knowing good and evil" (Gen. 3:4-5). Thus not only did the serpent accuse God of lying, but he claimed that the reason for the lie was a deliberate intention to deprive man of equality with Himself. The battle was to be fought in the mind.

Man's response to these statements was essentially an intellectual process, based on a choice as to whom to believe. Grudem suggests that this process brought into question three distinct concepts, namely, "what is true?", "what is right?", and "who am I?"[6] The first dealt with the basis for knowledge, and Eve chose to believe the serpent's misrepresentation of the facts. The second related to the basis for moral standards; God had forbidden man to eat of the fruit of one tree, and it was therefore wrong to do so (Gen. 2:16-17). The serpent postulated an alternative rule, suggesting that it would be right to eat of the fruit and that in so doing mankind would become as "gods" (Gen. 3:5). Eve elected to trust in her Satan-inspired evaluation of the moral code, rather than accepting God's direction. Thirdly, was the question of identity; Adam and Eve had been made in the image of God, to be dependent on Him for all things as He was both Creator and Lord. Now Eve asserted her independence and aspired to be like God, to elevate herself from the position of the creature to that of the Creator. It is clear from this process that the attack centred on the mind.

Berkhof gives a slightly different appraisal of the temptation process. He states:

---

[6]Grudem, 493.

> The course followed by the tempter is quite clear. In the first place
> he sows the seeds of doubt by calling the good intention of God in
> question and suggesting that his command was really an
> infringement of man's liberty and rights. When he notices from the
> response of Eve that the seed has taken root, he adds the seed of
> unbelief and pride, denying that transgression will result in death,
> and clearly intimating that the command was prompted by the
> selfish purpose of keeping man in subjection. He asserts that by
> eating from the tree man would become like God. The high
> expectations thus engendered induced Eve to look intently at the
> tree, and the longer she looked, the better the fruit seemed to her.
> Finally, desire got the upper hand, and she ate and also gave unto
> her husband, and he ate.[7]

It could also be argued that when the serpent suggested that by
partaking of the fruit Adam and Eve could become "as gods" (Gen.
3:5), he provoked the woman's imagination to consider this
possibility. Ignoring the fact that the statement was totally deceptive
for, as Genesis 1:27 teaches, man had been made in the very image of
God Himself, Eve chose to accept Satan's opinion and resentment
arose in her heart that God should deprive her of this great privilege.
She looked and saw three things, namely that "the tree *was* good for
food, and that it *was* pleasant to the eyes, and a tree to be desired to
make *one* wise" (Gen. 3:6). Finally, she succumbed, took of the fruit
and gave some to her husband who was with her. The serpent had
gained entrance via the senses, by appealing to "the lust of the flesh,
and the lust of the eyes, and the pride of life" (1 John 2:16). Thus
Eve was beguiled in her imagination to disregard the commandment
of God and to make an independent decision based on her own
judgement; incited by the serpent she chose to abandon rational
thought.[8] However, in summary, it is clear that whatever analysis is
adopted, the focus of the attack was the mind of man.

Satan had a definite strategy in view, namely to induce
disobedience. His first attack was launched against the woman as she
was perceived to be the more vulnerable. Berkhof suggests that Eve

---

[7]Louis Berkhof, *Systematic Theology* (Edinburgh: The Banner of Truth Trust, 2000),
223.

[8]Grudem, 493. Grudem points out that all sin is ultimately irrational. It did not
make sense for Adam and Eve to think that there could be any gain in
disobeying the words of their Creator. It was a foolish choice. It is the "fool" in
the book of Proverbs who recklessly indulges in all kinds of sins (see for
example, Prov. 10:23; 12:15; 14:7,16; 15:5; 18:2).

was the initial target of the serpent for three reasons, ". . . (a) she was not the head of the covenant and therefore would not have the same sense of responsibility; (b) she had not received the command of God directly but only indirectly, and would consequently be more susceptible to argumentation and doubt; and (c) she would undoubtedly prove to be the most effective agent in reaching the heart of Adam."[9]

The process for Adam was slightly different in that he made a definite and wilful choice to take of the forbidden fruit. He was not deceived by the serpent but chose to accept the lie because it appeared to be to his advantage to do so: "The essence of that sin lay in the fact that Adam placed himself in opposition to God, that he refused to subject his will to the will of God, to have God determine the course of his life; and that he actively attempted to take the matter out of God's hand, and to determine the future for himself."[10] As George Fox observed: "So they both forsook God's Voice and Commandment; and then that brought them into Sorrow, by hearkning to the Serpent, who was out of Truth, and disobeying the Voice and Command of the God of Truth."[11] Man chose independence from God and in so doing he lost fellowship with the Creator. Man also lost his dominion over the enemy and was driven out of the Garden under the curse of a brief and difficult life. Satan was the apparent victor in the first round of the battle and it was all on the basis of deception. The attack had focused on the mind and man had disregarded his only protection against the wiles of the enemy--obedience to the express will of God. The real problem was not the power of the devil, but man's willingness to disobey the commands of the Creator. Disobedience was the key issue (Rom. 5:19) and man was led astray only because he had abandoned the truth and accepted the lie.

Subsequently, the Old Testament refers very little to the Fall. "Nevertheless, the Fall is the silent hypothesis of the whole Bible doctrine of sin and redemption; it does not rest on a few vague passages, but forms an indispensable element in the revelation of

---

[9]Berkhof, 223.

[10]Ibid., 222.

[11]George Fox, *Gospel-Truth* (London: T. Sowle, 1706), 722.

salvation."[12] Thus Adam and Eve's fall was representative of the entire human race (Rom. 5:12-21).

The noun "Satan" appears only twenty-four times in the whole of the Old Testament and he is never depicted as a direct opponent of God.[13] The word "demon" is not used in the KJV; "devils" appears in four places; and "evil spirit" occurs on eight occasions, all of which shows clearly that the evil spirit was sent by, and consequently, under the control of God.[14]

It might be logical to conclude, therefore, that there is little indication of demonic activity in the Old Testament. However, the children of Israel often sinned by serving false gods. Deuteronomy 32:16-17 states: "They provoked him to jealousy with strange *gods*, with abominations provoked they him to anger. They sacrificed unto devils, not to God; to gods whom they knew not, to *new gods* that came newly up, whom your fathers feared not." The same terminology is found in Psalm 106:34-37 (NIV), where the people of Israel stand accused of sacrificing "their sons and their daughters unto demons" in accordance with the idolatrous practices of the Canaanites.

Some scholars claim that these references demonstrate that God viewed the worship offered to idols in all the nations surrounding Israel as worship of Satan and his demons. On that basis, the battles that the Israelites fought against pagan nations were essentially battles against peoples who worshipped demonic forces. In that sense, it could be argued that they were as much spiritual as physical battles.[15]

However, the actual meaning of the Hebrew word *sedim* (or *shedim*), which is translated as "demons" in both Deuteronomy 32:17 (NIV) and Psalm 106:37 (NIV), is not entirely clear. "*Shedim* was understood by the translators of the Septuagint as demons, but, as it is made parallel with 'foreign gods' (see Deut. 32:16 (NIV)), and is

---

[12]*The International Standard Bible Encyclopaedia*, s.v. "The Fall," by Hermen Brvinck, in *PC Study Bible: Complete Reference Library*, ver. 3.0 [CD ROM], (Seattle, WA: Biblesoft 1992-1999).

[13]See "Theological Themes and Issues" in the relevant section of this chapter.

[14]Judg. 9:23; 1 Sam. 16:14-16, 23; 18:10; 19:9. There is also the account in 1 Kin. 22 and 2 Chr. 18 of God sending a lying spirit to deceive the prophets and King Ahab.

[15]Grudem, 416-417.

the equivalent of the Assyr. *sedu,* or bull deity, it is probable that it is used here as the name of a foreign deity. The fact that the root *shed* became in later Judaism the general term for 'demon' . . . does not prove this inference wrong."[16] Whether "demons" or "foreign gods" is the correct translation, there is certainly no record or indication that God's people were instructed to engage in confrontation with unseen spiritual forces. God merely commanded them to destroy heathen practices--"Break down their altars, smash their sacred stones and cut down their Asherah poles" (Exo. 34:13 NIV),[17]--and heathen people.[18]

There are a number of incidents in the Old Testament, however, which may be interpreted fundamentally as clashes between good and evil. It is necessary to examine some of these in order to assess the nature of the warfare. First Samuel 17 recounts the well-known history of David and Goliath. Daily the Philistine champion presented his challenge to Saul's terrified troops: "I defy the armies of Israel this day; give me a man, that we may fight together" (1 Sam. 17:10).[19] David recognised this provocation for what it was, an affront not only to the Israelite people but to "the armies of the living God" (1 Sam. 17:26). Goliath invoked "spiritual" help by cursing David in the name of his god. However, David's faith was in the One who had delivered the lion and the bear into his hand; he saw beyond the size of the giant to the infinite greatness of his God. There was no warfare prayer or binding of spirits, just a total confidence that God would give him the victory: "This day will the LORD deliver thee into mine hand; and I will smite thee, and take thine head from thee . . . that all the earth may know that there is a God in Israel . . . for the battle *is* the LORD'S" (1 Sam. 17:46-47).

Similarly, the prophet Elijah was a man of confrontation, and nowhere is this better portrayed than in his contest with, and subsequent victory over, the 450 prophets of Baal on Mount Carmel (1 Kin. 18). The time had come for the people of Israel to make a

---

[16]*Encyclopaedia of Religion and Ethics,* vol. 4 of 13, ed. James Hastings, s.v. "Demons and Spirits" (Edinburgh: T and T Clark, 1981), 595-96.

[17]See also Num. 33:52; Deut. 7:5,25; 12:2-3.

[18]Deut. 20:17-18; 33:27.

[19]*Strong's Exhaustive Concordance,* s.v. "defy" (Grand Rapids, MI: Baker Book House, 1987). He takes it to mean blaspheme, defy, rail, reproach or upbraid.

choice between their idolatry and the true worship of Jehovah. The biblical account is extremely dramatic as the man of God waited for the priests of Baal to complete their increasingly desperate sacrificial rites: "And they cried aloud, and cut themselves after their manner with knives and lancets, till the blood gushed out upon them" (1 Kin.18:28).[20] Elijah showed no sign of fear but openly mocked them and ridiculed their god, suggesting he was talking, pursuing, on a journey, or asleep (1 Kin.18:27). Once again, there was no reference to, or necessity for, a spiritual conflict in order to bind unseen demonic powers. When the pagan priests finally conceded defeat, having produced nothing other than their own blood, Elijah made his own preparations in obedience to the word of the Lord (1 Kin. 18:30-36). To the waiting congregation his actions must have appeared totally self-defeating but they served to reinforce the impact of what was to be an incontestable miracle. "Then the fire of the LORD fell, and consumed the burnt sacrifice, and the wood, and the stones, and the dust, and licked up the water that *was* in the trench. And when all the people saw *it*, they fell on their faces: and they said, The LORD, he *is* the God; the LORD, he *is* the God" (1 Kin. 18:38-39). Elijah's final act of the day was to kill all the 450 prophets of Baal,[21] who had effectively demonstrated the total powerlessness of themselves and their god.

The account of the fall of Dagon (1 Sam. 5) is also interesting in respect to the implications for spiritual warfare. The Philistines had defeated the men of Israel in battle, and the Ark of the Covenant, symbolic of God's presence with His people, was taken captive. At that time, it was customary in all nations to dedicate the spoils of war to the gods. This was for two reasons; firstly, as a show of gratitude

---

[20]Adam Clarke, *Adam Clarke's Commentary*, in *PC Study Bible: Complete Reference Library*, ver. 3.0 [CD ROM] (Seattle, WA: Biblesoft 1992-1999), s.v. "1 Kings 18:28." "This was done according to the rites of that barbarous religion; if the blood of the bullock would not move him they thought their own blood might; and with it they smeared themselves and their sacrifice. This was not only the custom of the idolatrous Israelites, but of the Syrians, Persians, Greeks, Indians, and in short of all the pagan world."

[21]Ibid. "They had committed the highest crime against the state and the people by introducing idolatry and bringing down God's judgments upon the land; therefore their lives were forfeited to that law which had ordered every idolater to be slain."

to the deity who had supposedly given them the victory; and secondly, as a proof that their god was more powerful than the god of the conquered nation.[22] To place the ark of God in the temple of Dagon was, therefore, intended to insult the God of Israel, and to terrify His people. However, this action had unforeseen consequences because the following morning the idol was found to have fallen on its face--the first indication of the superiority of the God of Israel. It was replaced, but on the subsequent day was found again face downward "before the ark of the LORD" (1 Sam. 5:4), only this time the head and hands of the idol had been severed from the body.[23] This was the final proof of Jehovah's power and authority and was followed by His judgement upon the men of Ashdod and the consequent release of the ark of the tabernacle.[24] It was also the culmination of a series of sovereign acts of Almighty God without the requirement for a spiritual battle or involvement of any human agency.

Old Testament Summary

On the basis of the above analysis, two clear principles relating to spiritual warfare may be established. The first relates to the location and nature of the battle. Adam and Eve had a choice as to whom to believe and whom to obey, and their assessment involved a mental process. Both David and Elijah faced a similar decision.[25] They could respond to an apparently hopeless situation on the basis of the facts presented in the natural realm; alternatively, they could allow their thoughts and actions to be governed by obedience to God and His word.

Secondly, it is apparent that warfare in the sense of engaging demonic forces in a spiritual conflict was a complete non-issue. There

---

[22]For example, when the Philistines conquered Saul, they put his armour in the temple of Ashtaroth (1 Sam. 31:10). Similarly, after his encounter with Goliath, David deposited the giant's sword in the tabernacle of the Lord (1 Sam. 21:8-9).

[23]Clarke, s.v. "1 Samuel 5:4." Dagon had the head, arms and hands of a human, and the rest of the idol was in the form of a fish.

[24]Ibid.

[25]There are many other instances, too numerous to mention, including for example, Gideon, Joshua, Samson and Elisha. It is interesting to note that when the eyes of Elisha's servants were opened to the invisible realm (2 Kin. 6:8-23), he saw only God's angelic army.

is no foundation in the Old Testament for this practice, nor any indication that the devil has any intrinsic power or authority. No Dagon or any other idol can survive in the presence of the Living God and all powers must bow before Him. Too often, Old Testament stories have been allegorised to accommodate extra-biblical theories which have been devised without any real scriptural foundation.[26]

The battlefield is in the mind. The issue is obedience to the King of Kings. Satan's only weapon is deception; his only sphere of operation is that which God permits within His own eternal purposes.

New Testament Basis

The Gospels

The temptation of Jesus

The purpose of Jesus in coming to earth was to do the will of the Father (Heb. 10:7). The disobedience of the First Adam had brought death and destruction to mankind. Conversely, by His obedience, Jesus came to bring reconciliation between God and man (Rom. 5:19), to reinstate the potential for every man to repossess that which was lost through sin, namely his inheritance as a child of God.

The earthly ministry of Jesus was ushered in at the time of His baptism with the proclamation from heaven, "This is my beloved Son, in whom I am well pleased" (Matt. 3:17). Directly after this experience, Jesus was "led up of the Spirit into the wilderness to be tempted of the devil" (Matt. 4:1). Clearly, therefore, this encounter was within the purposes of God, for Jesus, the Second Adam, had to face and win the same battle which the First Adam had lost so many years before.

Satan waited his opportunity until forty days and nights had passed and Jesus was weak with hunger. Once again the devil's aim was to induce disobedience to the will of the Father. There were three prongs to his attack, two of which called on Jesus to prove His position as the Son of God (Matt. 4:3, 6). In response to these, Jesus

---

[26]For example, references to the king of Babylon in Isaiah 14:12-15 and the king of Tyre in Ezekiel 28:12-19 are often allegorised and interpreted to be references to Satan. See appendix A.

consistently refused to use the power He knew He possessed in order to benefit Himself or demonstrate His own authority. He held that power in sacred trust to be used only as the Father directed; His role was to do only what He saw the Father do (John 5:19-20). In the third temptation, Satan offered the kingdoms of the world in return for worship, but this was not to be the method of redemption. Jesus had come to earth because "God so loved the world" (John 3:16). Death on the cross at Calvary was the only way and there could be no easier alternative; that was the truth to which He adhered for, as Isaiah prophesied, He had set his face like a flint (Isa. 50:7) for what lay ahead.

In response to each temptation Jesus answered with the word of God: "it is written," "it is written," "it is also written" (Matt. 4:4, 7, 10). The word was His only weapon and it was used in a defensive, as opposed to an offensive, fashion. He did not engage in "Strategic Level Spiritual Warfare" (SLSW),[27] He did not bind Satan or evict him from the territory; He simply stood in truth and an attitude of obedience to God the Father. The Scripture teaches that Jesus "was in all points tempted like as *we are, yet* without sin" (Heb. 4:15). Just as with Adam, the battle was fought in the mind,[28] for Satan's approach to Jesus targeted "the lust of the flesh, and the lust of the eyes, and the pride of life" (1 John 2:16). The choice once again was based on whom to believe and whom to obey.

How Jesus dealt with the spirit powers during His earthly ministry

Throughout the earthly ministry of Jesus the gospels record many clashes between Him and spirit powers. This is in marked contrast to the apparent inactivity of the demonic world in the Old Testament. What then was the reason for this dramatic shift? The answer lies in the Intertestamental era. Most of the Old Testament writings are rooted firmly in a deep-seated conviction as to the

---

[27]C. Peter Wagner, *Warfare Prayer: Strategies for Combating the Rulers of Darkness* (Crowborough, England: Monarch Publications, 1997), 53. Wagner, on the contrary, believes that Christ did engage in SLSW during His temptation. See also Cindy Jacobs, *Possessing the Gates of the Enemy: An Intercessionary Prayer Manual* (London: Marshall Pickering, 1993), 230. Jacobs also believes that the temptation of Christ provides a "New Testament pattern for warring against principalities and powers."

[28]Michael Reid and Judson Cornwall, *Whose Mind Is It Anyway?* (Loughton, England: Sharon Publications, 1993).

sovereignty and dominion of Jehovah. However, in the latter part of the Old Testament era and during the 400 "silent years" prior to the opening of the New Testament, there had been a significant shift in Judaic thought in respect to demonic power and activity.[29] The fall of Jerusalem and the Diaspora had forced the Jews to re-evaluate their understanding of the nature of evil. It was convenient to shift the blame for their misfortunes away from the problem of sin and disobedience to God, and on to the malevolent interference of unseen devilish powers. The Intertestamental literature reveals a fascination with angels in particular and there are many references to exorcisms. For example, the Pseudepigrapha,[30] which offer a variety of techniques for deliverance from evil spirits, although it is doubtful as to how effective these practices really were.[31] However, many Jews had adopted such teachings as authentic and it is against this background that the apparent prevalence of demonic activity in the gospels must be understood.[32]

Mark records that Jesus "preached in their synagogues throughout all Galilee, and cast out devils" (Mark 1:39) .[33] His

---

[29]Conrad E. Smith, "Spiritual Warfare: An Analysis of Modern Trends Based on Historical Research and Biblical Exegesis" (M.A. diss., Capital Bible Seminary, Lanham, Maryland, 1994), 6.

[30]*Concise Oxford Dictionary*, 10th ed., s.v. "Pseudepigrapha." "Spurious or pseudonymous writings, especially Jewish writings ascribed to various biblical patriarchs and prophets but composed 200BC – AD200."

[31]Flavius Josephus, *The Antiquities of the Jews*, bk. 8, chap. 2, par. 5, in *Josephus: Complete Works*, trans. William Whiston (London: Pickering and Inglis, 1960), 173. However, Josephus does record an apparently successful exorcism by a Jew named Eleazar using an incantation said to be derived from Solomon--This depended on a ring which contained a special root purportedly prescribed by Solomon. As the victim smelled it, the demon was expelled via his nostrils. When the demon left, the man collapsed and the exorcist adjured it never to return employing the incantations which Solomon had purportedly written. As proof that the demon had departed, Eleazar placed a bowl of water nearby and commanded the demon to upset the bowl as it left, which it did.

[32]Grudem, 418. He suggests an extended discussion of Jewish exorcism is to be found in Emil Schurer, *The History of the Jewish People in the Age of Jesus Christ: 175 B.C. – A.D. 135, Part 2*, vol. 3 of 3, rev. English ed., eds. Geza Vermes, Fergus Millar, and Martin Goodman (Edinburgh: T. and T. Clark, 1987), 342-61, 376, 440.

[33]See also Matt. 4:23-24; 8:16-17; Mark 1:32-34; 3:7-12; Luke 4:40-41; 6:17-19; 7:21.

authority over the spirit world was absolute and demons were banished "with *his* word" (Matt. 8:16). In this He completely broke with the then current Judaic traditions because He used no ritual, no sacrifice, and no incantation. He just spoke the word with authority. In the synagogues the Jews had been diverted from the word of God and coached in the precepts of man and legalistic ritualism. This had resulted in a highly superstitious attitude in respect to the spirit world and how to deal with demons.[34] In contrast, the way in which Jesus dealt with demons was both simple and effective. He had no need of methodology because He was the incarnate word of God. The people were amazed, saying, "What thing is this? what new doctrine *is* this? for with authority commandeth he even the unclean spirits, and they do obey him" (Mark 1:27). The common people recognised the difference between Jesus and the hypocritical pedantry of the scribes and Pharisees.

However, Jesus rarely appeared to take the initiative in His encounters with evil spirits. On many occasions, He was approached by relatives of the possessed person (Matt. 15:21-28; Mark 7:24-30; 9:14-29; Luke 9:37-43), but frequently the demons themselves provoked His attention (Matt. 8:28-29.; Mark 1:23-24; 5:2-7; Luke 4:33-34; 8:27-28). There was certainly no consistent modus operandi which characterised His approach. He simply commanded the demons to leave without requesting any detailed information either from God or from the spirit powers. In many instances He prohibited the demons from speaking (Mark 1:34; 3:12; Luke 4:41). They never resisted Him, but often screamed for mercy (Mark 1:24; 5:7, 10, 12), begging only for another host in whom to dwell (Mark 5:12). As Chuck Lowe comments, "This is not spiritual 'warfare'; this is abject surrender."[35] Lowe also argues that "the casting out of demons carries two broader and interrelated messages: the kingdom of God has come; (Matt. 12:28); and, Satan has been dethroned as ruler of this world" (Matt. 12:29; Luke 11:21-22).[36]

---

[34]For further detail in respect to the Late Judaic and Intertestamental teachings please refer to the appropriate section of this chapter.

[35]Chuck Lowe, "Defeating Demons: A Critique of Strategic-Level Spiritual Warfare," TMs (diskette), n.p., n.d., 122.

[36]Ibid., 119. It is the author's opinion that Satan was finally defeated at Calvary (Col. 2:15).

How the Apostles Dealt with the Spirit Powers in the Book of Acts

Some SLSW protagonists explain the demonic activity of the New Testament as a direct result of the manifestation of Jesus Christ.[37] However, they fail to note that Calvary spelt the end of the Old Covenant and the final defeat of the devil. Only after the ascension, did Jesus take on His High Priestly office, and the Holy Spirit was sent forth ten days later so that believers would be endued with power to become witnesses to the total victory in Christ (Luke 24:49; Acts 1:8; 2:1-42).

The apostles lived and taught in a society that was essentially pagan. First century historians record the continued syncretism of heathen influences into Jewish thought and religious life. For example, Josephus recounts the assimilation into the Jewish religious tradition of pagan rituals designed to ward off evil spirits.[38] He also records the accepted use of Solomon's names of spirits in ritualistic practices because of the latter's reputation for healing and exorcism.[39] Even the ascetic Essene community at Qumran, who were extremely critical of the laxness of Jewish religious life in general, incorporated curses against Satan and the demonic realm into their worship of God. In some liturgical curses, these worshippers addressed Satan directly.[40] Clearly, dualistic philosophy had penetrated to the heart of the Jewish faith, and there was a fascination with the spirit realm which had not been evident in early Judaism. Accordingly, manifestations of demonic activity had to be faced and dealt with by first century Christians.

The book of Acts provides the record of the first twenty years of the early church and its pioneer evangelistic campaigns. The ministry of Peter dominates the first twelve chapters of this book; the ministry

---

[37]Michael Harper, *I Believe in Satan's Downfall* (Grand Rapids, MI: William B. Eerdmans Publishing Co., 1981), 26-27; quoted in C. Peter Wagner, *Confronting the Powers: How the New Testament Church Experienced the Power of Strategic-Level Spiritual Warfare* (Ventura, CA: Regal Books, 1996), 122.

[38]Francis X. Gokey, *The Terminology for the Devil and Evil Spirits in the Apostolic Fathers* (Washington, DC: The Catholic University Press, 1961), 19; quoted in Smith, 15.

[39]Josephus, 173.

[40]Chuck Lowe, *Territorial Spirits and World Evangelisation?: A Biblical, Historical and Missiological Critique of Strategic Level Spiritual Warfare* (Fearn and Kent: OMF and Mentor, 1998), 49.

of Paul characterises the remaining sixteen. The approach of both to the spirit world largely follows the model set by Jesus, and was both simple and effective. Acts 5:16 shows that all the needy who came to Peter were healed of their diseases or freed from unclean spirits. In Acts 19:11-12 the reader is informed that contact with one of Paul's handkerchiefs or aprons was sufficient to effect both healing and deliverance. Once again there was no need for sophisticated spiritual warfare techniques. The power of God at work via the apostles overcame the powers of darkness.

In terms of evangelism, revival in the early church was always directly connected with the word of God; the apostles lived the life and preached the word. On the day of Pentecost, the expectation of the Old Testament was at last fulfilled, for the Holy Spirit came to fill the waiting disciples just as their Lord had promised (Luke 24:49; John 14:26). These human vessels had already been prepared, and their strategy of evangelism developed spontaneously from this point because He who was the incarnate word of God was now alive within them.

Peter, who had denied his Lord, was transformed into a bold and courageous evangelist. His sermon on the day of Pentecost set the work and life of Jesus in the context of the prophecy of Joel, and the result was, "they that gladly received his word were baptised: and the same day there were added *unto them* about three thousand souls" (Acts 2:41). Throughout the book of Acts the same pattern emerges. Revival was birthed by the preaching of the word,[41] in the power of the Holy Ghost: "So then faith *cometh* by hearing, and hearing by the word of God" (Rom. 10:17).

The disciples had a simple gospel--they were convinced that Jesus, the promised Messiah, had come and they faithfully declared this truth. They had no gimmicks but they both proclaimed and lived what they believed. Persecution merely increased the geographical area covered by these early Christians as they went "every where preaching the word" (Acts 8:4). Initially, the main thrust of their witness was to the Jews but it was not long before the Gentiles also received "the word of God" (Acts 11:1). For example, at Antioch in Pisidia, when Paul and Barnabas visited, almost the whole city came

---

[41]For example, see Acts 4:4; 10:44; 11:19-21.

"together to hear the word of God" (Acts 13:44). Similarly, as a result of Paul's ministry in Ephesus "all they which dwelt in Asia heard the word of the Lord Jesus, both Jews and Greeks" (Acts 19:10). "So mightily grew the word of God and prevailed" (Acts 19:20). Wherever the apostles ministered, whether to Jew or Gentile, the word was the weapon that was used to destroy the works of darkness and establish the reality of the gospel in the hearts and minds of men. The real battle was the battle for truth (John 8:31-32).

The Teaching of Paul on Spiritual Warfare in the Epistles

There is very little space given to discussing demonic activity in the Pauline epistles. Rather, the primary focus, in respect to both evangelism and the growth in maturity of individual Christians, is on the choices and actions taken by people themselves (for example, Gal. 5:16-26; Eph. 4:1-7; Col. 3:1-2, 8-9).[42] Many of Paul's writings deal specifically with problems within the church context.

His first letter to the Corinthians refers to the dissension which had arisen amongst them (1 Cor. 1:11) because of misunderstanding in respect to the nature of the body of Christ, the message of the gospel and the nature of ministry (1 Cor. 1-4). Later in the epistle he deals with other problems of immorality, legal wrangling and licence (1 Cor. 5-6). Paul did not attempt to identify and rebuke the "spirit of dissension" but methodically set out corrective teaching aimed to bring them back into an understanding of their status in Christ Jesus and the impact this must have upon their lives and relationships (1 Cor. 6:11-12, 19-20).

Similarly, in Paul's letter to the church at Galatia, one of his aims was to uncover the erroneous teaching of the Judaisers (Gal. 6:12-13), in order to prevent his readers from embracing a false gospel. The Galatians had lost their focus. They had forgotten that salvation is all of faith and made the deadly assumption that there was something they had to do to merit it (Gal. 3:1-3). Again, the great apostle deals with the issue systematically, explaining how he received the revelation of Jesus Christ (Gal. 1-2) and then defining the true message of the gospel (Gal. 3-4). Throughout this process Paul's aim was to re-establish the truth in the hearts and minds of his readers, not to evict some demonic enemy. His real warfare was not against

---

[42]Grudem, 420.

spiritual powers, but against the wrong thinking and wrong believing which had taken these Christians into bondage.

However, Paul was not unaware of the influence of idolatrous practices and the fascination with the demonic realm in the world of the New Testament. Many of the cities in the ancient Mediterranean were full of temples devoted to the worship of idols. He warned "that in the latter times some shall depart from the faith, giving heed to seducing spirits, and doctrines of devils; Speaking lies in hypocrisy; having their conscience seared with a hot iron; Forbidding to marry, *and commanding* to abstain from meats, which God hath created to be received with thanksgiving of them which believe and know the truth" (1 Tim. 4:1-3).

Adam Clarke comments on this as follows: "They will apostatize from the faith, i.e. from Christianity; renouncing the whole system in effect, by bringing in doctrines which render its essential truths null and void, or denying and renouncing such doctrines as are essential to Christianity as a system of salvation. A man may hold all the truths of Christianity, and yet render them of none effect by holding other doctrines which counteract their influence; or he may apostatize by denying some essential doctrine, though he bring in nothing heterodox."[43] It is interesting to note, that the basis of this apostasy is clearly a matter of erroneous belief induced by deception, and leading to the choice of a wrong lifestyle. These features are the hallmark of the devil's mode of operation. The method of escape is "by repentance to the acknowledging of the truth" (2 Tim. 2:24-26).

The sixth chapter of Ephesians is probably the most well known source of Paul's teaching concerning spiritual warfare. Arnold contends that the spiritual warfare imagery was because of Paul's need to address those converts from a background of occultism.[44] Before examining the passage itself, it is necessary to look at the overall context and underlying message of the letter as a whole.

The first three chapters of Ephesians deal with the great fundamentals of the Christian faith. Paul informs his readers "who

---

[43]Clarke, s.v. "1 Timothy 4:1."

[44]Clinton E. Arnold, *Powers of Darkness: A Thoughtful, Biblical Look at an Urgent Challenge Facing the Church* (Leicester: InterVarsity Press, 1992), 150.

they are, what they are, and how they have become what they are."[45]
He explains that believers have been blessed "with all spiritual
blessings in heavenly *places* in Christ" (Eph. 1:3). He wanted them to
understand "the hope of his calling," "the riches of the glory of his
inheritance in the saints," and "the exceeding greatness of his power
to us-ward who believe" (Eph. 1:18-19). He teaches that Jesus is
exalted "far above all principality, and power, and might, and
dominion" (Eph. 1:21). He prays that they may both "know the love
of Christ, which passeth knowledge" and "be filled with all the
fullness of God" (Eph. 3:19). In other words, Paul's desire was that
the Ephesians should comprehend the immense privileges of the
Christian life, for such understanding could not but revolutionise
their walk of faith. Having set out the facts, Paul then goes on to
plead with them to "walk worthy of the vocation wherewith ye are
called" (Eph. 4:1-7). He points out the vital necessity of a mind
which is alive to the truths of God and the importance of the will in
this process (Eph. 4:18-27).

It is against this background that the sixth chapter of Ephesians
must be understood. Believers operate from a position of blessing
and of victory. They are those who have been made heirs to the
"unsearchable riches of Christ" (Eph. 3:8), and the gift of life within
(Eph. 2:1) is to be protected from every assault of the enemy. At one
time they were "children of disobedience" (Eph. 2:2), but now by
God's great love and grace they have been raised up and made to sit
together "in heavenly *places* in Christ Jesus" (Eph. 2:6).

So the epistle closes with the following exhortation, "Finally, my
brethren, be strong in the Lord, and in the power of his might" (Eph.
6:10). The strength of the believer is in God, the Almighty, All-
conquering One, and because of their relationship with Christ, each
and every child of God has access to His power.[46] Paul then goes on
to explain that the armour is God's, emphasising that this will enable
them to stand against the best devised schemes and strategies of the
devil (Eph. 6:11). The instruction to "stand" is repeated in verses 13

---

[45]D. Martyn Lloyd-Jones, *The Christian Warfare: An Exposition of Ephesians 6:10 to 13* (Edinburgh: The Banner of Truth Trust, 1976), 12.

[46]Andrew T. Lincoln, *Ephesians*, vol. 42, *Word Biblical Commentary*, eds. Bruce M. Metzger, David A. Hubbard, and Glenn W. Barker (Dallas, TX: Word Books, 1990), 442.

and 14, and, as Lincoln comments, it involves "holding one's position, resisting, not surrendering to the opposition but prevailing against it" (compare 1 Thess. 3:8; 2 Thess. 2:15; Gal. 5:1).[47] The underlying emphasis is that the decisive victory has already been accomplished by God in Christ Jesus. Believers, therefore, are not required to go on the offensive but to stand, preserving and maintaining the victory that has been won. This is a dramatically different situation from that described in Ephesians 2:2-3, where resistance was impossible because the enemy held them in bondage. Lincoln concludes, "So the call to the readers to stand against the powers is also a reminder of their liberation from the tyranny of these powers."[48]

In Ephesians 6:12, the nature of the enemy is described, and it is noteworthy that this is the only place in the Pauline writings where believers are said to be in conflict with evil powers.[49] "Although the opposing forces are formidable, the fact that they are in the heavenly realms need no longer pose a threat to believers, because they are not fighting to break through the hold of such powers . . . but are to see themselves as fighting from a position of victory, having already been seated with Christ in the heavenly realms (see also Eph. 2:6)."[50]

Divine resources are available to enable every Christian to withstand spiritual attack, simply by taking up the "whole armour of God" (Eph. 6:13), which provides all that is needed to prevail. The various protective elements of this armour include truth, righteousness, peace, faith and salvation. The only offensive weapon is the "sword of the Spirit, which is the word of God" (Eph. 6:17). This is the gospel of good news (John 3:16-17; Rom. 1:16). Significantly, it is as believers lay hold of and proclaim this gospel, that they are enabled to overcome in the battle. The gospel conquers

---

[47]The author points out that these verses do not call on Christians to be strategic, to be generals or to direct the battle. Believers just hold their place in the line as God directs; very much in keeping with the way Romans fought.

[48]Lincoln, 443.

[49]Ibid., 440. ". . . whereas in Colossians, on which this letter is based, these powers had played a specific role in the false teaching addressed, here there is no such controversy in view. The significant part which the powers played in the consciousness of the Gentile readers and in particular their continuing malevolent influence is simply assumed."

[50]Ibid., 445.

all hostile powers and brings about salvation by the power of the Holy Spirit. Paul's use of the battle imagery assists him in conveying the urgency and challenge of their task as he calls for courage, determination, prayerfulness, alertness and perseverance. "At the same time, his focus on Christ's strength and God's full armour enables him to leave them with a sense of security and confidence."[51]

New Testament Summary

There is no evidence in the New Testament to suggest that Christians are called to engage in an ongoing conflict with spiritual forces in the cosmic realm. There is, however, real evidence of a spiritual battle for truth. Jesus came to establish His truth in the hearts and minds of men; this was the promise of the New Covenant as foretold by the prophet Jeremiah, "I will put my law in their inward parts, and write it in their hearts; and will be their God, and they shall be my people" (Jer. 31:33). The apostles understood that truth alone brought freedom and life (John 8:31-32). Contending for truth, whilst standing in truth is the New Testament pattern of spiritual warfare.

Theological Themes and Issues

The Sovereignty of God

Discussions about the existence and being of God have fascinated mankind from the very dawn of time. The Bible starts with God: "In the beginning God" (Gen. 1:1). He is over all. Louis Berkhof comments that creation ". . . is the beginning and basis of all divine revelation, and consequently also the foundation of all ethical and religious life . . . It stresses the fact that God is the origin of all things, and that all things belong to Him and are subject to Him."[52]

Similarly, Johnson and Webber argue that everything is absolutely dependent on God for its existence, meaning and well-being. God Himself is the centre that makes the world a cosmos rather than a chaos. He created all things out of nothing--ex nihilo (Gen. 1:2), and His word alone sustains the universe (Heb. 1:3).[53] The

---

[51]Ibid., 460.

[52]Berkhof, 126.

[53]Alan F. Johnson and Robert E. Webber, *What Christians Believe: A Biblical and Historical Summary* (Grand Rapids, MI: Zondervan Publishing House, 1989), 60.

entire creation was intended to show God's glory (Psa. 19:1-6; Rom. 1:20). It was not a necessary act but something that God chose to do (Rev. 4:11). "God's wisdom forms the foundation of all he creates so that the world stands as an expression and witness to his intrinsic nature. Therefore as God chooses to create, to sustain, and to direct his creation he simultaneously discloses himself in these acts, for they are rooted in his wisdom (compare with Proverbs 8:22-31)."[54] This understanding of God is in direct opposition to the philosophies of materialism, dualism, pantheism and deism.[55] He is the "Lord of heaven and earth" (Acts 17:24) and depends on nothing other than His own being. The two essential and personal names of God in the Hebrew Scriptures are Elohim and Jehovah (or Yahweh), and these portray essential facets of God Himself; the former focuses on the fullness of His divine power, and the latter describes His self-existence, "He who is."

Scripture describes God by means of self-revealed attributes or qualities.[56] Of His natural attributes, He is spirit (John 4:24), changeless (Heb. 1:12), omnipotent (Gen. 1:3; 17:1; 18:14, 25; Isa. 40:27-31; Heb.1:3), all knowing (Psa. 139:1-6, 13-16; 147:5; Rom. 11:33-36), omnipresent (Psa. 139:7-12; Matt. 6:1-18) and eternal (2 Pet. 3:8; Rev. 1:8). His moral attributes include holiness (Isa. 6:1-3; Eph. 4:24), righteousness (Gen. 18:25; Deut. 32:4; Rom. 1:16-17; 2:6-16; 3:24-26), love (Deut. 7:8; Mal. 1:2; John 3:16; 1 Tim. 1:14; 1 John 4:8-10), wisdom (Prov. 2:6; 3:19; 1 Tim. 1:17; James 1:5) and truth (Deut. 32:4; Psa. 31:5; John 14:6).

Based on His perfection, it is God's prerogative to be sovereign (Psa. 50:1; 66:7; 93:1; Isa. 40:15, 17; 1 Tim. 6:15; Rev. 11:17). It is possible to oppose His will (John 1:13; Rom. 7:18), but ultimately His perfect will prevails and His purposes cannot be frustrated (Acts 4:28; Eph. 1:11; Phil.2: 13), merely resisted for a time (Luke 7:30). Charnock states, "We cannot suppose God a Creator, without supposing a sovereign dominion in him . . . It is such a dominion as cannot be renounced by God himself. It is so intrinsic and connatural

---

[54]Ibid., 61.

[55]Grudem, 268-69.

[56]Theologians differ in their statements, varying in their use of terms as well as in classification and arrangement. But they generally agree on those named here.

to him, so inlaid in the nature of God, that he cannot strip himself of it, nor of the exercise of it, while any creature remains."[57]

Hodge describes this concept of the omnipotence of God as follows: "This simple idea of the omnipotence of God, that He can do without effort, and by a volition, whatever He wills, is the highest conceivable idea of power, and is that which is clearly presented in the Scriptures . . . The Lord God omnipotent reigneth, and doeth his pleasure among the armies of heaven and the inhabitants of the earth, is the tribute of adoration which the Scriptures everywhere render unto God, and the truth which they everywhere present as the ground of confidence to his people."[58] God's absolute and irresistible dominion extends over all, including angels and devils, wicked and good, rational and irrational creatures. As Charnock points out, "All things essentially depend on him. . . . The heaven of angels, and other excellent creatures, belong to his authority . . . The hell of devils belong to this authority. They have cast themselves out of the arms of his grace into the furnace of his justice; they have, by their revolt, forfeited the treasure of his goodness, but cannot exempt themselves from the sceptre of his dominion. . . . He rules over the good angels as his subjects, over the evil ones as his rebels. In whatsoever relation he stands, either as a friend or enemy, he never loses that of Lord."[59] George Fox states, "Christ is a top of the head of them all, for he was before they were, and will be when they are gone, Glory to GOD for ever."[60]

In contrast, the scriptural doctrine of Satan is not systematically developed. References to him are both scattered and incidental.[61] However, with respect to an understanding of the sovereignty of God, it is of paramount importance to have a true biblical understanding of Satan's character, his capabilities, his methods and his limitations.

---

[57]Stephen Charnock, *The Existence and Attributes of God*, vol. 2 of 2 (Grand Rapids, MI: Baker Book House, 1979), 366.

[58]Charles Hodge, *Systematic Theology*, vol. 1 of 3 (Grand Rapids, MI: Wm. B. Eerdmans Publishing Co., 1981), 407.

[59]Charnock, 2:381-82.

[60]Fox, *Gospel-Truth*, 465.

[61]*ISBE*, s.v. "Satan," by Louis Matthews Sweet.

The word "Satan" appears a total of twenty-four times in the Old Testament. It is developed from a general term to an appellation and later to a proper name. In eight of these appearances, the name means "enemy" or "adversary" (Num. 22:22; 1 Kin. 5:4; 11:23) but it is also used in the sense of "accuser," as in Psalm 109:6.

His name is mentioned in Job 1:6, "when the sons of God came to present themselves before the LORD, and Satan came also among them." In this passage, there is a hint of opposition between God and Satan, and the latter is permitted to bring severe temptations against Job. This narrative shows two truths: a) that Satan is an accuser; and b) that he is not an independent rival of God, but is able to go only as far as God permits. He plays this same role in Zechariah 3:1 where the priest has a vision of "Joshua the high priest standing before the angel of the LORD, and Satan standing at his right hand to resist him." In this account the Lord is invoked to rebuke Satan, and once again it is clear that the latter can operate only within well-defined parameters.

There is a further reference to the influence of Satan in the book of Chronicles, where he supposedly enticed David to number the children of Israel (1 Chro. 21:1). The account in 2 Samuel 24:1, however, has the Lord inciting David to take the census. This was done to punish Israel. "God, in order to bring about his purposes, worked through Satan to incite David to sin, but Scripture regards David as being responsible for that sin."[62]

In the Old Testament, Satan never openly appears as the enemy of God. Conversely, in the New Testament, his malevolent character is well known and he is consistently portrayed as the opponent of both God and man (Matt. 13:25, 28). However, his power remains strictly limited (Luke 4:6; 2 Thess. 2:7-8).

It is clear that he has become the leader of the anarchic order of evil (1 Cor. 15:24; Col. 2:15; Eph. 6:12) and so operates in conjunction with a plurality of other evil spirits (Matt. 8:28-31). He is called the "prince of the power of the air" (Eph. 2:2); the "prince of this world" (John 12:31; 14:30); the "god of this world" (2 Cor. 4:4); and the "prince of the devils" (Matt. 12:24). However, the biblical emphasis upon the characteristic of falsehood in respect to Satan

---

[62]Grudem, 324.

(John 8:44) may imply that his kingdom is more limited than appears.[63] He continually seeks to defeat the divine plans of grace toward mankind (1 Pet. 5:8); causes spiritual blindness (2 Cor. 4:4) and may also inflict physical infirmities (Luke 13:16). He is subtle (2 Cor. 11:3); the tempter (Matt. 4:1; 1 Cor. 7:5; 1 Thess. 3:5); a liar and a murderer (John 8:44); a thief and a destroyer (John 10:10). He masquerades as an angel of light, and his servants as servants of righteousness (2 Cor. 11:14-15). Paul indicates the reason for his fall was pride or conceit (1 Tim. 3:6). He even disputed with the archangel Michael about the body of Moses (Jude 9).[64] Jesus Himself gives the fundamental moral description of Satan in the parable of the sower when He refers to Satan as the "wicked one" (Matt. 13:19, 38), in other words, one whose nature and will are given to evil.

Satan's power consists principally in his ability to deceive (Rev. 20:3, 8). He is fundamentally a liar, and his kingdom therefore is founded on deception. He operates by direct suggestion (Luke 22:3; John 13:2, 27), human agency (2 Cor. 2:11), misrepresentation (2 Cor. 11:13, 15; 1 John 4:1-2; 2 Thess. 2:8-9; Rev. 12:9; 19:20) or via a person's own weakness (1 Cor. 7:5).

The Scripture is quite clear in its teaching that Christ defeated Satan completely at Calvary (Col. 2:15; compare with Gen. 3:15), and that Christians have been freed from his power (Col. 1:13). He is a conquered enemy (John 12:31; 16:9-19; 1 John 3:8; Col. 2:15). He is bound (Rev. 20:1-3); he is already judged (John 16:11). He is to be cast out of this world (John 12:31) and into the lake of fire (Matt. 25:41; Rev. 20:10). One can only conclude from this evidence that Satan is not a rival of equivalent power to good and God; he is totally subordinate.

Contrary to a number of the Church Fathers,[65] and some present-day populist authors,[66] much of modern scholarship is of the

---

[63]*ISBE*, s.v. "Satan" by Sweet.

[64]Page, 209-210.

[65]For example, Tertullian, *Contra Marcion*, bk. 2, chap. 10, in vol. 1, *The Writings of Tertullian*, in vol. 11 of 23, *Ante-Nicene Christian Library: Translations of the Writings of the Fathers; Down to A.D. 325*, eds. Rev. Alexander Roberts and James Donaldson (Edinburgh: T. and T. Clark, 1869), 80-81. See also Origen, *De Principiis*, bk. 1, chap. 5, paragraphs 4 and 5, in vol. 1 of *The Writings of Origen*, in *Ante-Nicene Christian Library*, 10:49-53.

opinion that the Old Testament does not actually say anything about the original fall of Satan.[67] The most commonly quoted passages in this context are Isaiah 14:12-15 and Ezekiel 28:12-19, where the kings of Babylon and Tyre respectively are erroneously allegorised as Satan. Each passage is a description of a funeral dirge lamenting the death of a tyrant pagan ruler. In both, the king is depicted as having come to ruin because he exalted himself beyond what was right. The mythological, metaphorical language of the laments in both passages is extremely sarcastic and mocking, revealing that the demise of the kings was most welcome.[68] Page uses biblical and historical evidence to prove that these are earthly monarchs, not supernatural beings, and therefore there is no valid basis for the assumption that these passages allude to Satan.[69]

Without the false backing of these passages, Satan is reduced to his true stature, a fallen angel, a created being who has chosen to disobey God. He is not the "choice cherubim." There is no biblical foundation for ascribing to him such superior intelligence and power as to be almost equal to those of God Himself. Neither is there any evidence of a theodicy or philosophy of evil in the biblical treatment of Satan. As Sweet states, "The doctrine of Satan corresponds, item for item, to the intellectual saneness and ethical earnestness of the Biblical world-view as a whole. . . . The restraint of chastened imagination, not the evidence of mythological fancy, is in evidence throughout the entire Biblical treatment of the subject. Even the use of terms current in mythology (as perhaps Genesis 3:1,13-14; Revelation 12:7-9; compare 1 Peter 5:8) does not imply more than a literary clothing of Satan in attributes commonly ascribed to malignant and disorderly forces."[70]

---

[66]For example, Michael Green, *I Believe in Satan's Downfall* (Grand Rapids, MI: William B. Eerdmans Publishing Company, 1981), 36-41; and Merrill F. Unger, *Biblical Demonology* (Wheaton, IL: Scripture Press, 1952), 15.

[67]John D. W. Watts, *Isaiah 1-33,* vol. 24, *Word Biblical Commentary,* eds. David A. Hubbard and Glenn W. Barker (Waco, TX: Word Books, 1985), 24:212; H. L. Ellison, *Ezekiel: the Man and his Message* (London: Paternoster Press, 1956), 108-109; and Grudem, 72-73, 149-203.

[68]Page, 37.

[69]See Appendix A for a more thorough discussion of this subject

[70]*ISBE,* s.v. "Satan," by Sweet.

The Word of God

The word of God is the means by which God makes Himself known, declares His will and brings about His purposes. By His word God spoke the worlds into being (Gen. 1; 2 Pet. 3:5), and by His word He destroyed the world in the days of Noah (2 Pet. 3:6). God communicates Himself (1 Sam. 3:21), His promises, His blessings and His commandments by His word (Gen. 12:1-3). It is the primary means by which He is present and working in the world. God's word is eternal, as He is eternal (Isa. 40:8), and can discern every thought and intention of the human heart (Heb. 4:12). His word contains creative power (Ezek. 37:4-5) and always fulfils His purposes (Isa. 55:11; Jer. 23:29).[71] Charles Hodge comments, "His word can never fail, though heaven and earth pass away. The truth of God, therefore, is the foundation of all religion. It is the ground of our assurance . . . He certainly is, and wills, and will do, whatever He has thus made known."[72]

However, throughout the course of history there has been considerable theological debate in respect to the efficacy of the word as a means of grace. Nomism[73] contends that the truth revealed in the word of God operates only via moral persuasion. Conversely, Antinomianism disregards the external word, focussing on the mystical inner word or light from the immediate operation of the Holy Spirit; its slogan is "The letter killeth, but the Spirit giveth life." However, the Reformers held that in the work of redemption, the word and the Spirit operate in unison. As Lutheran doctrine developed, it taught that the converting power of the Holy Spirit was a divine deposit intrinsic to the word of God.[74] This was slightly different from the true Reformed position which was based on the belief that the word could only become efficacious by an accompanying operation of the Spirit in the hearts of men.[75]

---

[71]*Nelson's Bible Dictionary*, s.v. "Word of God," in *PC Study Bible: Complete Reference Library* ver. 3.0 [CD ROM] (Seattle, WA: Biblesoft 1992-1999).

[72]Hodge, 1:437.

[73]Nomism includes Judaism, Pelagianism, Semi-Pelagianism, Arminianism, Neonomianism, and Rationalism.

[74]In order to explain the differing results consequent on preaching the word, they also adopted the doctrine of free will.

[75]Berkhof, 611-12.

However, the Scripture makes it clear that God's revelation of Himself culminated in the sending of His Son, Jesus Christ, the incarnate word of God (John 1:1, 14; Heb. 1:1-2), empowered by the Spirit of God (Luke 4:18-19). Jesus recognised His own calling and purpose as recorded by the prophet Isaiah: "The Spirit of the Lord *is* upon me, because he hath anointed me to preach the gospel to the poor; he hath sent me to heal the broken-hearted, to preach deliverance to the captives, and recovering of sight to the blind, to set at liberty them that are bruised, To preach the acceptable year of the Lord" (Luke 4:18-19). He came to communicate in word and deed the heart of the Father and His great plan of salvation.

The common people recognised the authority of the words of Jesus, "For he taught them as *one* having authority, and not as the scribes" (Matt. 7:29). Healing and deliverance came by His word (Matt. 8:8; John 4:50); He forgave sins by His word (Matt. 9:2); He stilled the storm by His word (Mark 4:39); He cast out demons by His word (Matt. 8:32), and death was banished at His word (Mark 5:41-42; Luke 7:14-15; John 11:43-44). In the eyes of the average Jew, Jesus was a radical. He employed no ritual or methodology, but simply spoke the words of life in total obedience to the direction of the Father. His ministry was based on one immutable principle, "I do nothing of myself; but as my Father hath taught me, I speak these things" (John 8:28).

Thus the ministry of Jesus in the gospels was wholly word-based and this pattern was continued by the apostles in the early church. The great New Testament theologian Paul declared, "For I am not ashamed of the gospel of Christ: for it is the power of God unto salvation to every one that believeth; to the Jew first, and also to the Greek" (Rom. 1:16). New birth is accomplished by the word of God (1 Pet. 1:23), and the book of Acts reveals that not only the expansion of the church, but the destruction of witchcraft was effected by the simple exposition of the word (Acts 19:18-20).

Thomas Watson comments, "It was by the ear, by our first parents listening to the serpent, that we lost paradise; and it is by the ear, by hearing of the Word, that we get to heaven. 'Hear, and your souls shall live' (Isaiah 55:3)."[76] Preaching is the God-ordained tool in evangelism (Rom. 10:14) for, "faith *cometh* by hearing, and hearing by the word of God" (Rom. 10:17). Based on these verses, Haldane demonstrates that Paul's doctrine is that, "the Gospel must be communicated to the minds of men through the external instrumentality of the word, as well as by the internal agency of the Spirit. Men are not only saved through Christ, but they are saved through the knowledge of Christ, communicated through the Gospel."[77] Such hearing is "not merely a registering of a sequence of words on the mind, but a hearing with an understanding of the significance of those words and a response appropriate to that significance."[78] This is what theologians have defined as the effective calling of God, speaking through the human proclamation of the gospel, by which He calls individuals to Himself in such a way that they respond in saving faith. Such a call is particular, internal and always effective.[79] Grudem comments: "He [God] does not save us 'automatically' without seeking for a response from us as whole persons. Rather, he addresses the gospel call to our intellects, our emotions, and our wills. He speaks to our intellects by explaining the facts of salvation in his Word. He speaks to our emotions by issuing a heartfelt personal invitation to respond. He speaks to our wills by asking us to hear his invitation and respond willingly in repentance and faith--to decide to turn from our sins and receive Christ as Savior and rest our hearts in him for salvation."[80]

Spurgeon describes the process of conversion as follows:

> By the Word of the Lord you were brought to the cross, and comforted by the atonement. That Word breathed a new life into you; and when, for the first time, you knew yourself to be a child of God, you felt the enobling power of the gospel received by faith . . . Whoever may have been the man who spoke it, or whatever may have been the book in which you read it, it was not man's Word, nor

[76]Thomas Watson, *The Golden Treasury of Puritan Quotations* (Chicago, IL: Moody Press, 1975), 221.

[77]Robert Haldane, *A Commentary on the Epistle to the Romans* (London: The Banner of Truth Trust, 1960), 513.

[78]James D. G. Dunn, *Romans 9-16*, vol. 38B, *Word Biblical Commentary*, eds. Bruce M. Metzger, David A. Hubbard, and Glenn W. Barker (Dallas, TX: Word Books, 1988), 38B:628.

[79]Grudem, 693.

[80]Ibid., 695.

man's thought upon God's Word, but the Word itself, which made you know salvation in the Lord Jesus. It was neither human reasoning, nor the force of eloquence, nor the power of moral suasion, but the omnipotence of the Spirit, applying the Word itself, that gave you rest and peace and joy through believing.[81]

He also asserted that, "The Scriptures in their own sphere are like God in the universe--All-Sufficient. In them is revealed all the light and power the mind of man can need in spiritual things."[82]

The operation of the devil and his minions is to blind the minds of men, "lest the light of the glorious gospel of Christ, who is the image of God, should shine unto them" (2 Cor. 4:4). The light of God is contained in the word of God (Psa. 119:105; Prov. 6:23). Similarly, Jesus, the incarnate word (John 1:14), came to be the light of the world (John 8:12). At new birth the believer is delivered from the power of darkness and translated into the kingdom of His dear Son (Col. 1:13). The battle is in the mind and will; it is simply a question of who and what to believe.

In this great fight of faith the only weapon is "the sword of the Spirit, which is the word of God" (Eph. 6:17). Its purpose is "casting down imaginations, and every high thing that exalteth itself against the knowledge of God, and bringing into captivity every thought to the obedience of Christ" (2 Cor. 10:5). John Flavel describes these "imaginations" as the "subtleties, slights, excuses, subterfuges, and arguings of fleshly-minded men; in which they fortify and entrench themselves against the convictions of the word."[83] However, ultimately by God's sovereign grace, the gospel overthrows the strongholds erected against it in the mind and will. "Many staggerings, hesitations, irresolutions, doubts, fears, scruples, half-resolves, reasonings for and against, there are at the council-table of man's own heart, at this time . . . The soul yields not at the first summons, till its provisions within are spent, and all its towers of pride, and walls of vain confidence, be undermined by the gospel,

---

[81]Charles H. Spurgeon, *The Greatest Fight in the World* (Belfast, Northern Ireland: Ambassador Publications, 1999), 26-27.

[82]Ibid., 19.

[83]John Flavel, *The Works of John Flavel*, vol. 1 of 6 (Edinburgh: The Banner of Truth Trust, 1968), 199. John Flavel (1628-1691) was the son of a Puritan minister who died in prison for his nonconformity. He belonged to a tradition which believed that preaching should be "hissing hot," searching and expository.

and shaken down about its ears: and then the soul desires a parley with Christ."[84] Truly the gospel "is the power of God unto salvation" (Rom. 1:16).

Flavel writes further, concerning the efficacy of the word that: "No heart so hard, no conscience so stupid, but this sword can pierce and wound; in an instant it can cast down all those vain reasonings and fond imaginations, which the carnal heart hath been building all its life long, and open a fair passage for convictions of sin, and the fears and terrors of wrath to come, into that heart that never was afraid of these things before."[85] Thus on the day of Pentecost the gathered assembly responded to the words which Peter spoke: "when they heard *this*, they were pricked in their heart, and said unto Peter and to the rest of the apostles, Men *and* brethren, what shall we do?" (Acts 2:37). The word of God, spoken in the power of the Spirit of God, had done its work, "Then they that gladly received his word were baptised: and the same day there were added *unto them* about three thousand souls" (Acts 2:41).

This is the biblical pattern for evangelism. It requires none of the elements of SLSW, simply the preaching of the word of God in the power of the Spirit of God. It has been said of C. H. Spurgeon that: "There was no more solemn place in the world than the pulpit for this great man of God. To him, preaching wasn't child's play; it was spiritual warfare against the powers of darkness. In every sermon Spurgeon stood toe to toe with the devil himself. Every convert was a jewel snatched from Satan's crown and presented to the Savior."[86] His philosophy was, "Preach the gospel, the gates of hell shake. Preach the gospel, prodigals return. Preach the gospel, to every creature, it is the Master's mandate and the Master's power to everyone who believes."[87] He believed, "I am content to live and die as the mere repeater of scriptural teaching, as a person who thought out nothing and invented nothing, as one who never thought invention to be any part of his calling, but who concluded that he was

---

[84]Ibid., 202.

[85]Flavel, 2:56-57.

[86]Charles H. Spurgeon, *2200 Quotations from the Writings of Charles H. Spurgeon*, ed. Tom Carter (Grand Rapids, MI: Baker Books, 1988), 4.

[87]Ibid., 158.

simply to be a mouthpiece for God to the people, mourning that anything of his own should come between."[88]

The Holy Spirit[89]

Theologians have described the plan of redemption as a covenant between the three members of the Godhead.[90] On the part of the Father, this involved an agreement to accept the death of His own Son as a full, perfect and sufficient sacrifice for all sin forever (Heb. 10:12). Correspondingly, the Son determined that He would come to earth, live as a man and that He would be perfectly obedient to the will of the Father, even to the laying down of His own life as a "ransom for many" (Matt. 20:28). For His part, the Holy Spirit agreed, "to do the will of the Father and fill and empower Christ to carry out his ministry on the earth (Matthew 3:16; Luke 4:1,14,18; John 3:34), and to apply the benefits of Christ's redemptive work to his people after Christ returned to heaven (John 14:16-17; Acts 1:8; 2:17-18,33)."[91]

The study of pneumatology (like Christology) is primarily a New Testament development. But the roots of the doctrine may be found in much earlier periods of revelation.[92] The first reference to God's Spirit is in Genesis where, at the time of creation, the Spirit of God is said to have "moved upon the face of the deep" (Gen. 1:2). As Grudem points out, this gives the indication that the Holy Spirit's work "is to complete and sustain what God the Father has planned and what God the Son has begun."[93]

In the Old Testament, the Holy Spirit is seen primarily as a Spirit of enablement, endowing an artisan, judge, prophet, priest or king with the ability to perform certain functions or tasks. Such

---

[88]Ibid., 161-62.

[89]Given the constraints of space, the author foregoes an effort toward an exhaustive interpretation of the role of the Holy Spirit and accordingly limits himself in scope to two areas only: prayer and evangelism.

[90]Grudem, 518.

[91]Ibid., 518-19.

[92]Johnson and Webber, 148.

[93]Grudem, 635.

endowment was generally transitory rather than an abiding reality.[94] Old Testament prophecy also points to the coming Messiah who would fulfil His divine mission in the power of the Holy Spirit (Isa. 11:1-2), and it is clear in the New Testament that the gift of the Spirit in fullness to Jesus at His baptism constituted the formal and public anointing for His Messianic work (Acts 10:38).[95]

Towards the end of His earthly ministry, Jesus placed an increasing emphasis on the training of His disciples. They were to take His place and carry on the work He had begun, in His name and with His help.[96] Prior to His death, Jesus had told His followers, "Ye have not chosen me but I have chosen you, and ordained you, that ye should go and bring forth much fruit, and that your fruit should remain" (John 15:16).

In the same passage, Jesus sets out the requirements for fruitfulness, drawing the analogy of the relationship between the vine and the branches. The principle He illustrates is that of abiding. From a theological standpoint, Bruce distinguishes two types of abiding in this teaching--structurally, that of the branches abiding in the vine; and vitally, that of the vine abiding in the branches through its sap. He explains further:

> What, then would one say most nearly corresponded to the structural abiding of the branch in the tree? We reply, abiding in the doctrine of Christ, in the doctrine He taught; and acknowledging Him as the source whence it had been learned. In other words, "Abide in me" means, Hold and profess the truth I have spoken to you, and give yourselves out merely as my witnesses. The other abiding, on the other hand, signifies the indwelling of the Spirit of Jesus in the hearts of those who believe. Jesus gave His disciples to understand that, while abiding in His doctrine, they must also have His Spirit abiding in them; that they must not only hold fast the truth, but be filled with the Spirit of truth. The two abidings . . . cannot be separated without fatal effects.[97]

On the day of Pentecost, these "two abidings" came together in the hearts and minds of the followers of Jesus gathered in the upper

---

[94]William J. Rodman, *Renewal Theology: Systematic Theology from a Charismatic Perspective* (Grand Rapids, MI: Zondervan Publishing House, 1996), 155-60.

[95]*ISBE*, s.v. "Holy Spirit."

[96]Alexander Balmain Bruce, *The Training of the Twelve* (New Canaan, CT: Keats Publishing, 1979), 411.

[97]Ibid., 414-15.

room. The words that He had spoken to them now came alive within them by the power of the Holy Spirit. The Holy Spirit, who had been part of creation, was, with the inauguration of the new creation at Pentecost, now sent to empower the church.

The Role of the Holy Spirit in Prayer

Of the many broad definitions of prayer, one point on which theologians agree is that prayer is communion with God, as a result of a personal relationship with Him (for example, Grudem,[98] Lloyd-Jones,[99] Kenyon,[100] Hodge,[101] and the Catholic Encyclopaedia[102]). Spurgeon writes:

> True prayer is an approach of the soul by the Spirit of God to the throne of God. It is not the utterance of words, it is not alone the feeling of desires, but it is the advance of the desires to God, the spiritual approach of our nature towards the Lord our God. True prayer is not a mere mental exercise, nor a vocal performance, but it is far deeper than that--it is spiritual commerce with the Creator of heaven and earth. God is a Spirit unseen of mortal eye, and only to be perceived by the inner man; our spirit within us, begotten by the Holy Ghost at our regeneration, discerns the Great Spirit, communes with him, prefers to him our requests, and receives from him answers of peace. It is a spiritual business from beginning to end; and its aim and object end not with man, but reach to God himself.[103]

Just as a child is birthed and genetically belongs to his parents,[104] so at new birth a person comes into relationship with God, crying "Abba, Father" (Gal. 4:6). Prayer then becomes the Christian son's "vital contact with the Father."[105] It is not therefore a passive

---

[98]Grudem, 376.

[99]D. Martyn Lloyd-Jones, *The Christian Soldier: An Exposition of Ephesians 6:10-20* (Edinburgh: The Banner of Truth Trust, 1977), 339.

[100]E. W. Kenyon, *In His Presence: The Secret of Prayer* (Lynnwood, WA: Kenyon's Gospel Publishing Society, 1999), 8.

[101]Hodge, 3:692.

[102]*The Catholic Encyclopedia*, ed. Roberts C. Broderick, s.v. "Prayer" (Nashville, TN: Thomas Nelson Publishers, 1986), 485-87.

[103]Charles H. Spurgeon, *Spurgeon's Expository Encyclopedia*, vol. 12 of 15 (Grand Rapids, MI: Baker Book House, 1978), 203.

[104]Charles H. Spurgeon, *Sermons Preached and Revised by C. H. Spurgeon, During the Year 1885*, in *The Metropolitan Tabernacle Pulpit* (Pasadena, TX: Pilgrim Publications, 1973), 31:505.

[105]Kenyon, 8.

doctrine, but a way of life. William Penn said of George Fox, the great revivalist and founder of the Quaker movement, "above all he excelled in prayer," and continued to define prayer as "living near to the Lord."[106] Significantly, there is no scriptural basis for the notion that a preliminary combat with the devil is necessary to ensure the effectiveness of prayer.

The divine cooperation of the whole Trinity is at work in prayer: "God the Holy Ghost writes our prayers, God the Son presents our prayers, and God the Father accepts our prayers."[107] Further, it is ". . . the living experience of the truth of the Holy Trinity. The Spirit's breathing, the Son's intercession, and the Father's will become one in us."[108] Prayer, in its fullest sense, is addressed to the Father (Matt. 6:9-12), in the power of the Spirit (Eph. 6:18), and in the name of the Son (John 14:13-14).[109] Prayer is "an activity inspired by God himself, through his Holy Spirit. It is God siding with his people, and, by his own empowering presence, the Spirit of God himself, bringing forth prayer that is in keeping with his will and his ways."[110] A man or woman whose mind is under God's government prays as his Father does.[111]

God as Father is the object of Christian prayer.[112] The majority of scholars find enough New Testament warrant for addressing directly the Son as well as the Father, but only a few scholars include prayer to the Holy Spirit.[113] However, in this context Grudem cautions that, whilst finding nothing to forbid addressing the Holy Spirit, it is "not the New Testament pattern, and it should not

---

[106]William Penn, introduction to *The Journal of George Fox*, by George Fox, 3d ed. (London: W. Richardson and S. Clark, 1765), 28.

[107]Charles H. Spurgeon, *Sermons Preached by C. H. Spurgeon. Revised and Published During the Year 1908*, in *The Metropolitan Tabernacle Pulpit* (Pasadena, TX: Pilgrim Publications, 1978), 54:342-43.

[108]Andrew Murray, *With Christ in the School of Prayer* (North Brunswick, NJ: Bridge-Logos Publishers, 1999), 213.

[109]*ISBE*, s.v. "Prayer," by J. C. Lambert.

[110]Gordon D. Fee, *Paul, the Spirit and the People of God* (Peabody, MA: Hendrickson Publishers, 1996), 149.

[111]Hodge, 3:695.

[112]John Nolland, *Luke 9:21-18:34, Word Biblical Commentary*, eds. David A. Hubbard and Glenn W. Barker (Dallas, TX: Word Books, 1993), 35B:612.

[113]See for example, Grudem, 381, and Hodge, 3:700.

become the dominant emphasis in our prayer life."[114] In contrast, biblical scholar, Fee, sees quite a distinct role for the Spirit: "It has sometimes been noted, as a word either against the personality of the Spirit or against Paul's trinitarianism, that the Spirit is never invoked in prayer, as are the Father and the Son. Precisely, but the conclusion being drawn is incorrect. The role of the Spirit in prayer is a different one; he is our divine 'pray-er,' the one through whom we pray, not the one to whom prayer is directed."[115]

In Romans 8:26 the Holy Spirit is described as the one who "helpeth our infirmities" specifically in the context of prayer "for we know not what we should pray for as we ought." The word translated "helpeth" is the same as is used in Luke 10:40 where Martha asked Mary to come and "help" her.[116] Interestingly, the particular word for "pray" (Gk. *huperentugchano*) in this verse is not used anywhere else in Scripture,[117] making it the rarest prayer word[118] (see Kittel,[119] and Renner[120]). This word, "is not used in connection with us; rather, it is used in connection with the Holy Spirit."[121] Intercession rightly belongs to God, not to man.[122]

There is no New Testament pattern of Jesus, Paul or any apostle engaging in prayer evangelism, in the sense of praying specifically for world evangelisation (John 17:9). According to Fee, Paul's prayers for others were two-fold: a concern for their growth as Christians, and a concern for the growth of the Gospel. Paul wanted them to bear fruit

---

[114]Grudem, 381.

[115]Fee, 151.

[116]D. Martyn Lloyd-Jones, *Romans: The Final Perseverance of the Saints, An Exposition of Chapter 8:17-39* (Edinburgh: The Banner of Truth Trust, 1975), 133.

[117]Grudem, 382-83.

[118]Rick Renner, *Dressed to Kill: A Biblical Approach to Spiritual Warfare and Armor* (Tulsa, OK: Pillar Books and Publishing, 1991), 287. Renner identifies six types of prayer for the believer in the New Testament: consecration, petition, urgent need, thanksgiving, supplication and intercession.

[119]Gerhard Friedrich, ed., s.v. "*huperentugchano*", *Theological Dictionary of the New Testament*, vol. 8 of 10 (Grand Rapids, MI: Wm. B. Eerdmans Publishing Company, 1974), 243.

[120]Renner, 299.

[121]Ibid.

[122]Friedrich, 8:243; and John Calvin, "On Prayer," online posting, http://www.ccel.org/pager.cgi?file=c/calvin/prayer/prayer1.0.html&from=RTFTo.../prayer.htm; accessed 14 Feb. 2001.

in every good work, grow in their knowledge of God, to be strengthened for endurance, and to joyfully give thanks to the Father who "is creating a *people* among whom he can live and who in their life together will reproduce God's life and character."[123] Paul exhorted the believers to pray that the word of the Lord would spread rapidly, and those who carry the word would be rescued from evil (2 Thess. 3:1-2).

Prayer is not therefore a spiritual weapon,[124] nor is it an accompaniment to spiritual warfare,[125] but rather our intimate relationship with God. The emphasis is placed on the evidence of *The Christian in Complete Armour*, [126] where "the presence of his general" means "all" prayer at "all times."[127] Kenyon's poignant statement is a fitting conclusion to this discussion on the Holy Spirit and prayer, "We become so utterly ruled and governed by the Word and by the Holy Spirit that we become Masters of demons and of their work. We cast out demons with the Word. We pray for sick folks and the diseases leave them. Weakness is destroyed by the strength of God. The very life of God flows out through our lips."[128]

The Role of the Holy Spirit in Evangelism

The Great Commission (Matt. 28:18-19) was not just an instruction but also a pronouncement of victory by the risen Saviour through His disciples.[129] He told His followers to "Go," "Teach," and "Baptise all nations," on the basis of the fact that He had been given

---

[123]Fee, 149.

[124]A. Scott Moreau, "Gaining Perspective on Territorial Spirits" from the Lausanne Committee for World Evangelization, online posting, http://www.gospelcom.net/lcwe/dufe/Papers/terspir.htm; accessed 29 June 2001.

[125]Chuck Lowe, "Prayer, Evangelization and Spiritual Warfare," paper presented at the Inaugural Billy Graham Center Evangelism Roundtable, Billy Graham Center, Wheaton College, Wheaton, Illinois, 19 Jan. 2001.

[126]William Gurnall, *The Christian in Complete Armour*, vol. 2 of 3 (Edinburgh: The Banner of Truth Trust, 1995), 288.

[127]Charles E. Lawless, "A Response to Dr. Charles Lowe Regarding 'Prayer, Evangelization and Spiritual Warfare,'" paper presented at the Inaugural Billy Graham Center Evangelism Roundtable, Billy Graham Center, Wheaton College, Wheaton, Illinois, 19 Jan. 2001.

[128]Kenyon, 9.

[129]*The King James Study Bible* (Nashville, TN: Thomas Nelson Publishers, 1988), notes to Matt. 28.

all power in heaven and in earth. This was a divine mandate, requiring divine authority.

The promise of the Spirit was fulfilled at Pentecost, but was not to be limited to the original band of disciples.[130] When any man or woman is birthed by the word of God, through the agency of the Holy Spirit, he or she receives the reality of God's presence and enters into the realm of the miraculous, becoming a living witness to His life and power. In this context, Richard Roberts notes, "God gives you the power of the Holy Spirit so you can win the lost to Christ!"[131] American Baptist scholar, Howard M. Ervin, correspondingly states, "The purpose of Pentecost is unmistakably world evangelism."[132]

Jesus defeated Satan fully and finally by His death and resurrection. As Lockyer has said, "The cross nullifies the doings of the devil. Every regenerated, transformed life is a fresh evidence of Christ's conquest of Satan."[133] The first disciples were given power to be effective witnesses, not to embark upon a cosmic duel with the forces of darkness. Scripture clearly teaches that Satan is finally overcome by the blood of the Lamb and the testimony of the saints (Rev. 10:12). Lockyer also states, "Satan was defeated, prophetically, in Eden; actually, at Calvary; and is defeated practically in our lives as day by day we exercise faith in the overcoming principle."[134]

The real battle in evangelism is not with demonic powers, but in contending for the truths of the gospel. In this conflict, the Holy Spirit is sent to "reprove the world of sin, and of righteousness, and of judgment" (John 16:8). In other words, firstly, He points out the need of redemption, the greatest sin being that of unbelief (John. 16:9). This has been defined by Drummond as not mere ignorance of Christ, but rather "the willful rejection of the Lord and His salvation." He then cites Ethelbert Stauffer as commenting, "It was

---

[130]Ibid.

[131]Richard Roberts, *The Unlimited Power Within You* (Tulsa, OK: n.p., 1986), 22.

[132]Howard M. Ervin, *Spirit Baptism: A Biblical Investigation* (Peabody, MA: Hendrickson Publishers, 1987), 38.

[133]Herbert Lockyer, *All the Promises of the Bible: A Unique Compilation and Exposition of Divine Promises in Scripture* (Grand Rapids, MI: Zondervan Publishing House, 1962), 241.

[134]Ibid., 239.

necessary that the Holy Spirit himself should open our eyes," and continues, "This forensic work of the Spirit is absolutely essential to see unbelief for all it really is in God's sight."[135] Spurgeon gave a personal testimony of his own conversion as follows:

> I knew what sin meant by my reading, and yet I never knew sin in its heinousness and horror, till I found myself bitten by it as a fiery serpent, and felt its poison boiling in my veins. When the Holy Ghost made sin to appear sin, then was I overwhelmed with the sight, and I would fain have fled from myself to escape the intolerable vision. A naked sin stripped of all excuse, and set in the light of truth, is a worse sight than to see the devil himself. When I saw sin as an offence against a just and holy God, committed by such a proud and yet insignificant creature as myself, then was I alarmed.[136]

Secondly, the Holy Spirit demonstrates the possibility of redemption, on the basis that Jesus has ascended to the Father (John 16:10), having made full atonement for sin. Drummond comments, "believers are declared righteous because of Christ's atoning work,"[137] but goes on to point out:

> These salvation truths, however, do go against the grain of humanistic pride. Many feel they can do enough good things to be acceptable in God's sight. That line is the grand satanic deception. It is the blindness of the mere moralist. It is the core of all other world religions, and the mind-set of the masses. . . . Only the Holy Spirit can cause those scales to fall off one's eyes, as He did for the self-righteous Saul of Tarsus. The power of God alone can make people see the efficacy of the work of Christ, their position before God, and the utter need of Christ's righteousness, but that is exactly what the Spirit came into the world to do. He came to reveal the Jesus of the cross.[138]

Thirdly, the Holy Spirit reveals the reality of redemption, which is founded on the fact that the prince of this world is judged (John 16:11). The power of Christ to judge Satan and overthrow his kingdom is not in the future but was eternally established by His

---

[135]Lewis A. Drummond, *The Word of the Cross: A Contemporary Theology of Evangelism* (Nashville, TN: Broadman & Holman Publishers, 1999), 175-76 (original emphasis).

[136]Charles H. Spurgeon, *Sermons Preached and Revised by C. H. Spurgeon, During the Year 1891*, in *The Metropolitan Tabernacle Pulpit* (Pasadena, TX: Pilgrim Publications, 1975), 37: 224-25.

[137]Drummond, 177.

[138]Ibid., 177-178.

Cross and resurrection.[139] As Beasley-Murray has expressed it: "The ejection of [Satan] from his vaunted place of rule took place as the Son of Man was installed by God as Lord of creation and Mediator of the saving sovereignty of God to the world."[140] Jesus is the power of God (1 Cor. 1:24); Jesus is the gospel. However, as W.T. Conner has commented: "Pentecost [the giving of the Holy Spirit] was just as essential for the realisation in the lives of men of the values of the gospel as was Calvary and the resurrection. Without the death and resurrection of Jesus there could be no gospel. Without Pentecost there would be no gospel so far as our apprehension and experience are concerned."[141]

Accordingly, Drummond is correct in his conclusion that "the witness of the church has power only as the gospel is communicated in the strength and wisdom of the Holy Spirit."[142] The Holy Spirit fulfils His divine role, not only in the hearts of the hearers but also in those who minister the word by the foolishness of preaching (1 Cor. 1:18). Thus Kittel declares in respect to the gospel message:

> The preaching of the gospel is the continuation of the saving activity of Jesus Christ; the preachers of the Gospel are logically the continuators of this activity. . . . the apostles stand in the place of Jesus and are as He is. The risen Lord associates Himself with them and gives them His power in which they work. In the power of Jesus the apostles stand in the place of Jesus, and continue His work. . . . He endows His disciples with this power, they continue His activity in His place . . . proclaiming the Christian message and also working miracles.[143]

As the Spirit of grace (Heb. 10:29), the Holy Spirit makes available all that the Son of God has done to bring about salvation and new life.[144] There is no experience of the Spirit that is not somehow the experience of Christ; similarly, there is no experience of

---

[139]*King James Study Bible,* notes to John 16.

[140]George R. Beasley-Murray, *John,* 2d ed., *Word Biblical Commentary,* eds. Bruce M. Metzger, David A. Hubbard and Glenn W. Barker (Nashville, TN: Thomas Nelson Publishers, 1999), 36:282.

[141]W. T. Conner, *The Work of the Holy Spirit* (Nashville, TN: Broadman Press, 1949), 57-58.

[142]Drummond, 179.

[143]Gerhard Kittel, ed., *Theological Dictionary of the New Testament,* s.v. "The Power of the Disciple" (Grand Rapids, MI: Wm. B. Eerdmans Publishing Company, 1964), 2:310-11.

[144]Rodman, 143.

Christ that is not mediated by the Spirit.[145] As the Spirit of Adoption (Rom. 8:15-17), He is sent to witness within every child of God to the fact that he/she has been born into the family of God, with all the inherent privileges of sonship. As the Spirit of Holiness (Rom. 1:4), He comes to reproduce the holiness of God within the hearts and minds of everyone who turns to God for salvation. That is to say, the Holy Spirit manifests the whole life of Jesus Christ in the born-again believer and the fruits of the Spirit are the natural product of that life (Gal. 5:22-23). As the Spirit of Truth (John 14:17), He will not speak of Himself but will bear witness to the truth incarnate in Jesus Christ.[146]

God is vitally and centrally involved in the whole work of evangelism. New birth is the sovereign act of a sovereign God. In the final analysis, He alone is the Great Evangelist;[147] He is the One who empowers the speaker and prepares the hearer. There is no devil or demon that can stand in the way of His eternal purposes. As Spurgeon said: "The only salvation that can redeem from hell is a salvation that comes from heaven. Eternal salvation must come from an eternal God. Salvation that makes you a new creature must be the work of him who sits on the throne and makes all things new."[148]

Theological Summary

Having considered the sovereignty of God, the authority of His Word, and the power of the Holy Spirit with specific reference to His role in prayer and evangelism, the whole issue of SLSW fades into insignificance. A comprehension of divine sovereignty will result in assurance of salvation both on eternal and temporal scales. An appreciation of the authority of God's Word will bring a sound foundation to that assurance, and a true understanding of the role of the Holy Spirit will produce prayer and evangelism practices that will not be isolated from His intrinsic nature.

With reference to Satan's abject defeat, Spurgeon summarises the position as follows: ". . . His power is gone; he is fighting a lost battle;

---

[145]John O'Donnell, "Theology of the Holy Spirit, I: Jesus and the Spirit," *The Way* 23 (1983): 48.

[146]Rodman, 141.

[147]Drummond, 197.

[148]Carter, 181.

he is contending against omnipotence. He has set himself against the oath of the Father, against the blood of the incarnate Son, and against the eternal power of the blessed Spirit--all of which are engaged in the defence of the seed of woman in the day of battle. Therefore, beloved, be steadfast in resisting the Evil One, being strong in faith, giving glory to God."[149]

Historical Perspective

Old Testament Background

Early Judaic Thought

Apart from limited references to the origin of evil in Job, Chronicles, Daniel, and Zechariah,[150] the Old Testament Canon is silent on the subject of spiritual warfare. Early Judaic thought simply accepted the "destroyer" as one of God's angels executing divine judgement. For example, the smiting of the first born sons in Egypt (Exo. 12:23; Heb. 11:28) was seen as the action of the angel of death operating in accordance with God's will.[151] The angel was therefore regarded as the "emissary of Yahweh" and at times was not distinguished from Yahweh Himself.[152] God's total sovereignty and omnipotence were both assumed and accepted.

Later Judaic Thought

Clearly, the fall of Jerusalem in 586 BC and the subsequent period of exile (586-539 BC) were catastrophic events which moved the Jewish people to speculate on the nature of evil, as they searched for answers to explain these disasters. The writings of the era look back on the concept of God's sovereignty in the Torah, seeking to re-interpret this in the light of current events. As the Jews' national condition deteriorated, so apocalyptic thinking thrived, fostered also by the dualistic philosophy of their captors. Conjectural analysis of the situation developed into the firmly held belief that the coming of the messianic kingdom was imminent; and effectively, this was seen

---

[149]Charles H. Spurgeon, *Power Over Satan* (New Kensington, PA: Whitaker House, 1997), 141-42.

[150]The author has excluded the two highly debated passages in Isa. 14 and Ezek. 28 which modern scholarship claims do not directly refer to Satan. See Page, 37-42.

[151]For another example, see 2 Kin. 19:35.

[152]*ISBE*, s.v. "Destroyer," by D. Miall Edwards.

as the only hope of deliverance from oppression.[153] Russell comments as follows: "The Jews of the Apocalyptic period did not understand why Yahweh had abandoned Israel. If he had, they mused, then there could be no more hope for Israel as a nation among nations. Evil ruled the world in their time; the Messiah, they thought, must soon come."[154]

The period of exile also exposed the Jewish people to new influences in terms of religious thought and practice.[155] Thus, the later Jewish theology of the Targums and Midrash described the "destroyer" under the name of Sammael, meaning the poison of God. This thinking was highly influenced by Zoroastrianism, the dualistic Persian religion, which viewed good and evil as independent opposing forces. Samuel E. Karff comments concerning this era:

> As civil strife and foreign pressures plagued the Judeans, a more urgent vision seized their imagination. This was expressed in a form of literature called apocalypses (Greek for 'disclosures' or 'revelations'). These writings depicted a dramatic confrontation between the forces of light and darkness . . . Angels were transformed from anonymous, featureless agents of Yahweh into distinct personalities with names (cf. Dan. 8:16; 10:13, 20). Satan went from being a member of the divine entourage to the chief of a kingdom of demonic spirits opposed to God. Indeed, he even acquired independent power. Rather than against sinful humanity alone, Yahweh was cast in battle against supernatural powers.[156]

Hence, the Jews of the Diaspora came to regard the devil as a distinct and autonomous individual, who acted from evil desires. He was thought to have been an archangel at the throne of God and the motivating force behind the serpent's temptation of Eve.[157]

---

[153]Smith, 11.

[154]Jeffrey Burton Russell, *The Devil: Perceptions of Evil from Antiquity to Primitive Christianity* (Ithaca: Cornell University Press, 1977), 185; quoted in Smith, 8.

[155]Henry H. Milman, *History of Christianity from the Birth of Christ to the Abolition of Paganism in the Roman Empire* (London: John Murray, 1840), 70-71.

[156]Samuel E. Karff, *Religions of the World* (New York: St. Martin's Press, 1993), 306.

[157]Russell, *The Devil*, 188-89; "The names of the Devil vary, particularly in the Apocalyptic period: he is Belial, Mastema, Azazel, Satanail, Sammael, Semyaza, or Satan. These names have different origins, and the beings they denote differ in their origins and functions one from another. But gradually they coalesce. The Devil becomes a spiritual being personifying the origin and essence of evil: there can only be one Devil." The influence of extra-biblical Judaism is found in the

In addition, Babylonish thought was deeply embedded in magic which was viewed as a necessary protection from evil spirits. Certain diseases were believed to be due to demonical possession for which exorcism was the cure. It is of note that there is no mention whatsoever of demons being exorcised from humans in the Old Testament. The literature of the dispersion era, however, is full of superstition, including numerous incantations for exorcism.

Intertestamental Period

"When we enter the inter-testamental period we find that belief in angels has grown to proportions unknown in the Old Testament writings. Details of their numbers, their names, their functions, their natures are given which, though in many cases having their beginning in the canonical Scriptures, far outstrip anything to be found there."[158] The Apocrypha as a whole, contains fantastic tales of the supernatural. For example, Tobit and 2 Maccabees record Jewish exorcisms through the burning of fish organs, a ritual which involved specifying the name of the demonic angel.[159] Tobit also records the names of one good angel and one bad demon, with 2 Esdras giving additional detail as to angelic function and hierarchical status.[160]

Further speculation concerning heavenly authorities and various techniques for deliverance from evil spirits are presented in the Pseudepigrapha. The Testament of Levi sets out a three-fold hierarchy of angels, but gives no details of evil spirits, and in 2 Enoch ideas relating to angelic hierarchy are also developed. Jubilees and 1 Enoch 60:11-24 also describe various angelic categories, with the latter making a clear distinction between angels who dwell in heaven

---

use of the term Azazel in Lev. 16:8,10, and Paul's use of Belial in 2 Cor. 6:15; quoted in Smith, 11-12.

[158]Russell, *The Devil*, 20; quoted in Lowe, *Territorial Spirits*, 77.

[159]*The Catholic Encyclopaedia*, s.v. "Exorcism," by P. J. Toner, online posting, http://www.newadvent.org/cathen/05809a.htm; accessed 17 July 2001. The editor of the entry believes that this instance is part of an angel's plan for concealing his own identity.

[160]Ezra mentions Uriel, an archangel. Tobit identifies a) Raphael, one of seven holy angels, who presents the prayers of the saints, and b) Asmodeus, a wicked demon.

and demons who dwell on earth; demons are clearly presumed to be the offspring of angels and humans.

New Testament Background

In the New Testament era the majority of Jewish exorcisms were complex affairs, involving rigid formulae, ritual and mechanical or physical aids.[161] The theory of the Rabbis was that the air was full of demons and that men were in danger of swallowing them, thereby contracting some deadly disease.[162]

The Life of Jesus

The Gospels show that, in dealing with the spirit realm, Jesus was distinctive in His simplicity and completely inconsistent in His methodology. As a result of His teaching, the accepted authority of the demonic began to disintegrate. Jesus demonstrated that He had absolute power over demons (Matt. 12:22-23, 28; Luke 11:20) simply by His personal authority (Mark 9:25), not because He used more effective methods. Similarly, He gave His disciples power to cast out evil spirits and that same authority is available to every child of God.

However, it could be argued that the real spiritual conflict during the earthly ministry of Jesus was with the religious leaders of His day. When He began to teach in Palestine, all knowledge of God and His authority was exercised via the rabbis and scribes, based on their interpretation of the Old Testament. Jesus challenged that interpretation (Matt. 23:13-16), asserting His own absolute authority in the realm of religion and morals.[163]

It is clear from Scripture that Jesus confronted the Pharisees more than any other group of people (Matt. 9:3, 11, 34; 12:2,10, 14). They had maintained a position of spiritual authority despite all the changes of government under the Romans and Herodians. Schurer comments: "They had the bulk of the nation as their ally, and women especially were in their hands. They had the greatest influence upon the congregations, so that all acts of public worship, prayers, and sacrifices were performed according to their injunctions. Their sway

---

[161]*ISBE*, s.v. "Exorcism," by L. M. Sweet.
[162]*The Catholic Encyclopaedia*, s.v. "Demonology," by W. H. Kent, online posting, http://newadvent.org/cathen/04713a.htm; accessed 5 June 2001.
[163]*ISBE*, s.v. "Authority," by T. Rees.

over the masses was . . . absolute."[164] Therefore, they both feared and
hated the growing popularity of Jesus with the common people. The
righteousness of the Pharisee was external but Jesus placed faith on a
totally different basis. He emphasised that the heart must be right
before God, challenging the Pharisaical teaching of servile adherence
to the letter of the law (including their man-made precepts), and
denouncing its leaders for their hypocrisy. Jesus came to reveal the
heart of God, to demonstrate the forgotten principles that
undergirded the law, to fulfil the law (Matt. 5:17), not to confirm, as
many suppose it to mean.[165] He confronted what was false in order
that He might establish the truth.

The Book of Acts

The Book of Acts also reflects the widespread popular reliance
throughout the ancient world of the first century upon magical
charms, amulets and incantations (Acts 16:16-18; 19:18-19).[166]
However, as a result of the apostles' preaching of the victory in
Christ, "no longer could Satan and his demonic and human servants
harass and torment at will. Satan's kingdom was splintering around
him, and his authority was no longer acknowledged by all."[167]

In addition, the combat with the religious fraternity continued.
For example, within days of his conversion, Paul preached in
Damascus confounding the Jews and "proving that this is the very
Christ" (Acts 9:22). Their former hero was now their foe and Paul's
teaching enraged the Jews to the point of plotting to kill him. This
form of violent reaction was to be a feature of the lives and ministries
of all the apostles, as they proclaimed the truths of the gospel. Even
within the church, it was not long before error manifested itself and
threatened the faith of the new believers. The epistle to the Galatians,
for instance, was written by Paul in response to a crisis situation--they
were in danger of adopting another gospel (Gal. 1:6-10), for legalism
had been introduced by the Judaisers. Machen states: "The Judaizers
are dead and gone, but not the issue that they raised. Faith or works--
that is as much as ever a living issue. 'Salvation by character' is just a

---

[164]Schurer, div. 2, 2:28; quoted in *New Unger's Bible Dictionary*, in *PC Study Bible*, s.v.
"Pharisees."

[165]*New Unger's Bible Dictionary*, s.v. "Pharisees."

[166]Arnold, 71.

[167]Ibid., 108-109.

modern form of Judaizing, and a modern form of bondage to the law. Christ crucified needs still to be held up before our eyes; and still we need to receive by faith the gracious, life-giving power of his Spirit. Paul in Galatians was fighting the age-long battle of the Christian Church."[168]

The Early Church

The Apostolic or Church Fathers

The death of John, the beloved disciple, brought the end of the Apostolic period and the beginning of what is known as the era of the Apostolic or Church Fathers (AD 100-150). At this time, the epistles had been circulated around the churches but there was no formal canon of the New Testament, and church tradition began to exert a very real influence in the realm of interpretation and practice. The writings of such men as Clement of Rome, Ignatius, Polycarp and an author who uses the pseudonym, Barnabas, were influential during this era, when typology and allegory were popular modes of interpretation. It was a time of persistent and severe persecution, and the tradition of martyrdom entered deep into the Christian consciousness.[169] Thus, contemporary Christian writings reflect the attempt to come to terms with suffering from a theological viewpoint.

Clement of Rome (AD 30-100) wrote a letter addressing the cause of, and remedy for, the factions which had formed in the Corinthian church. He saw the devil as the adversary who through his suggestions causes men to do evil.[170] He exhorted Christians to recognise this spiritual conflict and that victory could be sustained by resisting the wiles of Satan.[171]

---

[168]J. Gresham Machen, *The New Testament: An Introduction to its Literature and History* (Edinburgh: The Banner of Truth Trust, 1976), 129.

[169]Kenneth Scott Latourette, *Beginnings to 1500*, vol. 1 of 2, *A History of Christianity* (New York: Harper & Row, 1975), 81.

[170]Clement of Rome, *Epistle to the Corinthians*, chap. 45, in *The Apostolic Fathers*, in *Ante-Nicene Christian Library*, 1:39-40.

[171]Gokey, 68-69; quoted in Smith, 17.

Ignatius (AD 30-107) presented the keys to victorious Christian living as meekness,[172] avoidance of heresy,[173] steadfastness in the faith,[174] and subjection to the higher authorities in the church.[175] He declared that it is Christ, the King of heaven within a man's heart, who destroys all the devices of evil spirits, since the devil is under His feet.[176] He also believed that Christians are enabled to tread the devil underfoot by joyful submission to persecution and martyrdom,[177] but that the final victory over Satan would not be realised until the Parousia.[178] Similarly, Polycarp of Smyrna (AD 65-ca.155, martyred) taught that there was victory in spiritual warfare through positive confession and perseverance in prayer.[179]

The *Pastor of Hermas* (AD 160) was one of the most popular books in the church of the second, third and fourth centuries. "Though the form of the book is apocalyptic and visionary, its object is practical and ethical."[180] It occupied a place analogous to Bunyan's *Pilgrim's Progress* in modern times and was regarded by many churches as divinely inspired.[181] The writer exhorts believers to "love the truth and let nothing but truth proceed from your mouth."[182] In respect to the devil he states, "Fear not the devil; for, fearing the Lord, you will

---

[172]Ignatius, *The Epistle to the Trallians*, chap. 4, in *The Apostolic Fathers*, in *Ante-Nicene Christian Library*, 1:193.

[173]Ignatius, *The Epistle to the Philadelphians*, chap. 2, in *The Apostolic Fathers*, in *Ante-Nicene Christian Libary*, 1:223; *The Epistle to theTrallians*, chapters 10-11, in *The Apostolic Fathers*, in *Ante-Nicene Christian Library*, 1:201-204.

[174]Ignatius, *The Epistle to Polycarp*, chapters 1-3, in *The Apostolic Fathers,* in *Ante-Nicene Christian Library*, 1:257-61.

[175]Ignatius, *The Epistle to the Philadelphians*, chap. 2, in *The Apostolic Fathers*, in *Ante-Nicene Christian Library*, 1:223.

[176]*The Martyrdom of Ignatius*, chap. 2, in *The Apostolic Fathers*, in *Ante-Nicene Christian Library*, 1:292.

[177]*The Martyrdom of Ignatius*, chap. 7, in *The Apostolic Fathers*, in *Ante-Nicene Christian Library*, 1:297.

[178]Jeffrey Burton Russell, *Satan: The Early Christian Tradition* (Ithaca, NY: Cornell University Press, 1981), 34.

[179]Polycarp, *The Epistle to the Philippians*, chap. 7, in *The Apostolic Fathers*, in *Ante-Nicene Christian Library*, 1:73.

[180]Gokey, 121-22; quoted in Smith, 20.

[181]*Pastor of Hermas*, Introductory Note, in *The Apostolic Fathers*, in *Ante-Nicene Christian Library*, 1:319.

[182]*Pastor of Hermas*, Book Second, Commandment Third, in *The Apostolic Fathers*, in *Ante-Nicene Christian Library*, 1:350.

have dominion over the devil, for there is no power in him;"[183] and "The devil has fear only, but his fear has no strength. Fear him not, then, and he will flee from you."[184]

It is apparent from this brief survey of the Church Fathers that despite the emphasis on the spiritual benefits of martyrdom, many writers had a clear understanding of the victory in Christ and the strict limitations on the devil's power. However, the highly allegorical *Epistle of Barnabas* (ca., 96-131) presents a somewhat different view of spiritual warfare. He depersonalised the conflict, teaching that the real struggle was in the angelic realm between the forces of good and evil.[185] This approach is analogous to that of the Intertestamental period when the Jews adopted the dualistic philosophy of their captors in an attempt to rationalise the outcome of their own sin and disobedience. Significantly, aspects of this teaching were to re-emerge in the 1900s; initially propounded by Sandford in 1901 and, in the latter part of the century, within the context of strategic level spiritual warfare.

The Apologists

The early church had to face much opposition, primarily from within the ranks of Judaism, but later from the pagan population round about. Intellectuals of the day were caustic in their criticism of these early believers. For example, Porphyry, an early leader of neo-Platonism, pointed out some supposed contradictions in the Christian scriptures. Not only did Christians reply to these attacks, they counter-attacked, highlighting weaknesses in pagan religions and demonstrating the many positive reasons for accepting the Christian faith.[186]

In addition to opposition from outside, the early believers also had to contend with error which assailed the church from within,[187]

---

[183] *Pastor of Hermas*, Book Second, Commandment Seventh, in *The Apostolic Fathers*, in *Ante-Nicene Christian Library*, 1:361.

[184] *Pastor of Hermas*, Book Second, Commandment Twelfth, chap. 4, in *The Apostolic Fathers*, in *Ante-Nicene Christian Library*, 1:373.

[185] Barnabas, *The Epistle of Barnabas*, chap. 18, in *The Apostolic Fathers*, in *Ante-Nicene Christian Library*, 1:130-31.

[186] Latourette, 1:81-84.

[187] For example, Montanism (2d century), Gnosticism (2d and 3d centuries) and Arianism (4th century).

and many Christian thinkers began to wrestle with key doctrines and beliefs. Given their struggle to defend the faith, it is not surprising that the issue of spiritual warfare is evident in various of these apologetic writings. For example, Justin Martyr (ca., 110-165) wrote that spiritual warfare consists in contending for the truth in a world where that truth is often misrepresented by mythology and fables.[188] He accepted healing,[189] and exorcism,[190] as part of the Christian ministry and spoke of Christians driving "the possessing devils out of men though they could not be cured by all the other exorcists, and those who used incantations and drugs."[191] He said, "And though the devil is ever at hand to resist us, and anxious to seduce all to himself, yet the Power of God sent to us through Jesus Christ, rebukes him and he departs from us."[192]

The writings of Irenaeus, bishop of Lyons (ca., 140-202), also constitute an exposé of the erroneous teaching of his era. His task was twofold: namely, to ensure that Gnosticism could never be confused with Christianity and to "make it impossible for such a monstrous system to survive, or ever to rise again." In so doing, "Irenaeus demonstrated its essential unity with the old mythology, and with heathen systems of philosophy."[193]

Irenaeus clearly recognised the supremacy and sovereignty of God, berating the followers of Marcion for their belief in two opposing powers.[194] He declared that heretics deceive themselves and, "wallowing in falsehood" are those who have "lost the bread of

---

[188]Justin Martyr, *The First Apology*, chap. 64, in *Justin Martyr and Athenagoras*, in *Ante-Nicene Christian Library*, 2:62-63; *Dialogue with Trypho, a Jew*, chap. 69, in *Justin Martyr and Athenagoras*, in *Ante-Nicene Christian Library*, 2:184.

[189]Justin Martyr, *The Second Apology*, chap. 13, in *Justin Martyr and Athenagoras*, in *Ante-Nicene Christian Library*, 2:83; *Dialogue with Trypho, a Jew*, chap. 39, in *Justin Martyr and Athenagoras*, in *Ante-Nicene Christian Library*, 2:136.

[190]Justin Martyr, *The Second Apology*, chap. 6, in *Justin Martyr and Athenagoras*, in *Ante-Nicene Christian Library*, 2:76-77; *Dialogue with Trypho, a Jew*, chap. 30, in *Justin Martyr and Athenagoras*, in *Ante-Nicene Christian Library*, 2:124.

[191]Justin Martyr, *The Second Apology*, chap. 6, in *Justin Martyr and Athenagoras*, in *Ante-Nicene Christian Library*, 2:77.

[192]*Dialogue with Trypho, a Jew*, chap. 116, in *Justin Martyr and Athenagoras*, in *Ante-Nicene Christian Library*, 2:245.

[193]Irenaeus, *Against Heresies*, Introductory Note, 614, in *The Master Christian Library*.

[194]Irenaeus, *Against Heresies*, bk. 3, chap. 12, in vol. 1 of *The Writings of Irenaeus*, in *Ante-Nicene Christian Library*, 5:310.

true life, and have fallen into vacuity and an abyss of shadow."[195] He believed that the devil had been defeated at Calvary, explaining that God, "by means of the second man did . . . bind the strong man, and spoiled his goods, and abolished death, vivifying that man who had been in a state of death."[196] His work was a battle against the errors that would destroy true faith, and he clearly recognised the extreme subtlety of many of the false teachings of his contemporaries: "Error, indeed, is never set forth in its naked deformity, lest being thus exposed, it should at once be detected. But it is craftily decked out in an attractive dress, so as, by its outward form, to make it appear to the inexperienced . . . more true than the truth itself."[197] Irenaeus maintained that Satan was conquered by the incarnate word of God and so his lies may still be defeated in the lives of individual Christians by simple proclamation of the truth. [198]

The teaching of the prolific and brilliant writer, Tertullian (ca., 155-240) in respect to spiritual warfare is less clear. He held that reason, the weapon of the philosophers, was a false guide to truth, and that truth was only to be found in the revelation of God in Christ Jesus.[199] Described as a warrior of the faith, Tertullian's writings were pitted against those he considered to be enemies of the truth, namely, Jews, pagans and heretics. He explicitly excluded the idea that angels are restricted to a particular geographical area, observing that "they are everywhere in a single moment; the whole world is as one place to them."[200] However, he also taught that the key to victory in combating Satan was a disciplined, ascetic life and, due to his increasing disillusionment with what he considered to be a lack of moderation in the Christian community, eventually adopted Montanist views.

---

[195]Irenaeus, *Against Heresies*, bk. 2, chap. 11, in vol. 1 of *The Writings of Irenaeus, in Ante-Nicene Christian Library*, 5:146.

[196]*Irenaeus Against Heresies*, bk. 3, chap. 23, in vol. 1 of *The Writings of Irenaeus*, in *Ante-Nicene Christian Library*, 5:363.

[197]*Irenaeus Against Heresies*, preface to bk. 1, in vol. 1 of *The Writings of Irenaeus*, in *Ante-Nicene Christian Library*, 5:2.

[198]*Irenaeus Against Heresies*, bk. 2, chap. 6, in vol. 1 of *The Writings of Irenaeus*, in *Ante-Nicene Christian Library*, 5:133.

[199]Latourette, 1:84.

[200]Tertullian, *Apologeticus*, par. 22, in vol. 1, *The Writings of Tertullian*, in *Ante- Nicene Christian Library*, 11:97.

The writings of the apologists were clearly addressed to a particular time and a particular situation but have a continuing significance for the Bible scholar of every generation. As the Introductory Note to *Irenaeus Against Heresies* states: "In the divine economy of Providence it was permitted that every form of heresy which was ever to infest the Church should now exhibit its essential principle, and attract the censures of the faithful. Thus testimony to primitive truth was secured and recorded: the language of catholic orthodoxy was developed and defined, and landmarks of faith were set up for a perpetual memorial to all generations."[201]

The Theologians

In the years AD 150-400, the two main centres of Christian teaching were located in Antioch and Alexandria respectively. The former stressed the historical study of the gospels and the humanity of Jesus Christ. The latter continued the tradition of allegorical methodology propounded by Philo in the previous century, minimised the historical and gave great weight to the divinity of Christ. Clement of Alexandria (AD 153-193-217) taught there towards the end of the second century. He was immersed in the philosophy of the neo-Platonists[202] which emphasised the supremacy of ideas. His interpretative approach was to identify two levels of meaning in any passage of Scripture, the hidden spiritual one being the more significant. Thus every detail of a story was spiritualised and evil was characterised as a loss of being.[203] He described Satan as the "wicked tyrant and serpent" who enslaves men with "the miserable chain of superstition."[204]

---

[201]Irenaeus *Against Heresies*, Introductory Note, 613; in *The Master Christian Library*.

[202]Neoplatonism combined much from philosophies which had gone before, including Platonism, Aristotelianism, Stoicism, and Neopythagoreanism. "It had a deeply religious quality with a strong mystical trend. It sought through asceticism to curb the flesh and its desires, to purify the human soul of the taint acquired by its departure from its original estate, and by contemplation to attain union with God. Again and again through the centuries Christian mysticism was to be deeply indebted to it." Latourette, 1:27.

[203]W. E. G. Floyd, *Clement of Alexandria's Treatment of the Problem of Evil*, (London: Oxford University Press, 1971), 99; quoted in Smith, 23.

[204]Clement of Alexandria, *Exhortation to the Heathen*, chap. 1, in vol. 1 of *Clement of Alexandria*, in *Ante-Nicene Christian Library*, 4:23.

Clement was succeeded by his pupil, Origen (ca., 185-254), who rejected the literal interpretation of Scripture, and carried the allegorical method even further. Thus he distinguished a third moral meaning, supposedly in line with the fact that man is a tripartite being, consisting of body, soul and spirit. Origen believed in territorial spirits[205] (citing the prince of Persia in Daniel, and the prince of Tyre in Ezekiel as his examples), and attributed to such spirits the dissemination of error.[206] He identified the warfare between angels and demons in every aspect of life, as they struggle for ascendancy over individuals and nations. Russell comments on Origen's beliefs as follows: "After the human race was divided at the Tower of Babel, God gave each nation, province and region into the control of two powerful angels, one good and the other evil. The latter are responsible for causing persecutions and unjust wars."[207] Despite this, Origen insisted that man has nothing to fear from demons because God will protect him, either directly or through the agency of angels. He taught that the provision outlined by Paul in Ephesians 6:11-12 is always available for the protection of Christians.

Origen also identified various supposed angelic functions. For example: Raphael supervised curing and healing; Michael attended to the prayers of man; and Gabriel oversaw the conduct of war.[208] He also referred to the fact that demons flee at the laying on of hands.

Throughout Origen's writings there is a strong emphasis on the importance of human choice. He states: "a soul is always in possession of free will . . . and freedom of will is always directed to either good or evil."[209] Thus, right choices bring "increased being" and freedom; and conversely, wrong choices result in "loss of being" and spiritual defeat. However, he believed that eventually all men,

[205]Origen, *De Principiis*, bk. 3, chap. 3, par. 2, in vol. 1 of *The Writings of Origen*, in *Ante-Nicene Christian Library*, 10:239.

[206]Origen, *De Principiis*, bk. 3, chap. 3, par. 3, in vol. 1 of *The Writings of Origen*, in *Ante-Nicene Christian Library*, 10:239.

[207]Russell, *Satan*, 134; quoted in Smith, 25.

[208]Origen, *De Principiis*, bk. 1, chap. 8, par. 1, in vol. 1 of *The Writings of Origen*, in *Ante-Nicene Christian Library*, 10:65.

[209]Origen, *De Principiis*, bk. 3 chap. 3 par. 5, in vol. 1 of *The Writings of Origen*, in *Ante-Nicene Christian Library*, 10:243.

and even devils, would be fully saved through repentance, learning and growth.[210]

The influence of Platonic idealism and dualism is also seen in the writings of Athanasius (ca., AD 300-373), Bishop of Alexandria and outstanding champion of Nicene orthodoxy. He viewed spiritual warfare as a struggle between the flesh, Satan and his demons on the one hand, and the soul, Christ and his angels on the other. Like Tertullian, he emphasised strict asceticism as the means of victory in spiritual warfare and his work, "The Life of St. Anthony," pictures monks as warriors against the powers of darkness through intense prayer and fasting.[211] The sign of the cross,[212] and the very name of Jesus,[213] were extolled as efficacious against all kinds of demonic activity.

Hilary of Poitiers (AD 315-367), another proponent of Nicene orthodoxy, believed that each church had its guardian angel.[214] However, in respect to angelic rank and society the pre-eminent theologian, Augustine (AD 354-430) commented, ". . . these questions let those answer who can, provided they have proof of

---

[210]Latourette, 1:151.

[211]St. Athanasius, *Life of St. Anthony*, paragraphs 21-23, in vol. 10 of *Ancient Christian Writers: The Works of the Fathers in Translation*, eds. Johannes Quasten and Joseph C. Plumpe, trans. Robert T. Mayer (Westminster, MD: The Newman Press, 1950), 38-40.

[212]St. Athanasius, *De Incarnatione*, n. 47, In *Contra Gentes and De Incarnatione*, trans. and ed. Robert W. Thompson (Oxford: Clarendon Press, 1971), 253. "Previously demons cheated men with their illusions, taking possession of springs or rivers or stones, and thus by their tricks stupefying the simple. But now that the divine manifestation of the Word has taken place, their illusion has ceased: for a man has only to make the sign of the cross to drive away their deceits." See also n. 48, p. 255.

[213]Ibid., n. 30, 209· "For where Christ and his faith are named, thence all idolatry is uprooted, all the deceit of demons is refuted, and no demon endures that name, but as soon as he hears it, takes to flight." See also n. 50, p. 261.

[214]Hilary of Poitiers, *Homilies on the Psalms*, 129:7, in vol. 1 of 3, *The Faith of the Early Fathers*, ed. William A. Jurgens (Collegeville, MN: Liturgical Press, 1970), 387; quoted in Lowe, *Territorial Spirits*, 87. See also, Origen, *De Principiis*, bk. 1, chap. 8, par.1, in vol. 1 of *The Writings of Origen*, in *Ante-Nicene Christian Library*, 10:65; and Origen, *De Principiis*, bk. 2, chap. 10, par.7, in vol. 1 of *The Writings of Origen*, in *Ante- Nicene Christian Library*, 10:144.

what they say. For my part, I admit my ignorance."[215] Augustine wrote about Satan and spiritual warfare but seemed more concerned with questions of theodicy than victory in spiritual conflict.[216]

By the end of the fifth century, the impact of neo-Platonism on mystical Christian thought was becoming very evident. Influential writings of this era were mistakenly ascribed to Dionysius the Areopagite, who was converted under the ministry of Paul in Athens (Acts 17:34). This supposed association with the great apostle meant that the writings carried great weight, their influence continuing into the Middle Ages. Significantly, although some of the terminology is Christian, the underlying concepts are based on heathen philosophy. Perhaps in an attempt to counteract the prevailing acceptance of dualism, Pseudo-Dionysius propounded the notion that nothing is inherently evil and that in all evil is some good. However, this reasoning was itself borrowed from Platonism and neo-Platonism.[217] He identified nine orders of celestial beings,[218] over whom God reigns supreme, and suggested that each nation has its own guardian angel.[219]

Throughout this period there was an obvious interest in the spirit world but it was evaluated within the context of God's total sovereignty. Thus relatively little attention was given to the demonic realm, and much more to God and His angelic messengers.

The Middle Ages

In AD 312, the Roman Emperor Constantine converted to Christianity and by the year 500 the overwhelming majority of the

---

[215]St. Augustine, *Enchiridion or Manual to Laurentius Concerning Faith, Hope and Charity*, chap. 15.58, trans. Ernest Evans (London: SPCK, 1953), 51.

[216] St. Augustine, *The City of God*, bk. 11, chap. 9, trans. John Healey (London and Toronto: J. M. Dent and Son, 1931), 234-36. See also bk. 12, chap. 3, p. 6-8.

[217]Latourette, 1:210-211.

[218]Pseudo-Dionysius, *The Heavenly Hierarchy and The Ecclesiastical Hierarchy*, caput 6, in pt. 2, *The Works of Dionysius the Areopagite*, trans., Rev. John Parker (London: James Parker, 1899), 23.

[219]Ibid., caput 9, sec. 2, p. 37-38. "Hence, the Word of God has assigned our Hierarchy to Angels, by naming Michael, as Ruler of the Jewish people, and others over other nations. For the Most High established borders of nations according to the number of Angels of God."

population of the Empire were calling themselves Christians.[220] Accordingly, state persecution of the church ceased and this decline in oppression was accompanied by a parallel decline in interest in spiritual warfare. The monastic movement gathered force as increasing numbers withdrew from a society they considered to be corrupt, electing to live in isolated communities which would supposedly embody the Christian ideal.[221]

The church became increasingly institutionalised, and it was a period of much internal wrangling and debate. There were also increasing problems with the question of the ultimate authority of Scripture. The canon was closed but as Hugh of St. Victor (1096-1141), an early scholastic theologian comments, the "limits are still fluid, and some writings outside the Canon as such, share in the inspirational power of the Holy Scripture."[222] Inevitably, therefore, the church at large had lost its anchorage.

It was against this background that Thomas Aquinas, the main exponent of scholasticism, produced a comprehensive summary of doctrine in the form of his *Summa Theologica*. He argued that the literal sense of scripture was the most important and contained everything that was necessary to faith. In his *Summa*, Aquinas debated the corporeality of angels and demons,[223] as well as arguments relating to spirit hierarchies.[224] He also came to the conclusion that the devil had chosen wickedness "by the fault of his own will in the first instant of his creation,"[225] rather than being intrinsically wicked.[226]

The fourteenth and fifteenth centuries saw a notable revival of mysticism, particularly in Germany. John ("Meister") Eckhart (ca., 1260-1327), the main founder of Dominican mysticism, taught the deification of man and assimilation of the creature into the Creator

---

[220]Latourette, 1:236.

[221]Ibid., 1:221-34.

[222]George H. Tavard, *Holy Writ or Holy Church: The Crisis of the Protestant Reformation* (New York: Harper and Row, 1959), 16; quoted by Johnson and Webber, 41.

[223]Thomas Aquinas, *Summa Theologica*, first pt., question 50, art. 1, in vol. 19 of 60, *Great Books of the Western World*, ed. Robert Maynard Hutchins (Chicago, IL: Encyclopaedia Britannica, 1952), 269-70.

[224]Ibid., first pt., question 63, art. 7, p. 331-32.

[225]Ibid., first pt., question 63, art. 5, p. 329-30.

[226]Ibid., first pt., question 63, art. 4, p. 338.

through contemplation.[227] A later mystic, Jakob Böhme (1574-1624), claimed to have received many of his ideas by visions and direct revelation. In his *Aurora* he conceived the nature of God as containing both good and evil, and taught that the human soul may kindle the fire of good or the fire of evil by operation of its free will.[228]

The Reformation

The Reformation period (AD 1500-1650) brought with it a total revolution in interpretation of Scripture. There had already been conflict between the traditional approach of scholasticism and the new thinking of Christian humanists such as Erasmus, who longed to see a return to the simplicity of faith characteristic of the early church. This period must be set within the context of the Renaissance (1300-1600) which had reawakened interest in classical Greek and Roman art and philosophy. In religious terms, this engendered a new enthusiasm for studying the word of God in the original languages, and in 1516 Erasmus published a modern edition of the Greek New Testament with Latin translation as well. However, the inaccuracies of the Vulgate translation were very apparent, and because this had been so closely associated with the Catholic Church, the authority of both was brought into question.

It was Martin Luther who spearheaded many of the dramatic changes within the church during this time. He dismissed the authority of tradition, establishing the revolutionary principle of *Sola Scriptura*. Luther disdained the speculative theology of the medieval church, including such teachers as Pseudo-Dionysius and his penchant for angelic hierarchies.[229] Luther often spoke of demons but restricted himself to Scripture rather than conjecture. He taught that

---

[227]"Archiv fur Literatur und Kirchengeschichte des Mittelalters" (Berlin, Germany: H. Denifle, 1886); quoted in *The Catholic Encyclopedia*, s.v. "Mysticism," by George M. Sauvage; online posting, http://www.newadvent.org/cathen/10663b.htm; accessed 7 May 2001.

[228]Paul Deussen, "Jakob Böhme: Über sein Leben und seine Philosophie" (Germany, Kiel, 1897); quoted in *The Catholic Encyclopedia*, s.v. "Mysticism," by Sauvage.

[229]Martin Luther, *Table Talk*, in *Luther's Works* (Philadelphia, PA: Fortress Press, 1977), 54:318.

each individual has a guardian angel,[230] and that holy angels contend with the devil for every human soul.[231] Luther fervently believed that the preaching of the word is the key to victory over Satan, exhorting reliance on Scripture and sacrament: "God provided his church with audible preaching and visible sacraments. Satan resists this holy ministry in all earnestness, and he would like it to be eliminated altogether because by it alone is Satan overcome. The power of the oral Word is truly remarkable. To think that Satan, that proud spirit, may be put to flight and thrown into confusion by such a frail word on human lips!"[232]

John Calvin (1509-1564) also specifically addressed the question of spirit hierarchies and the views of Pseudo-Dionysius.[233] With regard to spiritual warfare, he believed in God's total sovereignty and that accordingly, the man who trusted in God need not fear the devil. He said: "By faith we repel all the attacks of the devil, and by the Word of God the enemy himself is slain outright. In other words, if the Word of God shall be efficacious in us through faith, we shall be more than sufficiently armed both for repelling and for putting to flight the enemy."[234] Calvin viewed victory over sin and Satan as a simple matter of faith in the power which raised Jesus Christ from the dead: "To conclude in one word, the cross of Christ then only triumphs in the breasts of believers over the devil and the flesh, sin and sinners, when their eyes are directed to the power of his resurrection."[235] He believed strongly that demons would assail

---

[230]Martin Luther, *Watchwords for the Warfare of Life*, pt. 4, trans. The author of Chronicles of the Schönberg-Cotta Family (London: T. Nelson and Sons, Paternoster Row, 1869), 96-97.

[231]Ibid., 93-94. "It would not be fit that we should know how earnestly the dear holy angels contend for us with the devil; what a hard and severe strife and warfare it is. . . . The good angels are wiser and know more than the evil angels . . . . They are also much mightier; for they stand before Him whose name is Almighty."

[232]Martin Luther, *Table Talk*, in *Luther's Works*, 54:318.

[233]John Calvin, *Institutes of the Christian Religion*, bk. 1, chap. 14, par. 4 (Grand Rapids, MI: Wm. B. Eerdmans Publishing Company, 2001), 144.

[234]John Calvin, *Commentaries on the Epistles of Paul to the Galatians and Ephesians*, in vol. 21 of 22, *Calvin's Commentaries* (Grand Rapids, MI: Baker Book House, 1979), 339.

[235]Calvin, *Institutes*, bk. 3.9.6, 30.

unbelievers but that the elect were not subject to oppression.[236] With respect to the necessity for intercessory prayer he said, "The Sophists are guilty of the merest trifling when they allege that Christ is the Mediator of *redemption,* but that believers are mediators of *intercession;* as if Christ had only performed a temporary mediation, and left an eternal and imperishable mediation to his servants."[237]

The Puritans and the Quakers

The work of the Reformers brought back into focus the primacy of Scripture and its exposition in the anointing of the Holy Spirit. As Zacharias comments, "The Puritans took over this emphasis with great seriousness and devoted themselves to biblical learning and application."[238] They were saturated in Scripture and knew the whole canon, but especially referred to the epistles of Paul for practical living. They took the existence of devils seriously, accepting the reality of spiritual warfare. However, as Zacharias comments, "They are not indulging in occult speculation for its own sake, to satisfy their curiosity. One might say their demonology is a subset of their doctrine of sanctification, or of their ecclesiology. That is, their pastoral concern is to help the church."[239] Many Puritan theologians wrote about spiritual warfare, including such well-known classics as John Bunyan's *Pilgrims Progress* and *Holy War,* Thomas Brooks' *Precious Remedies Against Satan's Devices* and William Gurnall's *The Christian in Complete Armour.*

The Puritans believed that Satan and his minions possess power over the human race because of man's own rebellion. "Their power over the wicked is an aspect of the judgment of God; their harassment of the saints, under the sovereign hand of God, serves to build up God's people, and to undo the devil's work even as they perform it."[240] Thus the spiritual battle only begins at regeneration; until then a person is Satan's "tame slave."[241] In the conflict, the devil seeks to pinpoint the remaining sin in believers, and bring them into

---

[236]Calvin, *Institutes,* bk. 1.14.18, 153.

[237]Calvin, "Of Prayer," (original emphasis).

[238]Bryan G. Zacharias, *The Embattled Christian: William Gurnall and the Puritan View of Spiritual Warfare* (Edinburgh: The Banner of Truth Trust, 1995), 115.

[239]Ibid., 5.

[240]Ibid., 113.

[241]Ibid., 116.

defeat. The Puritans demanded discipleship and encouraged vigorous activity in the battle against sin and Satan, believing the armour of Ephesians 6 to be Christ Himself.

William Perkins pointed out that Jesus used Scripture to overcome the devil, rather than His divine power or by summoning the angelic hosts.[242] The pre-eminence of the word of God as the weapon to bring about Satan's defeat is found in many Puritan writings. For example, William Gurnall denounced the papacy for denying people the only weapon with which they could defend themselves.[243]

The Puritans believed that spiritual victory was born out of relationship with God, and not via ritual, spiritual mechanics or magic. "It is a life lived in fellowship with God, with others and with oneself."[244] With regard to "doctrines of angels," Baxter wrote authoritatively as follows:

> . . . Be satisfied in knowing so much of angels as God in nature and Scripture hath revealed, but presume not to inquire further, much less to determine of unrevealed things . . . Almost all the Heretiks in the first ages of the Church did make their Doctrines of Angels the first and chief part of their Heresies: Arrogantly intruding into unrevealed things, and boasting of their acquaintance with the orders and inhabitants of the higher World. These being risen in the Apostles Days, occasioned Paul to say, Colossians.2.18, *Let no man beguile you of your reward in a voluntary humility and worshipping of angels, intruding into those things which he hath not seen, vainly puffed up in his fleshly mind.*[245]

James Naylor's tract, "The Lamb's War," is a compact summary of early Quaker understanding of the basic conflict between good and evil. Naylor clearly identified the power of darkness as being that which operates within the human heart, rather than in the cosmic realm of the demonic. Victory consists in bringing every thought and aspiration of the heart into the obedience of Christ, by the power of the Holy Spirit. Quakers knew the uselessness of self-made

---

[242]William Perkins, *The Combat Between Christ and the Divell Displayed*, 2d ed. (London: Melchisedech Bradwood, 1606), 19; quoted in Zacharias, 101.

[243]Gurnall, 2:231-32.

[244]Zacharias, 118.

[245]Richard Baxter, *The Christian Directory*, vol. 1 of 4, *The Practical Works of the Late Reverend and Pious Mr Richard Baxter* (London: T. Parkhurst, I. Robinson and L. Lawrence, 1707), 615 (original emphasis).

commitment, recognising that self-will continues to rebel against the leadings of the Spirit even when new life had begun.[246]

Methodism

The mid-eighteenth century saw a marked awakening in Protestantism in the British Isles, particularly in England. The most famous leader of this Evangelical movement was John Wesley (1703-1791) who inaugurated the Methodist societies. Doctrinally he did not wish to be an innovator but simply to spread scriptural holiness over the land.[247] Wesley was open to supernatural manifestations but maintained that Scripture alone was his touchstone; he had no faith in either the Church Fathers or contemporary writers of his day. In respect to the angelic realm, he wrote: "Of angels, indeed, we know nothing with any certainty but by revelation; the accounts which are left by the wisest of the ancients, or given by the modern Heathens, being no better than silly, self-inconsistent fables, too gross to be imposed even upon children."[248] Lowe observes that Wesley firmly believed in the fact that Satan is subject to the sovereignty of God. Thus Satan wars only "so far as God permits!"[249] The Christian's focus is to look to God, in Christ Jesus, the One who reigns and who has defeated Satan already.[250]

Pre-Pentecostal

Charles Spurgeon was born in 1834 and died in 1892. He viewed his ministry as that of a reformer, bringing men back to the truths of the gospel.[251] This was the true nature of spiritual warfare. He stated, "Our fathers used to speak of 'The Cause of God and Truth'; and it is for this that we bear arms, the few against the many, the feeble against the mighty. Oh, to be found good soldiers of Jesus Christ!"[252]

---

[246]Hugh Barbour and Arthur Roberts, eds., *Early Quaker Writings* (Grand Rapids, MI: William B. Eerdmans Publishing Company, 1973), 23.

[247]Kenneth Scott Latourette, *Reformation to the Present*, vol. 2, *A History of Christianity* (San Francisco, CA: Harper Collins, 1975), 1022-28.

[248]John Wesley, *Sermons on Several Occasions*, vol. 6 of 14, *The Works of The Rev. John Wesley, A.M* (London: Wesleyan Conference Office, 1865), 350.

[249]Ibid., 374.

[250]Ibid., 30-40.

[251]Arnold Dallimore, *Spurgeon: A New Biography* (Edinburgh: The Banner of Truth Trust, 1999), 67.

[252]Spurgeon, *The Greatest Fight*, 15.

In terms of warfare against Satan, Spurgeon taught that Jesus fought and won the battle for mankind on Calvary; He is already the Victor.[253] He demonstrated that God's Word is all that is needed by each individual believer in order to stand, for "to become mighty in the scriptures will be to become mighty through God."[254] With reference to evangelism he taught, "Nothing else but the living Word of God will convince, convert, renew and sanctify. He has promised that this shall not return unto Him void; but He has made no such promise to the wisdom of men, or the excellency of human speech. The Spirit of God works with the Word of God."[255]

On the other side of the Atlantic, one of the significant figures who preceded the Pentecostal revival was Frank Weston Sandford (1862-1948). He had a tremendous concern for world evangelisation, and in 1895 opened his own Bible School, named "The Holy Ghost and Us," to train a band of co-workers for this great task.

Some two years later, Sandford was to reveal his strategy for global evangelism in a series of lectures entitled *The Art of War*. He adopted the battle plan used by Joshua in the conquest of Canaan, as the basis for this operation. It was defined as comprising four stages-- the conquest of Joshua, the conquest of Israel, the conquest of Canaan (or the Gentiles), and the conquest of Conquests.[256] Stage Three commenced on 1 January 1901, at the turn of the century. Sandford announced that there would be a 24 hour prayer vigil at the prayer tower in Shiloh, and, in fact, this was to continue for the next twenty years.[257] He was convinced that the primary battle was with Satan and his hosts, who held the world in bondage. It was therefore necessary to enlist spirit-filled warriors in intercessory prayer as the

---

[253]Charles H. Spurgeon, *Spurgeon on Prayer and Spiritual Warfare* (New Kensington, PA: Whitaker House, 1998), 545-50.

[254]Spurgeon, *The Greatest Fight*, 33.

[255]Charles H. Spurgeon, Address on "Beaten Oil for the Light," *Sword and Trowel*, ed., Charles H. Spurgeon (London: Passmore and Alabaster, 1892), 687; quoted in Iain H. Murray, *Spurgeon v. Hyper-Calvinism* (Edinburgh: The Banner of Truth Trust, 2000), 12-13.

[256]For full details, please refer to Frank W. Sandford, *The Art of War for the Christian Soldier* (Amherst, NH: The Kingdom Press, 1966).

[257]William C. Hiss, "Shiloh: Frank W. Sandford and the Kingdom 1893-1948" (Ph.D. diss., Tufts University, Boston, Massachusetts, Apr. 1978), 266.

first line of attack, which was to be followed by an extensive campaign of evangelisation.

A team of twelve was sent to Jerusalem to mount a prayer vigil there as well.[258] Sandford believed that Christ would return to the ancient city to lead His forces in the final battle of Armageddon and so this was the place chosen to "remove the covering cast over the earth."[259] Ships were purchased,[260] so that teams could sail around the seven continents engaging in intercessory prayer to break the stranglehold of Satan over the nations, prior to the work of evangelism.[261] It is not difficult to see the similarities between this methodology and modern day SLSW, which many believe originated with C. Peter Wagner.

Pentecostal

The Pentecostal Movement of the twentieth century may be described as a time of restoration. Faupel comments, "This included the restoration of apostolic doctrine, apostolic power, apostolic authority, and apostolic practice."[262] Taking the early church as their pattern, the adherents of this movement identified their overall purpose in the words of Jude 3, namely, to "earnestly contend for the faith which was once delivered unto the saints." They looked to church history to provide evidence of New Testament Christianity in every generation. This was compiled into litanies, drawing on passages from "The Doctrines of the Twelve Apostles," Irenaeus, Justin Martyr, Tertullian, Origen, Cyprian, Augustine, Ignatius and Polycarp. Reference was also made to the faith and practice of various Christian groups including the Montanists, Waldensians, Huguenots, and Irvingites, all of whom had advocated the practice of speaking in tongues.[263]

---

[258]Ibid., 279-81.

[259]Ibid., 417.

[260]For example, the Wanderer in 1903 (Hiss, 339); the Barracouta (Hiss, 374); the Overcomer (Hiss, 381); and the Coronet (Hiss, 389).

[261]Victor P. Abram, foreword to *The Golden Light upon the Two Americas*, by Frank W. Sandford (Amherst, NH: The Kingdom Press, 1974), 8.

[262]D. William Faupel, *The Everlasting Gospel: The Significance of Eschatology in the Development of Pentecostal Thought* (Sheffield: Sheffield Academic Press, 1996), 39.

[263]Ibid., 37.

The early Pentecostal message had a strongly eschatological flavour, and the restoration of signs and wonders to the church was interpreted in this context. For example, Maria Woodworth-Etter spoke of the ministry of Peter, Stephen and Paul in the book of Acts as follows: "God says before Jesus comes, these same 'signs and wonders' shall come to pass: the sick shall be healed, devils cast out, people shall speak with tongues--just before he comes."[264] The movement was to be racked with controversy, both internally,[265] and externally,[266] but on their fundamental purpose they were agreed, "the early Pentecostals proclaimed their mission to be the *evangelisation* of the world. "[267]

The great apostle of faith, Smith Wigglesworth ministered during this era. He was born in 1859 but did not embark upon his ministry until he was aged 48, when he was baptised in the Holy Spirit. "Suddenly he had a new power that enabled him to preach, and even his wife was amazed at the transformation."[268] The characteristics of Wigglesworth's ministry included an unflinching belief in the word of God and a tremendous desire to see people enlarge their faith in God. He was aware that man's greatest weakness in spiritual conflict was lack of knowledge of the Scriptures and said, "There is no fear . . . for those who know the Word of God. . . . God's Word is the great antidote to evil."[269]

Maria Woodworth-Etter, whose ministry was characterised by tremendous signs and wonders, was also a significant figure of this era. She explained the word of Jesus in the great commission as follows, "Go and proclaim this good news everywhere to everyone

[264]Maria B. Woodworth-Etter, *Signs and Wonders God Wrought in the Ministry for Forty Years* (Indianapolis, IN: The Author, 1916), 534-35; quoted in Faupel, 39.

[265]For example, William Durham's teaching on the finished work of Christ led to a schism over sanctification as a second work of grace. For further details, see Vinson Synan, *The Century of the Holy Spirit: 100 Years of Pentecostal and Charismatic Renewal* (Nashville, TN: Thomas Nelson Publishers, 2001), 149-52.

[266]Synan, 143-48.

[267]Faupel, 22 (original emphasis).

[268]Smith Wigglesworth, *Smith Wigglesworth on Healing* (New Kensington, PA: Whitaker House, 1999), 8.

[269]Smith Wigglesworth, "God's Word: Antidote to Evil," *Cry of the Spirit: Unpublished Sermons of Smith Wigglesworth*, ed. Roberts Liardon, online posting, http://bornagain.port5.com/wigglesworth3.htm; accessed 17 July 2001.

that whosoever will may benefit by My atoning death and victory over the kingdom of Satan and share in My triumph, that now they may enjoy freedom from satanic supremacy and power . . . and enjoy the security and protection of the bloodstained banner of King Emmanuel."[270] With reference to preaching, she believed that the word of God, spoken in the power of the Holy Ghost was the vehicle of God's creative, life transforming power. She said: "Through the Holy Ghost, His words come like coals of fire burning the brains and hearts of men. They are shot out like arrows dipped in the blood of Jesus; like lightning, piercing the king's enemies in the head and lodging in the heart. . . . They are like David's little pebbles, we throw them at a venture, and God directs them so that they never return void, but they bring life or death; heaven or hell . . . Woe to us if we do not preach the whole truth or are ashamed or offended at any of His mighty works."[271]

The writings of Dr. T. L. Osborn, whose international ministry of mass evangelism was birthed during the first half of the twentieth century but was to continue far beyond the Pentecostal era, are also a declaration of the total victory in Christ Jesus. He dismisses Satan as a "deceiver, a liar, a bluff, a peddler of non-truths, a farce and an empty noise,"[272] asserting that his trickery "works only on those who attribute reality and substance to his *wiles*."[273] Osborn cites the definition of "wiles" as that set out in Kittel's Theological Dictionary of the New Testament; this includes the following terminology: "Corrupt or irrational human thoughts of persons lacking in understanding. Adverse religious judgments *by those deficient in an understanding of salvation*."[274] He proclaims that "*the fight of faith against principalities and powers* is the Christian's struggle to *make known the mystery of the Gospel*,"[275] but rejects the notion that this requires preliminary agonising in prayer about devils. "We do not have to do that. Our part is to give the Gospel to our hurting world and to give

---

[270]Roberts Liardon, ed., *Maria Woodworth-Etter: The Complete Collection of Her Life Teachings* (Tulsa, OK: Albury Publishing, 2000), 590.

[271]Ibid., 697-98, 701.

[272]T. L. Osborn, *The Message that Works* (Tulsa, OK: OSFO Publishers, 1997), 319.

[273]Ibid., 325 (original emphasis).

[274]Ibid., 325 (original emphasis).

[275]Ibid., 369 (original emphasis).

it with faith. God will confirm it. Salvation is *His* idea. We do not have to agonize with Him to get Him interested in delivering people from Satan's captivity."[276] With respect to the concept that a Christian may be demon-possessed, Osborn dismisses this as mere superstition,[277] having more in common with pagan methodology than spiritual warfare.

The Charismatic Movement and the Third Wave

In 1936, Wigglesworth prophesised concerning the coming revival in mainline denominations, which is now known as the Charismatic Movement or The Third Wave. Its benchmark was the formation in 1951 of the Full Gospel Businessmen's Fellowship International, under the leadership of Demos Shakarian. This was to become the catalyst for integrating the Pentecostal experience into established churches, straddling the entire denominational spectrum.

Once again the overall focus was on baptism in the Spirit, bringing greater power and impetus to evangelism, and the restoration of supernatural gifts to the church. Charismatic teaching has also encouraged lay ministry, exhorting Christians to discover and function in their role in the body of Christ.[278] This emphasis on ministry has opened the door to much that is erroneous.

In terms of spiritual warfare implications, Nigel Scotland observes: "In general terms charismatics have a heightened awareness of the presence of evil and the personal devil and powers of darkness. They are conscious that life is a spiritual struggle against Satan and his demon hosts. They frequently engage in what they term 'spiritual warfare.' This involves 'putting on the armour' in the way

---

[276]Ibid., 374 (original emphasis).

[277]Ibid., 368.

[278]For example, John Wimber taught "what could be called the 'democratization' of healing. . . . What makes Wimber different is a conscious, sustained effort to help as many believers as possible to pray for the sick effectively. . . . Whatever one thinks of the content of his teaching, one certainly must admit that Wimber is doing everything possible to share the ministry of healing with as many people as possible." Ronald Kydd, *Healing Through The Centuries: Models for Understanding* (Peabody, MA: Hendrickson Publishers, 1998), 55.

that Paul urges in his letter to the Ephesians. It also involves 'intercessory prayer', fasting, deliverance and exorcisms."[279]

Typically, many in the Charismatic Movement and the early stages of the subsequent Third Wave became involved in aggressive and highly vocal SLSW that aims to bind so-called territorial spirits which manifest themselves. It is taught that this is a prerequisite for evangelism. To the observer, it would appear that the focus has shifted away from the mighty miracle power of God to heal, deliver and save which characterised early Pentecost, and towards the power of an "almost-as-mighty devil" whose purpose is to prevent such things from happening. In fact, C. Peter Wagner, who is commonly recognised as a leading figure in the SLSW movement, expresses his agreement with S. D. Gordon, who wrote in 1904 concerning prayer, "the pitch is not God-ward, but Satan-ward."[280] In this essentially dualistic tension, the believer effectively holds the balance of power, for his role is vital in releasing the power of God to overcome the enemy.[281] It appears to the author that later in the Third Wave, the initial emphasis on aggressive warfare techniques lessened and strategic-level intercession became the adopted tool.[282]

Much of this teaching has reached the popular market via the fictional press. Frank Peretti's novels, *This Present Darkness* and *Piercing the Darkness* have particularly captured the public imagination. Scotland comments on the former: "[The story] invests a great deal of power in the evil angels and the good angels only seem to get into action in response to the prayer and intercession of Christians here on earth. In places the book leaves the reader with an almost fatalistic

---

[279]Nigel Scotland, *Charismatics and the New Millennium: The Impact of Charismatic Christianity from 1960 into the New Millennium* (Guildford, England: Eagle, 2000), 33-34.

[280]S. D. Gordon, *Quiet Talks on Prayer* (New York: Fleming H. Revell Company, 1904), 120; quoted in Wagner, *Warfare Prayer*, 106. The concept of the Satanward view was popularised by James Kallas in *The Satanward View: A Study in Pauline Theology* (Philadelphia, PA: The Westminster Press, 1966).

[281]George Otis Jr., *The Last of the Giants: Lifting the Veil on Islam and the End Times* (Grand Rapids, MI: Chosen Books, 1991), 246-48; and George Otis Jr., *Informed Intercession: Transforming Your Community Through Spiritual Mapping and Strategic Prayer* (Ventura, CA: Renew Books, 1999), 58-59. See also Dutch Sheets, *Intercessory Prayer: How God Can Use Your Prayers to Move Heaven and Earth* (Ventura, CA: Renew Books, 1996), 204-206, 208-210.

[282]Wagner, *Confronting the Powers*, 13.

feeling that what happens in this world is simply dependent on angelic warfare in the heavens."[283]

In reality, there is no clear charismatic theology. There are also many different opinions as to the extent or otherwise of satanic power. However, as Scotland succinctly observes, "Christians and charismatics in particular must guard against investing Satan with more power than the Scriptures accord him."[284]

In his early years, John Wimber also wrote on spiritual warfare.[285] His book, *Power Evangelism*, defines the concept of kingdom power and its relationship to evangelism. Power evangelism is preceded and undergirded by supernatural demonstrations of God's presence.[286] Although Wimber believed in "custodian" territorial spirits, he rejected the concept of aggressive warfare against the spirits, concluding that it is God who determines the strategy, engages the enemy, and wins the victory. He believed that Christians must oppose Satan but they do not confront the ruling spirits, only the low-level demons, stating that the battle does not take place in the heavenlies between angels and demons but "in the hearts and minds of men and women."[287]

Historical Summary

History demonstrates that Christian doctrine and experience must be firmly grounded in the word of truth. The apologists of the early church fought to defend the faith, not only against syncretism from pagan philosophies but against internal errors propounded by other Christians. Irenaeus in particular recognised the extreme subtlety of error which masquerades as truth. It is clear that the church entered its darkest age when it abandoned the supremacy of the authority of Scripture, thus allowing the entrance of superstition and witchcraft; the same seeds of error have produced SLSW in contemporary Christendom.

---

[283]Scotland, 131.

[284]Ibid., 137.

[285]John Wimber and Kevin Springer, *The Dynamics of Spiritual Growth* (London: Hodder and Stoughton, 1990), 183-92.

[286]John Wimber, *Power Evangelism* (San Francisco, CA: Harper and Row, 1986), 35.

[287]Wimber and Springer, 184.

The work of the great Reformers, Luther and Calvin, revolutionised the contemporary Christian basis for faith, by pointing once again to the reality of God's great plan of redemption as revealed in His word by His Spirit. Through their love of the Scriptures the Puritans reinforced that teaching and the early Methodists, under the influence of John Wesley and George Whitefield, also maintained the total authority of the word of God.

However, in the nineteenth century, Spurgeon was to forsee troubled times ahead. As Iain Murray points out, the great preacher "found himself like Jeremiah, warning that the promises being made by his religious contemporaries were false."[288] Spurgeon warned, "We are only at the beginning of an era of unmingled unbelief and fanaticism. . . . The hurricane is coming. . . . Men have ceased to be guided by the Word and claim to be themselves prophets."[289]

The Pentecostal-Charismatic revolution of the twentieth century was a great move of God when the reality of the presence and power of the Holy Spirit was restored to many churches. However, its weakness was to be the paucity of associated biblical exegesis and doctrinal understanding. Increasingly, experience-based analysis rather than truth has become the touchstone of the charismatic world, and Christendom today is in danger of slipping once more into the spiritual dark ages.

---

[288]Iain H. Murray, 4-5.
[289]Spurgeon, *The Metropolitan Tabernacle Pulpit*, 29:214.

CHAPTER 3

REVIEW OF RELATED LITERATURE

Introduction

The author's hypothesis is that the systematic exposition of the word of God is the fundamental pre-requisite in relation to the understanding and practice of any spiritual truth. When viewed in this light, it is clear that much that is taught in the context of "Strategic Level Spiritual Warfare" (SLSW) is without scriptural foundation and is based on experiential evaluation and questionable empirical evidence. It is interesting to note that for most of the twentieth century, a large proportion of church members and an even higher proportion of church leaders in most major Protestant denominations failed to recognise the Bible as being wholly revealed by God and inerrant.[1] In addition, some Charismatics claim to have received special revelation from God which carries the same divine authority as the Scriptures.[2] These trends, allied with the focus on the experiential, have caused a dramatic shift in the approach to truth within much of Christendom and nowhere is this more clearly demonstrated than in the context of Christian literature.

According to Veith, a common saying in the Christian publishing world is that when a trend occurs in the secular arena, six months later a Christianised-version of it will appear.[3] For example, in the early 1980s there was a tremendous upsurge of interest in the occult engendered by the New Age movement. This produced a rash of books on angels and spirit-guides within the secular context, and the same phenomenon was soon mirrored in the Christian marketplace. Frank Perretti's fictitious work *This Present Darkness*,[4] was one of the first Christian novels written in this context and proved to be a vital catalyst in the emergence of SLSW in the Christian consciousness.

---

[1] John MacArthur, Jr., *2 Timothy*, in *MacArthur's New Testament Commentary*, in *QuickVerse*, ver. 7 [CD-ROM] (Omaha, NE: Parsons Technology, 1997).

[2] Ibid.

[3] Gene Edward Veith, Jr., "Whatever Happened to Christian Publishing?" online posting at http://www.worldmag.com/world/issue/07-12-97/cover_1.asp; accessed 21 Aug. 2001.

[4] Frank Peretti, *This Present Darkness* (Westchester, IL: Crossway Books, 1986); reached the Christian bestseller list in 1987. This work presents the demonic but without any theory of territoriality. See Duane A. Garrett, *Angels and the New Spirituality* (Nashville, TN: Broadman & Holman, 1995) for a critique.

Between 1960 and 1986, a total of 509 volumes were added to the spiritual warfare section of "WorldCat," a database which records the holdings of over 23,000 libraries worldwide. In his recent research on the subject, Steve Matthews has identified that in respect to this total, the majority appeared during 1985 and 1986, representing an overall increase of an amazing 523 percent. Since that time, "the trend does not seem to be slowing down."[5] He also discovered that at the later date of 1989, the editors of the secular "Cumulative Books Index," a compilation of books printed in the United States of America, saw the phrase "spiritual warfare" appear sufficient times to warrant its use as a classifying term.[6]

As the world moved towards the end of the second millennium, the concept of confrontation between good and evil with the associated use of warfare imagery seemed to reach fever pitch in the Christian media. Christians were instructed that the key to successful Christian living and evangelism was via 'pulling down strongholds' in the unseen spirit realm. For example, George Otis Jr. asserted:

> Demonic deceptions, offensives and strongholds are both real and sophisticated and represent a blend of unilateral initiatives against and considered responses to divine deployments. Understanding today's spiritual battlefield means negotiating our way through enemy zones of control or extraordinary influence (strongholds), and grappling with matters such as the strength and purposes of rival belief systems (such as Islam, Hinduism or materialism). If these systems and strongholds are to be overcome, they must first be identified with precision and then engaged with steadfastness and courage.[7]

Such modern day SLSW involves a variety of techniques, including identifying the relevant territorial spirit or demon by name, and engaging in spiritual battle by means of aggressive prayer.[8] Thus, in 1990, Larry Lea appeared on the front cover of *Charisma* magazine

---

[5]Steve Matthews, "Building Upon 'Missiological Syncretism: A New Animistic Paradigm': An Empirical Study of the 'Spiritual Warfare Movement'" (M.A. diss., Columbia Biblical Seminary and Graduate School of Missions, Columbia, South Carolina, 1999), 10-11.

[6]Ibid., 9.

[7]George Otis Jr., *The Last of the Giants: Lifting the Veil on Islam and the End Times* (Grand Rapids, MI: Chosen Books, 1991), 39.

[8]For example, C. Peter Wagner, *Engaging the Enemy: How to Fight and Defeat Territorial Spirits* (Ventura, CA: Regal Books, 1991).

in combat fatigues calling 300,000 "prayer warriors" to join him in taking America for God.

In this atmosphere, a plethora of literature continued to spill from the racks of retailers' shelves, with titles such as *Wrestling with Dark Angels* (Regal, 1990), *99 Answers to Questions about Angels* (InterVarsity, 1997), *Demons & Spiritual Warfare* (InterVarsity, 1997), *Handbook for Spiritual Warfare* (Thomas Nelson, 1996), and, *End Time Warriors* (Renew, 1999). Publishers also met the burgeoning market demand with sponsored author conferences and seminars, full page advertising in Christian magazines and on the Internet, and other resources in the form of CD-ROMs and video and audio cassettes. Furthermore, a growing host of "spiritual warfare" internet sites and articles sprang up to deal with what is an undeniably lucrative label.[9] Hits via the World Wide Web, using the search engine "Google" for the topic "spiritual warfare," totalled 50,900 on 23 August 2001.

Specific literature and associated products were also geared to the youth market. For example, the computer game *The War in Heaven* produced by Valusoft, was based on the underlying concept of a battle between opposing forces where players become angel warriors in heaven "who hold shields of faith while brandishing swords and spears to slay squatty, toad-like demons who pop up unexpectedly along the paths of good and evil."[10] In addition, contemporary Christian songbooks routinely incorporated spiritual warfare as a category, and explicit references were made by Christian music artists. Graham Kendrick wrote in the introduction to his *Make the Way Song Book and Instruction Manual:* "Satan has the real estate of villages, towns and cities overshadowed by ruling spirits which work untiringly at his command to bring about his malevolent will fostering fear, violence and deception."[11]

The popularity and attraction of spiritual warfare concepts have been unquestionable from the outset. Not unlike secular marketing,

---

[9]T. L. Osborn, *The Message That Works* (Tulsa, OK: OSFO Publishers, 1997), 267.

[10]Tara Dooley, "Battle of Good and Evil," online posting, http://www.star-telegram.com/news/doc/1047/1:RELIGION13/1:RELIGION130320100.html; accessed 20 May 2001.

[11]Nigel Scotland, *Charismatics and the New Millennium: The Impact of Charismatic Christianity from 1960 into the New Millennium* (Guildford, England: Eagle, 2000), 136.

this industry generates new products and ideas regularly in order to inspire new enthusiasms which unearth new targets to assault. However, the fundamental question remains, "What is spiritual warfare?" Today, the once accepted historical definition is just one of many.[12] Wagner has distinguished three generalised levels of spiritual warfare which he claims are broadly recognised by Christians specialising in this type of ministry. The first is the ministry of casting out demons and is classified as ground level spiritual warfare; the second, occult-level spiritual warfare, concerns the type of demonic power which operates via "shamans, New Age channelers, occult practitioners, witches and warlocks, Satanist priests, fortune-tellers and the like." The third category is that of SLSW, in which the focus of the Christian's contention is with the "even more ominous" territorial spirits.[13] These are generally defined as "geographically located" demons of various ranks, which exercise authority within their "assigned areas."[14] As Priest and others have commented, such concepts have been "formulated, systematized, publicized, accredited, and institutionalized in mainstream and missionary institutions,"[15]

---

[12]The Puritan concept is that warfare commences in the soul at new birth. Michael Reid and Judson Cornwall, *Whose Mind Is It Anyway?* (Loughton, England: Sharon Publications Ltd, 1993), 18; they posit that the battle is in the mind and the Christian's role is to tear down the strongholds (the lies of the devil) in the mind with the truth of the Word of God (2 Cor. 10:3-5). Clinton E. Arnold, *Spiritual Warfare: What Does The Bible Really Teach?* (London: Marshall Pickering, 1997), 1-72; the first chapter entitled, "What is Spiritual Warfare?" shows spiritual warfare as an all encompassing power struggle between the Evil One and Jesus in every area of the Christian's life; Thomas B. White, *The Believer's Guide to Spiritual Warfare* (Ann Arbor, MI: Vine Books, 1990); spiritual warfare is "to learn to detect and deal with the subtleties of Satan"; C. Peter Wagner, "Territorial Spirits," in C. Peter Wagner and F. Douglas Pennoyer, eds., *Wrestling with Dark Angels: Toward a Deeper Understanding of the Supernatural Forces in Spiritual Warfare* (Ventura, CA: Regal, 1990), 49-72; it is everything "within the context of this cosmic-earthly spiritual warfare dimension of reality."

[13]C. Peter. Wagner, *Warfare Prayer: Strategies for Combating the Rulers of Darkness* (Crowborough, England: Monarch Publications, 1997), 18.

[14]Chuck Lowe, *Territorial Spirits and World Evangelisation?: A Biblical, Historical and Missiological Critique of Strategic-Level Spiritual Warfare* (Fearn and Kent: OMF and Mentor, 1998), 18.

[15]Robert J. Priest, Thomas Campbell, and Bradford A. Mullen, "Missiological Syncretism: The New Animistic Paradigm" in Edward Rommen, ed., *Spiritual*

and this integration, in itself, demands an honest analysis. Wagner himself has noted that "Among those who do recognize the phenomenon of territorial spirits, there is ignorance in the area of methodology. Few know how to go about breaking high-level powers of evil systematically, and fewer yet are doing it effectively. For this reason much more research is needed in this field. I consider it one of the top-drawer challenges in the years to come."[16]

Since its inception in the 1980s, the SLSW movement has been dogged by conflict and controversy, despite its unquestionable popularity. Scores of authors give testimonies of monumental success (see for example, *Engaging the Enemy* (ed. Wagner, 1991), *Breaking Strongholds in Your City* (ed. Wagner, 1993), *Informed Intercession* (Otis, 1999), *Warfare Prayer* (Wagner, 1998), *Could You Not Tarry One Hour?* (Lea, 1987), *Prayer Power in Argentina* (Silvoso in Wagner, 1991), *Christianity with Power* (Kraft, 1989), and many others). Only a handful, however, voice concern and criticism (see for example *Territorial Spirits & World Evangelization?* (Lowe, 1998), *Do Demons Rule Your Town?* (Taylor, 1993), *Whose War Is It Anyway?* (Cornwall & Reid, 1993), *Whose Mind Is It Anyway?* (Reid & Cornwall, 1993), and, Section 7 of *The Message That Works* (Osborn, 1997). By means of this ongoing controversy, many key issues have been broached. These include, for example, concepts relating to territorial spirits and strategic-level spiritual warfare practices set in the context of global evangelisation and changing worldviews. Clearly, biblical and theological contextuality are also fundamental to the arguments and in examination of the relevant literature this will be the primary area of analysis. However, before evaluation of the theory and practice of SLSW, it is proposed to provide an analysis of the underlying influences.

Power and Missions: Raising the Issues, Evangelical Missiological Society Series no. 3 (Pasadena, CA: William Carey Library, 1995), 9-87.

[16]Wagner, "Territorial Spirits," in *Wrestling with Dark Angels*, 88.

Underlying Influences

Proponents of SLSW claim that it carries the promise of "unprecedented forward advances of the Kingdom of God,"[17] offering mission *"the greatest power boost it has had since the time that William Carey went to India in 1793."*[18] As Lowe points out, "Warfare prayer is credited with bringing down the Berlin Wall and the Iron Curtain, with penetrating Albania with the gospel, with deposing dictators like Manuel Noriega of Nicaragua, with lowering the crime rate of American cities, and with reviving the economies of Third World nations."[19]

However, given the paucity of biblical and theological evidence in support of the practice, many Christians have expressed unease. As theologian R. C. Sproul writes, "We are inconsistent and confused because we fail to understand where Christianity ends and paganism begins. We do not know where the boundary lines are."[20] The question must be raised--what is the basis for the theory and practice of SLSW? In 1996, Wagner published *Confronting the Powers* in response to this very question. The book has been described by Arnold as "the first and only serious attempt to provide biblical, theological and historical evidence for the practice of directly engaging territorial spirits,"[21] and for this reason it has been chosen in preference to other works by Wagner as the authoritative textbook representing his point of view in this context.

The author's analysis of this and other representative literature reveals three significant and interrelated concepts which are central to

---

[17]C. Peter Wagner, ed., *Breaking Strongholds in Your City: How to Use Spiritual Mapping to Make Your Prayers More Strategic, Effective and Targeted* (Ventura, CA: Regal Books, 1993), 25.

[18]C. Peter Wagner, *Confronting the Powers: How the New Testament Church Experienced the Power of Strategic-Level Spiritual Warfare* (Ventura, CA: Regal Books, 1996), 46 (original emphasis).

[19]Lowe, *Territorial Spirits*, 114; quoting Wagner in *Warfare Prayer*, 163-64.

[20]R. C. Sproul, in a press release about Luis Palau and David Sanford, *God Is Relevant: Finding Strength and Peace in Today's World* (New York: Doubleday, 1997); quoted in Elmer Towns and Warren Bird, *Into The Future: Turning Today's Church Trends into Tomorrow's Opportunities* (Grand Rapids, MI: Fleming H. Revell, 2000), 65.

[21]Arnold, *Spiritual Warfare*, 231.

the whole hypothesis of SLSW. These are (1) hermeneutical approach, (2) worldview, and (3) observation/experience. Although there is considerable overlap between the three subjects, it is proposed to deal with these, as far as possible, separately and in order.

Hermeneutical Approach

Wagner posits that "the major part of the criticism of strategic-level spiritual warfare that has come in during the last few years has revolved around issues of hermeneutics." He details the misgivings expressed by one of his critics as follows: "There is no model in Scripture of anyone doing what you are encouraging people to do. How can strategic-level spiritual warfare be God's clearly biblical method when the apostles themselves are not seen exercising that prerogative?"[22] Wagner describes this as the "apostles' example principle," which he dismisses on the following basis: "If it is a correct hermeneutical principle that we reject any form of Christian ministry if we do not find precedent in the teachings of Jesus or in the lives and writings of the apostles, we then must also reject many other forms of Christian behaviour."[23] In the author's opinion this is a non-argument; there are various so-called Christian practices which owe more to tradition and faulty exegesis than to biblical precedent. A negative argument cannot be used to confirm a positive proposition. However, Wagner then cites various examples of commonly accepted Christian teachings and practices which supposedly do not pass the apostles' example test. His list fails to differentiate between concepts which are fundamental to the faith and those which are a question of practice; it includes such varied topics as the doctrine of the Trinity, emancipation of slaves, Sunday as the primary day of worship, validation for a canon of sixty-six books, and celebration of Christmas and Easter. In the author's opinion, the way in which Wagner then uses some of these examples to illustrate his point is highly questionable. He refers in particular to the issue of whether or not a Christian can be demonised. He is of the opinion that this is a valid possibility, but sets out the arguments postulated by scholars of the opposite persuasion who conclude that

---

[22] Wagner, *Confronting the Powers*, 82.
[23] Ibid., 83.

the practice is erroneous, due to lack of scriptural validation in terms of teaching or practice.[24] Wagner admits the Bible is silent on the subject but this silence is at variance with his personal experience in the area. He, therefore, lists four points as the basis of his belief in the potential demonisation of Christians, namely:

> Our personal ministry experience has led us to believe that Christians can be invaded by demons.
>
> We have arrived at consensus that this is true from many others who have ministered in the area of deliverance.
>
> We have seen many positive, even dramatic, results in the lives of those Christians who have been delivered from demons. . .
>
> None of the previous three *contradicts* any explicit biblical teaching.[25]

This rationale is crucial to understanding Wagner's hermeneutical approach. Basically, experience is elevated to a position of high authority when it is confirmed by consensus opinion and apparently positive results; accordingly, it may supplant biblical truth. As Lowe succinctly comments, "where the silence of Scripture leaves [them] with no reliable criterion by which to distinguish truth from error, animism is used to fill in the gaps."[26] The only caveat is where the practice concerned specifically contradicts Scripture and in this context Wagner totally ignores teaching which is implicitly understood from the word of God. Thus, for example, although there is no explicit biblical teaching relating to the demonisation of Christians, by implication the Scripture makes it quite clear that this is an impossibility. Any individual who has had a true new birth becomes a living temple of the Holy Spirit (1 Cor. 3:16), and Jesus has promised that He and the Father will make their abode within him (John 14:23). It is therefore inconceivable that he or she can subsequently be demon possessed. As the apostle John wrote, "whosoever is born of God keepeth himself, and that wicked one toucheth him not" (1 John 5:18; see also 1 John 4:4). Wagner summarises his position as follows:

> I am not claiming biblical *proof* for the validity of strategic-level spiritual warfare, spiritual mapping or identificational repentance. I will, however, claim that we do have sufficient biblical *evidence* to warrant:

---

[24]Ibid., 85-86.

[25]Ibid., 86 (original emphasis).

[26]Lowe, *Territorial Spirits*, 111.

1) At the *least,* a working hypothesis that we can field test, evaluate, modify and refine;

2) At the *most,* a significant, relatively new spiritual technology God has given us to meet the greatest challenge to world missions since William Carey went to India more than 200 years ago. If this is the case, refusing to use it on the part of some might be to run the risk of unfaithfulness to the Master.[27]

Ed Murphy, who has produced a definitive handbook on the topic of spiritual warfare, adopts a position similar to that elucidated by Wagner. He deliberates somewhat tersely, "Why do we evangelicals so distrust experience with the spirit world? Why do we develop theologies about this dimension of reality about which we are personally ignorant except through biblical exegesis? Can a theology of Satan and demons that is both true and useful for ministry really be developed by theologians studying their Hebrew and Greek Bibles while sitting in their air-conditioned offices apart from at least some personal experience?" He continues, "correct biblical interpretation is that interpretation which is most consistent with experience . . . We cannot sacrifice people on the altar of theological presuppositions."[28] This is emotive language but it reveals the same assumption--experience rules in the field of hermeneutics.

In respect to the lack of biblical evidence to substantiate his theories concerning the supernatural, Charles Kraft asserts that God may have deliberately excluded some spiritual truths from the Bible, in order that these may be discovered in much the same way as man unearths scientific knowledge.[29] The implication is that man's observations can supplement the word of God in terms of spiritual understanding. One cannot fail to be reminded of Jonathan Edwards' observation:

> And why cannot we be contented with the divine oracles, that holy, pure word of God, which we have in such abundance and clearness now that the canon of Scripture is completed? . . . Why should we not rest in that standing rule that God has given to his church, which, the apostle teaches us, is surer than a voice from heaven?

---

[27]Wagner, *Confronting the Powers,* 89 (original emphasis).

[28]Edward F. Murphy, *The Handbook for Spiritual Warfare* (Nashville, TN: Thomas Nelson, 1996), xiii.

[29]Charles H. Kraft, "Christian Animism or God-Given Authority," in Rommen, 113.

And why should we desire to make Scripture speak more to us than it does? Or why should any desire a higher kind of intercourse with heaven than by having the Holy Spirit given in his sanctifying influences, infusing and exciting grace and holiness, love and joy, which is the highest kind of intercourse which saints and angels in heaven have with God, and the chief excellency of the glorified man Christ Jesus?[30]

Worldview

The concept of worldview is a recurring theme in much of the SLSW literature and is intrinsically connected with the hermeneutical approach. Wagner comments as follows: "Does our worldview influence our hermeneutics or how we interpret the Bible? Of course it does. Our worldview implants in each of us a certain mental grid through which we process *all* information that comes our way. . . . Although we wish it were not true, our understanding of Scripture is also limited to one degree or another by our worldview."[31] It is therefore vital to address the question of worldview in terms of understanding the rationale behind much of the SLSW philosophy.

In his comprehensive study of the subject, James Sire postulates the following definition: "A worldview is a set of presuppositions (assumptions which may be true, partially true or entirely false) which we hold (consciously or unconsciously, consistently or inconsistently) about the basic makeup of our world."[32] Phillips and Brown offer a similar interpretation, "A worldview is, first of all, *an explanation and interpretation of the world* and second, *an application of this view to life.* In simpler terms, our worldview is a view *of the world* and a view *for the world.*"[33] Charles Kraft suggests that a worldview consists in "*culturally structured assumptions, values and commitments underlying a people's perception of REALITY.* Worldview is the major influence on how we perceive REALITY. . . . People interpret and react on this basis reflexively

---

[30]Jonathan Edwards, *The Works of Jonathan Edwards*, vol. 1 of 2, rev. and corrected by Edward Hickman (Edinburgh: The Banner of Truth Trust, 1974), 404.

[31]Wagner, *Confronting the Powers*, 76-77.

[32]James W. Sire, *The Universe Next Door: A Basic Worldview Catalog*, 3d ed. (Downers Grove, IL: InterVarsity Press, 1997), 16.

[33]W. Gary Phillips and William E. Brown, *Making Sense of Your World* (Chicago, IL: Moody Press, 1991), 29 (original emphasis).

without thinking."[34] Kraft differentiates between the "big R" REALITY both material and non-material, which is outside of the mind, and the subjective reality which pertains to the perceptions of the individual. He argues that biblical revelation is part of the "big R" REALITY; conversely, the diversity of interpretation in respect to the Scriptures is an example of the subjective reality of human perceptions. He states, ". . . we need to learn as much as possible about REALITY and to adjust our perception of reality accordingly. To do this we must learn to be open to understandings that lie beyond those we now have."[35] Given Kraft's proposition that Scripture does not contain a totally comprehensive record of spiritual truth,[36] such learning may be from sources other than the word of God. It is in this context that the concept of worldview becomes relevant.

It must be remembered that the basic concept of SLSW came into being as a result of frustrated missionary endeavour and the resultant search for an effective church growth methodology.[37] It appeared that some traditional peoples of the undeveloped world were resistant to the gospel message as presented by missionaries who themselves originated in the West. For example, when Kraft first went to the mission field, he found himself totally unprepared for the worldview differences that he encountered.[38] Similarly, as a missionary to India, Paul Hiebert was shocked to discover that he had no answers to the questions of pagan villagers about the spirit

---

[34] Charles H. Kraft, *Christianity with Power: Your Worldview and Your Experience of the Supernatural* (Ann Arbor, MI: Servant Books, 1989), 20 (original emphasis).

[35] Ibid., 15 (original emphasis).

[36] Wagner, *Confronting the Powers*, 70-71.

[37] For example, Ralph Winter said, "We cannot reasonably expect to achieve the marvellous goals of the AD 2000 Movement without a significant change in strategy. More of the same will not be enough." Cited in Garrard, "Contemporary Issues in Mission." Also, in an interview between the author and Chuck Lowe (Chuck Lowe, interview by author, documented personal notes, Wheaton College, Wheaton, Illinois, 19 Jan. 2001), the latter related his discussions with disillusioned missionaries in Japan who adopted this method.

[38] James Flynn, review of *Anthropology for Christian Witness* by Charles Kraft, (Maryknoll, NY: Orbis. 1997), online posting, http://www.amazon.com/exec/obidos/ASIN/1570750858/ref=ase_.../102-5213116-639852; accessed 9 May 2001.

world; his brand of rational Western Christianity was totally ineffective in addressing animistic concerns. He writes, "As a Westerner, I was used to presenting Christ on a basis of rational arguments, not by evidences of His power in the lives of people who were sick, possessed and destitute."[39] "As a scientist I had been trained to deal with the empirical world in naturalistic terms. As a theologian, I was taught to answer ultimate questions in theistic terms. For me the middle zone did not really exist."[40]

On the mission field Hiebert discovered that Indian thinking assumed an extensive middle zone from which spirit powers exerted influence, either for good or evil, on the natural domain. Clearly his experience compelled him to re-evaluate his own Christian beliefs and he set out his thinking in an influential article, in which he defined what is described as the "Western Two-tiered View of Reality". He called for a "theology of God in human history" including "a theology of divine guidance, provision and healing; of ancestors, spirits and invisible powers of this world; and of suffering, misfortune and death."[41] Almost twenty years later he was to point out that most of the contemporary literature on spiritual warfare has been produced "by western missionaries who have been forced to question their Western denial of this-worldly spiritual realities through encounters with witchcraft, spiritism, and demon possession." He warns, "Too often they base their studies in experience and look for biblical texts to justify their views. They fail to examine the worldviews they use to interpret both Scripture and experience."[42]

Murphy asserts that apart from the agnostic position there are only two conceivable worldviews. Firstly, the spiritualistic worldview which affirms that the ultimate reality is spiritual/immaterial as opposed to physical, which is accepted by the vast majority of the world's five to six billion inhabitants. Secondly, the materialistic or naturalistic worldview which concludes that ultimate reality is

---

[39]Paul G. Hiebert, "The Flaw of the Excluded Middle" *Missiology: An International Review* 10, no. 1 (Jan. 1982): 35-47.

[40]Ibid.

[41]Ibid.

[42]Paul G. Hiebert, "Spiritual Warfare and Worldviews," online posting, http://www.missiology.org/ems/bulletins/hiebert.html; accessed 9 May 2001.

material/physical rather than spiritual.[43] The latter is assumed to be dominant in the Western world and as Murphy states is "the view of reality that arose out of the historical movement of the eighteenth century called the Enlightenment. It is often summed up in one word, *naturalism*." He then cites Ferm who has defined this as "the name for that characteristic of scientific method which constructs its patterns of thought on the basis of natural causation as distinguished from a supernatural or occult explanation."[44] Although naturalism has largely been rejected by Christians, Murphy argues that it has influenced Western theology "more than most of us are aware,"[45] the implication being that the typical Western Christian has little awareness of the spirit realm. Murphy goes so far as to claim that although both the spiritualistic (or traditional) worldview and the Western worldview are full of error, nevertheless the former "stands closer to the biblical world view because it fully acknowledges the reality of the spirit world."[46] He exhorts, "We must remove our Western-world view eyeglasses, which blind us to the biblical view of the spirit world, and be willing to become incarnate into the same world into which our Lord entered--a world of deadly spiritual warfare."[47]

Kraft also promotes the hypothesis that Westerners divide the world into two realms, the natural and the supernatural, and then proceed to disregard the latter. He draws the conclusion that this clouds their understanding of the great majority of people for whom the supernatural is part of daily life.[48] Greg Boyd holds a similar viewpoint, asserting that other non-Western cultures take the spirit realm for granted, assuming that there are spiritual beings whose behaviour impacts humanity. He argues that because of the "scientific, post-Enlightenment, rationalistic, naturalistic revolution" the average Western Christian has been "blinded to that reality." Boyd continues, "And if you're ever going to be involved in spiritual

---

[43]Murphy, 3-4.

[44]*Encyclopedia of Religion*, ed. Vergilius Ferm, s.v. "naturalism" (New York: The Philosophical Library, 1945), 518; quoted in Murphy, 4.

[45]Murphy, 4.

[46]Ibid., 7.

[47]Ibid., 8.

[48]Charles Kraft, *Christianity with Power;* quoted in Wagner, *Warfare Prayer*, 99.

warfare, or even begin to be aware of spiritual warfare, you've got to break the stronghold of Western naturalism, our scientific worldview, and begin to see the world in terms of this warfare."[49]

Such reasoning implies that the individual is totally subservient to the prevailing view of the culture in which he lives. Thus, Wagner, Kraft and other proponents of SLSW promote the assumption that the so-called Age of Reason has stifled the ability of the average Western Christian to comprehend the supernatural and the existence of good and evil in spiritual terms.

This assessment totally ignores a number of important issues. The first of these is that Christianity is a supernatural faith. The God of the Bible is a God of miracle power who confirms His word with signs and wonders (Mark 16:20). The Scripture teaches that there are evil forces at work which seek to deceive the minds of men, but their power is and always has been strictly limited.

Secondly, to quote the words of Dennis McCallum:

> God is also the Creator of *rationality* and *reason*. Reason isn't just a product of European culture, but a quality inherent in the Word and nature of the eternal God. God appealed to lost sinners by saying, 'Come, let us reason together' (Isaiah 1:18). Long before anyone ever dreamed of the Enlightenment, Paul said the truth about God is 'evident' and 'clearly seen' even by people without the Bible (Romans 1:19-20). Truth is 'evident from what has been created.' In other words, people can use their minds to draw reasonable conclusions from nature--that God exists, and that his nature is infinite and personal.[50]

As McCallum goes on to point out, "Enlightenment Europe" made the mistake of abusing reason by arguing that "reason *alone* could tell us all things."[51] However, this error does not invalidate the whole concept of rationality, nor prove that it is an unbiblical

---

[49]Greg Boyd, "Spiritual Warfare: Free Will and the Legacy of Augustine," online posting, http://www.eternalwarriors.com/lesson1.html; accessed 22 Aug. 2001.

[50]Dennis McCallum, *The Death of Truth: Responding to Multiculturalism, the Rejection of Reason and the new Postmodern Diversity* (Minneapolis, MN: Bethany House Publishers, 1996), 250 (original emphasis).

[51]Ibid., 252 (original emphasis).

concept. Clearly, it is impossible to acquire revelation by reason, but revelation in itself is not irrational.[52]

Thirdly, the assumption also ignores the fact that the Enlightenment delivered the churches of the west from a period of superstition and fear in respect to witchcraft, which even the Reformation failed to eradicate. Helen Ellerbe comments:

> As people adopted the new belief that the world was the terrifying realm of the devil, they blamed witches for every misfortune. Since the devil created all the ills of the world, his agents--witches--could be blamed for them. Witches were thought by some to have as much if not more power than Christ: they could raise the dead, turn water into wine or milk, control the weather and know the past and future. Witches were held accountable for everything from a failed business venture to a poor emotional state. A Scottish woman, for instance, was accused of witchcraft and burned to death because she was seen stroking a cat at the same time as a nearby batch of beer turned sour. Witches now took the role of scapegoats that had been held by the Jews. Any personal misfortune, bad harvest, famine, or plague was seen as their fault.[53]

Similarly, SLSW protagonists advance the notion that spirit powers are the source of many human problems and accordingly, it is not surprising that the Lausanne 1993 Statement on Spiritual Warfare noted with concern that there was a danger that SLSW could cause Christendom to "revert to think and operate on pagan worldviews."[54]

What then is the basis for SLSW teaching? In addition to a reaction against the supposed rationalism of Western theology, Hiebert identifies two worldviews which are shaping the current Christian debate regarding the nature of spiritual warfare. The first of these is the tribal worldview.

Tribal or Traditional Worldview

Hiebert states, "For most tribal peoples ancestors, earthly spirits, witchcraft and magic are very real. The people see the earth and sky as full of beings . . . that relate, deceive, bully and battle one another for power and personal gain. These beings are neither totally good

---

[52]Ibid., 253.

[53]Helen Ellerbe, "The Witch Hunts: The End of Magic and Miracles 1450-1750 C. E.," online posting, http://www.positiveatheism.org/hist/ellerbe1.htm; accessed 17 July 2001.

[54]"Lausanne 1993 Statement on Spiritual Warfare," online posting, http://www.gospelcom.net/lcwe/statements/spwar.html; accessed 31 July 2001.

nor totally evil. They help those who serve or placate them. They harm those who oppose their wishes or who neglect them or refuse to honor them. Humans must placate them to avoid terrible disasters."[55] It is significant that tribal religions, or animism, totally deny rationality. As McCallum notes, "Faith in these systems is blind faith--reason cannot confirm or deny any aspect of their spirituality, according to adherents. Most tribal religious views are accepted from early childhood as part of what it means to be a member of the tribe."[56]

Territory is basic to animistic understanding of spirit powers, which reside in specific places or objects and provide protection for people who live within their sphere of influence. Warfare between such beings is ongoing and when a community is defeated its people are expected to switch allegiance to the victorious god.[57] However, in this context David Neff outlines Hiebert's conclusion that, "missiologists who try to deliver populations by praying against territorial spirits sell human sinfulness short by treating people as the hapless victims of invisible forces rather than as moral agents responsible before God."[58]

According to Kraft, animistic people have "power needs" that a Western worldview does not address. He writes, "We were well-prepared [for the mission field] --except, as it turned out, in the area the Nigerians considered the most important: their relationships with the spirit world. These spirits, they told me, cause disease, accidents and death, hinder fertility of people, animals and fields, bring drought, destroy relationships, and harass the innocent. But I could not help these people, for I was just plain ignorant in this area."[59] He

---

[55]Hiebert, "Spiritual Warfare and Worldviews."

[56]McCallum, 207.

[57]Hiebert, "Spiritual Warfare and Worldviews."

[58]David Neff, "The Future of Missions?" *Christianity Today*, 1 Nov. 1999, online posting, http://www.christianitytoday.com/ct/1999/144/12.0.html; accessed 21 Aug. 2001.

[59]Charles Kraft; quoted in Gary D. Kinnaman, *How to Overcome the Darkness: Personal Strategies for Spiritual Warfare* (Grand Rapids, MI: Baker Book House, 1999), 26. Kraft is also cited in Otis, *The Last of the Giants*, 244; he states, "As missionaries we had brought an essentially powerless message to a very power conscious people. The Nigerians "knew" that whatever Christianity brought, it wasn't adequate to deal with such things as tragedy, infertility, relational

therefore suggests that old animistic forms should be given new meaning. Kraft's wife, Marguerite, insists that missionaries should not challenge the animistic worldview but allow the gospel to be adapted in order to accommodate it.[60] In face of opposition, Charles Kraft has brushed aside the scholarly criticisms of Priest, Campbell and Mullen, by branding them as classroom theorists, with no practical knowledge of the subject of the Spirit's power or effective ministry in animistic environments.[61]

Indo-European Paganism

The second worldview identified by Hiebert in respect to its spiritual warfare emphasis is found in cultures shaped by Indo-European paganism. This includes Zoroastrianism, Manicheism and Hinduism which focus on a supposed cosmic struggle between good and evil gods for the control of the universe. The outcome is dubious because both opponents are equally strong and humanity is trapped as the innocent victim in the ongoing combat. "Central to this worldview is the myth of redemptive violence. Order can be established only when one side defeats the other in spiritual warfare."[62] Hiebert highlights the analogy between contemporary teaching on SLSW and this Indo-European worldview: "The battle is fought in the heavens, but it ranges over sky and earth. The central question is one of power--can God defeat Satan? Because the

---

breakdowns, and troublesome weather. It didn't meet many of their deepest spiritual needs. Even though this was puzzling to them—given the fact that Christian leaders talked such a good game—they simply accommodated by developing a kind of dual allegiance: a loyalty to Christianity to handle certain needs paralleled by a continuing loyalty to traditional religious practitioners to handle their power needs. As missionaries we decried this practice, but we had no effective antidote."

[60]Marguerite Kraft, "Spiritual Conflict and the Mission of the Church: Contextualisation," paper presented at Lausanne Committee for World Evangelization: "Deliver Us from Evil" Consultation, 21 Aug. 2000, Nairobi, Kenya, online posting, http://www.gospelcom.net/lcwe/dufe/Papers/MKraft.htm; accessed 20 May 2001.

[61]Charles H. Kraft, "Christian Animism or God-Given Authority," in Rommen, 88-136.

[62]Hiebert, "Spiritual Warfare and Worldviews."

outcome is in doubt, intense prayer is necessary to enable God and his angels to gain victory over the demonic powers."[63]

Wagner and Charles Kraft each testify to having experienced paradigm shifts in their theological understanding.[64] Charles Kraft comments, "People never change their whole worldview. Yet worldviews change because people change parts of them. The reason for this is that a worldview is made up of a large number of distinguishable perspectives or 'paradigms.' It is these perspectives that can be changed. Indeed, many of them do get changed over the course of a person's lifetime."[65] Both Wagner and Charles Kraft now accept the animistic belief that spirits determine events and therefore teach that a Christian should be concerned properly with self-protection as well as endeavouring to control demonic powers.[66] In addition to giving credence to the animistic three-tiered world view,[67] Wagner also sees redeemed man as equidistant between God and Satan, and liable to being preyed upon by evil spirits if he fails to invoke warfare prayer. He writes, "When Facius mentioned the spirit of death I shuddered."[68] "I prayed for protection . . . I felt chills up and down my spine."[69] This megashift theology is described by Veith as an attempt "to soften the hard edges of Biblical orthodoxy and to accommodate contemporary society's values and mind-set."[70]

In any discussion of the concept of worldviews, it is all too easy to lose sight of the fact that these are essentially philosophical devices which at best express an average position and at worst, a distortion of reality. Such generalisations cannot be imposed as being of universal application. Even Charles Kraft is reluctant to speak of a single

---

[63]Ibid.

[64]C. Peter Wagner, *The Third Wave of the Holy Spirit: Encountering the Power of Signs and Wonders* (Ann Arbor, MI: Vine Books, 1988), 22-23; and Kraft, *Christianity with Power*, 1-10.

[65]Kraft, *Christianity with Power*, 82.

[66]Ibid., 123.

[67]Hiebert, "The Flaw of the Excluded Middle."

[68]Wagner, *Warfare Prayer*, 188.

[69]Wagner, *The Third Wave*, 31-35.

[70]Gene Edward Veith, Jr., *Postmodern Times: Christian Guide to Contemporary Thought and Culture* (Wheaton, IL: Crossway Books, 1994), 214.

Christian worldview.[71] He describes "Conversion to and growth in Christianity" as "a series of paradigm shifts from one perspective to another in a number of areas. The first is a change in one's ultimate allegiance from the world and its values to God and his kingdom. It continues in a series of further paradigm shifts as one grows in the Christian faith."[72] He concludes that the vast majority of the paradigms that make up the individual convert's worldview undergo very little change. Rather, "these remain pretty much the same as those of the non-Christians around us."[73]

Whilst concurring with the concept that development in Christian maturity will involve change in terms of, "bringing into captivity every thought to the obedience of Christ," (2 Cor. 10:5) the author takes issue with the assumption that new birth has a minimal impact on the convert's worldview. This is in direct conflict with the scriptural position on conversion, as described by Paul: "Therefore if any man be in Christ, he is a new creature: old things are passed away; behold, all things are become new. And all things are of God" (2 Cor. 5:17-18). Paul also exhorted the church at Rome, "And be not conformed to this world: but be ye transformed by the renewing of your mind, that ye may prove what is that good, and acceptable and perfect will of God" (Rom. 12:2).

Christians do not have a worldview in the sense of a belief system that is determined by culture, but an eternal view, based on the eternal word of God. Christianity is not a philosophy which the individual simply accepts or rejects, but a life-transforming encounter with the living God, "who hath delivered us from the power of darkness, and hath translated us into the kingdom of his dear Son" (Col. 1:13). The carnal mind cannot understand or adopt the ways of God, for it is at enmity with God (Rom. 8:6-7); the understanding of such a mind is "darkened, being alienated from the life of God through the ignorance that is in them, because of the blindness of their heart" (Eph. 4:18). In salvation, man is totally dependent on the sovereign work of God. Veith comments on the whole concept of "decision theology" as follows:

---

[71]Kraft, *Christianity with Power*, 84.

[72]Ibid.

[73]Ibid.

> For Luther, Calvin, St. Augustine, and many other Biblical theologians, the human will is in bondage to sin, so that our choices drive us away from God. In salvation we do not choose God; He chooses us. We are not saved by our wills, but by God's grace which transforms our sinful wills by the power of the Holy Spirit. Then and only then can we be said to have freedom of the will and are enabled to 'choose Christ.' Even theologians such as Arminius, Wesley, and Aquinas, who believed that the human will is free and must cooperate in the process of salvation, did not view salvation as a sheerly autonomous choice.[74]

Salvation is of God. It is He who draws the human heart; it is He who brings the individual to new birth by the gift of His grace and His faith; it is He who gives those who receive Him "power to become the sons of God" (John 1:12). He alone is omnipotent. Against this truth, worldview is irrelevant.

Experience

It is clear from the above discussion that experience is a key factor in the teaching on SLSW. Wagner asserts that experience is a valuable source of understanding in this context and is valid unless contradicted by the word of God;[75] Kraft goes one step further by suggesting that the Scriptures are not necessarily a comprehensive record of spiritual truth;[76] and Murphy castigates evangelicals for their mistrust of experience, calling for "a newly formulated theology more consistent with both Scripture and experience."[77] It is clear from their reasoning that where experience is perceived to be at variance with the word of God, it is the understanding of the word rather than the experience which must be re-examined.[78]

---

[74]Veith, *Postmodern Times*, 212.

[75]See "Hermeneutical Approach" earlier in this chapter.

[76]Ibid.

[77]Murphy, xiv.

[78]A similar error was a feature of Judaism in the post-Diaspora era. See Niels C. Nielsen, Jr. et al, *Religions of the World*, 3d ed., ed. Robert K. C. Forman (New York, St. Martin's Press, 1993), 315. "When a biblical passage clashed with their own sensibility, the rabbis found ways of reinterpreting it. For example, Deuteronomy 21:18-21 specifies that if a man has a 'stubborn and rebellious' son, the son shall be put to death. The rabbis defined "stubborn and rebellious" so restrictively that they concluded: 'Never has there been a stubborn and rebellious son in the biblical sense' (Sanhedrin 71a)."

This rationale has led Lowe to conclude that "Proponents of SLSW reflect a typical evangelical piety toward Scripture, coupled with a familiar evangelical tendentious appeal to Scripture. Devotion to the Bible is a virtue only when coupled with a concern for the original meaning of the text. Otherwise veneration becomes a guise--albeit unwittingly--under which speculation captivates a credulous Christian public." He comments further, "SLSW is a pre-existing practice in search of justification. It finds what it is looking for, or creates what it needs."[79]

Both Charles Kraft and Peter Wagner support the view that people who are the product of Third World cultures have "an inherent ability to understand some biblical teachings more accurately than those of us who have been shaped by Western cultures."[80] As has already been discussed, rationalism is viewed as the inhibiting factor for the average Westerner who requires a paradigm shift in order to comprehend "the reality of the modus operandi of the invisible world."[81] Thus, much of what is currently taught within the context of SLSW has been gleaned from observation and evaluation of pagan practices and beliefs. Wagner states that, "I think it would be wise not to reject all forms of animism or all Indo-European mythology on an assumption that anything those systems or similar non-Christian systems affirm have absolutely *no validity*." Whilst acknowledging that the final authority must remain with the word of God, he continues, "When Scripture itself does *not* provide us with divinely revealed glimpses of reality, the validity of any extrabiblical claim to reality must obviously be confirmed or rejected on the basis of criteria other than biblical exegesis. It would be a mistake to assume that *all* oral history transmitted through various cultural streams is *per se* invalid. Rather, it seems more reasonable to assume that each tradition might reflect *some* true aspects of reality, but have varying degrees of distortion." He argues that spiritual discernment is part of the image of God in which all mankind is created and accordingly, "Indo-Europeans, Melanesians, Amerindians or whatever they may be, can and often do possess valid information

---

[79]Lowe, *Territorial Spirits*, 145.

[80]Wagner, *Confronting the Powers*, 49.

[81]Ibid.

about the spirit world. At the same time, some of the information they possess is clearly distorted and invalid."[82]

Sourcing information about the spirit world is not limited to human intelligence and in this context queries have been raised about the legitimacy of information garnered from the evil powers themselves.[83] Wagner claims that demons do possess some accurate information which they are able to communicate. He cites Murphy's proposition that *"every time the words of a demon are recorded in the New Testament, they speak the truth!"*[84] and consequently concludes that this is "biblical evidence that we can indeed get valid information from the world of darkness."[85] However, Jesus refers to the devil as the father of lies who "abode not in the truth, because there is no truth in him" (John 8:44). It is also difficult to see how Wagner and Murphy's view can in any way be reconciled with the biblical prohibition set out in, for example, Leviticus 19:31: "Regard not them that have familiar spirits, neither seek after wizards to be defiled by them."

Wagner summarises his position as follows:

> The primary source of knowledge about God and the spiritual realm is the Bible--the written Word of God. This, however, is not our exclusive source. When we have proper safeguards and are under the anointing of the Holy Spirit, we can also receive valuable information from the *rhema*--or spoken Word of God--from careful observation and analysis of the works of God in the world, and from representatives of the world of darkness whether in human or spiritual form, although they must always be approached and evaluated as hostile witnesses."[86]

In the author's opinion, all of these things are essentially subjective in that they rely primarily on the understanding of the individual, which itself may be distorted (Heb. 5:12-14). That is why the Scripture makes clear that the word is the only touchstone, it is the final and absolute measure by which all revelation must be tested. "For the word of God is quick, and powerful, and sharper than any twoedged sword, piercing even to the dividing asunder of soul and

---

[82]Ibid., 66-67 (original emphasis).

[83]Ibid., 69.

[84]Ibid., 69 (original emphasis).

[85]Ibid., 70.

[86]Ibid., 70-71.

spirit, and of the joints and marrow, and is a discerner of the thoughts and intents of the heart" (Heb. 4:12). As Hayford points out, "God's inspired Word of the Holy Scriptures, not personal experience, is the authority upon which we found our life and our faith in Christ."[87] Without the anchor of "orthodox epistemology and hermeneutics,"[88] the Christian is left to drift on the fickle sea of experience.

The emphasis on the experiential is not unique to the SLSW movement. It is also the focus of much of the charismatic, neo-Pentecostal church and as such is but one characteristic of the postmodern mindset which has become the guiding spirit of the age. This also includes the abandonment of absolute truth, the denigration of rationality and the elevation of self as the ultimate arbiter of reality.[89] As Iain Murray comments:

> The twentieth century has seen a more widespread and enduring defection from historic Christianity in the English-speaking world than has been witnessed in any period since the Reformation. This defection has occurred through the removal of the foundation to all Christian teaching, namely that the words of Scripture are so given of God that the teaching they contain is entirely trustworthy and authoritative . . . It alone is *the* Book which God has given us for the salvation of men. If, therefore, Scripture loses its true place in the church, nothing remains certain.[90]

The twentieth century opened with the battle for truth between the modernists and the fundamentalists, with the former attempting to demythologise the Bible in order "to make Christianity palatable to the twentieth-century mind."[91] Modernist heresies were doomed to eventual failure but, according to Veith, these have now been replaced by postmodern heresies. He comments, "Rationalism,

---

[87]Jack W. Hayford, *Grounds for Living: Sound Teaching for Sure Footing in Growth & Grace* (Kent: Sovereign World, 2001), 22.

[88]John F. Hart, "The Gospel and Spiritual Warfare: A Review of Peter Wagner's Confronting the Powers," *Journal of the Grace Evangelical Society* 10, no. 18 (Spring 1997), online posting, http://www.faithalone.org/journal/1997i/Hart.htm; accessed 11 Oct. 2001.

[89]For further discussion on postmodernism, please refer to Veith's *Postmodern Times* and McCallum's *The Death of Truth.*

[90]Iain H. Murray, *Pentecost - Today?: The Biblical Basis for Understanding Revival* (Edinburgh: The Banner of Truth Trust, 1998), 171 (original emphasis).

[91]Veith, *Postmodern Times,* 191.

having failed, is giving way to *ir*rationalism--both are hostile to God's revelation . . . Modernists did not believe the Bible is true. Postmodernists have cast out the category of truth altogether. In doing so, they have opened up a Pandora's Box of New Age religions, syncretism and moral chaos."[92]

As a result, Anthony Thiselton views the present postmodern religious arena as one where "everything is shifting, as every stable meaning is deferred and erased in an ever-moving, never-ending flux."[93] Percy points out that "traditional Protestants and Roman Catholics alike are losing their grip on the souls of the people, as the search for authentic, transformative and convincing religious experience gathers pace."[94] Percy makes reference to the somewhat similar evaluation posited by Harvey Cox, who suggests that revivalism has become the prey of new theologies which are enhancing the numerical growth of the movement but betraying its original foundations. Cox notes the present preoccupation with such features as excessive demonology and spiritual phenomena more usually associated with New Age beliefs.[95]

In Percy's opinion, there is a marked absence of systematic theology within the revivalist movement as a whole, despite a strong background in biblical fundamentalism. He says, "Adherents are offered experience, not knowledge. Theology, if you can call it that, is done through the hormones and not in the head. Experience always precedes reflection. There is no charismatic exegesis of scripture, only eisegesis."[96] As Anderson also observes, "We have a generation that is less interested in cerebral arguments, linear thinking, theological systems and more interested in encountering the

---

[92]Ibid., 192-93 (original emphasis).

[93]Anthony Thiselton, *Interpreting God and the Postmodern Self: On Meaning, Manipulation and Promise* (Edinburgh: T. and T. Clark, 1995), 81-85; quoted in Martyn Percy, *Power and the Church: Ecclesiology in an Age of Transition* (London: Cassell, 1998), 184.

[94]Percy, 186.

[95]Harvey Cox, *Fire From Heaven: Pentecostalism, Spirituality and the Reshaping of Religion in the Twenty-First Century* (New York: Addison-Wesley, 1994), 281; quoted in Percy, 188.

[96]Ibid., 190.

supernatural."[97] He continues, "The old paradigm taught that if you have the right teaching, you will experience God. The new paradigm says that if you experience God, you will have the right teaching."[98] All this has led Veith to conclude: "Not only is objective doctrine minimized in favour of subjective experience; experience actually becomes the criterion for evaluating doctrine. . . . This openness to personal feelings and experience is a point of contact with postmodernism, which has gone on to exaggerate the role of subjectivity beyond anything that a 'hot gospeller' of the nineteenth century would ever recognize."[99]

Focus on the experiential is reflected even in the hymn book. Under Wesley, Moody or Edwards, hymns were used as didactic material, but in charismatic revivalism the aim is very different. The emphasis once again is on the emotive and the experiential, with truth becoming a mere side issue.[100] As Percy argues, such a sidestepping of truth has led to various problems:

> Conservative evangelicals find it hard to accept phenomena that are not explicitly reflected in the canon of scripture. Neo-Pentecostals partly respond to this by searching for texts that connect with their experience, but the connections are usually very thin, if appropriate at all. In turn, the failure to locate biblical proof or scriptural legitimization for revivalist practice leads them to the very heart of the postmodern abyss. . . . It abandons the search for any ultimate truth, and engages in methodological pragmatism and playful experientialism.[101]

This pattern is very clearly seen in the debate relating to SLSW.

In much of his writing, Wagner makes extensive use of what can only be described as anecdotal evidence, much of it from observations made in the context of anthropological study. Lowe is unconvinced by the assumptions drawn from such evidence and has investigated some of the case studies used by SLSW protagonists. He draws the following conclusion: "Though phrased in the aura of

---

[97]Leith Anderson, *A Church for the Twenty-First Century* (Minneapolis, MN: Bethany House, 1992), 20; quoted in Veith, *Postmodern Times*, 211.

[98]Leith Anderson, 21; quoted in Veith, *Postmodern Times*, 211.

[99]Veith, *Postmodern Times*, 211-12.

[100]Percy, 192.

[101]Ibid., 197.

social-scientific terminology (such as 'hypothesis', 'evidence,' and 'research'), SLSW does not employ a rigorous method. The failure to critique and confirm case studies before publication leads to the inclusion of clearly unreliable reports, and therefore to uncertainty about the reliability of any report. Moreover, the assignment of particular interpretations to these reports is often arbitrary."[102]

Wagner seeks to justify the use of such anecdotal evidence on the basis that this was also used by Jesus and the gospel writers. He states, "Jesus pointed to anecdotes, perhaps better described as narratives. . . . Much of the validity of Christianity, including the Resurrection itself, is predicated on narrative accounts. The fact that such narratives are verified by their inclusion in the written Word of God is an important observation, but it does not thereby nullify the validity of other works of God that have not been reported in the Bible."[103] Whilst admitting that not every account is accurate, Wagner declares that the authenticity of such reported narratives is assessed on the basis of the credibility or otherwise of the people concerned.[104] He poses the rhetorical question, "How can we tell the true from the spurious?" and gives the somewhat unsatisfactory reply, "I know of no fail-safe methodology."[105] The reality is that once one adopts the concept that the Scriptures are not a totally comprehensive record of spiritual truth, there is no absolute standard of evaluation. In the author's opinion, biblical "silence" is no basis for the assessment of truth and error. As Hart concludes, "Strategic-level spiritual warfare strikes at the very heart of the spiritual experience--the all-sufficiency of the Scriptures."[106]

Territorial Spirits

The basic controversy surrounding the SLSW movement relates to the whole concept of territorial spirits and the associated strategies for 'pulling them down.' In his incisive analysis, Chuck Lowe states that "the first describes a newly postulated kind of demon, and the

---

[102]Lowe, *Territorial Spirits*, 127. For further details please refer to *Territorial Spirits*, 114-27.

[103]Wagner, *Confronting the Powers*, 56.

[104]Ibid., 59.

[105]Ibid., 63.

[106]Hart, "The Gospel and Spiritual Warfare."

latter refers to a new strategy designed specifically to defeat them."[107] The whole practice of SLSW assumes that unseating or 'pulling down' territorial spirits is a prerequisite to the successful advancement of the gospel.[108] Wagner deliberates this thought as follows: "We read in 2 Corinthians 4:4 that Satan has successfully blinded the minds of unbelievers so that they cannot receive the gospel. This undoubtedly refers to individuals, but could it also refer to territories? Could it mean nations? States? Cities? Cultural groups? Tribes? Social networks? . . . Church growth theory has long ago recognized the phenomenon of resistant peoples. Could it be that at least some of that resistance may be caused by the direct working of demonic forces?"[109]

In response to the tremendous interest in this area, the Spiritual Warfare Network was set up following the 1989 Lausanne II Conference in Manila, to promote understanding relating to territorial spirits in the context of world evangelization.[110] It was later renamed the Strategic Prayer Network and its purpose extended to include the linkage of prayer groups world-wide. Some four years later, the Intercession Working Group of the Lausanne Committee on World Evangelization made this statement, "We are cautious about the way in which the concept of territorial spirits is being used and look to our biblical scholars to shed more light on this recent development."[111]

---

[107]Lowe, *Territorial Spirits*, 16.

[108]See for example, Wagner, *Warfare Prayer*, 65: "I believe in evangelistic crusades and the Four Spiritual Laws. But these social and evangelistic programs will never work as well as they could or should by themselves if Satan's strongholds are not torn down. This is the real battle, and our weapon is prayer. Warfare prayer."

[109]C. Peter Wagner, ed., *Territorial Spirits: Insights on Strategic-Level Spiritual Warfare* (Chichester: Sovereign World, 1991), 43.

[110]Arnold, *Spiritual Warfare*, 164. The first meeting included, among others, C. Peter Wagner, Charles Kraft, Cindy Jacobs, Gary Clark, Larry Lea, John Dawson, Dick Bernal, Frank Hammond, Mary Lance Sisk, Edgardo Silvoso, Bobbie Jean Merck, Jack Hayford, Joy Dawson, Beth Alves, Ed Murphy, and Tom White: Wagner, *Warfare Prayer*, 45.

[111]"Statement on Spiritual Warfare: The Intercession Working Group Report, Lausanne Committee on World Evangelization," *Urban Mission* 13, no. 2 (1995): 52; quoted in Arnold, *Spiritual Warfare*, 182.

Clearly, the basic question to be addressed is whether or not there is any scriptural foundation for the somewhat controversial concept of territorial spirits. Wagner himself has recognised the importance of establishing a biblical framework, stating that, "Our working hypothesis will be of little value for strategizing world evangelization unless there is some biblical warrant for it."[112]

In terms of Old Testament examples, Daniel 10 is probably one of the most commonly quoted passages as evidence of territorial spirits. Wagner has described the "princes" referred to in this chapter as "world rulers of darkness,"[113] and Arnold has identified similar interpretations in works by Stephen R. Miller and Sydney H. T. Page.[114] According to Wagner, the three week delay in the arrival of Daniel's answer to prayer was on account of a fierce spiritual battle in the heavenly realm between territorial spirits who supposedly have the ability to "greatly influence human life in all its sociopolitical aspects." He was subsequently to claim "that the only weapon Daniel had to combat these rulers of darkness was warfare prayer. "[115]

Mike Taylor accepts that heavenly powers were involved but takes issue with the whole question of territoriality. He argues that demons are infamous liars who take advantage of pagan worship as a means to deceive. Thus the national deity becomes a front for demonic activity.[116] "The power which they exercise over people is mediated not through territory, but through the cultus, or worship system, which they maintain."[117] It is nothing more than an elaborate masquerade which is given credence by the faith of gullible people.

With respect to the same passage, Lowe concludes that the foundational thesis of territoriality is totally untenable. He argues that the "princes" of Persia and Greece did not rule over areas with

---

[112]Wagner, "Territorial Spirits," in *Wrestling with Dark Angels*, 78.

[113]Ibid., 79.

[114]Stephen R. Miller, *Daniel*, vol. 18, *The New American Commentary* (Nashville, TN: Broadman and Holman, 1994), 284-85; and Sydney H. T. Page, *Powers of Evil: A Biblical Study of Satan and Demons* (Grand Rapids, MI: Baker Books, 1995), 65; quoted in Arnold, *Spiritual Warfare*, 246.

[115]Wagner, *Warfare Prayer*, 66.

[116]Mike R. Taylor, *Do Demons Rule Your Town?: An Examination of the Territorial Spirits' Theory* (London: Grace Publications Trust, 1993), 44.

[117]Ibid., 45.

"explicitly defined boundaries" but "over imperialistic empires whose boundaries expand and contract." When the expansion of one threatened the territory of the other, by implication this would lead to "civil war in the kingdom of darkness," a concept which is contradicted by the teaching of Jesus in Matthew 12:25-26 and Luke 11:17-18.[118]

A third commentator, T. L. Osborn, points out that the Daniel 10 passage is an Old Covenant, pre-Calvary example, and therefore, not applicable to Christians. He states authoritatively, "No longer may demons impede our prayers to our Heavenly Father. Victory is ours."[119]

With reference to New Testament examples, Wagner ("Territorial Spirits" in *Wrestling with Dark Angels* (1990) and *Warfare Prayer* (1992)) has constructed various theories in respect to "binding the strong man" (Matt. 12:29; Luke 1:21-22), claiming that the account is indicative of "multi-leveled demonic activity." The event opens with Jesus casting the demon out of a dumb man (Luke 11:14), which Wagner interprets as an example of ground-level spiritual warfare. Jesus then proceeds to discuss Satan's kingdom, a palace, and Beelzebub (Luke 11:18 and 21), all of which are viewed by Wagner as evidence of an escalation in the scope of the warfare.[120] The power that the strong man is able to exert over a house is used to support the theory of territorial spirits, which must be bound before "the kingdom of God can flow into the territory."[121]

Taylor dismisses these arguments as erroneous, pointing out that binding the strong man does not refer to deliverance from individual demons, but "to the work done personally by the Lord Jesus Christ in immobilizing the devil in making him unable to engage in effective retaliation while his kingdom is plundered." He continues, "The ultimate coup was the death of Christ on the cross, but the work which He undertook during His earthly life was a foretaste of that ultimate work of deliverance." Taylor is equally dismissive of what he regards as Wagner's faulty process of exegesis. He emphatically

---

[118]Lowe, *Territorial Spirits*, 33-34.

[119]Osborn, 269.

[120]Wagner, *Warfare Prayer*, 60.

[121]Wagner, *Territorial Spirits*, 89.

declares, "We are not entitled to build upwards in logical steps from a single Biblical text. Such a procedure has been used frequently throughout history to justify false doctrine."[122]

In the New Testament context, Ephesians 6 is probably the most commonly quoted passage with respect to the whole debate concerning SLSW. According to Wagner it provides "a formidable challenge for those who wish to argue that the New Testament gives us no indication God's people are to engage in strategic-level spiritual warfare."[123] In verse 12 the apostle Paul explains that the Christian's warfare is not against flesh and blood, but against "principalities," "powers," "rulers of the darkness of this world," and "spiritual wickedness in high places." Andrew T. Lincoln comments as follows: "The writer has listed different groups of evil forces not for the sake of some schematic classification or completeness, but in order to bring home to the consciousness of his readers the variety and comprehensiveness of the power the enemy has at his disposal."[124] The warfare is real but as Osborn comments it relates to "Christians going out into a dangerous world to bear witness of Jesus Christ at the risk of persecution, arrest, imprisonment, physical torture, and death. That is the warfare *against spiritual wickedness in high places in* which those early believers were engaged. And it is the same today."[125] However, as Lowe points out, there is no indication that individual spirits are linked with specific nations. Paul merely affirms that Satan is the prince of the power of the air (Eph. 2:2) and that rulers and authorities occupy heavenly places (Eph. 3:10; 6:12).[126] Lowe refers to the views of John Wesley in this context particularly because of his "openness to the manifestations of supernatural power." Despite this, Wesley took the same position as both Luther and Calvin who insisted in restricting doctrine to the revelation of Scripture. Concerning demons, Wesley accepted that demons operate as "rulers of this world" but this is not interpreted in a geographic

---

[122]Taylor, 52.

[123]Wagner, *Confronting the Powers*, 244.

[124]Andrew T. Lincoln, *Ephesians*, vol. 42, *Word Biblical Commentary*, eds. Bruce M. Metzger, David A. Hubbard, and Glenn W. Barker (Dallas, TX: Word Books, 1990), 444-45.

[125]Osborn, 272 (original emphasis).

[126]Lowe, *Territorial Spirits*, 38.

sense. He also agreed that the forces of evil are "constantly warring against man in general and Christians in particular" but in view of the absence of biblical authority he consistently refused to entertain the "speculations characteristic of the medieval period."[127]

Wagner is open about the fact that, particularly in his earlier writings, his hypotheses are built upon scanty biblical authority,[128] and that there is only questionable New Testament evidence for the existence of territorial spirits.[129] However, in an emotive rather than scholarly argument, he has labelled those who shy away from the concept as cowardly.[130] According to Steven Lawson, Wagner suggests that a thorough search of church history is likely to produce the necessary evidence and therefore vindicate his position.[131] This notion is totally refuted by biblical scholar Gordon Fee who finds that, "The use of historical precedents as an analogy by which to establish a norm is never valid in itself." Fee continues "Such a process (drawing universal norms from particular events) produces a *non sequiteur* and is therefore irrelevant."[132]

Wagner's later publication, *Confronting the Powers,* was intended to provide biblical, theological and historical authority for his SLSW theories, but Hart describes it as "a shrewd apologetic to counter recent criticism of the author's strange approaches to world evangelization and prayer for the lost."[133] The scriptural evidence in support of SLSW is largely restricted to the New Testament. For example, Beelzebub is declared to be a "classic territorial spirit" serving "under the rulership of Satan."[134] Wagner gives his rationale

---

[127]Ibid., 99.

[128]B. J. Oropeza, *Answers to Questions about Angels, Demons and Spiritual Warfare* (Eastbourne: InterVarsity Press, 1997), 125.

[129]Wagner, *Confronting the Powers,* 164, 171, 175, 177, 191, 193, 196, 203; Lowe, *Territorial Spirits,* 18, 153.

[130]C. Peter Wagner, *Praying with Power: How to Pray Effectively and Hear Clearly from God* (Ventura, CA: Regal Books, 1997), 23.

[131]Steven Lawson, "Defeating Territorial Spirits," in Wagner, ed., *Territorial Spirits,* 39.

[132]Gordon D. Fee, *Gospel and Spirit: Issues in New Testament Hermeneutics* (Peabody, MA: Hendrickson Publishers, 1991), 94.

[133]Hart, "The Gospel and Spiritual Warfare."

[134]Wagner, *Confronting the Powers,* 149.

for this assumption as follows, "The reason I have concluded he is a principality under the command of Satan is that the consensus of written materials I have examined and of personal interviews I have conducted with experts about the occult lead me to that judgment."[135] As Hart points out, Beelzebub or the strong man, is then taken to be representative of any territorial spirit which must be bound (Matt. 12:29) or overcome (Luke 11:22) as an essential in the evangelism process; indeed, this interpretation is described as the most important contribution to the actual "nuts and bolts of evangelism."[136] Wagner states, "Territorial spirits or 'strong men' have succeeded throughout history in sending enormous populations of people to hell. In our generation, they currently have the upper hand with about 3 billion men, women and children. They shouldn't be getting away with this!"[137] On this basis man is the hapless victim of a superior and malicious power rather than a sinner with a moral responsibility before a holy and righteous God.[138]

Hart's analysis of *Confronting the Powers* demonstrates that Wagner identifies only a very limited number of supposed confrontations with territorial spirits in the ministry of the apostles.[139] Hart states, "Wagner labors to explain why only five experiences can be found in the book of Acts if confronting territorial spirits is so indispensable for evangelism. The defense offered is that Luke avoids being overly repetitious, and allows the reader to assume that this pattern of demon-confrontation continued on many other occasions." Wagner argues that Paul's greatest evangelistic success (Ephesus) and failure (Athens) is attributable to his use or otherwise of SLSW. He comments, "My hypothesis is that the territorial spirits assigned to the city of Athens were so powerful and so deeply entrenched that Paul was not able to overcome them. The strongholds that had furnished them the right to rule the city for centuries were awesome,

---

[135]Ibid., 148.

[136]Hart, "The Gospel and Spiritual Warfare."

[137]Wagner, *Confronting the Powers*, 150.

[138]Hiebert, quoted by Neff in "The Future of Missions?"

[139]These are (1) Peter versus Simon Magus, (2) Peter versus Herod, (3) Paul versus Bar-Jesus or Elymas, (4) Paul versus the Python Spirit and (5) Paul versus Diana (or Artemis) of the Ephesians.

at the time virtually impenetrable."[140] Thus Hart points out that
Wagner understands "the lack of converts at Athens as evidence that
Paul . . . failed to demonstrate the mighty Christian God in an open
power encounter."[141] Similarly, following the line of this argument,
Peter's confrontation with Simon the magician is "metamorphosed to
imply that Peter engaged in strategic-level warfare. . . . The exegetical
leap is made that since Simon exercised territorial influence, he must
have been under the power of a territorial spirit."[142]

It is abundantly clear from the above examples that the so-called
biblical validation for territorial spirits is extremely dubious. In his
study of 1993, Taylor refers to the works of Vernon Sterk and John
Dawson, both of whom are proponents of SLSW, but who are
forced to admit that there is little biblical foundation for the whole
concept of territoriality.[143] After consideration of a wide spectrum of
supposed evidence in both the Old and New Testaments, Taylor
goes further, commenting that, "nothing is stated in the Bible at all
concerning 'territorial spirits', other than where the beliefs of pagans
in such spirits are exposed as fallacious." He concludes that, "This is
certainly no accident. The Bible is the Word of God and does not
give us untrue information. If 'territorial spirits' do not exist, this
would be an adequate explanation of the lack of revelation
concerning them."[144]

Concurring with A. A. Anderson, Lowe also rejects the entire
notion of territorial spirits. Anderson concludes that there is
absolutely "no hint in the Old Testament of an alien order of spirits
or demons with a rival realm outside the Lord's dominion."[145] In

---

[140]Wagner, *Confronting the Powers*, 204.

[141]Hart, "The Gospel and Spiritual Warfare."

[142]Ibid.

[143]Vernon J. Sterk, "Territorial Spirits and Evangelization in Hostile
Environments," unpublished research paper written for Fuller School of World
Mission, Pasadena, California, 1989, quoted in Wagner, ed., *Territorial Spirits*,
153-54; quoted in Taylor, 59. See also John Dawson, *Taking our Cities for God:
How to Break Spiritual Strongholds* (Lake Mary, FL: Creation House, 1989), 156;
quoted in Taylor, 45.

[144]Taylor, 57.

[145]A. A. Anderson, *Psalms 72-150* (London: Marshall, Morgan & Scott, 1974), 82;
quoted in Lowe, *Territorial Spirits*, 37.

respect to the New Testament, Lowe also concludes that any evidence promoting the notion of particular demons assigned to specific world regions is strikingly absent.[146]

Hwa Yung is of the opinion that much more research is required in this area before a consensus can be reached and on the basis of his own evaluation believes that Lowe may have "overstated his case in his concern to demolish some of the fundamental tenets of SLSW."[147] Yung cites Page's affirmation of the existence and activity of territorial spirits as a better representation of the scriptural approach. Significantly, Page argues that this recognition "does not constitute grounds for thinking that Christians can or should attempt to identify them and the areas they control. The presence and influence of the princes were disclosed to Daniel, but not because he sought to discover their identity or functions. Nor is there any evidence that Daniel prayed for their defeat. . . . Moreover, there is the ever present danger of exaggerating the role of territorial spirits in such a way that the biblical teaching on divine sovereignty is compromised."[148] Clinton Arnold adopts a similar position. While asserting that the idea of territorial spirits is supported by both scriptural and historical evidence, he concludes that God has not given man the responsibility of engaging this enemy in spiritual warfare. He states authoritatively: "It is therefore not necessary for us to discern them, name them and try to cast them out. We are called to continue proclaiming the Word in the power of the Spirit and ministering the kingdom of God."[149] He comments further, "As ambassadors of Christ, we need to focus less on territorial spirits and more on the task of being ambassadors. We are representatives of the King sent out to do kingdom business."[150]

---

[146]Lowe, *Territorial Spirits*, 38.

[147]Hwa Yung, "Some Issues in a Systematic Theology that Takes Seriously the Demonic," paper presented at Lausanne Committee for World Evangelization: "Deliver Us from Evil" Consultation, 17 Aug. 2000, Nairobi, Kenya, online posting, http://www.gospelcom.net/lcwe/dufe/Papers/HYung.htm; accessed 29 June 2001.

[148]Page, 65; quoted in Yung, "Some Issues in a Systematic Theology."

[149]Arnold, *Spiritual Warfare*, 214.

[150]Ibid., 218.

According to Mike Wakely, SLSW "owes more to Frank Peretti than Scripture,"[151] and Wagner admits that there has been the tendency in practice to confuse fact with fiction. He comments as follows: "Undoubtedly, the single-most influential event that has stimulated interest in strategic-level spiritual warfare among American Christians was the publication of Frank Peretti's two novels, *This Present Darkness* and *Piercing the Darkness* . . . even though they know better, many find themselves reading *This Present Darkness* as a documentary rather than as somewhat fanciful fiction."[152]

Lowe agrees with Stephen Dray that the concept of territorial spirits "is the result of a sloppy interaction with the text of Scripture," which has been manipulated to support a theory already arrived at.[153] In answer to such statements from Wagner as, 'It would seem reasonable . . . ,' Lowe firmly responds that "It would seem reasonable only to those who already share the presupposition of the author."[154] Lowe states that "I believe" has become the "new hermeneutic."[155] Concurring with Howard Peskett's view on Wagner's tendentiousness, he further states that in the absence of explicit biblical teaching it has apparently become acceptable to offer implications, possibilities, opinions, and assumptions, no matter that no commentator supports the supposed interpretation.[156] Edgar McKnight defines such practice as "reader-oriented criticism" applied to the Bible,[157] and according to McKnight, Veith and McCallum it appears that a Christianity based on personal experience is now regarded as being perfectly compatible with postmodern

---

[151]Mike Wakely, "A Critical Look at a New 'Key' to Evangelization," *Evangelical Missions Quarterly* 31, no. 2 (Apr. 1995): 152, online posting, http://www.wheaton.edu/bgc/EMIS/1995/newkey.htm; accessed 9 Sept. 2001.

[152]Wagner, *Warfare Prayer*, 19 (original emphasis).

[153]Stephen Dray, foreword to Taylor, 7.

[154]Taylor, 52.

[155]Ibid., 145. See also Wagner, *Confronting the Powers,* 162, 163, 164, 186, 190, 196, and, 208.

[156]Howard Peskett, "God's Missionary Railway According to Stott and Wagner," *Evangelical Missions Quarterly* 32 (1996): 480-84; quoted in Lowe, *Territorial Spirits,* 145.

[157]Edgar V. McKnight, *Postmodern Use of the Bible: The Emergence of Reader-Oriented Criticism* (Nashville, TN: Abingdon Press, 1988), 16, 176; quoted in McCallum, 255-56.

constructivism.[158] Lowe emphatically refutes the validity of any manipulation of Scripture to support new teachings. He cites Calvin who specifically warned about the dangers of such speculative teaching and practices in his own time:

> If we would be duly wise, we must renounce those vain babblings of idle men, concerning the nature, ranks and numbers of angels, without any authority from the Word of God. I know that many fasten on these topics more eagerly, and take greater pleasure in them than in those relating to daily practice. . . . None can deny that Dionysius . . . has many shrewd and subtle disquisitions in his *Celestial Hierarchy*; but on looking at them more closely, every one must see that they are merely idle talk. The duty of the theologian, however, is not to tickle the ear, but to confirm the conscience by teaching what is true, certain, and useful.[159]

Paradoxically, as Lowe implies, the current fascination with Satan and SLSW may in itself be a ploy of the enemy to deflect the church of Jesus Christ from the pursuit and proclamation of truth. Terry Law writes, "Without realizing it, many of those who engage in 'pulling down' spirits today are really paying tribute to evil angels. To evil spirits and angels, attention amounts to worship. Angels of God shun attention to themselves and direct attention to Jesus."[160]

Spiritual Warfare Practices

In the early phase of the movement, Wagner wrote,

> I myself feel that God may be calling, equipping and enabling a relatively small number of Christian leaders to move out in frontline, strategic-level spiritual warfare. . . . He is raising up large numbers of Christians to back up these people with moral support, intercession, encouragement and material resources. God, I think, is in the process of choosing an expanding corps of spiritual Green Berets such as Eduardo Lorenzo, Cindy Jacobs, Larry Lea, Carlos

---

[158]McCallum, 281. "The postmodern belief that knowledge about the world is not discovered, but "constructed" in the minds of observers. Constructivism denies that people can ever understand an objective or fixed universal reality. Reality instead is a social construct—a creation in people's minds, colored by their social background." See also, McKnight, *Postmodern Use of the Bible, and Veith, Postmodern Times.*

[159]John Calvin, *Institutes of the Christian Religion*, bk. 1, chap. 14, par. 4 (Grand Rapids, MI: Wm. B. Eerdmans Publishing Company, 2001), 144; quoted in Lowe, *Territorial Spirits*, 97.

[160]Terry Law, *The Truth about Angels* (Lake Mary, FL: Charisma House, 1994), 179.

Annacondia, John Dawson, Edgardo Silvoso or Dick Bernal who will engage in the crucial high-level battles against the rulers of darkness and consequently see measurable increases in the numbers of lost people who 'turn them from darkness to light, and from the power of Satan to God' (Acts 26:18).[161]

It was Cindy Jacobs who first introduced Wagner to the practice of strategic-level spiritual warfare,[162] and in *Warfare Prayer* he recounts how he brought her to Argentina on a number of occasions in 1990 to teach this practice to hundreds of Christian leaders.[163] Those in Resistencia, having first identified the ruling spirits over the area, were led in confession and warfare prayer, which reputedly resulted in a release in the heavenlies as suggested by an assurance in their spirits and a doubling of the evangelical population over the next year.[164] Despite a great diversity of viewpoints within the SLSW camp,[165] biblical scholar, Clinton Arnold, has identified the 3-fold approach of (1) discerning and naming the territorial spirits, (2) identificational repentance and, (3) warfare prayer, as constituting the general approach in the practice of spiritual warfare techniques.[166]

Discerning and Naming the Territorial Spirit

Wagner asserted in his early writings, that it was important to learn the names and natures of the demonic spirits over an area, as a vital first step in spiritual warfare.[167] This strategy was also emphasized by other SLSW protagonists including Larry Lea,[168] and Dick Bernal.[169] Bernal refers to the ancient Greeks' approach as

---

[161]Wagner, *Warfare Prayer*, 58.

[162]C. Peter Wagner, a sermon entitled "Practical Holiness," presented at Oral Roberts University Students' Chapel meeting in Tulsa, Oklahoma, 16 Jan. 2001.

[163]Wagner, *Warfare Prayer*, 31.

[164]Ibid., 31-33.

[165]Chuck Lowe, "Defeating Demons: A Critique of Strategic-Level Spiritual Warfare," n.d., TMs (diskette). This was provided to the author by Dr. Lowe.

[166]Arnold, *Spiritual Warfare*, 165.

[167]Wagner, *Warfare Prayer*, 156.

[168]Larry Lea, *Could You Not Tarry One Hour?: Learning the Joy of Prayer* (Altamonte Springs, FL: Creation House, 1987), 93.

[169]Dick Bernal, *Storming Hell's Brazen Gates* (San Jose, CA: Jubilee Christian Center, 1988), 57.

evidence,[170] whilst Wagner cites the work of anthropologists,[171] validated by anecdotes. However, in later years, Wagner was to downplay the necessity of using exact names, implying that a functional name will suffice; and he is supported in this opinion by John Dawson.[172]

Arnold and Moreau, on the contrary, relate the whole practice to that of ancient magical rites where identification of a spirit's name is intrinsic to assuming power over it.[173] Arnold claims that he cannot identify any biblical or church history evidence for the practice, and comments rather tersely, "Why do we need to find the name of a territorial ruler if we are in union with a Lord who has been exalted high above every conceivable power, regardless of its name or title?"[174]

Wayne Grudem also dismisses the practice, emphatically insisting that, "in no instance does anyone in the New Testament (1) *summon a "territorial spirit"* . . . (2) *demand information from demons about a local demonic hierarchy*, (3) *say that we should believe or teach information derived from demons*, or (4) teach by word or example that certain '*demonic strongholds' over a city have to be broken* before the gospel can be proclaimed with effectiveness." [175]

Spiritual Mapping

Spiritual mapping is a strategy which goes hand in hand with "naming the powers." This term originated with George Otis Jr., and has been defined as "the discipline of diagnosing the obstacles to revival in a given community." This involves "fervent prayer and diligent research," by which "practitioners are able to measure the landscape of the spiritual dimension and discern moral gateways

---

[170]Ibid.

[171]Wagner, *Warfare Prayer*, 100.

[172]Dawson, 156.

[173]Clinton E. Arnold, *Power and Magic: The Concept of Power in Ephesians* (Grand Rapids, MI: Baker Books, 1997), 54-55; A. Scott Moreau, *Essentials of Spiritual Warfare: Equipped to Win the Battle* (Wheaton, IL: Harold Shaw Publishers, 1997), 174.

[174]Arnold, *Spiritual Warfare*, 186.

[175]Wayne Grudem, *Systematic Theology: An Introduction to Biblical Doctrine* (Leicester: InterVarsity Press, 1994), 421 (original emphasis).

between it and the material world".[176] It is argued that this information will facilitate effective prayer for the people in question and Otis has developed a 28-stage scale to measure the progress of a community from "spiritual beachhead" phase to "spiritual breakthrough" to "spiritual transformation." Spiritual mapping begins at stage nine and Otis claims that, "When you reach that point you have a core of intercessors in a community really petitioning God for a visitation."[177]

Although Arnold takes issue with the whole concept of spiritual mapping, describing it at the worst as a "syncretistic adaptation of occult beliefs,"[178] he does, however, see a certain value in the George Otis version of this practice, as a means "to guide intercessors" as they pray for the lost.[179] According to Otis, many who have a problem with SLSW have fewer doubts about spiritual mapping and it is significant that the practice has been gaining ground in evangelical circles over the last few years. In 1998, the World Prayer Center was dedicated to tasks which included the coordination of the worldwide prayer movement. Its resources include a spiritual mapping repository whose purpose is "to disseminate information to its constituents" so that they may engage in prayer. In January 2000, *Christianity Today* reported as follows: "Otis says spiritual mapping is especially needed now because Satan will increase his resistance to the church as it moves toward fulfillment of the Great Commission."[180]

Wagner considers this practice to be the key component in strategic level tactics for unleashing God's power. The web page of the Observatory (the research division of Global Harvest Ministries, founded by Peter and Doris Wagner and located at the World Prayer Center), gives a more extensive description of spiritual mapping. It is defined in terms of intelligence reports: "An intelligence report is

---

[176]George Otis, Jr., *Informed Intercession: Transforming Your Community Through Spiritual Mapping and Strategic Prayer* (Ventura, CA: Renew Books, 1999), 256.

[177]Art Moore, "Spiritual Mapping Gains Credibility Among Leaders," *Christianity Today* 42, no. 1 (Jan. 1998), 55, online posting, http://www.christianitytoday.com/ct/8t1/8t1/055.html; accessed 21 Aug. 2001.

[178]Arnold, *Spiritual Warfare*, 202.

[179]Ibid.

[180]Moore, "Spiritual Mapping Gains Credibility."

designed to provide the type of reconnaissance needed to plan an effective strategy for dislodging an enemy from it's (sic) stronghold. By itself a report is of nominal value, but used within the context of a Holy Spirit inspired strategy a report is an awesome tool. Consider those that will use your spiritual mapping information as allies with whom you have a common goal."[181]

However, once again the question must be posed as to the biblical validation for this practice. Otis, who has been described as the pioneer of spiritual mapping within the SLSW movement,[182] cites the accounts in Numbers 13 and Joshua 18 respectively, where spies are sent into Canaan to discover what the land and its people are like.[183] However, on examination of these passages, it is difficult to see how they can be applied in the context of spiritual warfare. On the first occasion, subsequent occupation of the territory is frustrated by the unbelief of the children of Israel and God's resultant judgment upon them. In the latter passage, Joshua instructs his men to "walk through the land, and describe it . . . that I may here cast lots for you before the Lord in Shiloh" (Josh. 18:8). Clearly, the purpose of the survey is not spiritual but natural--it merely facilitated the division of the land between the various tribes. Otis also makes reference to Nehemiah's survey of the broken down walls of Jerusalem as a further example of spiritual mapping (Neh. 2).[184] Once again he seems to have drawn a spiritual conclusion from an event which has a specifically natural interpretation, namely the need to assess the physical damage prior to commencement of the restoration work.

In the New Testament context, Otis refers to Acts 17 where the apostle Paul is disturbed to discover that the whole city of Athens is consumed with idolatry (Acts 17:16). He states, "While there is no explicit evidence that the apostle took the results of this urban reconnaissance into spiritual warfare--specifically prayer against

---

[181]The Observatory, Global Harvest Ministries, "How to Submit Spiritual Mapping Data," online posting, http://www.globalharvestministries.org /home.qry?ID=446; accessed 27 Sept. 2001.

[182]C. Peter Wagner, foreword to *Informed Intercession,* by Otis.

[183]Otis, *Informed Intercession,* 90-91.

[184]Ibid., 91.

prevailing spiritual powers--we may speculate that he did."[185] This is indeed a shaky foundation for any evaluation of truth.

Wagner claims that "at least one" specific example of spiritual mapping is given in Scripture and cites Ezekiel 4:1, where God initially instructs the prophet to portray the city of Jerusalem on a clay tablet, and then to "lay siege against it." This is interpreted as spiritual mapping prior to spiritual warfare.[186] However, such interpretation is completely without contextual validation. The symbolic act in which Ezekiel was divinely ordered to engage spoke of the coming siege and fall of Jerusalem and the fate of those who lived in the city. This impending doom was not the result of demonic intervention but of God's judgment on the persistent iniquity of His people (Ezek. 4:4-6).[187]

Page refers to Daniel's teaching on the princes as an alternative source used by various authors in support of spiritual mapping. Whilst commending their attempt to take the reality of the unseen world seriously, Page concludes that "the practice of spiritual mapping lacks scriptural warrant and should not be embraced uncritically." He continues, "Proponents of spiritual mapping run the risk of indulging in the sort of speculation that Scripture consistently avoids and of falling into an unhealthy subjectivism."[188]

Lowe comes to a similar conclusion. He states that "the Bible shows little interest in the taxonomy of the demonic world. It merely affirms that opposition to the work and people of God is Satanic in origin. This is intended to serve as a counter to apostasy, and as motivation for perseverance, not as stimulus for 'spiritual mapping.'"[189]

The Scripture makes it clear in Colossians 2:8-10 that the traditions of men, such as witchcraft, superstition, idol worship, and anthropology are potential traps for the unsuspecting believer. There

---

[185]Ibid., 92.

[186]Wagner, *Warfare Prayer*, 152.

[187]For a full explanation of the Ezekiel passage, refer to Leslie C. Allen, *Ezekiel 1-19*, vol. 28, *Word Biblical Commentary*, eds., David A. Hubbard and Glenn W. Barker (Dallas, TX: Word Books, 1994), 46-80.

[188]Page, 65.

[189]Lowe, *Territorial Spirits*, 43.

is no place for conjecture or speculation about devils and demons (Col. 2:18-19). Christians ignore such advice at their peril.

Identificational Repentance

In recent decades the secular world has witnessed various high profile "national apologies" particularly in the context of historical war crimes. For example, in May 1995 the News & Observer Publishing Company reported as follows: "HIROSHIMA, Japan– In a surprise twist on the 50th anniversary of the world's first atomic bombing, the mayor of Hiroshima plans to break with tradition on Sunday and formally 'apologise' for Japan's action in World War Two."[190] Similarly, in June 1999, the *London Guardian* reported that "Serbia's wall of denial surrounding war crimes in Kosovo is about to be smashed by the Serbian Orthodox Church, which plans to tell its flock that the nation's soul is stained with the blood of ethnic Albanians. Church leaders will . . . defy the Yugoslav president, Slobodan Milosevic, by publicly admitting that Serb forces committed widespread atrocities."[191]

The whole concept of corporate sin has resurfaced in the Christian media in the days following the terrorist attacks on the World Trade Center and the Pentagon (11 September 2001). Some church leaders have declared that the tragedy was a direct result of God's judgment on America.[192] There have been emotive calls to Christians for national repentance, as a prelude to a move of God in evangelism, citing 2 Chronicles 7: 14. "If my people, which are called by my name, shall humble themselves, and pray, and seek my face,

---

[190]The News and Observer Publishing Co., "Hiroshima mayor to give Japan war apology," online posting, http://archive.nandotimes.com/newsroom/nt/805abomb8.html; accessed 11 Oct. 2001.

[191]National Council of the Churches of Christ in the U.S.A., "NCCCUSA Hails Courage of Pavle's July 4 Call for Repentance," online posting, http://www.ncccusa.org/news/99news77.html; accessed 20 Nov. 2001.

[192]See for example, Clifford Hill, "Moses Is Dead!" Editorial to *Prophecy Today*, Dec. 2001, 4-7; and Jon Garvey, "Manhattan and the Book of Revelation," *Prophecy Today*, Dec. 2001, 10-11; also David Wilkerson, "The Towers Have Fallen, But We Missed the Message," online posting, http://www.worldchallenge.org/first.htm; accessed 3 Jan. 2002. In the author's opinion, not only does this promote a totally wrong concept of God, but also it ignores the new covenant truth that it is the goodness of God which leads a man to repentance (Rom. 2:4).

and turn from their wicked ways; then will I hear from heaven, and will forgive their sin, and will heal their land."[193] In view of the current relevance of the subject it is therefore extremely important to examine the whole concept of identificational repentance and its biblical base.

The practice of identificational repentance has been heralded by protagonists of SLSW as a weapon which gives us "the awesome power to heal the past."[194] Whilst confession of sin has always been a fundamental element of Christian belief, this notion of corporate confession has been adopted and developed to become an integral feature of SLSW practice. The whole concept is based on the assumption articulated by Wagner that, "This sinful behavior has provided openings for high-ranking principalities and powers to establish spiritual strongholds that will not be loosened other than through corporate humility and repentance."[195] Thus it is argued that intercessors must confess not only their own personal sins, but also the corporate sins of the city or nation for which they are praying as part of the overall strategy for combatting territorial spirits.[196]

John Dawson is a leading exponent of this practice which he promotes as a method for breaking Satanic strongholds over a city and bringing reconciliation through confession and repentance for both community and national sins.[197] In his book, *Taking Our Cities for God*, he cites many instances where it has apparently been effective as a precursor to evangelism and spiritual renewal. He gives the example of a Christian leader in Sydney, Australia (1979), who led the crowd in a corporate act of forgiveness relating to Britain's wrong in establishing the country as a penal colony; this apparently opened the way for great blessing to come to the churches of Australia.[198] Dawson's subsequent publication, *Healing America's Wounds*, is now

---

[193]Murray argues that the confusion over this verse lies with lack of understanding of our privileges since Pentecost and the inception of the New Covenant. The promise of this scripture is specific to Old Testament Israel and her land. Iain H. Murray, *Pentecost - Today?*, 13-16.

[194]Wagner, "The Power to Heal the Past," online posting, http://www.pastornet.net.au/renewal/journal8/8d-wagnr.html; accessed 11 Oct. 2001.

[195]Wagner, *Warfare Prayer*, 177-78.

[196]Arnold, *Spiritual Warfare*, 167.

[197]Dawson, 183-89.

[198]Ibid., 80.

regarded as a textbook on the subject and Wagner declares that it provided the impetus for the AD 2000 Movement's designation of 1996 as the year to "heal the land." This involved a number of initiatives, including American whites repenting on the sites of Indian massacres and repentance for the atrocities perpetuated by the slave trade, which were viewed as opening the way for revival within the churches and a corresponding harvest of souls.[199]

In keeping with both Murphy and Wagner,[200] Jackson defines repentance as "the greatest weapon we have in warfare. It allows God to win the victory for us." He continues, "Territorial curses come from lack of repentance. . . . if enough people *corporately* repent on behalf of a nation for desiring abortion, immorality or any other number of sinful acts and ask God to remove sin, then He will heal and cast off the intended curse."[201]

Arnold initially took issue with the concept of remitting the sins of others as having more in common with Mormon doctrine than with biblical teaching.[202] He particularly objected to the AD 2000 & Beyond Movement's statement on their philosophy of prayer in the context of world evangelisation:

> Responsible spiritual mapping will frequently uncover sins of a nation or city which have been committed in the past, sometimes generations ago, and which have become strongholds of the forces of darkness, allowing them to keep multitudes in physical misery and spiritual captivity. When we corporately confess those sins of our nation through what many are calling 'identificational repentance,' they can be remitted through Jesus' blood shed on the cross, and the strongholds can be removed. God's people then can take back the place we have given to the Enemy, God's Spirit of grace can bring healing, and unsaved people can be open to receiving 'the light of the gospel of the glory of Christ' (2 Cor. 4:4).[203]

As Arnold points out, the logical application of this statement would lead one to believe that Christians can be instrumental in applying the atoning blood of Jesus Christ to the lives of other

---

[199]Wagner, "The Power to Heal the Past."

[200]Murphy, 537; Wagner, *Confronting the Powers*, 260.

[201]John Paul Jackson, *Needless Casualties of War* (Eastbourne: Kingsway Publications, 1999), 98-99 (original emphasis).

[202]Arnold, *Spiritual Warfare*, 206.

[203]Wagner, *Confronting the Powers*, 260.

people. Further discussion with Peter Wagner disclosed that the term "remit" was used only in the limited sense of removing the curse and penalty for the sins of others that is visited upon subsequent generations and on the land. Nonetheless, Arnold stresses that it is unwise for SLSW leaders to employ a term which carries a different connotation in biblical and Christian vocabulary. He comments, "at the minimum, it is quite confusing and could also lead to dangerous theology and practice."[204]

Otis has defined the practice of identificational repentance as involving two stages of intercessory action. These are, "(1) an acknowledgement that one's affinity group (clan, city, nation or organization) has been guilty of specific corporate sin before God and man, and (2) a prayerful petition that God will use personal repudiation of this sin as a redemptive beachhead from which to move into the larger community."[205] Biblical validation for this particular aspect of SLSW strategy is taken from the examples of Ezra, Nehemiah and Daniel who identified with the past sins of their people and confessed them before God. However, as Arnold has highlighted "they were fellow members of God's covenant community."[206] He believes there is a role for this practice within a church context but discounts the whole notion of vicarious repentance on behalf of unbelievers, explaining as follows: "We do not find, for instance, Daniel identifying with the sins of Nebuchadnezzar and confessing these to God in the hope that the Persians would soften their hearts to the living God." As far as the New Testament is concerned, Arnold draws on the example of Paul who never identifies "with the sins of Roman imperialism, sexual immorality and idolatry as a means of severing the ground held by ruling principalities."[207] One could also cite the preaching of Peter on the day of Pentecost; he confronted the Jews with the truths of the gospel and their sin in rejecting Jesus as the Messiah, but he did not repent on their behalf.

---

[204] Arnold, *Spiritual Warfare*, 207.

[205] Otis, *Informed Intercession*, 251.

[206] Arnold, *Spiritual Warfare*, 207.

[207] Ibid., 207-208.

Indeed, it is difficult to reconcile identificational repentance with a biblical understanding of the whole concept of repentance, as translated from the Greek word *metanoia*. Kittel discusses the meaning of *metanoia* as "a change of heart either generally or in respect of a specific sin" carrying with it the implication that "one has later arrived at a different view of something." He contrasts this with the word *metamelomai* which means to "experience remorse" implying that "one has a different feeling about it."[208] Kittel comments further, "In remorse (*metamelomai*) a man sees the bitter end of his sin, in repentance (*metanoia*) he breaks free from it. Remorse comes of itself at the end of a sinful and foolish way. But a man is called to repentance by the one who brings the divine Word (Mark 1:15)."[209] To illustrate the point, Kittel cites the examples of Judas (Matt. 27:3) and of Esau (Heb. 12:17), where the word used speaks of remorse and therefore "does not have the power to overcome the destructive operation of sin."[210] On the basis of this scholarly analysis, it is clear that there is no theological foundation for assuming that the practice known as identificational repentance has any spiritual value; it would more accurately be described as identificational remorse.

Grudem also discusses repentance as encompassing more than recognition of wrongdoing and regret for one's actions. He explains as follows: "Repentance, like faith, is an intellectual *understanding* (that sin is wrong), an emotional *approval* of the teachings of Scripture regarding sin (a sorrow for sin and a hatred of it), and a *personal decision* to turn from it (a renouncing of sin and a decision of the will to forsake it and lead a life of obedience to Christ instead)."[211] Accordingly, given that true repentance involves an individual turning from sin and determining to walk in God's principles, it cannot be undertaken vicariously. Even under the old covenant, the sin offering was made by the person concerned bringing an animal to the high priest for sacrifice; he then had to place his hands on the head of the animal, symbolically transferring his sin to the lamb or turtledove that was to die in his place; and finally he had to slit its throat. The sin of

---

[208]Gerhard Kittel, ed., *Theological Dictionary of the New Testament*, vol. 4 of 10 (Grand Rapids, MI: Wm. B. Eerdmans Publishing Company, 1967), 626.

[209]Ibid., 627-28.

[210]Ibid., 628.

[211]Grudem, 713 (original emphasis).

an individual had to be dealt with on an individual basis. Scripture makes it quite clear that "The son shall not bear the iniquity of the father, neither shall the father bear the iniquity of the son:" (Ezek. 18:20).

In the author's opinion, not only is the concept of identificational repentance wrong, but the whole argument underpinning the necessity for its practice is fallacious. The assumption that a person's response to the gospel is inhibited due to the curse imposed by satanic strongholds in a place or nation, is totally without biblical validation. Man is under the judgment of God because of sin; man was cursed because of sin (Gen. 3); and Jesus came to save his people from their sins (Matt. 1:21). By His sacrifice He took the curse of the law once and forever (Gal. 3:13). Salvation is based on the atoning work of Jesus Christ becoming a living reality within the heart and life of the individual and that is a sovereign act of Almighty God (John 1:13). The good news of the gospel "is the power of God unto salvation to every one that believeth" (Rom. 1:16) and against that omnipotence the devil is powerless.

Warfare Prayer

"THE WORLDWIDE PRAYER MOVEMENT IS OUT OF CONTROL! Never since Pentecost itself has history recorded a level of prayer on six of the continents comparable to what is happening today":[212] so claims Wagner in the opening paragraph of *Confronting the Powers*. Patrick Johnstone makes a similar declaration, when he said that the ". . . number of prayer initiatives and networks [are] unprecedented in the history of the world. There is, in fact, a **prayer awakening** under way." He continues, "The world is going to be evangelized only through prayer."[213] This philosophy undergirds the ministry of the United Prayer Track, which views intercessory prayer as the means enabling "the lost to be saved, the unevangelized to be evangelized, the unreached to be reached, the unchurched to be churched (Mt. 9:38; 24:14; 28:19), and churches to be multiplied

---

[212]Wagner, *Confronting the Powers*, 10 (original emphasis).

[213]Patrick Johnstone, *Biblical Intercession: Spiritual Power to Change our World*, Evangelical Missiological Society Series no. 3 (Pasadena, CA: William Carey Library, 1995), 144, 149 (original emphasis).

throughout the world."[214] Jack Hayford explains prayer in terms of partnership, "the redeemed child of God working hand in hand with God toward the realization of His redemptive purposes on earth."[215]

So strong is the emphasis on prayer within the SLSW movement, that children aged 12 and under have been incorporated into this worldwide prayer initiative. In 1993, Peter and Doris Wagner approached Esther Network International (a global intercessory prayer ministry), and as a result the Children's Sub-Track of the United Prayer Track was born. "That initial commitment soon grew into what is now The Children's Global Prayer Movement with over one million 'World Shapers' continuing to bombard the heavenlies on behalf of their generation."[216]

Wagner asserts that one of the results of "the increasing popularity of prayer" is "a growing awareness of the varieties of forms and functions of prayer."[217] Whilst prayer in general is viewed by some as the essential weapon of spiritual warfare,[218] there is also a considerable emphasis on specifically aggressive warfare prayer within the context of SLSW.[219] Both Wagner and Sheets[220] are of the opinion that this more technical form is the key to evangelism; they teach that binding Satan in warfare prayer enables sinners to receive Christ. Hayford exhorts believers that there is a viable method to deal with the impossible, namely, "*Invade it!* Not with a glib speech of high

---

[214]C. Peter Wagner, "The Philosophy of Prayer for World Evangelization Adopted by the A. D. 2000 United Prayer Track," in Wagner, *Confronting the Powers*, 254.

[215]Jack W. Hayford, *Prayer is Invading the Impossible*, rev. ed. (South Plainfield, NJ: Logos International, 1977), 92; quoted in Dutch Sheets, *Intercessory Prayer: How God Can Use Your Prayers to Move Heaven and Earth* (Ventura, CA: Regal Books, 1996), 33.

[216]Esther Ilnisky and Mary Tome, "Esther Network International Children's Global Prayer" (May 2000), online posting, http://www.ad2000.org/re01205.htm; accessed 15 Oct. 2001.

[217]Wagner, *Confronting the Powers*, 12-13.

[218]See for example, Arnold, *Spiritual Warfare*, 34, 38; Sheets, 209-10; and Wagner, *Warfare Prayer*, 48, 95.

[219]See for example, Lea, 85; Evelyn Christenson, *Battling the Prince of Darkness* (Amersham-On-The-Hill, England: Scripture Press, 1993), 104; and Murphy, 412.

[220]Wagner, *Warfare Prayer*, 48; Sheets, 177.

hopes. Not in anger. Not with resignation. Not through stoical self-control. But with violence. And prayer provides the vehicle for this kind of violence."[221]

Attempts to apply this teaching over the last ten years have resulted in numerous city-based, national and international "warfare" events, particularly geared to the unreached peoples of the 10/40 Window.[222] In 1997, "Operation Ice Castle" involved a group of intercessors climbing Mount Everest in what was described as a "frontal attack" on the "principal stronghold of Nepal." However as Tricia Trillin so pertinently asks, "Where are the results? Have the Roman Catholics stopped worshipping Mary? Has Nepal turned to Christ?"[223]

In 1999, the last big prayer thrust in the context of the 10/40 Window was "Operation Queen's Palace." This aimed to break a principal stronghold of the "Queen of Heaven" in Ephesus, Turkey, which had been identified as the hub of Mariolatry because this was where Mary was first declared to be the "mother of God" in AD 421.[224] In the year 2000, Wagner announced that the geographical focus for prayer and SLSW assault was to shift to the 40/70 Window, explaining that this area had now been claimed by the Queen of Heaven as her principal domain.[225] The new initiative is called "Operation Queen's Domain" and specifically targets the strongholds supposedly established because of Mariolatry and non-Arab Islamic worship of the Moon Goddess.

A whole range of language has grown up around the practice of warfare prayer, including such terminology as "storming the gates of hell," "green berets," "generals of intercession," and "capturing a city

---

[221]Hayford, 5; quoted in Sheets, 138 (original emphasis).

[222]For example, "Praying through the Window I, II, III and IV," "Cardinal Points Praying," "Praying through Ramadan," "The Day to Change the World," "Gideon's Army in Korea," "GCWOE 1995," "Prayer Journeys to the 100 Gateway Cities, March for Jesus," "The Reconciliation Walk," "Praying with Power" conferences, and "Celebration Ephesus," amongst others.

[223]Tricia Tillin, "The Lighthouse Movement," online posting, http://www.banner.org.uk/res/theglory9.html; accesssed 23 Aug. 2001.

[224]C. Peter Wagner, "The 40/70 Window Prayer Initiative: A New Directive of Prayer," online posting, http://globalharvestministries.org/home.qry?ID=204; accessed 27 Sept. 2001.

[225]Ibid.

for Christ." In 1993, however, the Lausanne Committee for World Evangelism expressed concern that this "language of violence and political involvement" pushed Christians into "adversarial attitudes with people."[226] World evangelist, T. L. Osborn, is also disturbed by both the language and practice of pulling down demonic powers. He states, "To me, this resembles what pagans abroad do, except that they use different vocabulary."[227] In 2000, ". . . representatives of evangelical mission groups signed a statement calling for an immediate halt to the inappropriate use of war imagery in mission work," which they described as counter-productive and noted that in extreme cases lives had been endangered.[228] Wagner promptly retorted, "They've developed some sort of pacifist paradigm . . . a direct statement against me and others who track with me."[229]

Both Moreau and White object to the whole concept of using prayer in a violent way.[230] Moreau comments, ". . . the orientation towards prayer as smart bombs vs scud missiles borrows too heavily on what Walter Wink explored as the myth of redemptive violence that pervades human cultures. Prayer was not intended to be a vehicle of violence, but a means of fellowship, growth and strength."[231]

Misgivings are also voiced by a number of other writers. Arnold states categorically that "The very idea of 'warfare prayer' is misleading." and repudiates any notion that "aggressive confrontation" with evil spirits may be termed prayer. He comments, ". . . it is inappropriate to speak of 'praying down' or 'praying against'

---

[226]Lausanne Committee for World Evangelization: "Lausanne 1993 Statement on Spiritual Warfare."

[227]Osborn, 278.

[228]Ted Olsen, ed., "Battle Brews Over Warfare Language (Or: Mission Minded Groups Attempt to Heal Each Others' Vocabularies)," *Colorado Springs Gazette*, 19 Aug. 2000; online posting, http://www.christianitytoday.com/ct/2000/138/42.0.html; accessed 21 Aug. 2001.

[229]Ibid.

[230]Thomas B. White, *Breaking Strongholds: How Spiritual Warfare Sets Captives Free* (Ann Arbor, MI: Vine Books, 1992), 141-42; quoted in A. Scott Moreau, "Gaining Perspectives on Territorial Spirits," paper presented at Lausanne Committee for World Evangelization, "Deliver Us From Evil" Consultation, Nairobi, Kenya, 22 Aug. 2000, online posting, http://www.gospelcom.net/lcwe/dufe/Papers/terspir.htm; accessed 21 Sept. 2001.

[231]Moreau, "Gaining Perspectives on Territorial Spirits."

a demonic ruler when we really mean exercising authority in Christ to directly command the spirit to leave."[232] Similarly, criticising the use of aggression, Hagin comments that, "You won't find any scripture in the Bible where Jesus yelled at the devil for hours, . . . He cast out demons with His Word. *His Word!*"[233] Concurring with Arnold,[234] and Moreau,[235] Hagin concludes that believers are not called on to engage in battle with demonic spirits in order to break strongholds; they are simply asked to proclaim the word of God in the power of the Spirit of God. Truth alone can dispel the satanic deception which clouds the minds and understanding of unbelievers. Hagin identifies this as the true context of the great fight of faith.[236] Osborn takes a similar stance, dismissing as erroneous the belief ". . . that by prayer and intercession, Christians can wage warfare against Satan and bring down his power in the *un*-converted world where he has the right to rule his own subjects."[237] He points out that, "When God created people, He gave them a free will and He never violates that right of choice . . . That is why Christians cannot reform people by casting evil spirits out of them. What they *can* do is teach God's Word to people, then people can embrace or reject His truths. . . . They have the right of choice and no one can *impose* God's Good Life Agenda."[238]

The question must be posed, therefore, as to the supposed biblical validation for this controversial aspect of SLSW. In 1992, Wagner wrote as follows: ". . . we have no biblical examples of the 12 apostles or any other first-century Christian leaders who challenged the devil to a direct power encounter as Jesus did. I would surmise the best explanation for this may be that God did not direct them to do so."[239] In this context, two issues must be addressed. Firstly, Wagner's assumption that the temptation of Christ may be interpreted as a 'power encounter' is highly questionable. Jesus

---

[232]Arnold, *Spiritual Warfare*, 186-87.

[233]Kenneth E. Hagin, *The Triumphant Church: Dominion Over All The Powers of Darkness* (Tulsa, OK: Faith Library Publications, 1993), 268 (original emphasis).

[234]Arnold, *Spiritual Warfare*, 214.

[235]Moreau, "Gaining Perspectives on Territorial Spirits."

[236]Hagin, *The Triumphant Church*, 222.

[237]Osborn, 280.

[238]Ibid., 282 (original emphasis).

[239]Wagner, *Warfare Prayer*, 56.

consistently refused to be drawn into the conflict on the terms set out by the devil. He did not discuss the lies, He proclaimed the truth. Accordingly, and this is the second point at issue, the means by which Jesus defeated the devil was not warfare prayer, but simple obedience to the will of the Father. The word of God, spoken in the power of the Holy Spirit, was His only weapon. He had need of no other.

In later writings, Wagner joins with others who cite Daniel 10:13 and 20 as the basis for warfare prayer.[240] Both are in the context of delayed answers to the prayers of Daniel and the appearance of an angelic being who brings encouragement to him. In verse 13, reference is made to a conflict in the heavenly realm between the angel, assisted by "Michael, one of the chief princes", and the prince of Persia. This same concept is expressed in verse 20 with respect to a future combat involving the angel with the princes of both Persia and Greece. There is, however, no indication of Daniel having engaged in spiritual warfare techniques.

As Garrard argues, it is clear from Old Testament history, that God fights on behalf of His people, so that against all odds, victories are assured (Exo. 14:19; 23:20; Judg. 5:19-20). Conversely, defeat for the children of Israel was an immediate indication that they had moved out of the protection of God and His word through disobedience (Exo. 32:35; Deut. 29:26-28). In this sense, what takes place on earth is a reflection of the heavenlies. However, Garrard further comments in respect to Daniel 10, ". . . although there are certainly heavenly beings involved, we should not exclude the presence of earthly rulers who are playing an important role in the outworking of what is revealed to Daniel in chapter 11." He continues:

> We know from history that the Persian empire was overthrown by the Grecian and we must consider what is written here as indicative of what takes place in the earthly sphere as first being determined in the heavenly. The final outcome does not depend upon man and his effort but upon God. This is vital, as man's inability and failure does not result in the failure of God's plan. Victory is assured, not because man has the right techniques for spiritual warfare, but because God is omnipotent, and Sovereign in all things and Satan is

---

[240]Wakely, "A Critical Look at the New 'Key' to Evangelization."

not co-existent and equally powerful with God. The cross has already made the difference.[241]

Some authors refer to Matthew 11:12 ("the kingdom of heaven suffereth violence and the violent take it by force") as the basis for an aggressive form of prayer.[242] However, as Hagner points out, the "violent person" of Matthew 11:12 is one who plunders and seizes for himself. The Greek word (and its cognates) is never used in a positive connotation to denote advancement of the kingdom of God. The overall meaning of the verse, therefore, does not refer to the demands of discipleship but concerns the reality of the persecution and opposition which must be faced by God's people.[243] In other words, the violence is directed against the kingdom of God rather than being used as a means whereby Christians are enabled to advance the kingdom.

In the author's opinion, much of what is taught in the context of warfare prayer and intercession arises from a total misunderstanding both of the nature of God in terms of His divine sovereignty and omnipotence and of the function of prayer itself.[244] For example, Walter Wink makes the emphatic assertion that the use of prayer "marks a decisive break with the notion that God is the cause of all that happens . . . Prayer changes us, but it also changes what is possible for God".[245] Dutch Sheets adopts a similar argument in his supposition that "Intercessory prayer is an extension of the ministry of Jesus through His Body, the Church, whereby we mediate between God and humanity for the purpose of reconciling the world to Him, or between Satan and humanity for the purpose of enforcing the victory of Calvary."[246] Two points arise in connection with this statement. The first is that Scripture is very clear that there is "one

---

[241]David J. Garrard, "Contemporary Issues in Mission," class lecture notes, M.A. in Missiology, Mattersey Hall, England, Spring 2001, p. 28.

[242]For example, see Wagner in *Confronting the Powers*, 138, 230.

[243]Donald A. Hagner, *Matthew 1-13*, vol. 33A, *Word Biblical Commentary*, eds. Bruce Metzger, David A. Hubbard, and Glenn W. Barker (Dallas, TX: Word Books, 1993), 307.

[244]For a theological examination of prayer, see chapter 2.

[245]Walter Wink, *Unmasking the Powers Powers*: The Invisible Forces that Determine Human Existence (Philadelphia, PA: Fortress Press, 1986), 88; quoted in Wagner, Warfare Prayer, 95.

[246]Sheets, 42 (original emphasis).

mediator between God and men, the man Christ Jesus" (1 Tim. 2:5); secondly, there is no biblical basis for the concept of mediation between Satan and humanity. To adopt such notions is to adopt the concept that man rather than God holds the balance of power in evangelism.

Interestingly, Hesselgrave draws the analogy between warfare prayer and the prayer typical of Indo-European paganism with its dualistic understanding of the eternal co-existence of good and evil. The latter is viewed as a means "to control the gods," but, in contrast, prayer in biblical thought is "submission" to God.[247] Osborn also comments in respect to his observations of pagan prayer, "They are preoccupied with the presence and power of evil spirits which they visualize as being destructive and that bring disasters, diseases and evil upon themselves and upon their communities."[248] It is not difficult to identify extremely similar concepts undergirding the practice of warfare prayer.

Certainly, much of what may be observed in this context is based on the implicit notion that the practice somehow compels God to act in a certain way. For example, Lighthouse of Prayer is another group which focuses on intercession for the immediate community. According to a Lighthouse resource, they "produce in reality a mantel of prayer that opens the heavens over the city so that the light of the gospel begins to shine through to the minds of lost people." The article goes on to state, "This kind of grass-roots prayer evangelism will create an atmosphere for effective evangelism. Your city will be prepared over a period of time for an effective proclamation of the gospel where all the spiritual IOU's that you have been collecting will be cashed in."[249] Sheets also teaches that prayers are accumulated in heaven for future use,[250] and that, correspondingly, lack of prayer may inhibit God's ability to intervene in a given situation. He makes the following staggering assertion: "The reality of it is that sometimes

---

[247]David Hesselgrave, *Scripture and Strategy: The Use of the Bible in Postmodern Church and Mission*, Evangelical Missiological Society Series no. 1 (Pasadena, CA: William Carey Library, 1994), 210.

[248]Osborn, 372.

[249]Pray Twin Cities, "How to be a Lighthouse of Prayer," online posting, http://www.praytwincities.org/howtobea.htm; accessed 21 Nov. 2001.

[250]Sheets, 208.

He cannot do what we've asked because we have not given Him enough power in our prayer times to get it done. He has poured out all there was to pour and it wasn't enough! It's not just a faith issue, but also a power issue."[251]

Acceptance of the hypotheses of Wink, Sheets and Silvoso, is tantamount to accepting that man, not God, is the fulcrum of redemption and that accordingly, man's efforts are the vital catalyst in the work of prayer evangelism. In the author's opinion this concept places a burden on people that God never intended, and has more in common with the "commandments of men" refuted by Jesus in Matthew 15:9 and Mark 7:7, than the truths of the gospel. Moreover, as Osborn so robustly declares: "WHEN CHRISTIANS IMAGINE demonic powers arrayed against them in spiritual conflict, and they believe that their warfare against these principalities requires long intercessions, then they are discrediting the victory that Christ won through His death and resurrection. To visualize Satan's power pitted against God's people in a struggle that may be lost if Christians do not wrestle long enough, negates Christ's victory and gives undue credit to the enemy."[252] As John Osteen writes, "God's people are destroyed for lack of knowledge. They need to know the Word of God. When they know the truth--the truth shall make them free!"[253] Kenneth E. Hagin makes a similar assertion. He writes, "One reason we, as Christians, live in unbelief and our faith has been hindered, is because we lack knowledge about redemption and our redemptive *rights*. We lack knowledge of what God's Word says about our redemption, and that lack of knowledge is the greatest enemy of faith."[254]

Clearly, the believer who desires to be an effective witness of the gospel must be in relationship with His Heavenly Father; and prayer is simply an expression of that relationship. However, assuming that the witness is prepared, is it possible to identify a specific role for prayer in the context of evangelism? The Scriptures record two

---

[251]Ibid., 209-10.

[252]Osborn, 279 (original emphasis).

[253]John Osteen, *The Truth Shall Set You Free* (Houston, TX: A John Osteen Publication, 1978), 10.

[254]Kenneth E. Hagin, *Understanding How to Fight the Good Fight of Faith* (Tulsa, OK: Faith Library Publications, 1996), 1 (original emphasis).

simple truths in this context. Speaking to the twelve disciples, Jesus said, "Pray ye therefore the Lord of the harvest, that he will send forth labourers into his harvest." (Matt. 9:38), and to the seventy His words were virtually identical (Luke 10:2). To pray for labourers is the first instruction, and the second is revealed by Paul in the epistles. Osborn deliberates the latter as follows: "*Praying always,* the apostle counseled. Praying for WHAT? Here is the key to Christian ministry as witnesses of Christ. Pray *that utterance may be given to us, that we may open our mouths boldly to make known the mystery of the Gospel.* Eph. 6:19 . . . *Pray for us, that the Word of the Lord may have free course...and that we may be delivered from unreasonable and wicked men.* 2Th.3:1-2. "[255] Paul knew the authority of the gospel. He defined it as the "power of God unto salvation to every one that believeth" (Rom. 1:16). Jesus Himself warned His disciples not to postpone bringing in the harvest of souls. He said, "Say not ye, There are yet four months, and *then* cometh harvest? behold, I say unto you, Lift up your eyes and look on the fields; for they are white already to harvest" (John 4:35).

In recent years the author has noticed a subtle shift in focus within the SLSW movement away from the extremes of warfare prayer and towards the more acceptable concept of strategic-level intercession. In the author's opinion this is merely a change in emphasis; the underlying philosophy remains the same. There is no biblical validation for the notion that the glorious truths of redemption are insufficient to destroy every satanic stronghold. The power of the enemy has already been defeated at Calvary (Heb. 2:14); Satan's only weapon is deception, and his lies are revealed for what they are when God's word is proclaimed in life and truth. Osborn makes it quite clear: "We do not win lost souls by interceding and struggling in prayer to defeat evil spirits and to bring down Satan's strongholds in their lives. We win over the principalities of darkness by giving to people the delivering truths of the Gospel. That is the power that pulls down Satan's strongholds and that brings salvation to the lost."[256]

---

[255]Osborn, 369 (original emphasis).

[256]Ibid., 283.

A Recurring Phenomenon?

In this dissertation some attention has been given to the influences underlying the current understanding of SLSW. For example, the thumbprint of postmodernism is seen in terms of the focus on the experiential at the expense of both rationality and scriptural truth. However, there are many features of SLSW which are far from contemporary. In this context, the author is grateful to the work of D. William Faupel whose scholarly publication, *The Everlasting Gospel,* traces the development of Pentecostal thought in respect to eschatology. His analysis of the pre-Pentecostal era pinpoints several men who were to have a significant influence in preparing the way for the coming spiritual awakening; one of these was Frank Weston Sandford (1862-1948).

Sandford was born in Bowdoinham, Maine, in 1862. Converted at age eighteen, he enrolled at the Theological School of Lewiston six years later, but shortly after abandoned his studies to enter the ministry. He was ordained as a Free Baptist minister but, "After holding several successful pastorates in Maine and New Hampshire, he left the denomination in 1892 to strike out on his own for God without organisational support."[257]

Sandford's formative period in the ministry coincided with the final years of the nineteenth century when there was much speculation about the imminency of the second coming. Expectations rose that God was about to restore apostolic authority and power to the church to empower it to fulfil His end time purposes. As F. S. Murray comments, "By the early nineties the groundswell of religious fervor was beating hard against the beaches of the world. . . . Ministers like Boston's A. J. Gordon and Chicago's R. A Torrey were confidently predicting the imminent [return] of the Lord."[258] Sandford himself was particularly influenced by the

---

[257]Frank W. Sandford, inside front cover to *The Golden Light upon the Two Americas* (Amherst, NH: The Kingdom Press, 1974).

[258]F. S. Murray, *The Sublimity of Faith: The Life and Work of Frank W. Sandford* (Amherst, NH: The Kingdom Press, 1981), 74; quoted in D. William Faupel, *The Everlasting Gospel: The Significance of Eschatology in the Development of Pentecostal Thought* (Sheffield: Sheffield Academic Press, 1996), 115.

restorationist teaching of John Alexander Dowie, and he also imbibed J. N. Darby's dispensational theology.

As the result of a missionary tour visiting India, Japan and China in 1890, Sandford came to the conclusion that present missionary efforts were falling short of the mark.[259] He later wrote:

> The trip demolished all my sermons on the world's speedy evangelization. I saw the utter foolishness of attempting such a vast undertaking by any of the methods then in existence . . . The following summer at Old Orchard, God revealed my future life on apostolic lines, and whispered the one, strange, dread word, 'Armageddon.' I knew then that the whole world was to be 'gathered to the great day of the battle of God Almighty,' and that a movement with signs, wonders and mighty deeds was to be used to the ends of the earth in separating the human race into two great divisions, one under the leadership of the Christ and the other under the leadership of the Antichrist.[260]

Sandford left his denomination and, in his own words, "began the journey back to apostolic life and power."[261] In 1895, he opened a Bible School with one student. The following year a permanent location for the School was selected and building began on a farm near New Durham, Maine. It was intended to be a centre for training co-workers for the great task of evangelising the world. "From 1896 to 1904, followers responded to Sandford's call to re-form an apostolic church modeled on the primitive Christianity of the Book of Acts and to prepare the world for the second coming of Christ and the millennium. . . . Since Sandford felt that conventional mission methods could not possibly evangelize the world, the primary activity of the community was 'prevailing prayer' for God to intervene in history and bring about His purposes."[262]

In 1900, Sandford revealed his strategy for world evangelisation in a series of lectures entitled, "The Art of War." He adopted the battle plan used by Joshua in the conquest of Canaan as the basis for this *modus operandi*. It comprised four stages--the conquest of Joshua,

---

[259]Faupel, *The Everlasting Gospel*, 144.

[260]Frank W. Sandford, *Seven Years with God* (Mount Vernon, NH: The Kingdom Press, 1957), 12-13.

[261]Ibid., 58.

[262]William C. Hiss, "Shiloh: Frank W. Sandford and the Kingdom 1893-1948," (PhD. diss., Tufts University, Boston, Massachusetts, Apr. 1978), 4.

the conquest of Israel, the conquest of Canaan (or the Gentiles), and the conquest of Conquests.[263] His autobiographical work, *Seven Years with God* (1901), contained a summary of that which had already been achieved. He writes: "During the first period the Son of God by fiery trials, tribulations and tests of nearly every conceivable kind, was preparing me personally to represent Himself among men. In the second, He was preparing a place where I might teach others the lessons I had learned, and thus fit them to reproduce the same to the ends of the earth."[264] Accordingly, it was announced that Stage Three commenced on 1 January 1901. Sandford declared that there would be a twenty-four-hour prayer vigil at the prayer tower in Shiloh, and in fact, this was to continue for a period of some twenty years. As Faupel points out, "Sandford was convinced that the primary battle was with Satan and his legions, who held the world in bondage. Spirit-filled warriors who engaged in intercessory prayer were the first line of attack. They would be followed by others who would engage in an extensive campaign of personal evangelism."[265]

In November of that year, Sandford made the further announcement that he was the Elijah, the one who is to come before the "great and dreadful day of the LORD" (Mal. 4:5-6). In this role, he restored numerous Biblical practices as part of his plan to create a small army of perfect Christians "who would be the 'white cavalry' at the Battle of Armageddon."[266] In overall terms, the year 1901 marked a significant watershed in the work at Shiloh. As Hiss comments:

> Shiloh became less of a missionary training school and more of a prayer fortress; the supplications of the saints were intended to support Sandford in his role as Elijah the Restorer, and to hasten God's intervention in the last days of history.
>
> To outsiders, Shiloh seemed more concerned with grand and symbolic actions than with "real" Christian work, the conversion of various categories of heathen. To Sandford, however, the new century marked the end of "the gospel age" and the beginning of the "millennial age." Convinced since 1891-1892 that traditional

---

[263] For full details on Sandford's battle plan, please refer to Frank W. Sandford, *The Art of War for the Christian Soldier* (Amherst, NH: The Kingdom Press, 1966), 21-146.

[264] Sandford, *Seven Years With God*, 15.

[265] Faupel, 154.

[266] Hiss, 5.

evangelistic methods had failed, he now was seeking in earnest the route to apostolic, pentecostal power, and a method of preparing the world for the Last Days.[267]

Significantly, his "theological authority" was validated by the "various messages and instructions he had received from God."[268] One of the most significant of these, (with the exception of the revelation of his role as Elijah), was the earlier command to "REMOVE THE COVERING CAST OVER THE FACE OF ALL THE EARTH" derived from Isaiah 25:7. In Sandford's understanding this seemed, "to empower him to strip from the whole world the carnal mist, the earthly perception that made God and spiritual things unreal." As far as he was concerned, "he was now the most powerful man since St. Paul, and . . . close members of his following realized that he was thinking once more of global conquest."[269]

From 1904 onwards, Sandford spent much of his time at sea. Ships were purchased so that select groups of spiritual warriors could circumnavigate the world praying off each continent for a breakthrough against the powers of darkness. "The 'Kingdom Yacht Club,' which would eventually own five sea-going vessels and a smaller fishing boat, represented a major new direction in Shiloh's history. Sandford's explanation for the change was that God was leading him toward world travel in order to 'symbolically' subdue the globe for Christ."[270] On these voyages, increasingly evangelistic work was abandoned and the "primary activity" was "prevailing prayer," which was viewed as the means of breaking Satan's power. It was therefore thought that "the voyage would 'remove the covering,' and allow the blinded inhabitants to see God's plan for the redemption of the 144,000 and the battle of Armageddon."[271]

In January 1907, Sandford set off on the Coronet for a voyage that was to last for three years. During that time the yacht "travelled 51,924 nautical miles, visited thirty-two ports and prayed off twice

---

[267] Ibid., 267-68.
[268] Ibid., 269.
[269] Ibid., 183.
[270] Ibid., 392.
[271] Ibid., 417.

that many foreign lands."[272] "For Sandford, the voyage was the pinnacle of his spiritual career; the cost in suffering and lives disappeared in spiritual victory."[273] He often said in later years, "It put the handcuffs on the globe for Jesus Christ, and I know it."[274]

The parallels between the Sandford methodology and that of SLSW are unmistakable; there are mutual hallmarks. Both are fuelled by a fervour for world evangelisation; both search for a new method of reaching the lost; both focus on prayer as the prime means to evict Satan from his worldly strongholds; both employ the strategy of using a select band of prayer warriors to effect this eviction; both place considerable emphasis on the need for personal holiness; and both came to view themselves as restoring the apostolic/prophetic ministry to the Church. There are also differences. Wagner and other proponents of SLSW effectively call into question the all-sufficiency of the word of God. This has led to the incorporation of 'facts' deduced from both observation and anecdotal evidence as an addendum to spiritual truth. Sandford had a tremendous respect for the word of God which Faupel has described as a "radical commitment to live out the gospel."[275] However, he adopted an extremely literalistic interpretation of Scripture often seeing himself as the fulfilment of prophecy as he supposedly received direct revelation from God.[276]

For both, the self-imposed pressure of eschatological emphasis is a significant feature. Yet Jesus told His disciples, "But of that day and hour knoweth no *man*, no, not the angels of heaven, but my Father only" (Matt. 24:36). "It is not for you to know the times or the seasons, which the Father hath put in his own power" (Acts 1:7). The prohibition is for man's good, and it appears that the root of error is often embedded in an unnecessary fascination with that which God has either forbidden or chosen not to reveal. Peter Martyr once wrote: "It is a miserable thing, that whereas we have so many clear and manifest things in the Holy Scriptures, concerning faith, hope,

---

[272]Ibid., 450.

[273]F. S. Murray, 612; quoted in Hiss, 450.

[274]F. S. Murray, 540; quoted in Hiss, 418.

[275]Faupel, 149.

[276]Sandford, *Seven Years with God*, 78.

charity and the bonds of other virtues, wherein there is nothing obscure, we will leave those utterly neglected and with so great superstition follow other things which are uncertain and serve less unto salvation."[277]

In a letter to the editor of *Messiah's Herald* in 1874, C. H. Spurgeon voiced a similar opinion: "The more I read the Scriptures as to the future, the less I am able to dogmatise. I see conversion of the world, and the personal pre-millenial reign, and the sudden coming, and the judgment, and several other grand points; but I cannot put them into order, nor has anyone else done so yet. I believe every prophetical work I have ever seen (and I have read very many) to be wrong in some points. I feel more at home in preaching Christ crucified than upon any other theme, and I do believe He will draw all men unto Him."[278]

Summary

Systematic evaluation of the literature demonstrates that the whole concept of SLSW stands on inadequate biblical and theological foundations. Where scriptural authority is claimed, this tends to be on the basis of proof texts which are manipulated to support the various hypotheses and Scripture itself is viewed through the dangerously subjective lens of experience.

In reality, most of the validation for SLSW is drawn from extra-biblical sources and empirical evidence which is largely unconfirmed.[279] Moreover, it appears to be acceptable to seek spiritual 'truth' outside of the word of God so long as this is not explicitly contradicted by Scripture. Thus, what is being proposed is effectively a sophisticated form of syncretism based on the observation of pagan beliefs and practices. However, as Lowe points out, "When a teaching finds more support from animism than from Scripture, Christopaganism looms near."[280] Even the lessons of

---

[277]Peter Martyr, *Common Places*, pt. 3. (n.p., 1583), 386; quoted in Iain H. Murray, *The Puritan Hope: Revival and the Interpretation of Prophecy* (Edinburgh: The Banner of Truth Trust, 1971), 86.

[278]C. H. Spurgeon, letter to the editor of *Messiah's Herald*, 1874; quoted in Iain H. Murray, *The Puritan Hope*, 263.

[279]Lowe, *Territorial Spirits*, 118.

[280]Lowe, *Territorial Spirits*, 112.

history demonstrate that any human attempt to augment the word of God with additional 'truth' inevitably opens the door to error.

The whole focus of SLSW is on the devil and his demonic host, and accordingly, such fundamental issues as sin, free will, and the moral responsibility of the individual before a holy God have been sidestepped. Man has become the fulcrum of redemption, holding the balance of power between God and the devil in the battle for the souls of men, and the gospel itself rendered impotent without the preliminary work of pulling down demonic strongholds. Many authors pay lip service to the concept of God's sovereignty but in real terms view His ability to intervene as being limited to the extent of man's willingness to cooperate in the process of salvation.

These are serious matters which call into question the very basis of the Christian faith. In the author's opinion, proponents of SLSW are effectively promoting "another gospel: Which is not another; but there be some that trouble you, and would pervert the gospel of Christ" (Gal. 1:6-7).

CHAPTER 4

METHODOLOGY OF APPLIED RESEARCH PROJECT

Introduction

The Christian faith is founded in the truths of God as revealed in His word. As Sir Robert Anderson has stated:

> God has given us a revelation. And, while doubt still lingers round innumerable questions on which we crave knowledge, Divine certainty is our privilege in respect of "all things that pertain unto life and godliness". The man who would force his opinions on others is a boor. He who would die for his opinions is a fool. But Christianity has not to do with *opinions*. It is founded on established facts and Divine truth; and faith based thereon is the heritage of the Church. Her martyrs knew the power of faith. The truth they died for was not "the general sense of Scripture corrected in the light of reason and conscience," and thus reduced to the pulp-like consistency of modern theology . . . We are not called upon to wear the martyr's crown, but it is ours to share the martyr's faith . . . Agnosticism is Greek for ignorance, and ignorance is both shameful and sinful in presence of a Divine revelation.[1]

As has been discussed in chapter three, the current teaching on SLSW challenges some of the "established facts and Divine truth" of the gospel; in the author's opinion, its widespread acceptance in Christian circles can only be as a result of a corresponding ignorance or misunderstanding as to those very truths and their implications for the Christian life.

The hypothesis to be tested was that the exposition of biblical and theological truth, applied in both an historical and a modern context, with the opportunity for study, discussion and re-evaluation of relevant concepts, would ensure that the understanding and practice of spiritual warfare was brought into alignment with the word of God. This hypothesis was put to the test in the context of a group of church leaders, men and women of integrity who hold to the principle that the Bible is the infallible word of God and who, it was assumed, would be prepared to amend their own thinking and practice where this was shown to be unbiblical. The author's conviction was that the concepts and teaching of SLSW have drawn people away from the eternal truths of scripture, but by refocusing their understanding on what the Bible actually teaches about spiritual

---

[1] Sir Robert Anderson, preface to *The Gospel and Its Ministry: A Handbook of Evangelical Truth*, 13th ed. (London: Pickering and Inglis, [1969]), vii.

warfare, individuals would be enabled to live and walk in Christ's total victory over the devil and all demonic powers, conquered at Calvary. The gospel of Jesus Christ is "the power of God unto salvation to every one that believeth; to the Jew first, and also to the Greek" (Rom. 1:16). It is the preaching of the gospel and not the best devised stratagems of SLSW that brings people to salvation in Christ.

Rationale

SLSW as now practiced, is a relatively recent phenomenon, and literature on the subject has only been published within the last twenty years. The influence of the thinking that undergirds this teaching can be traced in its seed form and development throughout church history. However, it is only now that its philosophy and practice are sweeping through Christendom like wildfire.

From his own study of the Bible and its foundational truths, as well as research into church history, theology, and a review of contemporary literature, the writer had come to the conclusion that many of the current practices advocated under the banner of SLSW are deficient in scriptural foundation. Review of history demonstrates that both biblical and unbiblical practices have often been accepted and/or adopted without question, either as a result of tradition or because of the standing of the leader of the group advancing the teaching. Unfortunately, there are few believers who display the diligence of the Bereans, "who searched the scriptures daily" (Acts 17:11) to ascertain whether or not Paul's teachings were true. The concepts of SLSW have mainly been propounded via populist books promoted by ingenious marketing; there are few scholastic publications on the subject.

As a bishop, the author has contact with many churches and church leaders in various nations. As a result of his discussions with pastors both within the United Kingdom and abroad, it became clear that few have studied the biblical base for the teachings of SLSW. The pressures of church responsibility and the needs of people have effectively precluded the time for individual research. Thus many church leaders are largely reliant on easily accessible and superficially attractive information, which has been pre-packaged in the form of popular books, CD-ROMs and articles from the internet, and is also advanced via Christian media, seminars and conventions.

The author's proposal was to isolate a sample group of pastors from their oft-interrupted, busy schedules and give them the opportunity to explore, examine and discuss primarily what the Scripture says about the issues and practices of SLSW. A secondary aim was to present and evaluate church history in the light of these findings. In view of inevitable time constraints and the problems of co-ordinating the existing commitments of the various participants over a longer term, it was decided to organise a seminar on an intensive basis. It was calculated that in order to have adequate time to cover a representative section of the wealth of material on the biblical, theological and historical aspects of SLSW, in addition to a review of current practices, a minimum of four days would be required to complete the seminar course.

Learner Differences Which Lead to the Choice of Teaching Methods

It was recognised from the outset that the teaching method adopted for the course must be sufficiently flexible to take into consideration vital differences between various participants. Each person learns and assimilates information at his or her own pace since the capacity, capability, background and set of experiences of each is unique.[2] The implication of this for teaching is that the level of explanation may need to be different for different students. In its guidelines for good teaching practice, the American Association of Higher Education recommends that teachers acknowledge students' different learning styles, in addition to their differing capacities.[3] Honey & Mumford observe that many teachers ignore this difference, assuming that learners are "empty buckets" waiting to be filled by the training method preferred by the instructor.[4]

---

[2]For a study of the learning process, please refer to Noel Entwistle, *Styles of Learning and Teaching: An Integrated Outline of Educational Psychology*, pt. 2 (New York: John Wiley & Sons, 1981), 65-116.

[3]"Seven Principles of Good Practice in Undergraduate Education," online posting, http://www.byu.edu/fc/pages/tchlrnpages/7princip.htm; accessed 1 Mar. 2002.

[4]Peter Honey and Alan Mumford, *The Manual of Learning Styles* (Berkshire: Peter Honey, 1982), 1.

There are numerous theories regarding different learning styles and D. A. Kolb is probably the most quoted of these.[5] He showed that learning styles could be seen on a continuum. These run from: (1) concrete experience, as a result of being involved in a new experience; (2) reflective observation, based on watching others or developing observations about one's own experience; (3) abstract conceptualisation, involving creating theories to explain observations; and (4) active planning, using theories to solve problems or make decisions.

Hartman took Kolb's classification and demonstrated how one might adapt the teaching style to cater for each. He suggested that for the concrete experience the key to effective learning would be via laboratories, field work, observations or trigger films; for the reflective learner, he advocated the use of logs, journals or brainstorming sessions; in respect to the abstract conceptualiser, lectures, papers and analogies facilitate learning; and for the active experimenter, Hartman identified simulations, case studies and homework as the most effective learning media.[6] However, it is the author's belief that students will select different learning styles depending on what is being learned. The author can certainly identify this tendency within his own learning and some research would also support this view. For example, in 1981, Entwistle observed the need to recognise that an individual student's learning strategy may vary from task to task.[7]

It was concluded, therefore, that the teaching should attempt to cater for a variety of learning styles. In order to do this, the author engaged his learners in both group and individual work. The variety of teaching methods used included lectures, discussions, group and

---

[5]"The Kolb Learning Cycle," The College of St. Scholastica, Duluth, Minnesota, online posting, http://www.css.edu/users/dswenson/web/PAGEMILL/Kolb.htm; accessed 1 Mar. 2002.

[6]V. F. Hartman, "Teaching and Learning Style Preferences: Transitions Through Technology," *VCCA Journal* 9, no. 2 (1995), 18-20. For further discussion, see Glenn Sullivan, "The Development of a Learning Style Measure for the Drake P3 Assessment System," TMs (photocopy), p. 3, Pacific Graduate School of Psychology, Palo Alto, California, n.d.

[7]Entwistle, 106.

individual question and answer times, set reading, trigger videos, power-point presentations, and questionnaires.

Teaching Philosophy

However, with regards to the philosophy of teaching the author is by inclination a dogmatist, concurring with the methods of C. H. Spurgeon who ". . . differed from so many of his contemporaries (and ours!) with regard to the manner in which students should be trained. Instruction, he maintained, should be given in definite, *dogmatic* form. Tutors should not teach their students in that broad, liberal manner which presents a number of 'view-points' and leaves the ultimate choice to the student; rather they should forcibly and unmistakably declare the mind of God and show a determined predilection for the old theology, being saturated in it and ready to die for it!"[8]

Measuring Instrument

In order to ascertain the delegates' beliefs before starting the course, and to test the impact of the teaching instrument afterwards, the pastors were asked to complete identical pre-course, post-course, and follow-up (three months later) questionnaires. A questionnaire is a key data collecting instrument and was selected for the purposes of this study because it is both simple to use and to analyse. This method has facilitated the measurement and evaluation of any change in the strength of foundation of each delegate's beliefs occurring as a result of the seminar.

A questionnaire of forty-two questions was designed which offered a five-point rating-scale answer to each question; generally 1 being low and 5 being high in value, all the answers being phrased to easily identify the various strengths of positive and negative opinion. Answers to some of the questions were inverted so that low values became more positive. The reason for doing this was that, in analysing the data, some lower values represented the more desirable outcomes. In addition, some questions were deliberately inverted to

---

[8]William Williams, *Charles Haddon Spurgeon: Personal Reminiscences* (London: The Religious Tract Society, 1895), 138; quoted by Iain H. Murray, Introduction to *An All-Round Ministry: Addresses to Ministers and Students* by Charles H. Spurgeon (Edinburgh: Banner of Truth Trust, 2000); (original emphasis).

avoid pastors from habitually answering according to pattern rather than thinking about the question and evaluating their answer first. For the same reason, other questions had a neutral response rather than the most negative one for the first answer.

The questions were divided into six groups, and each group was put on a different page of the questionnaire. The titles of the groups were: 1) What sources do you use for spiritual insight/inspiration? 2) Basis of successful evangelism. 3) Factors contributing to a lack of church growth. 4) Spirits and demons. 5) Spiritual warfare. 6) Role of speaking in tongues.

The reason for grouping the questions like this was to enable the author to ascertain the delegates' thinking on different aspects of SLSW. Consider, for example, the issue of fasting; it was important to discover what each delegate thought about this in a number of different contexts, namely: a) as a source for spiritual insight or inspiration, b) as a basis for successful evangelism, c) as a factor contributing to a lack of church growth, and d) as a pre-requisite for exorcising demons. By including a question on fasting in each of these groups, the author was able to determine if a delegate viewed fasting as being important or otherwise in each context.

Procedures

Since the purpose was to quantify the impact of teaching a specific course to pastors, the population was already defined. The most readily accessible target population was the regional Global Gospel Fellowship (GGF) pastors' meetings held at Peniel Church, Essex, England. This inter-denominational pastors' fellowship was set up in 1995 to facilitate informal communication and fellowship between pastors and church leaders on a monthly basis. The author was hosting between sixty and eighty pastors at each session, which take the form of a meal followed by a discussion or teaching session. The majority of these pastors minister in the UK, with congregations drawn from the international community. In addition, there were a small number of ministers who travelled regularly from Europe, as well as regular guests from Africa.

The sample, made up of a cross section of this target population, was largely self-defining, as it consisted of those who had recorded an interest in this subject and who were able to commit to a four-day seminar. To ensure that the final sample was representative of the group as a whole and that those of similar opinions did not distort the results, a method of purposive sampling of the available group ensured it included a range of different denominations, ages, sexes, ministerial status, ethnic origins, educational backgrounds, and attitudes to SLSW practice.

To entice this sample population to commit to a full four days, they were offered a seminar package that included paid hotel accommodation and meals. A local hotel was booked for bed and breakfast. Also, in order to facilitate the maximum opportunity for fellowship and discussion, church catering staff provided for midday and evening meals at the seminar site.

A sample population of some thirty pastors was in place approximately two months before the seminar date. This was largely drawn from GGF membership but a significant number of delegates had not been previously exposed to the author's ministry and made application to attend because of their particular interest in the subject.[9] Administration assistants were prepared to co-ordinate the seminar and questionnaires. One month before the seminar, each delegate received correspondence, giving the details of the seminar.

Since the purpose was to measure any changes in these pastors' attitudes and beliefs after the seminar, the previously described questionnaire was carefully prepared. It was developed from a detailed literature review and research into the biblical, historical and theological perspectives of SLSW, which have given rise to research questions. Having compiled the questionnaire, it was applied pre-seminar, post-seminar, and three months after the seminar.

On their arrival, each delegate received a registration pack containing an agenda, recommended book list, educational brochure, and a seminar badge. They were clearly informed of the significance of the project, the importance of answering the questionnaire honestly, and assured that all responses would be held in strict confidence and used only in the generation of statistics for this particular Doctor of Ministry Project. They were asked to sit apart from one another to complete the questionnaire at the commencement of the first session of the seminar. (They were not

---

[9]For example, this is evidenced by the large number of positive responses relating to the importance of SLSW given by many of the delegates in the Pre-test.

informed at this time that identical questionnaires would be completed following the course.) After a period of twenty minutes, the questionnaires were collected and stored. The programme for the seminar then commenced. For an outline of the curriculum, see appendix B.

The same approach was adopted for the post-course questionnaire. Following completion of the seminar the Pre-test questionnaires were counted. The results were recorded by administration assistants (the same procedure was followed Post-test and Follow-up).

Database Creation

First, the data from the questionnaire responses was split into two tables. The first table held the specific data concerning the individual, and the second contained the numerical results of the questionnaire for each of the three stages (Pre-test, Post-test and Follow-up). A unique identifier field linked the two tables. (All this was compiled using Microsoft Access.) The first table contained the forename and surname of the individual, country of origin, country of residence, ministerial status, age, level of education and denomination. The second table contained all the questionnaire answers as numbers from 1 to 5 and were uniquely identified by the individual identification number and the date. (The date was a choice field containing three options: Pre-test, Post-test, and Follow-up). Questionnaire answers from table two are summarised in the analysis of individual questions in chapter 5.

Analysing the Results

A purely numerical approach has limitations because of the different responses available to the questions. Since the responses were arranged as in a normal Likert scale, an initial method of weighting the responses was attempted by multiplying the number who ticked the "5" box by 5, the "4" box by 4, the "3" by 3 and so on. Adding these totals together and dividing by the number of delegates answering each question gave a resultant score which allowed the different answers to be compared. A weighted result of "1" would then have meant that the majority of delegates felt very negatively about that topic; a response of "5" would have indicated a very positive response. However, it was found that this method blurred many of the statistics. For example, a final weighted response of "3" could have meant that no delegates came with any opinion at all, or that half the delegates felt very negatively and the other half very positively.

Hence a further refinement of the results was made to group the responses into three categories, which can be generally described as positive, neutral and negative. The raw data was converted into percentages so the difference in responses for each of the three "lumped" categories between Pre-test, Post-test and Follow-up could be easily seen. Using this method highlighted any changes in the percentage responses very clearly, without any of the ambiguity which the previous method produced as explained above. Using this "lumping" method was also advantageous for another reason. The five parts of each response scale were not always even. For example, in the very first question the middle response "frequently" was probably more biased towards the positive than to the negative. Hence it was not a truly neutral response.

By taking each question individually, and "lumping" positives into one category and negatives into another, it was easier to identify the middle ground. The analysis thus highlighted how the delegates' views changed as a result of the seminar. The detailed structure for this refinement is given for each question in chapter 5.

Two approaches were made. The first considering individual questions in which there was a considerable shift in opinions, and the second by grouping a number of questions on a particular theme. This second phase demonstrated changes of opinion in six of the more predominant themes of SLSW. This is presented in both tabular and mini-chart form. The six themes are: the role of fasting; the practice of intercessory prayer; the concept of territorial spirits; the role of speaking in tongues in spiritual warfare, the main beliefs of SLSW; and the principal practices of SLSW. By taking all the data and individual post-course testimonies, it was possible to identify and correlate any changes in thinking and attitude. The testimonies were compared with the results of the post-course questionnaire.

CHAPTER 5

STATISTICAL RESULTS

TABLES

ILLUSTRATIONS

Page

Introduction

The following is a report on a series of questionnaires completed by delegates who attended a four day seminar entitled "Spiritual Warfare," which was held at Peniel Church in Brentwood, England from 26 February to 1 March 2001. The purpose was to examine the rationale and methodology currently being propagated as Strategic Level Spiritual Warfare (SLSW) in the light of biblical and theological truth and against the experience of history. The fundamental question to be addressed was whether or not such practices are biblical. The seminar therefore posed questions from a biblical point of view, such as, "Is there a hierarchy of evil spirits?" "How much control do evil spirits exert on mankind?" "Are the current practices of fasting, intercessory prayer, and prayer evangelism necessary?" "What is the true meaning of prayer?" "To what extent have eschatological considerations impacted the church's view of evangelism?" In order to evaluate the impact of the seminar teaching, questionnaires were completed by the delegates both before and after the course, and a final questionnaire was applied some two months later.

Applied Project

Review of the Seminar Teaching

The seminar emphasised the conclusions already outlined in chapter 2 that the battlefield is in the mind and the only issue for a Christian is obedience to the King of Kings. Thus SLSW, in the sense of engaging demonic forces in a spiritual conflict, is a complete non-issue. There is no foundation in the Old Testament for this practice, nor any indication that the devil has any intrinsic power or authority. Satan's only weapon is deception and his only sphere of influence that which God permits for His own eternal purposes.

In the New Testament the picture is similar; there is no evidence to suggest that Christians are called to engage in an on-going conflict with spiritual forces in the cosmic realm. The Scripture is quite clear in its teaching that Christ defeated Satan completely at Calvary and that Christians have been freed from his power. He is a conquered enemy, he is bound, he is already judged, and he is to be cast out of this world and into the lake of fire. He is not a rival of equivalent power to God; rather, he is totally subordinate.

In terms of evangelism, revival in the early church is always directly connected with the word of God, spoken and applied to hearts in the power of the Spirit of God. Its success requires none of the elements of SLSW. Thus, there is very little space given to discussing demonic activity in the Pauline epistles; the primary focus, in respect to both evangelism and the growth in maturity of individual Christians, is on the choices and actions taken by people themselves. In his opposition to this process, the operation of the devil is to blind the minds of men. It is, therefore, the battle for truth which constitutes the great fight of faith, in which the Christian's only weapon is the sword of the Spirit, which is the word of God. Its purpose is, "casting down imaginations and every high thing that exalteth itself against the knowledge of God, and bringing into captivity every thought to the obedience of Christ" (2 Cor. 10:5). Prayer, however, is not a spiritual weapon, nor is it an accompaniment to spiritual warfare; it is an expression of the Christian's intimate relationship with the Father.

History demonstrates that Christian doctrine and experience must be firmly grounded in the word of Truth. It could be argued that the Church entered its darkest age when it abandoned the supremacy of the authority of Scripture, thus allowing the entrance of superstition and witchcraft. Unfortunately, the weakness of the recent Pentecostal-Charismatic tradition has been the paucity of associated biblical exegesis and doctrinal understanding. Increasingly, experience-based analysis rather than truth has become the touchstone of the Charismatic world, and Christendom today is in danger of slipping once more into the spiritual dark ages.

The seminar also covered, as contained in chapter 3, a review of the contemporary teaching associated with SLSW. The whole practice of SLSW concerns strategies for unseating or "pulling down" territorial spirits as a pre-requisite to the successful advancement of the gospel. Consideration, therefore, was given to the supposed biblical validation for the entire concept of territoriality and to the various techniques which are advocated to depose them (including naming the spirits, spiritual mapping, identificational repentance and warfare prayer/intercession). On the basis of a systematic appraisal of the relevant literature, it was shown that the rationale for SLSW stands on extremely shaky biblical and theological foundations. Where scriptural authority is claimed, this tends to be on the basis of proof texts which are manipulated to support the various hypotheses, and Scripture itself is viewed through the subjective lens of experience. It was demonstrated that most of the validation for SLSW is drawn from extra-biblical sources and empirical evidence which is largely unconfirmed.

The seminar teaching also identified the main influences which undergird SLSW methodology, namely, hermeneutical approach, worldview and personal observation and experience. It was also shown that SLSW is not, as its proponents would claim, a new methodology but a recurring phenomenon. In this context, reference was made to the life and work of Frank W. Sandford, who in the early 1900s purchased ships to sail around the seven continents engaging in intercessory prayer to break the stranglehold of Satan's power over the nations. In the modern day, Wagner has published a six-book "Prayer Warrior" series, and, together with Ted Haggard, he is the co-director of the World Prayer Center in Colorado which holds a 24-hour prayer vigil. Ambulatory prayer has resulted in planes being chartered to engage in warfare prayer as they fly above supposed territorial spirits, to bind and pull them down. All this is strikingly similar to Sandford's activities, including the restoration of apostles to the Church.

The author concluded by turning the delegates' attention to the facts of the new covenant and the reality of redemption in Christ as a finished work at Calvary. Christians have actually been translated from the authority of Satan and birthed into the very family of God. The realities of the new creation were taught, including righteousness in Christ, the indwelling Christ making the believer a conqueror in every situation, and fellowship with the Father.

Method of Measuring Results of the Seminar

To ascertain the effectiveness of the seminar, all the delegates were asked to complete the same questionnaire on three separate occasions; namely, before they came to the seminar, immediately afterwards, and again two months later. A strong point of this method is that it enables the reader to see how the thinking of these delegates changed as a direct result of the seminar, and whether this change continued for some time afterwards. From this point on, the three occasions of completing the questionnaire will be referred to as the Pre-test, the Post-test, and the Follow-up. The numbers of delegates completing the questionnaire on each occasion were:

Pre-test	
Date 26/2/01	28
Post-test	
Date 1/3/01	27
Follow-up	
Date 8/5/01	19

The results are analysed in the following pages. However, it must be appreciated that as the Follow-up test involved only 19 delegates, care must be taken in using this particular group of percentages for the purposes of comparison.

Analysis of Results

The questionnaire was divided under six different headings, as follows:

A. What sources do you use for spiritual insight / inspiration?
B. Basis of successful evangelism.
C. Factors contributing to a lack of church growth.
D. Spirits and demons.
E. Spiritual warfare.
F. Role of speaking in tongues.

The six topics covered a total of 42 questions, with different numbers of questions in each topic. Although each question had five possible responses, the style of the responses varied from question to question, so the delegates were not tempted to always give the same level of response. Because of this variation in the question style they have been analysed individually. However, to do this for all 42 questions would not only have been cumbersome, but would also tend to hide important trends. For this reason only questions where a significant number of delegates changed their thinking will be analysed in detail. The question then arose as to how big a change would be statistically significant. As a rule of thumb, a shift of 30 percent was decided upon. This implied a 15 percent drop coupled with a 15 percent rise. Since 15 percent of 28 is only 4 delegates it was felt that to take less than this would be inappropriate.

Topic 5 on "Spiritual Warfare" produced some of the biggest changes in delegates' thinking, and, since this was also the title of the seminar, it has been analysed first. Questions are numbered according to their order in the questionnaire. To analyse each question two tables have been drawn. For the purposes of illustration the tables for question 28, which is the first question in the Spiritual Warfare topic, and the first to be analysed, have been reproduced below:

Question 28. What is your view of the need for strategic level spiritual warfare?

Table 1. Answers to Question 28 Showing Number of Delegates (as sample)

	Not necessary	Rarely necessary	No opinion	Necessary	Very necessary
Pre-test	8	3	3	11	3
Post-test	20	2	4	1	0
Follow-up	16	2	1	0	0

Table 2. Percentages and Changes to Question 28 (as sample)

	Pre-test	Post-test	Post – Pre	General change	Follow-up	Follow - Post	General change
Not necessary	28	74	+46		84	+10	
Rarely necessary	11	7	-4	+42	11	+4	+14
No opinion	11	15	+4	+4	5	-10	-10
Necessary	39	4	-35		0	-4	
Very necessary	1	0	-11	-46	0	0	-4

Column 1

Column 2-6

Column 7

Table 1 is fairly self-explanatory. Underneath the title are the possible responses for this question i.e.

- Not necessary
- Rarely necessary
- No opinion
- Necessary
- Very necessary

It can be seen that, in the Pre-test, 8 delegates felt that SLSW was "not necessary," 3 felt it was "rarely necessary" and so on.

In table 2 the raw data of table 1 has been converted into percentages, which can be found in column 1 for the Pre-test, column 2 for the Post-test, and column 5 for the Follow-up. Column 3 (Post – Pre) gives the differences between columns 1 and 2 i.e. the

Post-test percent minus the Pre-test percent. Column 6 (Follow – Post) gives the Follow-up percent minus the Post-test percent. This demonstrated how the responses changed over the three tests.

However, it was also useful to see the percentages of delegates who had generally positive or negative opinions concerning each question. To assess this some of the percentage responses for each question have been added together. To group them more generally, the percentage responses for "not necessary" and "rarely necessary" have been added together to give the negative opinion (28 + 11 =39 percent for the Pre-test, in Table 2, column 1). Similarly, "necessary" and "very necessary" have been added together to give the positive opinion (39 + 11 =50 percent for the Pre-test, in table 2, column 1). These figures are then shown in charts for each question. The 39 percent and 50 percent can be seen at the top of the first bars in each of the charts for question 28. The charts show at a glance how the general positive or negative opinions changed as a result of the seminar. These "general changes" are also shown in table 2 in columns 4 and 7.

"Lumping" responses together in this way naturally loses some of the statistical detail. For example, in the Follow-up there may have been some "bounce back" from one level to another. However, any large "bounce back" would still have shown up in the lumped categories, and to have kept all five categories separate would have resulted in complicated tables from which the changes in opinion would have been more difficult to identify.

Consideration was given to use of Chi Squared (χ^2) analysis but this was deemed inappropriate because the total frequency was less than 50.[1]

Analysis of Spiritual Warfare Topic

The questions in this topic were arranged in five pairs. The first question of each pair referred to a belief in some aspect of SLSW,

---

[1] For further consideration of this problem refer to Jane Miller, *Statistics for Advanced Level* (Cambridge: Cambridge University Press, 1989), 303-19. She states, "The χ^2-test should only be used when the sampling distribution of χ^2 approximates closely to a χ^2 distribution. The conditions for this are:
(i) the total frequency is not less than 50,
(ii) the expected class frequencies are not less than 5" (p. 305).

and the second referred to the frequency of engaging in the associated practice. To analyse the responses to the topic it was easier to separate the "belief" questions from the "frequency" questions.

Belief Questions for Spiritual Warfare

Question 28. What is your view of the need for strategic level spiritual warfare?

Table 3. Answers to Question 28 Showing Number of Delegates

	Not necessary	Rarely necessary	No opinion	Necessary	Very necessary
Pre-test	8	3	3	11	3
Post-test	20	2	4	1	0
Follow-up	16	2	1	0	0

Table 4. Percentages and Changes to Question 28

	Pre-test	Post-test	Post – Pre	General change	Follow-up	Follow - Post	General change
Not necessary	28	74	+46		84	+10	
Rarely necessary	11	7	-4	+42	11	+4	+14
No opinion	11	15	+4	+4	5	-10	-10
Necessary	39	4	-35		0	-4	
Very necessary	11	0	-11	-46	0	0	-4

Table 4 shows that, before the seminar, 50 percent of the delegates (39 + 11 in column 1) felt that strategic level spiritual warfare was "necessary" or "very necessary," and only 39 percent (28 + 11) felt it was "not necessary," or "rarely necessary;" i.e. many delegates had positive feelings about the need for SLSW. By the end of the seminar the figures had reversed quite dramatically. Those feeling it was "necessary" or "very necessary" had fallen by 46 percent (bottom figure in column 4), and there was a further 4 percent fall (bottom figure in column 7) by the Follow-up time. Immediately after the seminar (column 2) only 4 percent felt SLSW was "necessary" and none felt it was "very necessary." By the Follow-up time none of the delegates had any positive belief at all, as indicated by the two zero scores at the bottom of column 5.

Figure 1. Charts for Question 28

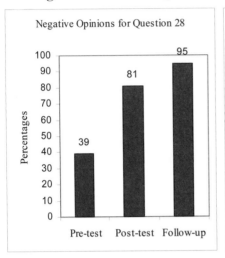

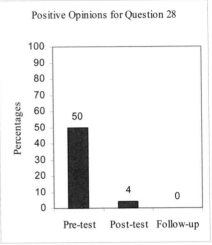

These charts illustrate the very large change in delegates' thinking over the course of the seminar, and the next few months. Before the seminar, the positive feeling about SLSW was at 50 percent, and only 39 percent felt negative about it. The sharp increase in the negative opinions, and the corresponding decrease in the positive ones, demonstrates that the seminar clearly convinced most delegates that SLSW is not a biblical concept.

Question 30. How much value do you place on warfare prayer?

Table 5. Answers to Question 30 Showing Number of Delegates

	No value	Little value	No opinion	Moderate value	Considerable value
Pre-test	7	2	4	7	8
Post-test	15	5	5	2	0
Follow-up	13	3	1	2	0

Table 6. Percentages and Changes to Question 30

	Pre-test	Post-test	Post - Pre	General change	Follow-up	Follow - Post	General change
No value	25	55	+30	+42	68	+13	+10
Little value	7	19	+12		16	-3	
No opinion	14	19	+5	+5	5	-14	-14
Moderate value	25	7	-18	-47	11	+4	+4
Considerable value	29	0	-29		0	0	

Before the seminar the majority of delegates (54 percent) placed "moderate" or "considerable value" on warfare prayer. This was comprised of 25 percent who placed "moderate value" on it, and an even higher number, 29 percent, who considered it to be of "considerable value" (two figures at the bottom of column 1). By the end of the seminar, the figures were 7 percent for "moderate value" (column 2), and 0 percent for "considerable value;" this represented a fall in the positive opinion of some 47 percent (column 4). The Follow-up figure for "moderate value" is 11 percent (column 5), with the "considerable value" remaining at zero.

The number placing "little" or "no value" on warfare prayer before the seminar was 32 percent (25 + 7 in column 1). This rose to 74 percent immediately after the seminar (55 + 19 in column 2), which was an increase of 42 percent (column 4). By Follow-up time the negative opinion had increased by a further 10 percent (column 7).

Figure 2. Charts for Question 30

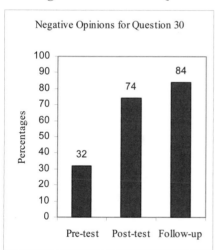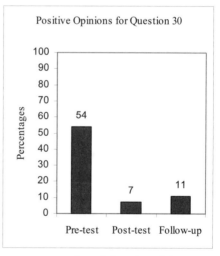

The charts illustrate that the importance placed by the delegates on the value of warfare prayer dropped dramatically after the seminar teaching. There was a very big change in their thinking. From a largely positive attitude towards the value of warfare prayer they became convinced there was "little" or "no value" to it at all.

Question 32. How effective do you believe prayer marches are?

Table 7. Answers to Question 32 Showing Number of Delegates

	Not effective	Not very effective	No opinion	Moderately effective	Very effective
Pre-test	5	7	4	9	3
Post-test	16	4	5	2	0
Follow-up	8	10	0	1	0

Table 8. Percentages and Changes to Question 32

	Pre-test	Post-test	Post - Pre	General change	Follow-up	Follow - Post	General change
Not effective	18	59	+41		42	-17	
Not very effective	25	15	-10	+31	53	+38	+21
No opinion	14	19	+5	+5	0	-19	-19
Moderately effective	32	7	-25		5	-2	
Very effective	11	0	-11	-36	0	0	-2

Before the seminar the negative and positive opinions were equal at 43 percent each (18 + 25, and 32 + 11 in column 1). The result of the seminar was to push the negative opinion to 74 percent (59 + 15 in column 2) in the Post-test figures, which was a rise of 31 percent (column 4). It then rose further to 95 percent (42 + 53 in column 5), a further rise of 21 percent (column 7), in the Follow-up results. The positive opinion dropped to 7 percent (column 2), and then 5 percent (column 5). After the seminar no one expressed the belief that prayer marches were "very effective," and only a small number felt they were even "moderately effective."

The charts on the following page show a very large increase in the negative opinion about the effectiveness of prayer marches. There is a corresponding decrease in the positive opinion. Most of the delegates were clearly convinced that prayer marches are not biblical, and this persuasion continued, as is reflected in the Follow-up percentages.

Figure 3. Charts for Question 32

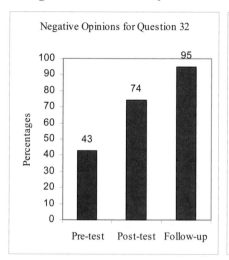
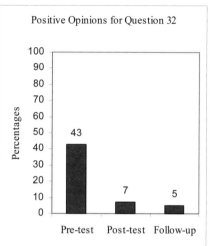

Question 34. Do you believe in the existence of territorial spirits?

Table 9. Answers to Question 34 Showing Number of Delegates

	Disbelieve strongly	Disbelieve	No opinion	Believe	Believe strongly
Pre-test	2	4	8	11	3
Post-test	10	8	5	4	0
Follow-up	5	9	3	2	0

Table 10. Percentages and Changes to Question 34

	Pre-test	Post-test	Post - Pre	General change	Follow-up	Follow - Post	General change
Disbelieve strongly	7	37	+30	+46	26	-11	+6
Disbelieve	14	30	+16		47	+17	
No opinion	29	18	-11	-11	16	-2	-2
Believe	39	15	-24	-35	11	-4	-4
Believe strongly	11	0	-11		0	0	

The belief in the existence of territorial spirits was very strong before the seminar. Some 50 percent held positive opinions (39 + 11 in column 1), as opposed to 21 percent negative (7 + 14 in column 1) i.e. more than twice the number believed in them compared with those who did not.

After the seminar the picture was very different. The "disbelief" figures more than trebled to 67 percent (37 + 30 in column 2), which was a total increase of 46 percent (column 4). By the Follow-up time it had increased by a further 6 percent to 73 percent (26 + 47 in column 5). The "belief" figure fell sharply to 15 percent, with no one recording any "strong belief" (column 2) and by the Follow-up time it had fallen by a further 4 percent to 11 percent (columns 7 and 5), again with no one "believing strongly."

It is worth noting that this question had the highest Pre-test "no opinion" response (29 percent in column 1). More delegates were unsure about this question than any other. The percentage response dropped down to 18 percent after the seminar (column 2), and then to 16 percent by the Follow-up time (column 5). Since the main swing was to disbelieve in the existence of territorial spirits, this would include many of those who were originally unsure.

Figure 4. Charts for Question 34

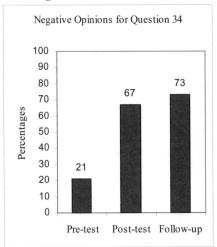
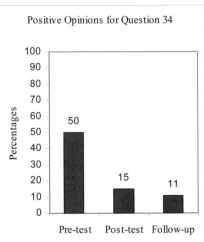

Before the seminar the charts show the large number of delegates who believed in the existence of territorial spirits (50 percent). By the end of the seminar the situation was completely reversed. The increase in negative opinion, and the decrease in the positive, is very marked.

Question 36. Do you believe it is possible to repent on behalf of another person?

Table 11. Answers to Question 36 Showing Number of Delegates

	Disbelieve strongly	Disbelieve	No opinion	Believe	Believe strongly
Pre-test	16	4	1	7	0
Post-test	12	11	1	3	0
Follow-up	11	7	1	0	0

Table 12. Percentages and Changes to Question 36

	Pre-test	Post-test	Post - Pre	General change	Follow-up	Follow - Post	General change
Disbelieve strongly	57	44	-13	+14	58	+14	+10
Disbelieve	14	41	+27		37	-4	
No opinion	4	4	0	0	5	+1	+1
Believe	25	11	-14		0	-11	
Believe strongly	0	0	0	-14	0	0	-11

This is the only one of the belief questions where the delegates were not initially more inclined towards a positive opinion. The negative feeling was already high at 71 percent (57 + 14 in column 1), but this was strengthened to 85 percent (44 + 41 in column 2), and then to 95 percent (58 + 37 in column 5) as a result of the seminar teaching. There was never any "strong belief," but by the Follow-up time there was no positive feeling at all (two zeros in column 5).

Figure 5. Charts for Question 36

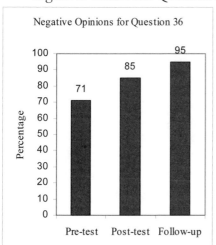
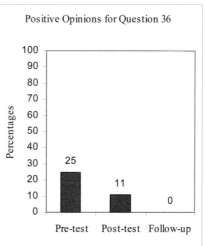

The charts show that, although the negative opinion was already high to start with, it still increased quite substantially as a result of the seminar; from 71 percent to 95 percent is an overall increase of 24 percent. The positive opinion dropped overall by 25 percent to zero.

Once again, of the delegates who had positive beliefs about the possibility of repenting on behalf of another person or region, most of them felt after the seminar that they could no longer continue with these beliefs.

Frequency of Practice Questions for Spiritual Warfare

The responses for these questions vary as to how many of the responses are positive or negative. They have been divided into "no practice" and "frequent practice."

Question 29. How frequently do you engage in spiritual warfare?

Table 13. Answers to Question 29 Showing Number of Delegates

	Never	Occasionally	Monthly	Weekly	Daily
Pre-test	7	11	8	2	0
Post-test	14	9	2	2	0
Follow-up	11	7	1	1	0

Table 14. Percentages and Changes to Question 29

	Pre-test	Post-test	Post - Pre	General change	Follow-up	Follow - Post	General change
Never	25	53	+28	+28	58	+5	+5
Occasionally	39	33	-6	-6	37	+4	+4
Monthly	29	7	-22		5	-2	
Weekly	7	7	0	-22	0	-7	-9
Daily	0	0	0		0	0	

"Monthly," "weekly," and "daily" are all fairly positive so they have been taken together as the "frequent practice" responses. "Never" is "no practice," while "occasionally" has been taken as the neutral ground.

Before the seminar only 25 percent (column 1) of the delegates said they would "never" engage in spiritual warfare but 36 percent (29 + 7 in column 1) practiced it fairly "frequently." This position changed greatly as a result of the seminar, with 53 percent (column 2) and later, 58 percent (column 5) saying they would "never" engage in it. This matches the change in their opinions as to the need for SLSW in question 28.

The charts show how the percentage of delegates who would "never" practice SLSW rose quite dramatically as a result of the seminar. Those who originally said they practiced it on any "frequent" basis can be seen to have fallen correspondingly.

Figure 6. Charts for Question 29

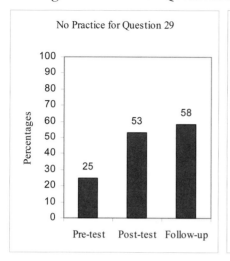

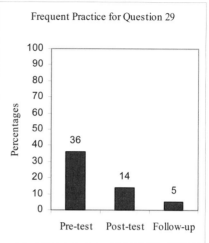

Question 31. How frequently do you engage in warfare prayer?

Table 15. Answers to Question 31 showing Number of Delegates

	Never	Occasionally	Monthly	Weekly	Daily
Pre-test	9	10	6	3	0
Post-test	16	9	1	1	0
Follow-up	13	6	0	0	0

Table 16. Percentages and Changes to Question 31

	Pre-test	Post-test	Post - Pre	General change	Follow-up	Follow - Post	General change
Never	32	59	+27	+27	68	+9	+9
Occasionally	36	33	-3	-3	32	-1	-1
Monthly	21	4	-17		0	-4	
Weekly	11	4	-7	-24	0	-4	-8
Daily	0	0	0		0	0	

The responses are the same as for question 29, and have been be analysed in the same way.

Before the seminar, 32 percent of delegates (21 + 11 in column 1) engaged in warfare prayer fairly "frequently." This was the same as the number who "never" practiced it (top figure in column 1). After the seminar those engaging in "frequent" practice dropped to 8 percent (4 + 4 in column 2), and then 0 percent (three zeros in column 5).

Figure 7. Charts for Question 31

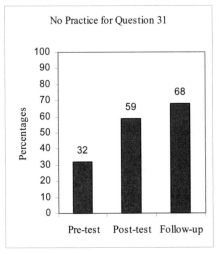
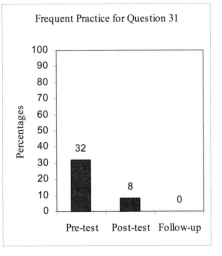

The sharp rise in "no practice" as a result of the seminar is easily seen from the first chart. The corresponding fall in "frequent practice" can be seen from the other chart.

Once again this matches the change in thinking related to question 30 as to the value the delegates placed on warfare prayer.

Question 33. How frequently are you involved in prayer marches?

Table 17. Answers to Question 33 showing Number of Delegates

	Inappropriate	Never	Occasionally	On most opportunities	At every opportunity
Pre-test	2	13	9	1	3
Post-test	6	16	4	0	1
Follow-up	3	13	3	0	0

Table 18. Percentages and Changes to Question 33

	Pre-test	Post-test	Post – Pre	General change	Follow-up	Follow - Post	General change
Inappropriate	7	22	+15	+28	16	-6	+3
Never	46	59	+13		68	+9	
Occasionally	32	15	-17	-17	16	+1	+1
On most opportunities	4	0	-4	-11	0	0	-4
At every opportunity	11	4	-7		0	-4	

"Inappropriate" and "never" have both been designated as "no practice," while "on most opportunities" and "at every opportunity" have been taken as "frequent practice."

Before the seminar, 53 percent of delegates said they would not engage in the practice of prayer marches, i.e. 7 percent said prayer marches were "inappropriate" and 46 percent said they would "never" be involved in them (column 1). After the seminar these figure rose to 22 percent, and 59 percent (column 2), representing a general increase of 28 percent (column 4). In the Follow-up figures (column 5), the number feeling it was "inappropriate" had dropped to 16 percent, while "never" continued to rise to 68 percent. None of the delegates replying to the Follow-up questionnaire felt they could be involved on "most" or "every opportunity" (two zeros in column 5).

An interesting set of figures are the "occasionally" ones. The Pre-test percentage was 32 percent (column 1), and this dropped to 15 percent after the seminar (column 2), and stayed fairly steady afterwards. Since the "frequent practice" dropped sharply, the fall in the "occasional" practice would mean these delegates had moved towards "no practice."

Figure 8. Charts for Question 33

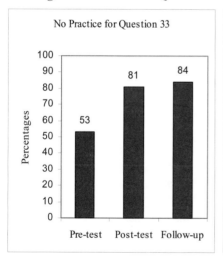
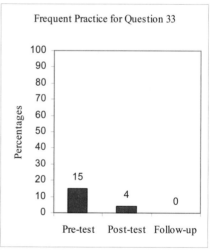

The charts show the large rise in "no practice," and the fact that, even though the "frequent practice" was low before the seminar, it fell almost to zero afterwards. As a result of the seminar, very few delegates felt they could be involved in any way. This matches the answers to question 32.

Question 35. How frequently do you take a stand against territorial spirits?

Table 19. Answers to Question 35 showing Number of Delegates

	Inappropriate	Never	Occasionally	Frequently	Very frequently
Pre-test	3	8	11	6	0
Post-test	6	15	6	0	0
Follow-up	5	11	3	0	0

Table 20. Percentages and Changes to Question 35

	Pre-test	Post-test	Post - Pre	General change	Follow-up	Follow - Post	General change
Inappropriate	11	22	+11	+38	26	+4	+6
Never	29	56	+27		58	+2	
Occasionally	39	22	-17	-17	16	-6	-6
Frequently	21	0	-21	-21	0	0	0
Very frequently	0	0	0		0	0	

Once again, the table shows a very large shift away from the practice of taking a stand against territorial spirits. Before the seminar 40 percent gave their response as "inappropriate" or "never" (11 + 29 in column 1). This figure rose to 78 percent (22 + 56 in column 2) immediately after the seminar, which was an increase of 38 percent (column 4). By the Follow-up time the figure was 84 percent (26 + 58 in column 5). After the seminar no delegates felt they could practice this "frequently" or "very frequently" (two zeros in columns 2 and 5). Their responses match the answers to question 34.

Figure 9. Charts for Question 35

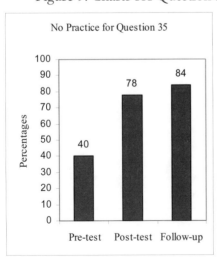

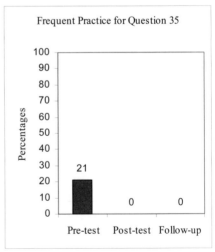

The first chart shows the large move away from the practice of taking a stand against territorial spirits. The other chart shows that, although the number who would take a stand frequently against territorial spirits did not start at a high level, even this dropped right to zero by the end of the seminar and stayed there.

Question 37. How frequently do you repent on behalf of another person or region?

Table 21. Answers to Question 37 Showing Number of Delegates

	Inappropriate	Never	Occasionally	Frequently	Very frequently
Pre-test	6	15	5	2	0
Post-test	8	15	4	0	0
Follow-up	6	12	1	0	0

Table 22. Percentages and Changes to Question 37

	Pre-test	Post-test	Post - Pre	General change	Follow-up	Follow - Post	General change
Inappropriate	21	30	+9	+10	32	+2	+10
Never	54	55	+1		63	+8	
Occasionally	18	15	-3	-3	5	-10	-10
Frequently	7	0	-7	-7	0	0	0
Very frequently	0	0	0		0	0	

This question produced the lowest positive response of all the Pre-test figures.

However, the negative feeling still increased as a result of the seminar. The Post-test responses demonstrate that after the seminar no delegates felt they could "frequently" or "very frequently" repent on behalf of another person or region (column 2). This persuasion continued (column 5). For those who felt they could do it "occasionally," the original figure (18 percent in column 1) had fallen to 5 percent by the Follow-up time (column 5).

The first chart shows that the number of delegates who felt they would not repent for another person or region "very frequently" was quite high, even before the seminar. However, this figure rose further as a result of the seminar and the small number in the second chart who practiced with any high frequency disappeared completely. Once again the responses match those given in relation to question 36.

Figure 10. Charts for Question 37

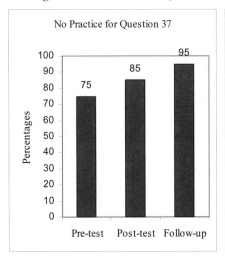
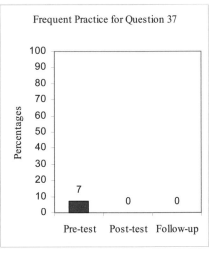

Significant Changes in Other Topics

Questions in other topics were analysed where there was a significant change in the delegates' thinking as a result of the seminar. Thus, questions showing a swing of more than 30 percent from the Pre-test to the Post-test have been included.

Basis of Successful Evangelism

The questions in this topic had the following possible responses:

No opinion   Not   Fairly   Important   Very
              important   important   important

In each one "not important" is taken as the negative opinion. "Fairly important," "important," and "very important" are taken together as the positive opinion.

Question 12. Intercessory Prayer

Table 23. Answers to Question 12 Showing Number of Delegates

	No opinion	Not important	Fairly important	Important	Very important
Pre-test	0	7	3	12	6
Post-test	3	17	4	2	1
Follow-up	3	11	4	1	0

Table 24. Percentages and Changes to Question 12

	Pre-test	Post-test	Post - Pre	General change	Follow-up	Follow - Post	General change
No opinion	0	11	+11	+11	16	+5	+5
Not important	25	63	+38	+38	58	-5	-5
Fairly important	10	15	+5		21	+6	
Important	43	7	-36	-49	5	-2	0
Very important	22	4	-18		0	-4	

Before the seminar 75 percent (10 + 43 + 22 in column 1) of delegates felt that intercessory prayer was "fairly" to "very important" as a basis for evangelism. After the seminar this figure had fallen to 26 percent (15 +7 +4 in column 2). The figure was the same for the Follow-up time (21 + 5 in column 5), with no one then of the opinion that it was "very important." The very large fall (49 percent in column 4) in the number of delegates who felt it was "important" or "very important" shows that the seminar had a profound effect on how the delegates viewed intercessory prayer as a basis for evangelism.

The fall in importance, and the corresponding increase in unimportance are clearly seen in the following charts.

Figure 11. Charts for Question 12

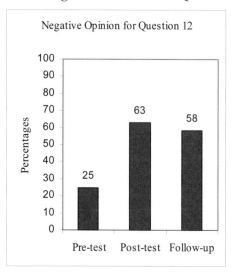

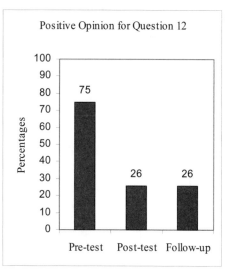

Question 13. Fasting

Table 25. Answers to Question 13 Showing Number of Delegates

	No opinion	Not important	Fairly important	Important	Very important
Pre-test	2	13	8	2	3
Post-test	3	21	3	0	0
Follow-up	2	14	3	0	0

Table 26. Percentages and Changes to Question 13

	Pre-test	Pos-test	Post - Pre	General change	Follow-up	Follow - Post	General change
No opinion	7	11	+4	+4	10	-1	-1
Not important	47	78	+31	+31	74	-4	-4
Fairly important	29	11	-18		16	+5	
Important	7	0	-7	-35	0	0	+5
Very important	10	0	-10		0	0	

Before the seminar 46 percent (29 + 7 + 10 in column 1) felt that fasting was a "very important," "important" or "fairly important" part of successful evangelism. After the seminar this had fallen to 11 percent (column 2). The Follow-up figures show a slight rise in this positive opinion to 16 percent (column 5), but only in respect to the somewhat qualified status of being "fairly important." In both the Post-test and Follow-up figures no delegate felt it was "important" or "very important." The increase in negative opinion, and the corresponding fall in the positive are clearly seen in the charts below.

Figure 12. Charts for Question 13

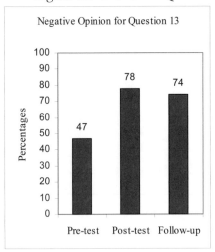

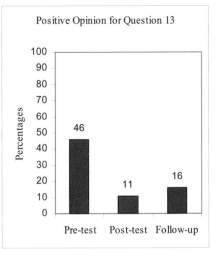

The charts again show how the importance of fasting as a basis for evangelism fell sharply as a result of the seminar. By the end of the seminar many of the delegates had changed their thinking, and accepted that fasting as part of evangelism is not a biblical concept.

Question 14. Binding demons

Table 27. Answers to Question 14 Showing Number of Delegates

	No opinion	Not important	Fairly important	Important	Very important
Pre-test	2	11	8	2	5
Post-test	2	20	3	1	1
Follow-up	1	17	1	0	0

Table 28. Percentages and Changes to Question 14

	Pre-test	Post-test	Post - Pre	General change	Follow-up	Follow - Post	General change
No opinion	7	7	0	0	5	-2	-2
Not important	39	74	+35	+35	90	+16	+16
Fairly important	29	11	-18		5	-6	
Important	7	4	-3	-35	0	-4	-14
Very important	18	4	-14		0	-4	

Before the seminar 39 percent of delegates (column 1) felt that binding demons as a basis for successful evangelism was "not important." This has to be compared with 54 percent (29 + 7 + 18 in column 1) who felt it was "fairly" to "very important." After the seminar the figures had changed dramatically with 74 percent (column2) now considering it to be "unimportant" (a rise of 35 percent, see column 3), while the "important" figures had dropped to only 19 percent (11 + 4 + 4 in column 2, which was a fall of 35 percent, bottom figure in column 4). It is easily seen from the Follow-up figures that this change in thinking continued to be strengthened. The charts below also illustrate the changes very well.

The charts show clearly the original "not important" responses of 39 percent rising to 74 percent and then even further to 90 percent. The bars on the right hand chart show the corresponding fall in the "fairly" to "very important" opinions.

Referring back to table 28, column 4, and also the "no opinion" row, it is interesting to note that the "no opinion" did not change. Accordingly, the whole 35 percent change went straight from the positive responses of "very important," "important" or "fairly important," directly to the negative response of "not important" (even if some moved to "no opinion," and some of the "no opinions" moved towards "important").

Figure 13. Charts for Question 14

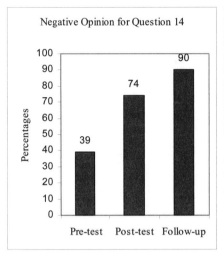
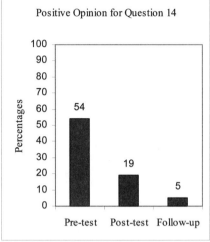

The result of the seminar was to convince many of the delegates that binding demons plays no role in evangelism.

Factors Contributing to a Lack of Church Growth

The questions in this topic had the following possible responses:

Totally irrelevant   Not a significant factor   Slight factor   A factor   Major factor

In each one "totally irrelevant" and "not a significant factor" have been taken together as the negative opinion. "A factor" and "major factor" have been grouped as the positive opinion.

Question 17. Inability of the church to combat social deprivation in the area

Table 29. Answers to Question 17 Showing Number of Delegates

	Totally irrelevant	Not a significant factor	Slight factor	A factor	Major factor
Pre-test	2	8	4	9	4
Post-test	3	14	8	2	0
Follow-up	3	8	3	4	1

Table 30. Percentages and Changes to Question 17

	Pre-test	Post-test	Post - Pre	General change	Follow-up	Follow - Post	General change
Totally irrelevant	7	11	+4	+26	16	+5	-5
Not a significant factor	30	52	+22		42	-10	
Slight factor	15	30	+15	+15	16	-14	-14
A factor	33	7	-26	-41	21	+14	+19
Major factor	15	0	-15		5	+5	

Before the seminar the percentage of delegates who felt the inability of the church to combat social deprivation was "a factor" contributing to lack of church growth was 48 percent (33 + 15 in column1). Immediately after the seminar this figure had fallen to 7 percent (column 2), a fall of 41 percent (column 4). This was one of the very few questions in the seminar where there was any real shift back again in the Follow-up. The positive opinion rose again to 26 percent (21 +5 in column 5). This was mainly due to some delegates changing to the more neutral "slight factor" which increased from 15 percent to 30 percent (columns 1 and 2) in the Pre and Post-tests. The position tended to revert again in the Follow-up (column 5). The charts below show the general increase in the negative opinion, and the corresponding increase in the positive results.

Figure 14. Charts for Question 17

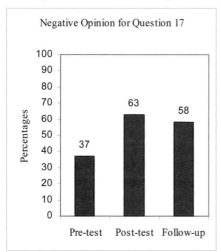
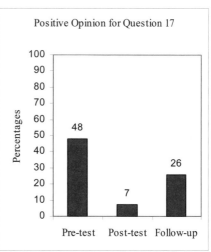

In question 21, most of the delegates came to the seminar with the strong opinion that "a major factor" contributing to a lack of church growth is the lack of a miracle ministry with signs and wonders following. This opinion was further strengthened by the seminar teaching. Other factors such as social deprivation were not seen to be so important in so far as church growth is concerned.

Question 18. Lack of intercessory prayer

Table 31. Answers to Question 18 Showing Number of Delegates

	Totally irrelevant	Not a significant factor	Slight factor	A factor	Major factor
Pre-test	4	5	4	13	1
Post-test	10	11	4	2	0
Follow-up	8	8	3	0	0

Table 32. Percentages and Changes to Question 18

	Pre-test	Post-test	Post - Pre	General change	Follow-up	Follow - Post	General change
Totally irrelevant	15	37	+22		42	+5	
				+44			+6
Not a significant factor	19	41	+22		42	+1	
Slight factor	15	15	0	0	16	+1	+1
A factor	47	7	-40		0	-7	
				-44			-7
Major factor	4	0	-4		0	0	

Before the seminar, 51 percent of delegates (47 + 4 in column 1), i.e. more than half, felt that lack of intercessory prayer was "a factor," or a "major factor" contributing to a lack of church growth. This figure fell dramatically to only 7 percent (column 2) after the seminar, with nobody considering it a "major factor." This was a fall in the positive opinion of 44 percent (column 4). The change in thinking continued and, by the Follow-up, no delegate even rated it "a factor." The negative opinions correspondingly rose from 34 percent (15 + 19 in column 1) to 78 percent (37 + 41 in column 2), and then to 84 percent (42 + 42 in column 5). The figures are clearly seen in the charts below.

Figure 15. Charts for Question 18

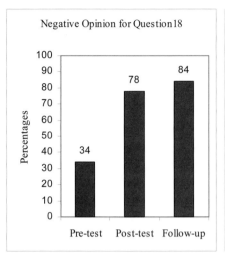

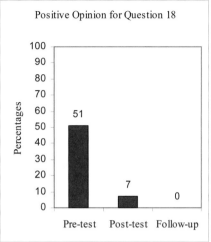

By the end of the seminar many of the delegates had changed their minds, and no longer considered the lack of intercessory prayer as a reason affecting church growth. The seminar had a profound effect on their thinking concerning this question. The changes in the responses to this question are similar to those for question 12, which dealt with the role of intercessory prayer in evangelism.

Question 19. Lack of prayer and fasting

Table 33. Answers to Question 19 Showing Number of Delegates

	Totally irrelevant	Not a significant factor	Slight factor	A factor	Major factor
Pre-test	5	8	5	7	2
Post-test	14	9	2	2	0
Follow-up	6	11	2	2	0

Table 34. Percentages and Changes to Question 19

	Pre-test	Post-test	Post - Pre	General change	Follow-up	Follow - Post	General change
Totally irrelevant	19	53	+34		32	-21	
Not a significant factor	29	33	+4	+38	58	+25	+4
Slight factor	19	7	-12	-12	10	+3	+3
A factor	26	7	-19		0	-7	
Major factor	7	0	-7	-26	0	0	-7

The negative opinion of "totally irrelevant" and "not a significant factor" before the seminar was 48 percent (19 + 29 in column 1). At the Post-test this had risen to 86 percent (53 + 33 in column 2), a rise of 38 percent (column 4); and in the Follow-up it was 90 percent (32 + 58 in column 5). The 33 percent who originally had positive opinions (26 + 7 in column 1) had fallen to 7 percent after the seminar (column 2), and none rated it as a "major factor." By the Follow-up test none even rated it as "a factor" (column 5).

Figure 16. Charts for Question 19

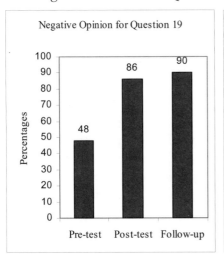
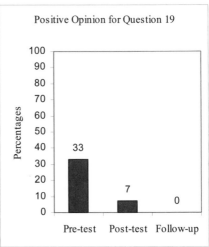

The charts show the steep increase in negative opinion as a result of the seminar, and the corresponding fall in the positive opinion. The result was to make most of the delegates conclude that lack of prayer and fasting is not a contributory factor to lack of church growth.

Question 20. Principalities and powers governing the area

Table 35. Answers to Question 20 Showing Number of Delegates

	Totally irrelevant	Not a significant factor	Slight factor	A factor	Major factor
Pre-test	9	4	6	6	2
Post-test	17	7	3	0	0
Follow-up	11	7	1	0	0

Table 36. Percentages and Changes to Question 20

	Pre-test	Post-test	Post - Pre	General change	Follow-up	Follow - Post	General change
Totally irrelevant	33	63	+30		58	-5	
Not a significant factor	15	26	+11	+41	37	+11	+6
Slight factor	22	11	-11	-11	5	-6	-6
A factor	22	0	-22		0	0	
Major factor	8	0	-8	-30	0	0	0

Before the seminar 30 percent of delegates (22 + 8 in column 1) felt positively about the fact that principalities and powers governing the area was "a factor" or a "major factor" contributing towards lack of church growth. Every one of these delegates had abandoned that position by the end of the seminar (two zeros in column 2). Conversely, 48 percent (33 + 15 in column 1) began with negative opinions about the question, i.e. it was "totally irrelevant," or "not a significant factor". This figure rose to 89 percent (63 + 26 in column 2) as a result of the seminar, an increase of 41 percent (column 4). Even the 22 percent in column 1 who felt it was "a slight factor" had reduced to 11 percent by the end of the seminar. The change in the negative and positive opinions is clearly illustrated in the charts below.

Figure 17. Charts for Question 20

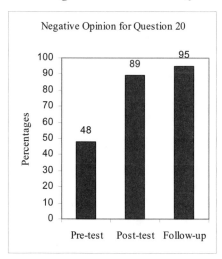
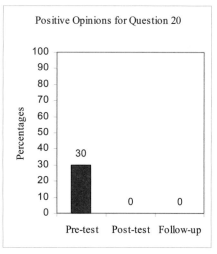

The overwhelming impact of the seminar was to destroy the notion that principalities and powers governing an area can be "a factor" or a "major factor" limiting church growth. The delegates, on the whole, were convinced that this concept is unbiblical.

Spirits and Demons

The responses to the questions in this topic were:

Disbelieve strongly   Disbelieve   No opinion   Believe   Believe strongly

They have been analysed on the basis of taking "disbelieve strongly" and "disbelieve" as the negative opinions, and "believe" and "believe strongly" as the positive ones.

Question 25. Do you believe some demons only come out by prayer and fasting?

Table 37. Answers to Question 25 Showing Number of Delegates

	Disbelieve strongly	Disbelieve	No opinion	Believe	Believe strongly
Pre-test	6	6	3	8	5
Post-test	11	9	5	2	0
Follow-up	6	10	2	1	0

Table 38. Percentages and Changes to Question 25

	Pre-test	Post-test	Post - Pre	General change	Follow-up	Follow - Post	General change
Disbelieve strongly	21	41	+20	+32	32	-9	+11
Disbelieve	21	33	+12		53	+20	
No opinion	11	19	+8	+8	10	-9	-9
Believe	29	7	-22	-40	5	-2	-2
Believe strongly	18	0	-18		0	0	

In the Pre-test the majority of delegates expressed a positive opinion in response to this question; 47 percent (29 + 18 in column 1) "believed," or "believed strongly" that some demons only come out by prayer and fasting. By contrast, only 42 percent (21 + 21 in column 1) "disbelieved," or "disbelieved strongly." By the end of the seminar, only 7 percent felt positively about it (column 2), with no one "believing strongly." This was a fall of 40 percent (column 4). The negative feeling had risen to 74 percent (41 + 33 in column 2) and it is noteworthy that of these, 41 percent now "disbelieved strongly." The negative opinion continued to increase to 85 percent (32 + 53 in column 5), while the positive opinion continued to fall to 5 percent, again with no one "believing strongly."

Figure 18. Charts for Question 25

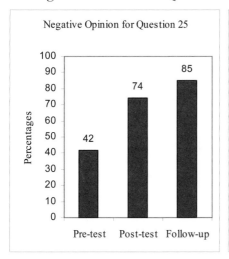
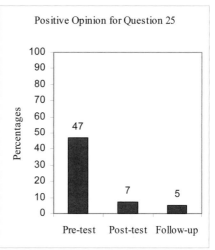

The charts show the enormous change in the delegates' opinions as a result of the seminar. From a starting position of a large positive percentage, most of the delegates came away convinced that prayer and fasting is "not necessary" for casting out demons.

Question 27. Do you believe that spirits have a hierarchical order?

Table 39. Answers to Question 27 Showing Number of Delegates

	Disbelieve strongly	Disbelieve	No opinion	Believe	Believe strongly
Pre-test	4	3	5	8	8
Post-test	6	11	7	3	0
Follow-up	3	6	7	2	1

Table 40. Percentages and Changes to Question 27

	Pre-test	Post-test	Post - Pre	General change	Follow-up	Follow - Post	General change
Disbelieve strongly	14	22	+8	+38	16	-6	-15
Disbelieve	11	41	+30		32	-9	
No opinion	17	26	+9	+9	37	+11	+11
Believe	29	11	-18	-47	10	-1	+4
Believe strongly	29	0	-29		5	+5	

There was initially a very high positive belief for this question. Over half the delegates (58 percent = 29 + 29 in column 1) "believed" or "believed strongly" that spirits have a hierarchical order. Only 25 percent (14 + 11 in column 1) "disbelieved" or "disbelieved strongly." The turn-around after the seminar was dramatic. The 58 percent positive fell to 11 percent (column 2), with nobody "believing strongly." This was a fall in the positive of 47 percent (column 4). The 25 percent negative opinion rose to 63 percent after the seminar (22 + 41 in column 2), a rise of 38 percent (column 4). There was a slight reversion in the Follow-up test, which was mainly due to an increased percentage of those who were "not sure" (37 percent for "no opinion" in column 5).

Figure 19. Charts for Question 27

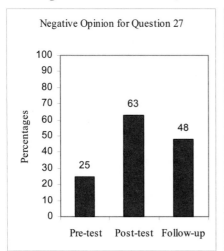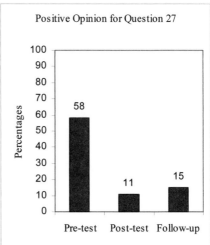

The charts show the overall rise in negative opinion, and the corresponding fall in the positive. From an initial position of mainly positive opinion, most of the delegates came away from the seminar convinced that the notion that spirits have a hierarchical order is not a biblical concept.

Role of Speaking in Tongues

In this topic the delegates were asked to respond with a number from 1 to 5 where

1 = "No role" ... 5 = "Very major role."

The questions will be analysed by taking 1 and 2 together as the mainly negative opinion, and taking 4 and 5 together as the mainly positive opinion.

Question 39. Rebuking evil powers

Table 41. Answers to Question 39 Showing Number of Delegates

	1 = No role	2	3	4	5 = Very major role
Pre-test	12	2	5	1	8
Post-test	21	1	3	0	2
Follow-up	17	1	1	0	0

Table 42. Percentages and Changes to Question 39

	Pre-test	Post-test	Post - Pre	General change	Follow-up	Follow - Post	General change
1 = No role	43	78	+35	+32	90	+12	+13
2	7	4	-3		5	+1	
3	18	11	-7	-7	5	-6	-6
4	4	0	-4	-25	0	0	-7
5 = Very major role	28	7	-21		0	-7	

A large number of delegates on the Pre-test (50 percent = 43 + 7 in column 1) already held a negative opinion i.e. that tongues plays "no role," or "very little role" in rebuking evil powers. Of these, the vast majority (43 percent in column 1) felt it had "no role" at all. However, this negative percentage became even higher as a result of the seminar, rising to 82 percent (78 + 4 in column 2), a rise of 32 percent (column 4). It was 95 percent (90 + 5 in column 5) by the Follow-up test. The positive opinion started at 32 percent (4 + 28 in column 1), fell to 7 percent after the seminar (column 2), and then to 0 percent (column 5) for the Follow-up test.

The charts show the shift away from the opinion that tongues can be used to rebuke evil powers. This view had already been rejected by 50 percent before the seminar, but their position was greatly strengthened by the seminar teaching. Very few delegates after the seminar felt it was a biblical concept.

Figure 20. Charts for Question 39

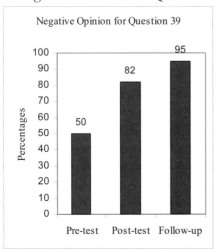
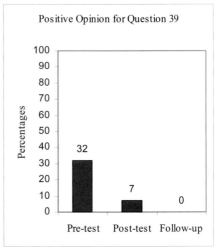

Question 41. Prophesying

Table 43. Answers to Question 41 Showing Number of Delegates

	1 = No role	2	3	4	5 = Very major role
Pre-test	2	2	7	5	12
Post-test	11	5	5	5	1
Follow-up	7	5	2	3	2

Table 44. Percentages and Changes to Question 41

	Pre-test	Post-test	Post - Pre	General change	Follow-up	Follow - Post	General change
1 = No role	7	42	+35	+46	37	-5	+3
2	7	18	+11		26	+8	
3	25	18	-7	-7	11	-7	-7
4	18	18	0		15	-3	
5 = Very major role	43	4	-39	-39	11	+7	+4

A large number of delegates before the seminar held the positive opinion that tongues can be used for prophesying (61 percent = 18 +43 in column 1). Of that 61 percent, 43 percent felt it played a "very major role" (the level 5 response). The seminar made an enormous difference. In the Post-test the 61 percent had fallen to 22 percent (18 + 4 in column 2).

Interestingly, the level 4 response stayed steady at 18 percent (columns 1 and 2), but the level 5 "very major role" fell to only 4 percent, a fall of 39 percent (column 4). The negative opinion delegates, i.e. those who felt tongues plays "no role," or "very little role," rose from a very small 14 percent (7 + 7 in column 1) to 60 percent (42 + 18 in column 2), a rise of 46 percent (column 4). Although the positive opinion rose again very slightly in the Follow-up test, so did the negative opinion.

Figure 21. Charts for Question 41

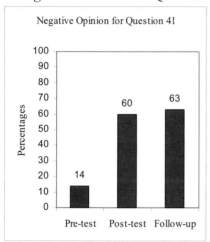
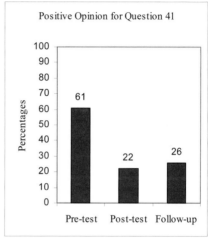

The charts show the small number (14 percent) who initially felt tongues should not be used for prophesying, and the large number (61 percent) who expressed the opposite opinion. The picture was very different after the seminar, showing that many delegates had been convinced it is not biblical to use tongues for prophesying.

Question 42. Pulling down strongholds

Table 45. Answers to Question 42 Showing Number of Delegates

	1 = No role	2	3	4	5 = Very major role
Pre-test	10	2	6	1	9
Post-test	21	2	3	1	0
Follow-up	16	1	2	0	0

Table 46. Percentages and Changes to Question 42

	Pre-test	Post-test	Post - Pre	General change	Follow-up	Follow - Post	General change
1 = No role	36	78	+42	+42	84	+6	+4
2	7	7	0		5	-2	
3	21	11	-10	-10	11	0	0
4	4	4	0		0	-4	
5 = Very major role	32	0	-32	-32	0	0	-4

Before the seminar 43 percent (36 + 7 in column 1) held the negative opinion that tongues has "no role" or "very little role" in pulling down strongholds. The effect of the seminar was to increase this percentage quite dramatically to 85 percent (78 + 7 in column 2), a rise of 42 percent (column 4); and 78 percent out of the 85 percent then felt that tongues plays "no role" at all in this question. The figure increased further to 89 percent (84 + 5 in column 5) in the Follow-up test. Those who initially had positive views on this question (36 percent = 4 + 32 in column 1) changed their minds almost entirely (only 4 percent in column 2, with no delegate giving it a "very major role"). By the Follow-up test nobody responded at levels 4 or 5 at all (two zeros in column 5). The "no opinion" (level 3 responses) percentages also fell from 21 percent in column 1 to 11 percent in column 2, and, since these must have gone towards the negative opinion, we see that many of the "unsure" delegates were also convinced.

Figure 22. Charts for Question 42

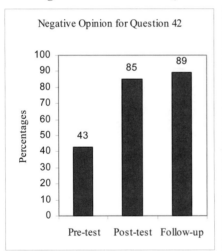
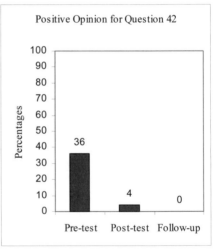

The charts show the large changes in the negative and positive responses. Although the positive opinion only started at 36 percent, it fell very sharply, and the substantial increase in the negative opinion shows that most delegates by the end of the seminar were convinced that pulling down strongholds by speaking in tongues is not a biblical concept.

Results Grouped by Theme

The themes considered were the role of fasting, the practice of intercessory prayer, the concept of territorial spirits, the role of speaking in tongues in spiritual warfare, and a summary of the main beliefs and practices of SLSW.

The wording of the response options varies between the questions, so in order to combine results a modified scale of "low, middle, high" was applied. The structure for this is given with each group, but it should be noted that in seeking to identify general trends there was some loss of detail. The raw data was initially combined and presented as a total number of responses, and then as percentages.

The Role of Fasting

The questions included in this theme were:

11. Fasting as a source of spiritual insight / inspiration
13. Fasting as a basis for successful evangelism
19. Lack of prayer and fasting as a factor contributing to the lack of church growth
25. Belief that some demons only come out by prayer and fasting

The responses were combined into "low, middle, high" as shown in table 43.

Table 47. The Role of Fasting - Responses

Re-scale	Wording of the original response options			
	Question 11	Question 13	Question 19	Question 25
Low	Never	Not important	Totally irrelevant	Disbelieve Strongly
Low			Not a significant factor	Disbelieve
Middle	Occasionally	No opinion	Slight factor	No opinion
High	Frequently	Fairly important	A factor	Believe
High	Very frequently	Important	Major factor	Believe strongly
High	Continuously	Very important		

Table 48. The Role of Fasting - Responses According to the Re-Scale.

| | Number in Pre-test | | | Number in Post-test | | | Number in Follow-up | | |
	Low	Middle	High	Low	Middle	High	Low	Middle	High
Q.11	11	11	6	11	13	3	11	8	0
Q.13	13	2	13	21	3	3	14	2	3
Q.19	13	5	9	23	2	2	17	2	0
Q.25	12	3	13	20	5	2	16	2	1
Total	49	21	41	75	23	10	58	14	4

Table 49. The Role of Fasting – Responses Expressed as Percentages

| | Percentage in Pre-test | | | Percentage in Post-test | | | Percentage in Follow-up | | |
	Low	Middle	High	Low	Middle	High	Low	Middle	High
Q.11	39	39	21	41	48	11	58	42	0
Q.13	46	7	46	78	11	11	74	11	16
Q.19	46	18	32	85	7	7	89	11	0
Q.25	43	11	46	74	19	7	84	11	5
Total	44	19	37	69	21	9	76	18	5

The final row in the table gives the average percentage responses to the four questions on the role of fasting. The percentage of delegates who viewed fasting as important reduced from 37 percent to 5 percent, a shift in belief of 32 percent.

The changes in delegates' views can be seen clearly in a diagram of the last row of data:

Figure 23. Charts for the Role of Fasting

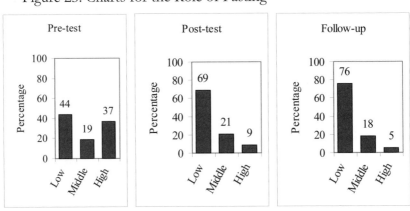

The percentage giving a "low" importance to the role of fasting increased from 44 percent before the seminar to 69 percent immediately after the seminar. It had attained a level of 76 percent in the Follow-up. Conversely, those attaching "high" importance to fasting dropped from 37 percent to 9 percent to 5 percent.

The Practice of Intercessory Prayer

The questions included in this theme were:

10. Intercessory prayer as a source of spiritual insight / inspiration
12. Intercessory prayer as a basis for successful evangelism
18. Lack of intercessory prayer as a factor contributing to the lack of church growth

The responses were combined into "low, middle, high" as shown in table 46.

Table 50. The Practice of Intercessory Prayer - Responses

	Wording of the original response options		
Re-scale	Question 10	Question 12	Question 18
Low	Never	No opinion	Totally irrelevant
Low			Not a significant factor
Middle	Occasionally	Not important	Slight factor
High	Frequently	Fairly important	A factor
High	Very frequently	Important	Major factor
High	Continuously	Very important	

Table 51. The Practice of Intercessory Prayer - Responses According to the Re-Scale

	Number in Pre-test			Number in Post-test			Number in Follow-up		
	Low	Middle	High	Low	Middle	High	Low	Middle	High
Q.10	5	7	16	11	5	11	11	5	3
Q.12	7	0	21	17	3	7	11	3	5
Q.18	10	4	14	21	4	2	16	3	0
Total	22	11	51	49	12	20	38	11	8

The majority of delegates considered the practice of intercessory prayer to be important prior to attending the seminar, as shown by the total of 51 responses out of 84 being in the "high" category in the Pre-test. Subsequent to the seminar and in the Follow-up the number of "high" responses fell considerably. The shift in viewpoint is shown more clearly when the same data is presented in percentages as in table 6.

Table 52. The Practice of Intercessory Prayer – Responses Expressed as Percentages

	Percentage in Pre-test			Percentage in Post-test			Percentage in Follow-up		
	Low	Middle	High	Low	Middle	High	Low	Middle	High
Q.10	18	25	57	41	19	41	58	26	16
Q.12	25	0	75	63	11	26	58	16	26
Q.18	36	14	50	78	15	7	84	16	0
Total	26	13	61	60	15	25	67	19	14

From the bottom line of the table, the percentage of delegates who considered the practice of intercessory prayer to be important fell from 61 percent prior to the seminar to 25 percent at the end of the seminar. The Follow-up results showed a further drop to a level where only 14 percent of delegates viewed intercessory prayer as important. A diagrammatic presentation of this shift is as follows:

Figure 24. Charts for The Practice of Intercessory Prayer

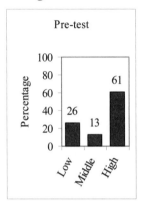
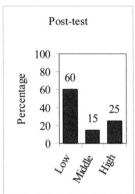
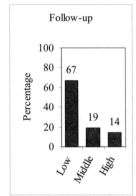

The shift was not just a reduction in the responses classified as "high" importance down to "medium" importance, but towards a viewpoint that considered intercessory prayer as of "low" importance (in the context of the particular questions). The percentages in the "low" category rose from 26 percent to 60 percent to 67 percent

The Concept of Territorial Spirits

The questions included in this theme were:

    16. Identifying territorial spirits as a basis of successful evangelism
    20. Principalities and powers governing the area as being a factor contributing to a lack of church growth
    34. Belief in the existence of territorial spirits
    35. Frequency of taking a stand against territorial spirits

This theme included a mix of questions relating to both belief and practice, but it was considered valid to combine them for the purpose of this themed analysis. The criteria for amalgamating the responses are given in table 53.

Table 53. The Concept of Territorial Spirits - Responses

	Wording of the original response options			
Re-scale	Question 16	Question 20	Question 34	Question 35
Low	No opinion	Totally irrelevant	Disbelieve strongly	Inappropriate
Low		Not a significant factor	Disbelieve	Never
Middle	Not important	Slight factor	No opinion	Occasionally
High	Fairly important	A factor	Believe	Frequently
High	Important	Major factor	Believe strongly	Very frequently
High	Very important			

Table 54. The Concept of Territorial Spirits - Responses According to the Re-Scale.

	Number in Pre-test			Number in Post-test			Number in Follow-up		
	Low	Middle	High	Low	Middle	High	Low	Middle	High
Q.16	16	2	10	21	4	2	18	0	1
Q.20	13	6	8	24	3	0	18	1	0
Q.34	6	8	14	18	5	4	14	3	2
Q.35	11	11	6	21	6	0	16	3	0
Total	46	27	38	84	18	6	66	7	3

Prior to the seminar a total of 38 responses affirmed of the concept of territorial spirits and the need to identify and contend with them. This dropped to 6 and then to 3 responses after the seminar, indicating an almost total rejection of the concept of territorial spirits. The data set is presented as percentages in table 55.

Table 55. The Concept of Territorial Spirits – Responses Expressed as Percentages

	Percentage in Pre-test			Percentage in Post-test			Percentage in Follow-up		
	Low	Middle	High	Low	Middle	High	Low	Middle	High
Q.16	57	7	36	78	15	7	95	0	5
Q.20	46	21	29	89	11	0	95	5	0
Q.34	21	29	50	67	19	15	74	16	11
Q.35	39	39	21	78	22	0	84	16	0
Total	41	24	34	78	17	6	87	9	4

From the percentage of the total responses, the effect of the seminar was to shift understanding away from a belief in the concept of territorial spirits (34 percent to 4 percent) and to convince those who had not made up their minds (24 percent to 9 percent). This resulted in a total of 87 percent viewing the concept as erroneous or irrelevant.

The changes in delegates' views can be seen clearly in a diagram of the data from the last row of table 55.

Figure 25. Charts for The Concept of Territorial Spirits

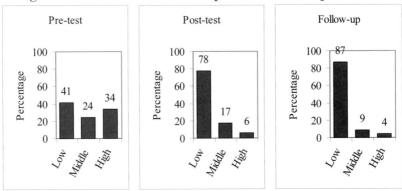

Summarising this in another way, 58 percent of responses were positive or undecided towards the concept of territorial spirits before the seminar, and subsequently only 13 percent were in this category. The remaining 87 percent were firmly against the existence, the relevance, or the need to stand against territorial spirits.

The Role of Speaking in Tongues in Spiritual Warfare

The questions included in this theme were:

39. The role of speaking in tongues for rebuking evil powers
41. The role of speaking in tongues for prophesying
42. The role of speaking in tongues for pulling down strongholds

For these three questions the available responses were all on a uniform scale from level 1 to level 5, even though the wording varied slightly. Hence the level 1 and level 2 are combined as "Low," the level 3 as "Middle," and the level 4 and level 5 as "High." This gives the numbers of responses set out in table 56.

Table 56. The Role of Speaking in Tongues in Spiritual Warfare - Responses

	Number in Pre-test			Number in Post-test			Number in Follow-up		
	Low	Middle	High	Low	Middle	High	Low	Middle	High
Q.39	14	5	9	22	3	2	18	1	0
Q.41	4	7	17	16	5	6	12	2	5
Q.42	12	6	10	23	3	1	17	2	0
Total	30	18	36	61	11	9	47	5	5

In each of the questions there was initially a strong response in support of speaking in tongues as a weapon in spiritual warfare, but this subsequently reduced dramatically. The totals in the last row of table 10 indicate this, but it is also helpful to view the results as percentages.

Table 57. The Role of Speaking in Tongues in Spiritual Warfare – Responses Expressed as Percentages

	Percentage in Pre-test			Percentage in Post-test			Percentage in Follow-up		
	Low	Middle	High	Low	Middle	High	Low	Middle	High
Q.39	50	18	32	81	11	7	95	5	0
Q.41	14	25	61	59	19	22	63	11	26
Q.42	43	21	36	85	11	4	89	11	0
Total	36	21	43	75	14	11	82	9	9

The percentage of responses rejecting the role of speaking in tongues for spiritual warfare rose sharply from 36 percent to 75 percent to 82 percent over the seminar and subsequent reflection. The totals in the last row of table 57 have been presented as a chart to show the extent of the change in viewpoint as a result of the seminar.

Figure 26. Charts for the Role of Speaking in Tongues in Spiritual Warfare

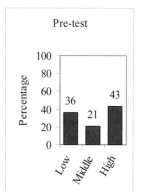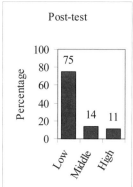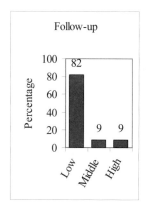

The bars shown in the Pre-test section of the diagram indicate a group of delegates with strong negative views, a similar group of delegates with strong positive views, and 21 percent occupying the "middle" ground. This position was modified considerably by the seminar so that over 80 percent of final responses suggested that speaking in tongues has "very little role" in spiritual warfare.

The Principal Tenets of SLSW

The questions included in this theme were:

14. Binding demons as a basis for successful evangelism
16. Identifying territorial spirits as a basis for successful evangelism
20. Principalities and powers governing the area contribute to lack of church growth
26. Belief that some spirits need to be identified by name before being cast out
27. Belief that spirits have a hierarchical order
28. View of the need for strategic level spiritual warfare
30. Value placed on warfare prayer
32. Belief in the effectiveness of prayer marches
34. Belief in the existence of territorial spirits
36. Belief in the possibility of repenting on behalf of another person

Table 58 below shows how the responses to this set of questions were grouped into the "Low," "Middle," and "High" categories.

Table 58. SLSW - Responses

	Wording of the original response options		
Re-scale	Questions 14, 16	Question 20	Questions 26, 27, 34, 36
Low	Not important	Totally irrelevant	Disbelieve strongly
Low		Not a significant factor	Disbelieve
Middle	No opinion	Slight factor	No opinion
High	Fairly important	A factor	Believe
High	Important	Major factor	Believe strongly
High	Very important		
Re-scale	Question 28	Question 30	Question 32
Low	Not necessary	No value	Not effective
Low	Rarely necessary	Little value	Not very effective
Middle	No opinion	No opinion	No opinion
High	Necessary	Moderate value	Moderately effective
High	Very necessary	Considerable value	Very effective

Table 59. SLSW – Responses According to the Re-Scale

	Number in Pre-test			Number in Post-test			Number in Follow-up		
	Low	Middle	High	Low	Middle	High	Low	Middle	High
Q.14	11	2	15	20	2	5	17	1	1
Q.16	16	2	10	21	4	2	18	0	1
Q.20	13	6	8	24	3	0	18	1	0
Q.26	16	3	9	22	3	2	19	0	0
Q.27	7	5	16	17	7	3	9	7	3
Q.28	11	3	14	22	4	1	18	1	0
Q.30	9	4	15	20	5	2	16	1	2
Q.32	12	4	12	20	5	2	18	0	1
Q.34	6	8	14	18	5	4	14	3	2
Q.36	20	1	7	23	1	3	18	1	0
Total	121	38	120	207	39	24	165	15	10

At the Pre-test stage, the responses show about equal numbers with a "high" view of SLSW compared to those with a "low" view. (120 responses and 121 responses – see bottom figures in columns 1 and 3 respectively). Relatively few responses were made in the undecided "middle" ground. All ten questions showed radical changes in thinking by the Post-test stage, with the total number of "high" responses falling to just 24. This trend continued over the next two months to the Follow-up stage in all questions except question 27, for which the numbers of "middle" and "high" responses remained constant (7 and 3 respectively).

Table 60. SLSW – Responses Expressed as Percentages

	Percentage in Pre-test			Percentage in Post-test			Percentage in Follow-up		
	Low	Middle	High	Low	Middle	High	Low	Middle	High
Q.14	39	7	54	74	7	19	89	5	5
Q.16	57	7	36	78	15	7	95	0	5
Q.20	46	21	29	89	11	0	95	5	0
Q.26	57	11	32	81	11	7	100	0	0
Q.27	25	18	57	63	26	11	47	37	16
Q.28	39	11	50	81	15	4	95	5	0
Q.30	32	14	54	74	19	7	84	5	11
Q.32	43	14	43	74	19	7	95	0	5
Q.34	21	29	50	67	19	15	74	16	11
Q.36	71	4	25	85	4	11	95	5	0
Total	43	14	43	77	14	9	87	8	5

The bimodal distribution of responses at the Pre-test stage is shown in the bottom line of the table with 43 percent holding "low" levels of belief and 43 percent holding "high" levels of belief in strategic level spiritual warfare. The changes in delegates' responses are stunningly shown by the figure of only 5 percent holding any positive view at the Follow-up stage. The last line of table 60 is displayed as a diagram thus:

Figure 27. Charts for the Principle Tenets of SLSW

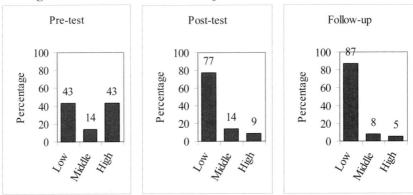

From an initial level of 43 percent, the proportion of delegates who considered that strategic level spiritual warfare was almost entirely erroneous rose to 87 percent. If one includes the undecided, then 95 percent could give no credence to strategic level spiritual warfare by the Follow-up stage.

Practices Associated with SLSW

The questions included for this theme were:

29. Frequency of engagement in spiritual warfare
31. Frequency of engagement in warfare prayer
33. Frequency of involvement in prayer marches
35. Frequency of making a stand against territorial spirits
37. Frequency of repentance on behalf of another person or region

The responses to these questions were grouped as shown in table 61.

Table 61. Practices Associated with SLSW – Responses

	Wording of the original response options		
Re-scale	Questions 29, 31	Question 33	Questions 35, 37
Low	Never	Inappropriate	Inappropriate
Low		Never	Never
Middle	Occasionally	Occasionally	Occasionally
High	Monthly	On most opportunities	Frequently
High	Weekly	At every opportunity	Very frequently
High	Daily		

With these criteria the numbers of responses are shown in table 62:

Table 62. Practices Associated with SLSW – Responses According to the Re-Scale

	Number in Pre-test			Number in Post-test			Number in Follow-up		
	Low	Middle	High	Low	Middle	High	Low	Middle	High
Q.29	7	11	10	14	9	4	11	7	1
Q.31	9	10	9	16	9	2	13	6	0
Q.33	15	9	4	22	4	1	16	3	0
Q.35	11	11	6	21	6	0	16	3	0
Q.37	21	5	2	23	4	0	18	1	0
Total	63	46	31	96	32	7	74	20	1

The number of responses indicating "high" frequency of activity in strategic level spiritual warfare reduced from 31 to 7 to 1 over the timescale of the survey. For further comparisons, the percentages of responses (given in table 63) have been considered.

Table 63. Practices Associated with SLSW – Responses Expressed as Percentages

	Percentage in Pre-test			Percentage in Post-test			Percentage in Follow-up		
	Low	Middle	High	Low	Middle	High	Low	Middle	High
Q.29	25	39	36	52	33	15	58	37	5
Q.31	32	36	32	59	33	7	68	32	0
Q.33	54	32	14	81	15	4	84	16	0
Q.35	39	39	21	78	22	0	84	16	0
Q.37	75	18	7	85	15	0	95	5	0
Total	45	33	22	71	24	5	78	21	1

The proportion of delegates who did not take any significant part in the practices of strategic level spiritual warfare rose steadily from 45 percent initially to 71 percent after the seminar, and then to 78 percent at the Follow-up stage. This is an endorsement of the shift in belief identified in the previous section being outworked in the lifestyles of the delegates, and is illustrated in the following diagrams.

Figure 28. Charts for the Practices Associated with SLSW

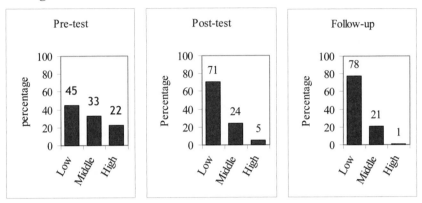

Before the seminar, the responses indicate 22 percent were zealous for the activities of warfare prayer, prayer marches, standing against territorial spirits, and repenting on behalf of others. This enthusiasm was seen, as a result of the seminar, to be misplaced.

CHAPTER **6**

RESPONSE TO FINDINGS

Introduction

The primary purpose of this research project has been to evaluate the impact of presenting the truths of God concerning biblical spiritual warfare in the context of understanding and assessing the modern day teaching on Strategic Level Spiritual Warfare ("SLSW"). In a wider sense, however, it could be argued that SLSW methodology is merely representative of the entire gamut of erroneous teaching which has infiltrated the church of Jesus Christ under the guise of divine revelation. Today, as always, the main threat to true faith comes from within the ranks of the church itself. As MacArthur comments:

> It is because of . . . distorted and destructive views of Scripture within professing Christendom that biblical believers must, more than ever before, "contend earnestly for the faith which was once delivered to the saints" (Jude 3) . . . Paul warned the godly, mature church at Ephesus, pastored first by the apostle and then by Timothy, and led by godly elders, "I know that after my departure savage wolves will come in *among you,* not sparing the flock; and from *among your own selves men will arise,* speaking perverse things, to draw away the disciples after them" (Acts 20:29-30, emphasis added).[1]

In line with the existential, subjectively orientated spirit of this present age, the current focus of error has been to promote an experience-led Christianity, supposedly emancipated from the limitations of "orthodox epistemology and hermeneutics. "[2]

In this context, the author has sought to address an issue which is essentially one of truth, for it is knowledge of the truth which alone can bring spiritual freedom (John 8:32). Accordingly, it has not been his purpose to engage in a personal attack on any individual or group, or in any sense to impugn their sincerity or motivation. Most protagonists of SLSW must be commended for their sincere and laudable desire to reach the lost and their emphasis on world

---

[1] John MacArthur Jr., *2 Timothy,* in *MacArthur's New Testament Commentary* (Chicago, IL: Moody Bible Institute, 1995), in *QuickVerse* ver. 7 [CD-ROM] (Omaha, NE: Parsons Technology, 1997).

[2] John F. Hart, "The Gospel and Spiritual Warfare: A Review of Peter Wagner's Confronting the Powers*," Journal of the Grace Evangelical Society* 10, no. 18 (Spring 1997), online posting, http://www.faithalone.org/journal/1997i/Hart.htm; accessed 11 Oct. 2001.

evangelism encourages an outward-looking church mentality. But the devil is a subtle foe; he comes not only with outright lies but with half-truths,[3] his purpose always being to deflect the believer from the simplicity of the gospel, which is "Christ in you, the hope of glory" (Col. 1:27). It is the author's heart-felt hope that this research project will promote dialogue on the whole understanding of SLSW within the body of Christ; his prayer is that of Paul in his letter to the Ephesians (chap. 1:17-23) :

> That the God of our Lord Jesus Christ, the Father of glory may give unto you the spirit of wisdom and revelation in the knowledge of him: The eyes of your understanding being enlightened; that ye may know what is the hope of his calling, and what the riches of the glory of his inheritance in the saints, And what *is* the exceeding greatness of his power to us-ward who believe, according to the working of his mighty power, Which he wrought in Christ, when he raised him from the dead, and set *him* at his own right hand in the heavenly places, Far above all principality, and power, and might, and dominion, and every name that is named, not only in this world, but also in that which is to come: And hath put all *things* under his feet, and gave him to *be* the head over all *things* to the church, Which is his body, the fullness of him that filleth all in all.

Interpretation of Results

The hypothesis under consideration was that the exposition of biblical and theological truth, applied in both an historical and a modern context, with the opportunity for study, discussion and re-evaluation of relevant concepts, would ensure that the understanding and practice of spiritual warfare was brought back into alignment with the word of God. This hypothesis was put to the test in the context of a group of church leaders, men and women who accept that the Bible is the inspired word of God and who would therefore be prepared to adjust their thinking and practice to bring them into alignment with what the scriptures teach.

---

[3]See also, Arthur W. Pink, "Another Gospel," online posting, http://users.aol.com/libcfl/another.htm; accessed 18 Dec. 2001. "Heresy is not so much the total denial of the truth as a perversion of it. That is why half a lie is always more dangerous than a complete repudiation. Hence, when the Father of Lies enters the pulpit it is not his custom to flatly deny the fundamental truths of Christianity, rather does he tacitly acknowledge them, and then proceed to give an erroneous interpretation and a false application."

The sample population was primarily drawn from the Global Gospel Fellowship (GGF) regional membership. This is an international and inter-denominational fellowship which was set up in 1995 to facilitate informal communication between pastors and church leaders on a monthly basis. In all twenty-eight delegates attended the seminar on Spiritual Warfare, of whom only three were women but this figure is probably representative of the relatively low ratio of women in full-time ministry. There were few delegates from the younger age groups but as all were church leaders or pastors this was to be expected.

Reactions to the teaching were assessed by means of a questionnaire which was applied before (the Pre-test), immediately after (the Post-test), and some two months later (the Follow-up test). All delegates completed the Pre-test, twenty-seven completed the Post-test and nineteen submitted the final Follow-up test by post. The high level of returns at the third and final stage is in itself an indication of the value placed upon the seminar teaching by the majority of the participants.

The time of intensive teaching and discussion made possible by the seminar had a significant impact on the thinking of individual delegates. Most appear to have had prior exposure to some aspect of SLSW methodology as, at the Pre-test stage, in response to question 28 (What is your view of the need for strategic level spiritual warfare?), only three recorded that they had no opinion. Eleven thought that SLSW was either "not necessary" or "rarely necessary," a total of 39 percent, but by the end of the seminar this had increased to 81 percent, of whom the vast majority (74 percent) took the more definitive view that SLSW was "not necessary" at all.

In terms of giving an overall interpretation of the results it has been decided to follow the format laid out in chapter 5, which begins with an analysis of individual questions and is followed by an analysis of the results grouped by theme. It must be remembered that the results obtained for the Follow-up questionnaire, whilst being exceptionally high for a postal return, represent the views of nineteen delegates and not the original twenty-eight. Accordingly, in order to retain statistical integrity, these figures have not been used comparatively with those relating to the Pre and Post-tests. They do, however, contain valuable information in showing that, in the vast majority of cases, the shift in opinion between the beginning and end of the seminar had been maintained, and so, will be referred to in this context.

Section One: Interpretation of the Responses to Individual Questions

(In this context, questions relating to the belief in, and practice of certain aspects of SLSW have been grouped together to facilitate the interpretative process.)

Questions Relating to the Belief in and Practice of Spiritual Warfare

Question 28: What is your view of the need for strategic level spiritual warfare?

Question 29: How frequently do you engage in spiritual warfare?

At the beginning of the seminar, 50 percent of the delegates expressed a positive opinion concerning the need for SLSW, and 36 percent practised it either "monthly" or "weekly." The Post-test showed that the belief figure had reduced to a mere 4 percent. By the Follow-up stage none of the delegates recorded the opinion that it was either "necessary" or "very necessary."

One of the main foci of the seminar teaching concerned the true nature of spiritual warfare, "the Peniel model," which is as outlined in 2 Corinthians 10:4-5, "(For the weapons of our warfare *are* not carnal, but mighty through God to the pulling down of strong holds;) Casting down imaginations, and every high thing that exalteth itself against the knowledge of God, and bringing into captivity every thought to the obedience of Christ." It was demonstrated the battle is in the mind, and is based on the individual's choice between God and truth, or Satan and lies. Thus, the biblical perspective on spiritual warfare has nothing to do with combating evil powers in the spirit realm but in using the word of God to cast down every thought or imagination which "exalteth itself against the knowledge of God." In the process of evangelism this is achieved by the simple proclamation of the gospel, applied to the heart by the Spirit of God. The shift in opinion over the course of the seminar is illustrated by the responses--the Post test showed that the vast majority of the delegates (74 percent) now believed that SLSW was not a biblical concept and therefore totally unnecessary.

Question 30: How much value do you place on warfare prayer?

Question 31: How frequently do you engage in warfare prayer?

Warfare prayer as a technique in SLSW is viewed as the chief weapon for engaging the enemy in battle. It is generally an aggressive and high volume challenge, taunting spirits to manifest themselves. Then Christ's power over the enemy can be displayed, the spirits are bound and the work of evangelism can proceed. At the beginning of the seminar 54 percent of the delegates were of the opinion that this practice was of "considerable" or "moderate" value; 36 percent engaged in the practice "occasionally," 21 percent "monthly" and 11 percent "weekly."

The teaching addressed the fundamental issue that prayer is never directed at the devil. It is, rather, the believer's expression of his relationship with God and as such is a channel of love and fellowship with the heavenly Father. The pattern in the New Testament is quite clear; Jesus never engaged in any form of warfare prayer, He simply banished demons with His word and the disciples followed His example. This aspect of the teaching also had a significant impact on the delegates and, at the Post-test stage, only 7 percent retained any positive opinion of warfare prayer.

Question 32:   How effective do you believe prayer marches are?

Question 33:   How frequently are you involved in prayer marches?

At the Pre-test stage the results show an even spread of opinion concerning the concept of prayer marches, with the negative and positive responses both being 43 percent. The notion derives from the belief that Christians must join together in the streets of a city as a method of breaking the powers of darkness, thus enabling unbelievers to respond to the gospel. Organisers and intercessors may walk the route seeking discernment on the particular needs of the area and identifying what spirits must be bound.

The seminar teaching pointed to the fact that Jesus defeated the enemy fully and finally at Calvary. The only weapon Satan has consists of lies and deception which he consistently uses to divert believers from their main task of proclaiming the gospel in the power of the Holy Ghost. The Post-test results show a very large increase in the negative opinion about the effectiveness of prayer marches. Most of the delegates (74 percent) were convinced that advocates of SLSW have interpreted prayer in a totally unbiblical way, viewing it as a weapon to be wielded against the enemy rather than a vehicle of communion with the Father. In terms of frequent practice, the numbers for this were relatively low before the seminar but fell to almost zero amongst the respondents at the Follow-up stage.

Question 34: Do you believe in the existence of territorial spirits?

Question 35: How frequently do you take a stand against territorial spirits?

The seminar teaching placed SLSW in a biblical context and demonstrated that there is no validation of territoriality in the word of God and that Jesus Christ has been given a place high above every principality and power (Eph. 1:21-23). The saints of God, therefore, have no need to engage in so-called cosmic warfare with non-existent territorial spirits. Jesus has won a full and complete victory, and conquered the power of the enemy forever. The indwelling Christ is the source of authority in the life of every believer who has been translated out of the power of darkness and into the kingdom of His dear Son (Col. 1:13).

Belief in territorial spirits is one of the main tenets of SLSW. This was very strong amongst the delegates before the seminar; 50 percent held positive opinions, with only 21 percent expressing a negative point of view. In addition, almost 30 percent were clearly confused about the whole issue and were unable to give a definite opinion.

The Post-test results display a very different picture, with the disbelief figures having trebled to almost 70 percent, representing a total increase of 46 percent. Similarly, no one retained a strong belief in territorial spirits at the end of the seminar and this was also true for the Follow-up test results. The change in beliefs was mirrored in the change in frequency of practice with 84 percent of the Follow-up respondents stating that conflict with territorial spirits was either "inappropriate" or a practice in which they would "never" engage. There was also a significant decrease in the percentage of those who initially had "no opinion" about territorial spirits. This fell to 18 percent directly after the seminar.

Question 36: Do you believe it is possible to repent on behalf of another person?

Question 37: How frequently do you repent on behalf of another person or region?

As has already been noted in chapter 5, this practice produced the lowest positive response level of all the Pre-test results, with 71 percent indicating a "disbelieve" or "disbelieve strongly" response. Most delegates obviously were suspicious of this aspect of SLSW.

The teaching was geared to the truth that repentance can never be undertaken by proxy and that what is being propagated is effectively identificational remorse, which is of no spiritual value whatsoever. At the Post-test stage the overall negative responses had increased by a further 14 percent; but for reasons which are not altogether clear, this involved a fall in the numbers of those who "disbelieved strongly" and a very large increase in those who "disbelieved." In terms of the actual practice of identificational repentance, there was an overall decrease in the levels of participation as a result of the teaching.

Questions Relating to the Basis for Successful Evangelism

In the original questionnaire, five factors were listed as possibly having an effect on the success or otherwise of evangelism. These included:

Question 12: Intercessory prayer

Question 13: Fasting

Question 14: Binding demons

Question 15: Proclaiming the word of God

Question 16: Identifying territorial spirits

In fact, analysis for question 15 was not produced because there was no significant change in the responses as the result of the seminar. Over 92 percent of the delegates came to the seminar with the strong conviction that the basis of successful evangelism is proclaiming the word of God. The teaching reinforced this opinion and at the Follow-up stage all nineteen respondents gave it the highest level of importance. The vast majority of the delegates accepted the fact that man's role in evangelism is primarily to preach the word. It was also stressed that where the word goes forth in truth God will faithfully confirm it with signs and wonders.

For each of the other factors there was a significant shift as a result of the seminar. Intercessory prayer was rated by 75 percent of the delegates to be "fairly important" (10 percent), "important" (43 percent), or "very important" (22 percent). This figure was higher than for any other factor. However, over the course of the seminar it was pointed out that the ministry of intercession is the work of the Holy Spirit (Rom. 8:26), and that it is never mentioned in the Scriptures as being the responsibility of individual Christians. To bring the unbeliever to new birth in Christ is the work of God, not of man. Many delegates saw this clearly and the re-alignment of their beliefs is seen in the Post-test results where the positive response had dropped to 26 percent.

Binding demons was ranked third in importance in the Pre-test responses, with 54 percent believing this to be a significant part of the evangelism process. Conversely, 39 percent said it was "not important," with the remaining 7 percent having "no opinion" on the subject. As has already been stated the seminar teaching stressed the victory in Christ and the fact that demonic interference never impeded the advance of the gospel in New Testament days. By the conclusion of the seminar, the percentage of those attributing importance to this issue had dramatically reduced to only 19 percent with 74 percent now expressing the opinion that it was of "no importance." In the Follow-up results 90 percent of the respondents viewed this subject as being unimportant in evangelism.

Question 16 related to the importance of identifying territorial spirits in progressing the gospel. This has already been referred to in the interpretation of individual questions (see chapter 5). To summarise briefly, the seminar resulted in the positive opinion dropping from 50 percent to 21 percent, and the negative opinion increasing from 21 to 67 percent.

The final issue under the heading of evangelism was the necessity of fasting. At the start of the seminar opinion was divided, with 46 percent believing it to be "fairly important," "important" or "very important," and 47 percent maintaining that it was "not important." Teaching in this context emphasised that under the new covenant the true fast of God is as is described in Isaiah 58:6 - "Is not this the fast that I have chosen? to loose the bands of wickedness, to undo the heavy burdens, and to let the oppressed go free, and that ye break every yoke?" Jesus made it clear that fasting, in terms of deprivation of food, was only appropriate in the absence of the bridegroom (Matt. 9:15). Accordingly, since He is come to indwell each believer by His Spirit, the days of fasting are at an end. This teaching clearly impacted the understanding of the delegates, and in the Post-test results 78 percent had come to the conclusion that it was "not important", with only 11 percent recording the somewhat qualified verdict that is was "fairly important."

Questions Relating to the Basis for Church Growth

In this context, four questions were selected for analysis due to the substantial shift in the responses as a result of the seminar. These will form the basis of the interpretation.

Question 17: Inability of the church to combat social deprivation in the area

Question 18: Lack of intercessory prayer

Question 19: Lack of prayer and fasting

Question 20: Principalities and powers governing the area

In terms of ranking in the Pre-test results, lack of prayer and fasting (Q19) and the problem of principalities and powers exerting control over the area (Q20) were virtually equal; under both headings 48 percent of the delegates considered that these factors were "totally irrelevant" or "not significant." By the end of the seminar, these figures had increased to 86 percent (Q19) and 89 percent (Q20), respectively. The vast majority of delegates had grasped the teaching concerning the true fast of God and the total irrelevance of demonic powers; Jesus said "I will build my church, and the gates of hell shall not prevail against it" (Matt. 16:18).

The Pre-test results concerning lack of intercessory prayer as a factor affecting church growth show that 34 percent considered this to be "totally irrelevant" or "not significant." By the time of the Post-test this had increased to 78 percent, as increasing numbers of delegates accepted the truth that intercession is the work of the Holy Spirit.

When the results for the above questions are reviewed from a Follow-up perspective, it is evident that 84 percent of the respondents continued to view lack of intercessory prayer as "totally irrelevant" or "not a significant factor" in church growth; at this stage, the equivalent figure for lack of prayer and fasting was 90 percent and for principalities and powers, the figure was 95 percent.

Question 17 dealt with the church's inability to combat social deprivation as a factor contributing to a lack of growth. Before the seminar opinion was divided, with 37 percent considering that it was either "totally irrelevant," or "not a significant factor," and 48 percent believing it to be either "a factor" or "a major factor." The seminar teaching focused on the fact that social deprivation has nothing to do with demonic influence but can generally be attributed to the lack of a basic work ethic; thus, when a person comes into the reality of new birth and lives according to biblical principles, his life will prosper in every area. In the Post-test, the numbers of delegates holding a positive opinion in this context had dropped from 48 to only 7 percent, with none considering it to be a "major factor." Conversely, the delegates considering it to be either "totally irrelevant" or "not a significant factor" had risen by 26 percent to 63 percent. It was interesting to note that some of the overall shift in opinion was accounted for by a rise in the numbers considering this to be a "slight factor," from 15 to 30 percent. This question was one of the very few in the seminar where there tended to be a reversion at the Follow-up stage; the negative opinion dropped slightly to 58 percent and the positive opinion increased to 26 percent. This may have been because the phrasing of the question itself appeared to have little relevance to the extremes of SLSW, and so in the longer term it was viewed as a more neutral question, leading to a slight distortion of results. Once again some of the change was accounted for by a variation in those recording a "slight factor" response; this fell from 30 percent at the Post-test stage to 16 percent at the Follow-up.

The figures relating to question 21 have not been analysed because there was not a significant change in the responses. However, reference to question 21, demonstrates that most of the delegates came to the seminar with the strong opinion that a miracle ministry is a very significant factor in church growth. This was strengthened by the seminar teaching.

Questions Relating to Spirits and Demons

Consideration of this topic involved the analysis of two separate questions:

Question 25:   Do you believe some demons only come out by prayer and fasting?

Question 27:   Do you believe that spirits have a hierarchical order?

Belief that the combination of prayer and fasting is the prerequisite for exorcism is based on Mark 9:29, "And he said unto them, This kind can come forth by nothing, but by prayer and fasting." However, this wording in the KJV is based on an error in one of the original manuscripts; the NIV which is translated from an earlier manuscript does not include the word "fasting." In respect to a parallel Scripture in Matthew 17:21, the whole phrase does not appear in the NIV.

Interpretation of the results demonstrates the impact of this corrective teaching on delegate opinion. At the Pre-test stage 42 percent "disbelieved strongly" or "disbelieved" in the requirement for prayer and fasting in casting out demons. By the Post-test stage this had increased to 74 percent, with only 7 percent continuing to believe in the practice.

The swing in opinion relating to spirit hierarchies was more dramatic. Before the seminar some 58 percent "believed" or "believed strongly." This had dropped to a mere 11 percent after the seminar. Teaching continually stressed that the focus of the Christian's life must be on Jesus Christ and that when He is fixed in the centre of one's vision, the demonic world lapses into insignificance.

Questions Relating to the Role of Speaking in Tongues

In this category three questions were considered:

Question 39: For rebuking evil powers

Question 41: For prophesying

Question 42: For pulling down strongholds

The seminar teaching made clear that the role of speaking in tongues is for the personal edification of the believer. Like prayer it is not a weapon to be used against the enemy.

In the Pre-test results, 32 percent viewed tongues as a means of rebuking the enemy By the Post-test some 82 percent had dismissed this opinion. Similarly, with respect to pulling down strongholds, the initial number who saw tongues as a weapon equated to 36 percent but after the teaching 85 percent viewed it as having either "no role" or a "minimal role."

The seminar teaching on prophesying emphasised that the use of tongues to induce prophetic revelation as to the names of spirits and demons in the context of SLSW was without biblical validation. The Pre-test results show that 61 percent believed that the use of tongues in this context played a "major" or "very major role" (level 4 and 5 responses) but this figure had dropped to 22 percent by the end of the seminar. Conversely, at the Pre-test stage the negative opinion was relatively low, with only 14 percent considering that tongues had "no role" or a "minimal role" in this context (level 1 and 2 responses). However, by the end of the seminar this figure had increased to 60 percent.

In the longer term, the Follow-up figures demonstrate that these changes had been maintained. In terms of using tongues to rebuke evil spirits, 90 percent recorded level 1 and 2 responses ("no role" or a "minimal role") with no one recording the belief that it has "major" or "very major" importance (levels 4 and 5). The figures in respect to using tongues to pull down strongholds were equivalent, with 95 percent recording levels 1 and 2 responses, and once again none at levels 4 and 5. As far as the use of tongues for prophesying in the context of SLSW was concerned, the negative opinion maintained a level of 63 percent but the positive opinion increased slightly to 26 percent. With the benefit of hindsight it may be that the wording of question 41 was not sufficiently specific and so caused some distortion in the final results.

Section Two: Interpretation of Results Grouped by Theme

The themes under consideration are the role of fasting, the practice of intercessory prayer, the concept of territorial spirits, the role of speaking in tongues in spiritual warfare and a summary of the main beliefs and practices of SLSW. Since the first four of these have already been considered from various aspects in section two, it was decided to merely provide an interpretative synopsis in this section and to consider the summary of the main beliefs and practice of SLSW in more detail.

The Role of Fasting

The questions included in this theme were fasting as a source of spiritual insight / inspiration (Q11); as a basis for successful evangelism (Q13); as a factor contributing to the lack of church growth (Q19); and, in terms of the belief that some demons come out only by prayer and fasting (Q25). The main thrust of the teaching on the role of fasting (in terms of deprivation of food), was that it is not part of the New Covenant experience. Accordingly, when the results were presented cumulatively, it was shown that the delegates who viewed fasting as important reduced from 37 percent to 9 percent over the course of the seminar. This trend was sustained in the longer term with only 5 percent of the respondents to the Follow-up test viewing it as important.

The Practice of Intercessory Prayer

The questions in this theme included the practice of intercessory prayer as a source of spiritual insight / inspiration (Q10); as a basis for successful evangelism (Q12); and the lack of intercessory prayer as a factor contributing to the lack of church growth (Q18). As a result of the teaching's emphasis on the fact that intercession is the role of the Holy Spirit, on a cumulative basis the delegates who placed a high importance on intercessory prayer decreased from 61 percent in the Pre-test results to 25 percent in the Post-test figures. This trend was maintained to the Follow-up stage with only 14 percent continuing to regard it as being of importance.

The Concept of Territorial Spirits

The questions in this theme included, identifying territorial spirits as a basis for successful evangelism (Q16); whether or not principalities and powers contribute to a lack of church growth (Q20); belief in the existence of territorial spirits (Q34); and the frequency of taking a stand against territorial spirits. The teaching challenged the whole notion of territoriality showing that it had no biblical or theological foundation. Rather, it is rooted in animism and pagan beliefs. As a result the percentage of delegates who placed a high importance on territorial spirits and their influence dropped from 34 percent before the seminar to a mere 6 percent afterwards. Conversely, 87 percent left the seminar viewing the concept as erroneous or irrelevant.

The Role of Speaking in Tongues in Spiritual Warfare

Questions 39, 41 and 42 have already been considered together, above. When the results are interpreted on a cumulative basis the percentage of delegates who considered speaking in tongues to be important in spiritual warfare fell from 43 percent in the Pre-test figures to 11 percent after the seminar teaching. Equally, those who considered it to be of low relevance increased from an initial reading of 36 percent to 75 percent in the Post-test results. This trend was continued at the Follow-up stage.

The Principal Tenets of SLSW

This subject was the focus of the seminar teaching and so the interpretation has been conducted on a more detailed basis. The questions included in this theme have been subdivided into three sections; namely, (1) Questions relating to beliefs about evil spirits, (2) Questions relating to beliefs about SLSW and its practices and, (3) Questions relating to beliefs about evangelism and church growth.

(1) Questions relating to beliefs about evil spirits

In this category there were three significant questions:

Question 26:   Belief that some spirits need to be identified by name before being cast out

Question 27:   Belief that spirits have a hierarchical order

Question 34:   Belief in the existence of territorial spirits

The seminar stressed the fact that there is very little evidence in Scripture concerning the taxonomy of the spirit world, and no evidence to support the concept of territoriality. The New Testament demonstrates that Jesus cast out demons by His word without the need for any sophisticated methodology of exorcism and that His power is available to every child of God today. It was also shown that many of the erroneous beliefs about demons date from the Intertestamental era when the Jews of the Diaspora adopted practices from the pagan religions of their captors. Accordingly, in respect to question 26, there was a resultant increase of 26 percent in the numbers who either "disbelieved" or "disbelieved strongly" in the necessity for the demon to be identified by name prior to successful exorcism. This was exactly mirrored by the corresponding decrease in the numbers who "believed" or "strongly believed" in the necessity for this practice.

As far as question 27 was concerned, a similar pattern emerged. The seminar teaching brought about an increase of 38 percent in those who "disbelieved" or "disbelieved strongly" in the notion of a hierarchical system in the spirit world, with an even greater decrease of some 47 percent in those who had initially "believed" or "believed strongly." It was also significant that out of the 29 percent of delegates who originally "believed strongly" none retained that level of belief by the end of the seminar.

Question 34 dealt with the issue of whether or not territorial spirits exist. Once again the impact of the seminar teaching was quite significant. By the time of the Post-test there was a rise of 46 percent in those who "disbelieved" or "disbelieved strongly" and a fall of 35 percent in those recording "belief" or "strong belief." Those who had previously indicated a neutral position also decreased by 11 percent.

If the answers to the three questions are grouped as a whole, the average results indicate that the teaching produced a 36.7 percent increase in those who "disbelieved" or "disbelieved strongly" and a parallel decrease of 36 percent in those who "believed" or "strongly believed."

Section Three: Questions Relating to Beliefs about SLSW and its Practices

This section included four questions:

Question 28: View of the need for strategic level spiritual warfare

Question 30: Value placed on warfare prayer

Question 32: Belief in the effectiveness of prayer marches

Question 36: Belief in the possibility of repenting on behalf of another person

In this context, the whole thrust of the seminar teaching was to demonstrate that there is no biblical or theological foundation for most of what is propagated under the auspices of SLSW. The author sought to bring the delegates back to the simple truths of the gospel that the enemy was defeated fully and finally at Calvary, and that each believer can therefore live in the reality of Christ's total victory. The Peniel model of spiritual warfare shows that the real battle is in the mind and is based on the choice to obey God and His word, or to accept the lies and deception of the devil. In this conflict the weapon is the word of God.

Most of the delegates attending the seminar appear to have been exposed to some aspect of SLSW methodology. At the Pre-test stage, only three (10.7 percent) recorded that they had no opinion on the need for SLSW, in response to question 28. As a result of the teaching there was a 42 percent increase in those who viewed it as "not necessary" or "rarely necessary" and a corresponding decrease of 46 percent in those who retained the opinion that it was "necessary" or "very necessary."

The figures given in response to question 30 were virtually identical, with a rise of 42 percent in those who considered it to be of "no value" or "little value," and a fall of 45 percent in those who placed a "moderate" or "considerable" value on the practice.

In respect to the less controversial question concerning prayer marches (question 32), the impact of the teaching remained substantial but to a lesser degree. After the seminar, there was a 31 percent increase in those who believed it was "not effective" or "not very effective," and a similar decrease of 36 percent in those who took the position that it was "moderately" or "very effective."

Question 36 addressed the issue of the efficacy of identificational repentance and in this case there was a swing of 14 percent away from "belief," in favour of "disbelief" or "strong disbelief." The apparently lower impact of the teaching with respect to this particular question was due to the fact that 71 percent did not believe that this was a valid practice at the commencement of the seminar. No one recorded a "strong belief" response at any stage.

Once again, if an average is calculated for the four questions, even allowing for the identificational repentance response, the increase in those who "disbelieved" or "strongly disbelieved" in the necessity for SLSW and its associated practices was 32.2 percent, with a parallel decrease in those who "believed" or "strongly believed" of 35.2 percent.

Section Four: Questions Relating to Beliefs about Evangelism and Church Growth

In this section three significant questions were identified:

Question 14:   Binding demons as a basis for successful evangelism

Question 16:   Identifying territorial spirits as a basis for successful evangelism

Question 20:   Principalities and powers governing the area contribute to lack of church growth

At the seminar the author argued that, as is illustrated in the book of Acts, the word of God spoken in the power of the Spirit of God has always been the key to successful evangelism and church growth. Additionally, he stressed that where this is in evidence, God will always faithfully confirm His word with signs and wonders.

In response to question 14, the percentage shift after the teaching was 35 percent away from the belief that it was "fairly important," "important" or "very important" to bind demons as a basis for evangelism. This was mirrored by a 35 percent increase in the "not important" position.

Question 16 dealt with the necessity or otherwise of identifying territorial spirits in advance of evangelism. There was an increase of 20 percent after the seminar in those who felt this was "not important" and a corresponding decrease of 28 percent in those who recorded a "fairly important," "important" or "very important" response. However, once again it is apparent from examination of the figures that 57 percent of the total delegates were already of the opinion before the seminar that this practice was "not important."

The final question in this section concerned the influence of principalities and powers in inhibiting church growth in any particular area (question 20). There was an increase of 41 percent in those who recorded a "totally irrelevant" or "not a significant factor" verdict at the end of the seminar. This was mirrored by the total decrease of 11 percent in those who thought it was a "slight factor" together with the 30 percent decrease in those who said it was "a factor" or a "major factor." On the basis of the average results for the three questions there was a shift of 32 percent away from belief in the relevance of dealing with evil spirits in evangelism.

As has already been pointed out in chapter 5, when the figures for all of the above ten questions were considered, the number of responses reflecting a positive view of SLSW were roughly equivalent to those reflecting a negative view, being 121 and 120 respectively. This is illustrated in table 13 in chapter 5. Relatively few responses were recorded in the undecided middle ground. All ten questions showed radical changes in thinking by the Post-test stage, with the total number of high responses falling to just 24. From an initial level of 43 percent, the proportion of delegates who considered that SLSW was almost entirely erroneous rose to 87 percent.

The author did not think it appropriate to analyse the results concerning the frequency of engaging in spiritual warfare between the Pre-test and Post-test stage as insufficient time had elapsed. However, on the basis of somewhat theoretical responses, the proportion of delegates who would not take any significant part in the practices of strategic level spiritual warfare rose steadily from 45 percent initially to 71 percent after the seminar. This was an endorsement of the shift in belief identified above.

Before the seminar, the responses indicate 22 percent were zealous for the activities of warfare prayer / strategic-level intercession, prayer marches, standing against territorial spirits, and repenting on behalf of others. This enthusiasm, as a result of the seminar, was seen to be misplaced, and virtually all delegates are now resolved to devote their time and energy to more valid activities. In contrast to this theme of spiritual warfare, the responses to question 15 reinforce the overwhelming conclusion of the delegates that the most important task is to proclaim the word of God.

Conclusions

A large proportion of the delegates came with quite strong positive beliefs about a number of aspects of SLSW. After the seminar some might have been tempted to register a neutral response, which would have been an indication that, although challenged on their positive beliefs, they were not ready to abandon them too quickly. One of the reasons in the analysis for simplifying the responses into "generally positive" and "generally negative" results was to test for this very situation. Had the delegates moved from a position of "strong belief" to one of "not sure," there would have been a large fall in the "positive" charts, but very little corresponding increase in the "negative" charts. However, in question after question, there was both a fall in the positive position accompanied by a large rise in the negative. The delegates were saying in effect that they had no need to go away and reconsider. They were so convinced by the seminar teaching that many abandoned their positive opinions about SLSW immediately. This is not unusual when survey instruments are applied immediately after a seminar but it was particularly interesting to note that the trend was generally maintained over the longer term, as exemplified by the Follow-up responses.

The success of the seminar was particularly encouraging since all the delegates were pastors or church leaders, who, in the author's experience are generally difficult to convince that they may have imbibed the wrong doctrine. In particular, pride and insecurity may conspire to prevent them from publicly acknowledging their error. The indications of the test results suggest that the delegates were sufficiently convinced by the seminar teaching that they were prepared to amend their thinking despite any such considerations.

The seminar teaching involved the exposition of Biblical truth and the scriptural meaning of spiritual warfare, as opposed to the false teaching of SLSW which clearly represents syncretised epistemology. A significant number of the delegates had developed a belief system derived from erroneous, non-Biblical teaching. This was demonstrated by many of the responses at the Pre-test stage. The seminar therefore sought to reinforce an exclusively Biblical epistemology as the only basis of sound doctrine.

The results bear effective witness to the liberating power of truth (John 8:32). Thus, when the delegates were confronted with the biblical teaching on spiritual warfare and a sound theological understanding of the sovereignty of God and the efficacy of the word of God proclaimed in the power of the Spirit of God, they recognised that most of what is currently propagated under the banner of SLSW is erroneous. Seminar teaching and discussion also focused on various SLSW practices, including discerning and naming of spirits, warfare prayer and strategic-level intercession, and spiritual mapping and identificational repentance. It was shown from Scripture that such concepts are not only unbiblical but also completely alien to the Christian gospel. In addition, the lessons of history were used to illustrate the very real danger that SLSW is re-introducing the age-old error of syncretism from pagan religions into the church of Jesus Christ.[4] Similarly, an examination of the relevant literature led to the overwhelming conclusion that SLSW teaching and methodologies are without balanced biblical validation. In fact, they are founded on observation, experience-based evaluation and largely unsubstantiated empirical evidence, rather than upon the word of God.[5]

As well as addressing erroneous beliefs, the seminar also presented the Peniel model of spiritual warfare based on 2 Corinthians 10:4-5. It was demonstrated on the basis of a biblical, theological and historical evaluation that the real battle has always been between truth and error. The choice in the Garden of Eden was essentially one of whom and what to believe--God and His word, or Satan and his lie. Man, on the basis of his subjective evaluation, abandoned the word of the Creator and adopted the

---

[4]Chuck Lowe has likened this to Christopaganism (Chuck Lowe, *Territorial Spirits and World Evangelisation?: A Biblical, Historical and Missiological Critique of Strategic-Level Spiritual Warfare* [Fearn and Kent: OMF and Mentor, 1998], 112). Other observers have described SLSW as the "New Montanism" or "New Gnosticism" (for example, Lonnie J. Allison, Director, Billy Graham Center, open discussion, the Inaugural Billy Graham Evangelism Roundtable, Wheaton College, Wheaton, Illinois, 18 Jan. 2001).

[5]Lowe, 127, 146, 151.

misrepresentations of the enemy; and ever since that day, the devil has used the same web of deceit to ensnare those who do not live in the reality of the tremendous victory achieved by Jesus Christ at Calvary. Satan seeks to blind the mind of the unbeliever, "lest the light of the glorious gospel of Christ, who is the image of God, should shine upon them" (2 Cor. 4:4); he seeks to distort the understanding of the believer, to effectively rob him of his great inheritance in Jesus Christ, who has "given us all things that *pertain* unto life and godliness, through the knowledge of him" (2 Pet. 1:3).

It is for these reasons that the Holy Spirit comes to pull down these mental strongholds, to cast down "imaginations and every high thing that exalteth itself against the knowledge of God" (2 Cor. 10:5). In evangelism, such pulling down is effected by proclaiming the simple gospel in the power of the Spirit in order to bring the unconverted into the reality of saving faith for, "faith cometh by hearing, and hearing by the word of God" (Rom. 10:17). In the Christian's walk of faith, victory is achieved by "acknowledging of the truth" (2 Tim. 2:25), so that those who have been caught in the lie may "recover themselves out of the snare of the enemy" (2 Tim. 2:26). In this process the Holy Spirit works within to bring every thought into captivity "to the obedience of Christ" (2 Cor. 10:5); and it is He who spiritually renews the mind (Titus 3:5; Rom. 12:2).

The seminar teaching also emphasised the true nature of redemption and Christ's eternal victory over the enemy, the essential differences between the Old and New Covenants, and the significance of Christ's post-ascension priestly ministry as advocate, intercessor, mediator and counsellor. The course content had a tremendous impact on a majority of the delegates, which was a vindication of the author's original conviction that when men and women of integrity are encouraged to refocus on the scriptures as the only basis of faith and truth, there will be a speedy rejection of error. There was therefore a dual aspect to the delegates' responses; not only did a significant number move away from positive belief in SLSW but, in addition, they adopted the Peniel Model of Christ's eternal victory on the cross.

In fact, a testimony session was held at the end of the course and many spoke of the benefit they had received from the seminar teaching.[6] For example, one pastor said, "It's actually unfortunate to review my life and realise that I was founded on all these teachings we've been hearing. Over the years, I've let it slip in favour of other things that simply aren't in the Book . . . Whatever happens, I'm going to hang on to this teaching and I'm not going to let it go again."

Another said, "I think the main thing it's done for me is to bring into focus a number of things linked to SLSW that we haven't been happy with . . . but we haven't known the reasons why, and the biblical base to the reasons why . . . has been a wonderful help to us."

A pastor of Ghanaian origin testified, "I have never been so challenged in my life . . . the only thing that's important is the Word, nothing else . . . it's the first time I've seen this in all my life."

A woman pastor from Australia spoke of the revolution in her thinking, "I would personally like to thank you for the relief that I now have that it's not up to me. It may have been my fault but I can change that by preaching the gospel and praying for the sick and doing what I'm supposed to do and leaving Him to do what He's supposed to do, instead of trying to do His job for Him."

There was also a pastor from Korea who had been heavily involved in teaching SLSW both in his own country and internationally. He said, "I want to confess one thing that, as a preacher, I greatly sinned because I didn't really examine carefully or exactly whether this SLSW teaching came from the Bible text or not. I read most of the books of Peter Wagner, John Dawson, John Wimber and I was quoting from all these books . . . I made a great mistake . . . I am going again to my country and will teach what I have learned here. It will be so different."

Recommendations

To Improve the Project

The main area of the study which could be strengthened relates to the mechanical process of gathering the information. For example, certain questions in the questionnaire were slightly ambiguous in that they referred to Spiritual Warfare and not to SLSW. This may have

---

[6]A full testimony is contained in appendix D.

skewed some of the results in certain instances. In addition, the subject matter of the questionnaire could have been broader to include the theological aspects of the teaching. This would have yielded valuable information as to the underlying reasons for the adoption of certain errors. In particular it would have been useful to have included questions determining the extent to which delegates (a) rejected SLSW and (b) accepted the Peniel model.

A more comprehensive reading list would also have assisted and in future courses this should be representative of the range of the opinion on the subject, including: C. Peter Wagner, *Confronting the Powers*; Charles H. Kraft, *Christianity with Power* (relevant section only); George Otis, Jr., *Land of the Giants*; Ed. Murphy, *The Handbook for Spiritual Warfare*; Chuck Lowe, *Territorial Spirits and World Evangelisation?*; Clinton E. Arnold, *Spiritual Warfare*; Michael Reid and Judson Cornwall, *Whose Mind Is It Anyway?*; Judson Cornwall and Michael Reid, *Whose War Is It Anyway?*; T. L. Osborn, *The Message That Works*; and Gene Edward Veith, Jr., *Postmodern Times*. In the context of reading material, it would also have been helpful for the delegates to have had a course textbook summarising the biblical, theological and historical basis of the study and a review of the related literature. A seminar pack was provided but a textbook would have ensured a more permanent record of the teaching. Video footage demonstrating different approaches to evangelism was also used in the course.[7] This presented some of the material in a form which may be more accessible to those whose learning style favours a visual presentation, so it is important to bear this in mind for future presentations.

Clearly, the hypothesis has only been put to the test statistically in one forum, although the author has taught much of the course content on a variety of occasions and in different countries. It would be strengthened by further successful application.

---

[7]For example, George Otis Jr., *Transformations: A Documentary*, prod. Global Net Productions, 58 min., The Sentinel Group, 1999, videocassette; and T. L. Osborn and Daisy Osborn, *Java Harvest: A Docu-Miracle Film*, prod. OSFO International World Missionary Church, 1990, videocassette.

For Further Research

Various topics for research presented themselves in the course of conducting the study. In view of the proliferation of populist material on the subject of SLSW, it would be interesting to evaluate the influence of the publishing industry and aggressive promotion in the media in this context. Several questions could be addressed; for example, is the industry driven by market demand or vice versa? In addition, there seems to be a direct connection between the current absorption with SLSW in the Christian world and a parallel fascination with the spirit realm in the secular world. The whole cause and effect relationship between contemporary trends in the secular world and those in the Christian world is one which demands investigation and could also include such topics as the influence of postmodernism and multi-cultural living.

Similarly, vital research could be conducted within mainstream Christian colleges, Bible seminaries and mission agencies to ascertain the extent to which current curriculae and teaching support the whole concept of SLSW. In addition, an investigation of the link between eschatological beliefs and evangelistic methodology would provide a fascinating field of study, as would evaluation of the causal factors promoting cyclical error within the church of Jesus Christ. It would also be interesting to establish whether there is any significant difference in the acceptance of SLSW teaching between those who hold Arminian beliefs and those who have a Calvinistic view of the work of salvation.

For Implementation in Ministry

At the end of the seminar, a pastor of Congolese origin, spoke of the need for the truths presented to be made available in other languages. He said, "I want to translate all this into other languages because so many people are dying because they are without this word." It may be that part of the future implementation of this project will involve making the material available in a number of key languages.

The author has been invited by some delegates from Nigeria, Ghana and the Congo to conduct the course on "Spiritual Warfare" in their native countries and has presented the material at the 2002 conference of the Global Gospel Fellowship, which was attended by pastors and church leaders from around the world. If the focus is primarily on the leadership, who may become links in the chain of communication, this should ensure that a wider church membership is impacted.

The course now forms one of the modules offered by Peniel College of Higher Education as part of the study for the Oral Roberts University degree in Practical Theology. It would be beneficial to make this available to a wider range of Bible colleges.

CHAPTER 7

THEOLOGICAL REFLECTIONS

Introduction

Throughout history, God has faithfully intervened to work all things together for the good of those who love Him (Rom. 8:28), and this applies even within the context of error. As the theologian, John Murray comments, "The promulgation of heresy has exercised a profound influence upon the development of theology. It has always compelled the church to examine the deposit of revelation with more care, to set forth the truth in opposition to error and right to wrong, and to awaken the faithful to greater vigilance against the inroads of unbelief."[1] Spurgeon echoes this same truth when he says, "We have no defences for our churches, either in Acts of Parliament or enforced creeds; but the regenerated hearts and consecrated spirits of men, who resolve to live and die in the service of King Jesus, have hitherto sufficed, in the hands of the Spirit, to preserve us from grievous heresy. I see no beginning to this business, this battle of truth commenced so long ago; and I see no end to it, except the coming of the Master and the eternal victory."[2]

In this section, the purpose is to reflect on the various questions and conclusions that have been raised through the course of this research. For the sake of clarity these will be dealt with under four sub-headings: Biblical Fact or Methodological Fiction?; Knowledge of the Truth; The Gospel of the New Covenant; and God's Remedy: The Preaching of the Gospel.

Biblical Fact or Methodological Fiction?

In the year 1859, the British naturalist, Charles Darwin produced his revolutionary paper on natural selection under the title *The Origin of Species*. Within a relatively short period of time this theory was to be elevated from what was essentially a highly speculative hypothesis, to an unchallenged dogma commanding almost universal acceptance. The underlying concepts of continuity and gradualism which were the basis of the whole model of evolution were in keeping with much socio-political thought in the nineteenth century and Darwin's

---

[1]John Murray, *Studies in Theology*, vol. 4 of 4, *Collected Writings of John Murray* (Edinburgh: The Banner of Truth Trust, 1982), 7.

[2]Charles H. Spurgeon, *An All-Round Ministry: Addresses to Ministers and Students* (Edinburgh: The Banner of Truth Trust, 2000), 151.

hypothesis was to become the *gestalt* imposed on every facet of biological activity.[3]

Darwin was essentially a scientific observer; between the years 1831 and 1836 he served aboard the H.M.S. Beagle as part of a British scientific expedition around the world. Upon his return to London, Darwin conducted thorough research of his notes and specimens, and out of this study grew several related theories, which were subsequently advanced in the scientific world as a rationale for understanding the origins and development of life on earth. Michael Denton has described the Darwinian revolution as "a dramatic overthrow of one particular interpretation of nature and its replacement by an entirely antithetical theory,"[4] pointing out that its "highly theoretical and meta-physical nature has been forgotten."[5`] Even D. M. S. Watson, the television presenter who popularised the whole concept of evolution for the British public, has admitted, "Evolution itself is accepted by zoologists not because it has been observed to occur or . . . can be proved by logically coherent evidence to be true, but because the only alternative, special creation is clearly incredible."[6]

It is quite clear from the review of literature relating to SLSW (see chapter 3) that much of what is currently promoted in this context stands on an equally shaky foundation. Even Wagner himself has admitted that he has no biblical proof for SLSW, spiritual mapping or identificational repentance, merely what he views as sufficient scriptural evidence to warrant "at the least, a working hypothesis that we can field test, evaluate, modify and refine."[7] The

---

[3]Ruth Deakin, "Christian Perspectives and Values in the Classroom, Session One," class lecture notes, M.A. in Christian Education, Cheltenham College of Higher Education, Cheltenham, England, Feb. 1998.

[4]Michael Denton, *Evolution: A Theory in Crisis* (Bethesda, MD: Adler and Adler, 1986), 74.

[5]Ibid., 76.

[6]Dave Hunt and T. A. McMahon, *The Seduction of Christianity: Spiritual Discernment in the Last Days* (Eugene, OR: Harvest House Publishers, 1985), 96.

[7]C. Peter Wagner, *Confronting the Powers: How the New Testament Church Experienced the Power of Strategic-Level Spiritual Warfare* (Ventura, CA: Regal Books, 1996), 89. Wagner also states, "It goes without saying that if this hypothesis concerning territorial spirits is correct, and if we could learn how to break their control through the power of God, positions on the resistance-receptivity axis could

problem is that despite this reservation, the "working hypothesis" of SLSW is being advanced throughout much of the church of Jesus Christ as divine truth, just in the same way as the theory of evolution is presented in most modern classrooms as the rationale for natural life. As Priest, Campbell and Mullen comment concerning SLSW, such concepts have been "formulated, systematized, publicized, accredited, and institutionalized in mainstream and missionary institutions."[8]

The tragic result is the promotion of a gospel methodology which bears little resemblance to the gospel of Jesus Christ; it is a man-made message divorced from divine authority; it is a gospel of works and not of sovereign grace, with the creature, rather than the Creator, placed assumptively in the spiritual driving seat. Thus, man becomes the lynchpin in the process of salvation; his experiences constituting the determining factor in the evaluation of biblical truth; his efforts in warfare prayer and/or intercession playing what is claimed to be a vital role in the ability of the unconverted to respond in saving faith to the gospel.

The great apologist Tertullian (ca.,155-240) was convinced that Christian faith and human wisdom are diametrically opposed. He believed that God had revealed His plan of salvation in scripture alone and to "mix Scripture with the philosophy of pagans could only distort God's message."[9] Yet this form of syncretism appears to be perfectly acceptable within the context of SLSW, proponents of which have abandoned the concept of *Sola Scriptura*, so integral to the message of the Reformers, and embarked on a dangerous quest

---

change virtually overnight"; quoted in John D. Robb, *Strategic Praying for Frontier Missions: Perspectives on the World Christian Movement, Study Guide* (Pasadena, CA: William Carey Library, 1997), 1-8.

[8]Robert J. Priest, Thomas Campbell, and Bradford A. Mullen, "Missiological Perspectives: The New Animistic Paradigm," in Edward Rommen, ed., *Spiritual Power and Missions: Raising the Issues,* Evangelical Missiological Society Series, no. 3 (Pasadena, CA: William Carey Library, 1995), 10.

[9]Tim Garrett, "Faith and Reason: *Friends or Foes?*" online posting, http://www.probe.org/docs/faithrea.html; accessed 27 Oct. 2001.

for "something more."[10] Wagner, for example, began his investigation into church growth by observation and research on the mission field; his focus,[11] therefore, was on experience and empirical evidence, not on biblical truth. Propelled by a highly commendable desire for successful evangelism, the underlying aim was to find a methodology for promoting church growth which could be replicated around the world, especially in areas not previously penetrated by the gospel. In the author's opinion, it is courting spiritual disaster to begin in the realm of experience, propose a hypothesis, and then seek biblical validation for one's conclusions.[12] Such tendentiousness throws open the door to error; through which, unfortunately, so many appear to have gone.

In the context of SLSW the tragedy has been that, increasingly, experiential evaluation has usurped the authority of the scriptures, and it has become acceptable to look outside the word of God for answers to spiritual problems and for methods of reaching the lost. As Iain Murray succinctly comments, "The true cause of all religious disunity is the addition of man's teaching to the Scripture. Satan's design in every age, ably abetted by sinful man's distaste for the word of God, is to mingle men's inventions with the institutions of Christ."[13] As has been already pointed out, the current generation is particularly vulnerable to this danger because of its postmodern focus on subjective experience rather than on objective truth.

In SLSW, the focus has shifted away from the eternal victory obtained by Jesus Christ when He defeated the enemy at Calvary (Col. 2:15), and is now firmly fixed on Satan and his demonic host. In effect, the devil is viewed not as a created being, dependent on God

---

[10]John F. MacArthur, Jr., "What is True Spirituality?" Pt. 11, *Charismatic Chaos*, online posting, http://www.biblebb.com/files/MAC/CHAOS11.HTM; accessed 14 Dec. 2001.

[11]C. Peter Wagner, "MC510: Genesis of a Concept," in C. Peter Wagner, ed., *Signs & Wonders Today* (Altamonte Springs, FL: Creation House, 1987), 39-49.

[12]Stephen Dray, foreword to *Do Demons Rule Your Town?: An Examination of the Territorial Spirits' Theory* by Mike R. Taylor (London: Grace Publications Trust, 1993).

[13]Iain H. Murray, quoted in Stephen Sizer, "The 'Toronto Blessing': A Theological Examination of the Roots, Teaching and Manifestations, and Connection Between the Faith Movement and the Vineyard Church," online posting, http://www.gospelcom.net/apologeticsindex/sva-tb01.html; accessed 21 May 2001.

for his very existence, but as a spirit of god-like status with power equivalent, or almost equivalent, to that of God Himself. Yet as A. W. Tozer observes, "The scriptural way to see things is to set the Lord always before us, put Christ in the center of our vision, and if Satan is lurking around, he will appear on the margin only and be seen as but a shadow on the edge of the brightness. It is always wrong to reverse this – to set Satan in the focus of our vision and push God to the margin. Nothing but tragedy can come of such invasion."[14]

In parallel with this elevation of Satan by the main protagonists in SLSW, there has been a corresponding demotion in respect to God, who is reduced to a position of passive attendance awaiting the initiative of man in order to act. For example, Dutch Sheets advances the notion based on Revelation 5:8 and 8:3-5, that Christians accumulate a reservoir of prayer in heaven "for use at the proper time."[15] However, according to his hypothesis, "In answer to our requests, He sends His angels to get our bowls of prayer to mix with the fire of the altar. But *there isn't enough in our bowls to meet the need!* We might blame God or think it's not His will or that His Word must not really mean what it says. The reality of it is that sometimes He cannot do what we've asked because we have not given Him enough prayer in our prayer times to get it done. He has poured out all there was to pour and it wasn't enough!"[16] Thus, not only is the Almighty Creator effectively treated as a "genie in a bottle" but a "genie" which is vitally dependent on man's prayer input in order to intervene successfully. Such is not the God of the Bible, Creator of heaven and earth. As Iain Murray points out, "Whenever wrong methods are popularised, on the basis of a weak or erroneous theology, the work of God is marred and confused. Dependence on men, whoever they are, or upon means, is ultimately the opposite of biblical religion."[17]

---

[14]A. W. Tozer, *Born After Midnight* (Camp Hill, PA: Christian Publications, 1989), 43.

[15]Dutch Sheets, *Intercessory Prayer: How God Can Use Your Prayers to Move Heaven and Earth* (Ventura, CA: Regal Books, 1996), 208.

[16]Ibid., 209-10 (original emphasis).

[17]Iain H. Murray, *Revival and Revivalism: The Making and Marring of American Evangelicalism* (Edinburgh: The Banner of Truth Trust, 1996), 412.

It is recognised that part of the driving force behind the SLSW movement has been the desire for world evangelisation. Worldwide evangelisation also forms the basis of what has come to be called the "World Christian Movement" (WCM),[18] which originally aimed to evangelise the world by A.D. 2000.[19] *The Reader for Perspectives on the World Christian Movement* is a substantial document containing messages about missions written by various notable Christian leaders. However, in this context, a striking distinction is made between "evangelism" and the broader concept of "evangelisation."[20] The latter, ". . . does include evangelism, but not exclusively, and not primarily to the unsaved in so-called Christianized nations. It promotes evangelism to 'people groups' who have not heard about Jesus Christ, and then only in terms that can be understood within the cultural context of these people groups . . . personal evangelism-- although a part of world evangelization is not the primary goal. Rather, the primary goal is the turning of whole people groups into Christianized organisms."[21] Significantly, the simple preaching of the gospel is only part of the overall scope of evangelisation, which places an equivalent emphasis on socio-political action. Wagner describes social and political action as the "cultural mandate" of the gospel. He states, "Both the cultural mandate and the evangelistic mandate are essential parts of biblical mission, in my opinion.

---

[18] The World Christian Movement is not a single organisation but a network of different organisations working towards the same goal.

[19] This is not an entirely modern phenomenon; for example, in the late 1800s, such notable Christian leaders as D. L. Moody and A. T. Pearson put out the challenge to evangelise the entire world by the turn of the century, as a result of which some 100,000 students committed their lives to working in foreign missions. The Student Volunteer Movement (forerunner of the Intervarsity Christian Fellowship and the Student Mission Association) took as its slogan "The evangelization of the world in this generation."

[20] This distinction is consistent with that recognised by the first International Congress on World Evangelization which grew out of the Lausanne Conference of 1974.

[21] Albert James Dager, "The World Christian Movement: Evangelism vs Evangelization," *Media Spotlight: A Biblical Analysis of Religious and Secular Media* 22, no. 1 (April 1999): 16, online posting, http://www.banner.org.uk/globalism/WCM1.html; accessed 3 Oct. 2001.

Neither is optional. There is a growing consensus on this point in Evangelical circles."[22]

Against this misconception of the Great Commission, the practice of SLSW becomes extremely relevant, as it offers a methodology for advancing the gospel on an individual, community, city or national basis.[23] Francis Frangipane is quoted in the WCM *Perspectives Study Guide*: "There are satanic strongholds over countries and communities . . . These fortresses exist in the thought patterns and ideas that govern individuals . . . as well as communities and nations. Before victory can be claimed, these strongholds must be pulled down, and Satan's armor removed. Then the mighty weapons of the Word and the Spirit can effectively plunder Satan's house."[24] Once again, the power of the gospel and of the Holy Spirit are being undermined and denigrated, and the operation of man is viewed as the pre-requisite in removing the obstacles to faith; without his involvement the "mighty weapons" of God are effectively immobilised. In identifying the problems facing the foundations of mission as a whole, Hiebert has given a very pertinent warning; he cautions that there is a "dangerous potential of shifting from God and his work to the emphasis of what we can do for God by our own knowledge and efforts." He concludes, "We become captive to a modern secular worldview in which human control and technique

---

[22]C. Peter Wagner, *On the Cutting Edge of Mission Strategy: Perspectives on the World Christian Movement, A Reader,* rev. ed. (Pasadena, CA: William Carey Library, 1992), 45-46; quoted in Dager.

[23]In the context of methodology in evangelism, Horatius Bonar stated in the mid-nineteenth century: "Our whole anxiety is, not how shall we secure the glory of Jehovah, but how shall we multiply conversions? The whole current of our thoughts and anxieties takes this direction. We cease to look at both things together; we think it is enough to keep the one of them alone in our eye; and the issue is that we soon find ourselves pursuing ways of our own. We thus come to measure the correctness of our plans, simply by their seeming to contribute to our favourite aim. We estimate the soundness of our doctrine, not from its tendency to exalt and glorify Jehovah, but entirely by the apparent facility with which it enables us to get sinners to turn from their ways. The question is not asked concerning any doctrine, Is it in *itself* a God-honouring truth, but will it afford us facilities for converting souls?"; quoted in Iain H. Murray, *The Forgotten Spurgeon,* 2d ed. (Edinburgh: The Banner of Truth Trust, 1998), 112 (original emphasis).

[24]Dager, 25.

replace divine leading and human obedience as the basis of mission."[25]

The underlying concept of evangelisation is also apparent as the *raison d'être* for such SLSW techniques as identificational repentance and specific targeting of certain latitudes of the world, (for example, the 10/40 Window and 40/70 Window), in terms of advancing the gospel. However, such notions ignore the biblical truth that Jesus alone provides the basis of reconciliation with the Father and He must be encountered on an individual and not a communal basis. SLSW has made a theology out of delivering nations, apparently discounting the fact that nations are made up of individuals each of whom needs a personal Saviour. Under the Old Covenant, the Jews as a whole were God's people and thus there was a national focus to, and expression of, their faith. But since the inception of the New Covenant on the day of Pentecost, the people of God as individuals have been called out of "every kindred, and tongue, and people, and nation" (Rev. 5:9). The gospel is a universal message, which transcends culture, creed and colour, and is sufficient in power to reach all men (Rom. 1:16).

One of the main themes that has emerged from this study of SLSW is that its proponents are effectively promoting a "gospel plus theory." However, it is impossible to tamper with the simple biblical message without "infringing the copyright" and moving inexorably into error. Error is ever with us, and from the days of the early church, the apostle Paul specifically warned against this very danger: "But I fear, lest by any means, as the serpent beguiled Eve through his subtilty, so your minds should be corrupted from the simplicity that is in Christ" (2 Cor. 11:3). The same admonition is given in his letter to the church at Galatia: "I marvel that ye are so soon removed from him that called you into the grace of God unto another gospel: Which is not another; but there be some that trouble you, and would pervert the gospel of Christ" (Gal. 1:6-7). As Martyn Lloyd-Jones comments, "[The church] must repent of her apostasy. She must repent of her perversion of, and her substitutes for, 'the faith which

---

[25]Paul Hiebert, "De-theologizing Missiology: A Response," *Trinity World Forum* 19 (Fall 1993): 4; quoted in Gailyn Van Rheenen, "The Theological Foundations of Missiology," *Monthly Missiological Reflection* 20 (August 2001), online posting, http://www.missiology.org/MMR/mmr20.htm; accessed 14 Nov. 2001.

was once delivered unto the saints' (Jude 3). She must repent of setting up her own thinking and methods over against the divine revelation given in Holy Scripture. Here lies the reason for her lack of spiritual power and inability to deliver a living message in the power of the Holy Ghost to a world ready to perish."[26]

Knowledge of the Truth

In the author's opinion, one of the greatest tragedies of the contemporary church has been the marginalisation of sound biblical exegesis and theological teaching so that too few Christians appear to have any real grasp of what the Bible really teaches concerning fundamental aspects of their faith. As Wayne Grudem states:

> I am convinced that there is an urgent need in the church today for much greater understanding of Christian doctrine, or systematic theology. Not only pastors and teachers need to understand theology in greater depth--the *whole church* does as well. One day by God's grace we may have churches full of Christians who can discuss, apply and *live* the doctrinal teachings of the Bible as readily as they can discuss the details of their own jobs or hobbies . . .Once that happens, I think that many Christians will find that understanding (and living) the doctrines of Scripture is one of their greatest joys."[27]

Thus, Grudem implies that understanding truth is a pre-requisite to living in truth (see John 8:32). The converse of this is also true and the author would argue that misapprehension or ignorance of truth will inevitably lead to the adoption of erroneous belief and practice. As Percy points out the root of many problems in the Pentecostal-Charismatic movement "lies with the absence of theology." It is for this very reason that the errors propagated under the auspices of

---

[26]D. Martyn Lloyd-Jones, *Knowing the Times: Addresses Delivered on Various Occasions 1942-1977* (Edinburgh: The Banner of Truth Trust, 1989), 57. Gordon Murray advances a similar viewpoint. He states. "The failure to act positively against doctrinal error is our greatest weakness at the present time. We refuse, apparently, to decide whether or not we believe others to be preaching another gospel in case the answer proves to be too embarrassing. Yet this is the question which must be asked and answered if we are to know what to do. A Church only exists where the true gospel is proclaimed"; quoted in Iain H. Murray, *The Fight of Faith 1939-1981*, vol. 2 of 2, *D. Martyn Lloyd-Jones* (Edinburgh: The Banner of Truth Trust, 1990), 447.

[27]Wayne Grudem, *Systematic Theology: An Introduction to Biblical Doctrine* (Leicester: InterVarsity Press, 1994), 18 (original emphasis).

SLSW have been able to command such widespread acceptance,[28] based on the fact that few really understand the glorious truth of redemption in Jesus Christ, and most have been kept in ignorance by the lack of sound preaching and teaching.

However, ignorance has never been part of God's intention for His people, "who will have all men to be saved, and to come unto the knowledge of the truth" (1 Tim. 2:4). In the epistle to the Hebrews, the writer refers to God's complaint against the children of Israel: "Wherefore I was grieved with that generation, and said, they do always err in *their* heart; and they have not known my ways" (Heb. 3:10; see also Psa. 95:10). He then continues, "Take heed, brethren, lest there be in any of you an evil heart of unbelief, in departing from the living God" (Heb. 3:12). God takes the issue of ignorance amongst believers very seriously, for the very reason that ignorance is so closely allied with error, and error induces apostasy. Thus, the word of God contains numerous warnings about this very danger: Proverbs 19:2 declares that it is not good "*that* the soul *be* without knowledge"; Isaiah 5:13 reveals that "my people are gone into captivity, because they have no knowledge"; God says in Jeremiah 4:22, "For my people is foolish, they have not known me; they are sottish children, and they have none understanding: they are wise to do evil, but to do good they have no knowledge"; and in Hosea 4:6, "my people are destroyed for lack of knowledge."

In the New Testament the same emphasis re-emerges; for example, part of the reason that the great letter to the church at Rome was penned by Paul, was to bring clarification on the fundamental doctrine of salvation so that Christians would be enabled to withstand the errors being propagated by the Judaisers. Similarly, Paul exhorts the Corinthian church to "be not children in understanding . . . but in understanding be men" (1 Cor. 14:20); and to the Ephesians he writes that unbelievers are those who are "alienated from the life of God through the ignorance that is in them" (Eph. 4:18).[29] As MacArthur also points out: "Knowledge is a

---

[28]Martyn Percy, *Power and the Church: Ecclesiology in an Age of Transition* (London: Cassell, 1998), 190.

[29]John MacArthur, Jr., *Colossians and Philemon,* in *MacArthur's New Testament Commentary,* in *QuickVerse* ver. 7 [CD-ROM] (Omaha, NE: Parsons Technology, 1997).

central theme in Paul's writings. He said of the Corinthians, 'In every thing you were enriched in him, in all speech and all knowledge' (1 Corinthians 1:5). He prayed that 'the God of our Lord Jesus Christ, the Father of glory' would give the Ephesians 'a spirit of wisdom and revelation in the knowledge of Him' (Eph. 1:17). To the Philippians he wrote, 'This I pray, that your love may abound still more and more in real knowledge and all discernment' (Phil. 1:9)."[30]

When Jesus was born the whole world lay shrouded in the lies of the devil, the spirit that even now continues to work in the children of disobedience (Eph. 2:2). Jesus defeated that power on Calvary, and at new birth the enemy's stranglehold on the individual's life is broken, and he or she is translated out of the kingdom of darkness into the kingdom of His dear Son (Col. 1:13). Thus, God intends that new birth should be the vehicle to a totally different realm; He intends that the believer should know the reality of an abundant and victorious Christian life. But so many sincere people become trapped in bondage because of ignorance or wrong teaching that leads to wrong thinking. It is therefore so important to understand what the word of God teaches so that faith may be grounded in truth. In a spiritual sense it is suicidal to evaluate one's beliefs on the basis of human experience. That is the road to disaster, but it is a road that many are travelling! As Leith Anderson has commented, "The old paradigm taught that if you have the right teaching you will experience God. The new paradigm says that if you experience God you will have the right teaching."[31]

In reality, the scriptures are the only measure by which to evaluate any spiritual experience; thus, if the experience does not accord with the word, the experience is false. Christians need a living knowledge of the word so that they may be able to discern between truth and error. This is more than an intellectual grasp of doctrine; it is rather, a deep inward knowing of the Almighty God and of His ways which impacts both the understanding and, consequently, the life of the individual believer who lives in the power of the Spirit. The

---

[30]Ibid.

[31]Leith Anderson, *A Church for the Twenty-First Century* (Minneapolis, MN: Bethany House, 1992), 20; quoted in Gene Edward Veith, Jr., *Postmodern Times: A Christian Guide to Contemporary Thought and Culture* (Wheaton, IL: Crossway Books, 1994), 211.

apostle Paul commended the Jews of Berea not only for their ready acceptance of the gospel, but for their painstaking eagerness to evaluate what was taught on the basis of the word of God. This is not to say that faith can be appropriated by the human intellect or that mental acquiescence to a set of beliefs brings about new birth. Only the Spirit of God can give true revelation of the things of God, but such revelation will always accord with the Scriptures.[32] As Charles Price comments, "The things of God receive their unveiling as the Hands of the Holy Spirit lift the curtains of our doubts and fears and misunderstandings and the Truth shines forth in all its radiance and in its unchangeable glory."[33] Robert Barclay also knew this wonderful truth. He wrote, ". . . the Testimony of the Spirit is that alone, by which the true knowledge of God hath been, is, and can be, only revealed . . . Moreover, these divine Inward Revelations, which we make absolutely necessary for the Building up of True Faith, neither do or can ever contradict the outward Testimony of the Scriptures."[34]

Traditionally, within Pentecostal and Charismatic circles, there has been an irrational underlying fear of education on the basis that it may adversely affect an individual's walk with God. Allied to this, the rejection of dead truth (namely, truth expounded without the quickening life of the Spirit of God), has inadvertently brought about a devaluing of the word of God and the elevation of an experience-based faith. However, it is God's desire that every believer should be able to elucidate the reasons which undergird his hope in the gospel

---

[32]John Flavel, *The Works of John Flavel*, vol. 2 of 6 (Edinburgh: The Banner of Truth Trust, 1968), 334-35. "The scriptures are by the inspiration of the Spirit, therefore this inspiration into the hearts of believers must either substantially agree with the scriptures, or the inspiration of the Spirit be self-repugnant, and contradictory to itself. It is very observable, that the works of grace wrought by the Spirit in the hearts of believers, are represented to us in scripture, as a transcript, or copy of the written word, Jer. xxxi. 33. 'I will write my law in their hearts.' Now, as a true copy answers the original, word for word, letter for letter, point for point; so do the works of the Spirit in our souls harmonize with the dictates of the Spirit in the scriptures; whatsoever motion therefore shall be found repugnant thereto, must not be fathered upon the Spirit of God, but laid at the door of its proper parents, the spirit of error and corrupt nature."

[33]Charles S. Price, *Made Alive* (Plainfield, NJ: Logos International, 1945), 27.

[34]Robert Barclay, *An Apology for the True Christian Divinity* (London: T. Sowle Raylton and Luke Hinde, 1736), 24.

(1 Pet. 3:15). The Bible alone sets out the basis for such knowledge; it is therefore vital to imbibe that word in order that it may be used by the Holy Spirit to establish truth in the Christian's heart and mind--otherwise, the Spirit is robbed of the very tool which has been ordained for development and blessing (2 Tim. 3:16-17).

Part of God's promise in the everlasting covenant was that His people would have an individual and personal knowledge of their Saviour: "And they shall teach no more every man his neighbour, and every man his brother saying, Know the Lord: for they shall all know me, from the least of them unto the greatest of them, saith the Lord" (Jer. 31:33-34). In the gospel of Jesus Christ, God has sovereignly chosen to reveal Himself, as the God who loved, the God who gave, the God who sent His only begotten Son to die in the place of sinful man (John 3:16). Just as Jesus came to make known the heart of the Father, so the Holy Spirit came to make known the things of Christ (John 16:13-15). Accordingly, the man or woman who comes to a living knowledge of the power of the gospel comes to a living knowledge of the God of the gospel.

Such knowledge, however, is not static.[35] The road to maturity involves development: "Till we all come in the unity of the faith, and of the knowledge of the Son of God, unto a perfect man, unto the measure of the stature of the fullness of Christ" (Eph. 4:13). It was for this reason that Jesus impressed upon His followers the vital necessity of continuance in His word as the means of knowing the liberating power of truth. This is the essence of true discipleship (John 8:31-32). Unfortunately, the corollary of this principle is equally true and many saints of God struggle in the Christian life through a basic lack of knowledge of the truth of full redemption. Belief is always subject to knowledge and so it is possible to live in an impoverished Christian experience because of ignorance, misunderstanding and false teaching.

The enemy seeks to promote such ignorance of the truth; he attempts to establish his strongholds in the minds of men with the sole aim of diverting them from truth. That was the strategy he used

---

[35]See for example Col. 1:10, ". . . that ye might be filled with the knowledge of his will in all wisdom and spiritual understanding; That ye might walk worthy of the Lord unto all pleasing, being fruitful in every good work, and increasing in the knowledge of God."

so successfully with Adam and Eve. They were created in the image of God but the serpent managed to convince them that somehow God had treated them unfairly, that they had been deprived. Acting upon that lie they directly disobeyed the instruction God had given them and became the servants of sin. Lying is the enemy's only weapon and he still continues to use it to great effect. However, Satan fears the power of truth, for it is truth that sets the captive free.

Lloyd-Jones declares, "Christian truth is not a matter of reason or of philosophy; it is something which is given. It is of God. It is God's truth. It is God speaking to man, not man trying to arrive at a knowledge of God, trying to understand his life and world, trying to concoct some proposals for dealing with the difficulties. No, it is the exact opposite. It is something that we *receive* entirely from God. It is revelation and it is all of grace."[36]

Barclay expresses a similar understanding: "This is not the best and truest knowledge of God, which is wrought by the labour and sweat of the Brain, but that which is kindled within us, by an heavenly Warmth in our Hearts . . . It is but a thin and airy knowledge, that is got by mere Speculation, which is ushered in by Syllogisms and Demonstrations; but that which springs forth from true Goodness . . . brings such a Divine Light into the soul, as is more clear and convincing, than any Demonstration."[37]

Spurgeon also writes:

> Blessedness is ascribed to those who treasure up the testimonies of the Lord: in which it is implied that they search the Scriptures, that they come to an understanding of them, that they love them, and then that they continue in the practice of them. We must first get a thing before we can keep it . . . God's word is his witness or testimony to grand and important truths which concern himself and our relation to him: this we should desire to know; knowing it, we should believe it; believing it, we should love it; and loving it, we should hold it fast against all comers. There is a doctrinal keeping of the word when we are ready to die for its defence, and a practical keeping of it when we actually live under its power. Revealed truth is precious as diamonds, and should be kept or treasured up in the memory and in the heart as jewels in a casket, or as the law was kept in the ark . . . If we keep God's testimonies they will keep us; they

---

[36] Lloyd-Jones, 289.

[37] Barclay, 24.

will keep us right in opinion, comfortable in spirit, holy in conversation, and hopeful in expectation . . . their designed effect does not come through a temporary seizure of them, but by a persevering keeping of them: "in keeping of them there is great reward."[38]

The Gospel of the New Covenant

Given the scriptural emphasis on knowledge of the truth as the God-ordained vehicle for spiritual freedom, it is vitally important for each and every believer to understand the gospel of Jesus Christ biblically. As J. I. Packer points out in respect to problems encountered by the church in the second half of the twentieth century:

> Modern Evangelicalism, by and large, has ceased to preach the gospel in the old way, and we frankly admit that the new gospel, insofar as it deviates from the old, seems to us a distortion of the biblical message . . . Our theological currency has been debased. Our minds have been conditioned to think of the Cross as a redemption which does less to redeem, and of Christ as a Saviour who does less than save, and of God's love as a weak affection which cannot keep anyone from hell without help, and of faith as the human help which God needs for this purpose. As a result we are no longer free either to believe the biblical gospel or to preach it. We cannot believe it, because our thoughts are caught in the toils of synergism . . . The resultant mental muddle deprives God of much of the glory that we should give Him as author and finisher of salvation, and ourselves of much of the comfort we might draw from knowing what God is for us.[39]

This same confusing synergism,[40] to which Packer refers, is also advocated by proponents of SLSW. However, the biblical truth is quite different, for "of his own will begat he us with the word of truth" (James 1:18); "which were born, not of blood, nor of the will of the flesh, nor of the will of man, but of God" (John 1:13); "so

---

[38]Charles. H. Spurgeon, *Psalms 111-150*, vol. 6 of 7, *The Treasury of David: An Expository and Devotional Commentary on the Psalms* (Grand Rapids, MI: Baker Book House, 1983), 13.

[39]J. I. Packer, introduction to *The Death of Death in the Death of Christ*, by John Owen (Edinburgh: The Banner of Truth Trust, 1983), 13-14.

[40]*The Shorter Oxford English Dictionary*, vol. 2 of 2 (London: Guild Publishing, 1983), s.v. "synergism," defined as "the doctrine that the human will cooperates with Divine Grace in the work of regeneration."

then it is not of him that willeth, nor of him that runneth, but of God that showeth mercy" (Rom. 9:16).[41] Salvation is the sovereign act of a sovereign God and as such, it cannot be frustrated. "We did not ask him to elect us. We did not ask him to redeem us. These things were done before we were born. We did not ask him to call us by grace, for alas! we did not know the value of that call, and we were dead in trespasses and sins, but he gave us freely of his unsought, but boundless love. Prevenient grace came to us, outrunning all our desires, and all our wills, and all our prayers."[42] It is that same 'prevenient grace' which reaches out to man and causes him to respond to the message of the gospel, transforming him into a totally new creature in Christ Jesus (2 Cor. 5:17; see also Gal. 6:15). As Flavel explains concerning the efficacy of salvation: "It is . . . an everlasting work, never to be destroyed . . . The exceeding greatness of God's power goes forth to produce it; and indeed no less is required to enlighten the blind mind, break the rocky heart, and bow the stubborn will of man."[43] He continues, "The new creature is a mercy which draws a train of innumerable and invaluable mercies after it . . . When God hath given us a new nature, then he dignifies us with a *new name,* Rev vii. 17. brings us into a *new covenant,* Jer xxxi. 33. begets us again to a *new hope,* 1 Pet i. 3.. intitles us to a *new inheritance,* John i. 12, 13. "[44]

The essence of the gospel of the new covenant is that it is entirely God-centred--it is God's plan, He fulfils it in and for us,

---

[41]In his last sermon, preached in London in July 1688, Bunyan speaks of John 1:13 and Romans 9:16 as follows: "Natural desires after the things of another world, are not an argument to prove man shall go to heaven whenever he dies. I am not a free-willer, I do abhor it, yet there is not the wickedest man, but he desires some time or other to be saved; he will read some time or other, or it may be, pray; but this will not do. 'It is not in him that wills, not in him that runs, but in God that shows mercy'; there is willing and running, and yet to no purpose . . . Though a man without grace may have a will to be saved, yet he cannot have that will in God's way; nature cannot know any thing but the things of nature; the things of God knows no man, but by the Spirit of God. Unless the Spirit of God be in you, it will leave you on this side of the gates of heaven." John Bunyan, "The New Birth," in vol. 2 of 3, *The Works of John Bunyan,* ed. George Offor (Edinburgh: The Banner of Truth Trust, 1991), 756.

[42]Iain H. Murray, *The Forgotten Spurgeon,* 81.

[43]Flavel, 2:367 (original emphasis).

[44]Ibid.

"according as he hath chosen us in him before the foundation of the world, that we should be holy and without blame before him in love" (Eph. 1:4):

> All true faith is really based in the belief, the certainty, that God cannot lie. He made an eternal promise before the foundation of the world that He would bring many sons unto Glory! For this purpose He sent His Son into the world, to redeem those whom He calls. The gospel is so simple, so sure, because it is based on the Covenant Word of our unchangeable God . . . He initiated the whole plan of salvation and He will also bring it to completion (Titus 3:3-5). Salvation is neither conditional upon our set beliefs nor our responses. It is all according to His wonderful mercy and grace.[45]

Viewed from this perspective, it is clear that Satan has no real power to obstruct the work of the gospel. He may lie and deceive but he is already defeated and he knows it. For every true child of God there is a time of divine appointment, when the word of God breaks through in the power of the Holy Spirit to convict, convince, cleanse and make alive. It is the moment of new birth; it is the moment when the reality of God's redeeming love bursts forth in the inner man, for life has come. Then and only then the human heart can, indeed must, open and respond in saving faith.[46] There is no devil that can prevent this impartation of the divine nature, for God is sovereign and He alone is omnipotent. The power of His grace and love to restore and redeem is infinitely greater than Satan's transient attempts to kill and destroy. And down through the ages men and women of God have given testimony to that moment of divine choosing when, like Saul of Tarsus, the scales of doubt and fear, rebellion and unbelief, fell from their eyes and the risen Christ was revealed within. For Martin Luther, the word which captivated his life and dominated his ministry

---

[45] Michael S. B. Reid, *Faith: It's God Given* (Brentwood, England: Alive UK, 2000), 117-18.

[46] Iain H. , *The Forgotten Spurgeon*, 87: "It is at the point of spiritual *death* that the Holy Spirit first meets men in saving power and raises them from sin's sepulchre. Not until life is implanted can repentance and faith be exercised and therefore these spiritual acts are the 'first apparent result of regeneration' . . . We are as helpless to co-operate in our regeneration as we are to co-operate in the work of Calvary, and as it is the Cross alone that meets the guilt of sin, so it is regeneration alone which meets its power."

was "The just shall live by faith" (Rom. 1:17);[47] George Fox's heart
was set on fire by the verse, "I am the light of the world: he that
followeth me shall not walk in darkness, but shall have the light of
life" (John 8:12);[48] and William Law had a life-transforming revelation
of God's love based on 1 John 4:19, "We love him, because he first
loved us."[49] In more recent church history, Amy Carmichael was
launched into life and ministry with the simple instruction "Go ye";[50]
similarly, for Benson Idahosa the words which opened the door of
life were, "Preach the gospel and I will confirm my word with signs
following";[51] and Oral Roberts received health and eternal life when

---

[47]H. J. Hillerbrand, *The Reformation in its Own Words* (London: SCM Press, 1964),
21; Roland Bainton, *Here I Stand* (Oxford: Lion Publishing, 1990), 65.

[48]Fox later wrote: "Now the Lord God opened to me by His invisible power that
every man was enlightened by the divine Light of Christ, and I saw it shine
through all; and that they that believed in it came out of condemnation to the
Light of life, and became the children of it; but they that hated it, and did not
believe in it were condemned by it, though they made a profession of Christ.
This I saw in the pure openings of the Light without the help of any man . . . I
was sent to turn people from darkness to Light, that they might receive Christ
Jesus; for to as many as should receive Him in His Light, I saw He would give
power to become the sons of God; which power I had obtained by receiving
Christ." George Fox, *A Journal of George Fox,* 3d ed., with an introduction by
William Penn (London: W. Richardson and S. Clark, 1765), 20.

[49]"Would you divinely know the mysteries of grace and salvation, would you go
forth as a faithful witness of gospel truths, stay until this fire of divine love has
had its perfect work in you. For till your heart is an altar, on which this heavenly
fire never goes out, you are dead in yourself, and can only be a speaker of dead
words, about things that never had any life in you . . . There is no knowledge in
heaven, but what proceeds from this birth of love, nor is there any difference
between the highest light of an angel, and the horrid darkness of a devil, but that
which love has made . . . And so it is, that we could not love God, but because
he first loved us, that is, because he first by our creation brought forth, and by
our redemption continued and kept up that same birth of his own Spirit of love
in us." William Law, *An Humble, Earnest, and Affectionate Address to the Clergy,* in
vol. 9 of 9, *The Works of William Law* (Canterbury: G. Moreton, 1893), 66-67.

[50]"I heard Him say 'GO YE' I never heard it quite so plainly before; I cannot be
mistaken for I know He spoke. He says 'Go', I cannot stay . . . Oh, nothing but
that sure word, *His* word, could make it possible to do it, for until He spoke, and
I answered, 'Yes, Lord', I never knew what it would cost." Frank Houghton,
Amy Carmichael of Dohnavur (London: SPCK, 1954), 45.

[51]Ruthanne Garlock, *Fire in His Bones: The Story of Benson Idahosa* (Tulsa, OK: Praise
Books, 1981), 69.

God spoke the words, "Son, I am going to heal you and you are to take My healing power to your generation. You are to build Me a university and build it on My authority and the Holy Spirit."[52] To the author himself, as a sceptical atheist seeking to prove that God did not exist, the divine voice spoke, "Give all that thou hast and the Lord will provide" and somehow those words not only became the gateway into life, but have proved to be life's sustaining power over many years. Scripture makes it quite clear that it is by His word that God has chosen to impart life to every believer (1 Pet. 1:23-25). As Kenyon comments, "He is not only in the Word, but He breathes His very life through it as it is unfolded . . . It is His word that gives birth to faith . . . It is God's faith expressed."[53]

A forceful and persuasive preacher may convince his audience on an intellectual basis; he may evoke an emotional response; but no lasting work of any spiritual value will be accomplished without the application of that word to the hearts of his hearers by the Holy Ghost. Only then does it become God's Word. As is made clear in the parable of the sower (Matt. 13:23), there are many different types of heart, each of which will receive the same word in a very different way: "But he that received seed into the good ground is he that heareth the word, and understandeth it; which also beareth fruit, and bringeth forth, some an hundredfold, some sixty, some thirty" (Matt. 13:13). To open the understanding of unregenerate man, convincing him of ". . . sin, and of righteousness, and of judgment" (John 16:8) is the work of God's Spirit. However, He also works within the people of God, as the Spirit of truth, revealing divine truth (John 14:7; Eph. 1:17-19). Putting this in simple terms, man is totally reliant on the intervention of God for his salvation and for his spiritual growth. He may give assent to a set of beliefs, but these will never become a living reality in his heart and life until they are spoken by

---

[52]"Bigger than my healing was my call. God had spoken in my spirit words that I heard audibly: 'You are to take My healing power to your generation. You are to build Me a university and build it on My authority and the Holy Spirit.' It was impossible for me to fully understand this awesome call, but I am grateful that I believed every word and that a *knowledge* came into my consciousness that I would be able to obey God and do those things." Oral Roberts, *Expect a Miracle: My Life and Ministry* (Milton Keynes, England: Nelson Word, 1995), 36.

[53]E. W. Kenyon, *New Creation Realities: A Revelation of Redemption* (Lynnwood, WA: Kenyon's Gospel Publishing Society, 2000), 6.

the Holy Spirit. Even within the context of the author's own teaching on the errors of SLSW, he is only too well aware that lasting results are in God's hands: "So then neither is he that planteth any thing, neither is he that watereth; but God that giveth the increase" (1 Cor. 3:17).

In a world in which salvation and spiritual development are so frequently predicated on the basis of the individual's personal choice, it has become spiritually unfashionable to speak of God's sovereignty in this context. Man demands the right to make his own decisions, insisting that a God of love must provide equal opportunity for all. However, "no man can come to [Jesus] except the Father . . . draw him" (John 6:44). The reality is that when God speaks the word, it has to be; conversely, without His word, it cannot be and no amount of SLSW or any other humanly inspired methodology will ever change that truth. As John Murray writes:

> The only gospel there is is a gospel which rests upon the assumption of total inability. It is this truth that lays the basis for the glory of the gospel of grace.
>
> . . . It is the doctrine of man's utter sinfulness and inability that leads men to cease to trust in themselves and shuts them up to reliance upon God's grace . . . This doctrine does not hinder evangelism. One of the greatest hindrances to the spread of the gospel is the lack of it. It is only on the presupposition of total depravity and complete human impotence that the full glory and power of the gospel can be declared.[54]

But when that gospel is declared and the divine voice is heard in the innermost depths of the soul speaking with life, with love, and with power, then the impossible is made possible and the sinner bows in glad surrender to the Lord of glory. It is a moment when eternity steps into time, as another precious blood-bought child of God is birthed into the family, a new creation in Christ Jesus. Just as God spoke the worlds into being, He speaks life into that which was dead in trespasses and sins (Eph. 2:1; see also 1 Pet. 2:9-10). Thomas Boston writes of the miracle of new birth as follows: "The work of the Spirit is felt; but his way of working is a mystery we cannot comprehend. A new light is let into the mind, and the will is renewed; but how that light is conveyed thither, how the will is fettered with

---

[54]John Murray, *Systematic Theology*, vol. 2 of 4, *Collected Writings of John Murray* (Edinburgh: The Banner of Truth Trust, 2001), 88.

cords of love, and how the rebel is made a willing captive, we can no more tell than we can tell how the bones do grow in the womb of her that is with child, Eccl. xi. 5. "[55]

In the light of biblical truth, the claims of SLSW have neither substance nor relevance to the regenerate man who lives in victory. New birth is the work of the Almighty, in accordance with His covenant promise. Just as He spoke the worlds into being, He speaks new life into the soul, "when he raises it from the death of sin to the life of righteousness."[56]

Under the Old Covenant, man was responsible to keep the law; man was required to live up to God's standard of righteousness; man provided the sacrifices for sin; man strove for victory; and man was in bondage to his own failure. But for those who have come into the reality of New Covenant truth, everything is so different. Now salvation is of God; Jesus Christ is become the eternal sacrifice for sin; He is "made unto us wisdom, and righteousness, and sanctification and redemption" (1 Cor. 1:30); He "giveth us the victory" (1 Cor. 15:57); He "always causeth us to triumph" (2 Cor. 2:14); and "the law of the Spirit of life in Christ Jesus hath made [us] free from the law of sin and death" (Rom. 8:2). Speaking of the transition from the Old to the New Covenant, Kenyon makes the following comment:

> [Jesus] had fulfilled the Old Covenant and there had been the annulling of the Priesthood and the Law of the Sacrifices with the Old Covenant. Now a New Covenant has come into being and there must be a new Priesthood. There must be a New Law. The old

---

[55]Thomas Boston, *Human Nature in its Fourfold State* (London: The Religious Tract Society, 1837), 191. See also John Wesley, "Sermon 45: The New Birth," *Sermons on Several Occasions,* in vol. 6 of 14, *The Works of John Wesley,* with the last corrections of the author (London: Methodist Publishing House, 1865), 69. Wesley writes of the mystery of the new birth. " 'The wind bloweth where is listeth,'--not by thy power or wisdom; 'and thou hearest the sound thereof;'--thou art absolutely assured, beyond all doubt, that it doth blow; 'but thou canst not tell whence it cometh, not whither it goeth;'--the precise manner how it begins and ends, rises and falls, no man can tell. 'So is every one that is born of the Spirit:'--Thou mayest be as absolutely assured of the fact, as of the blowing of the wind; but the precise manner how it is done, how the Holy Spirit works this in the soul, neither thou nor the wisest of the children of men is able to explain."

[56]Wesley, "The New Birth," *The Works,* 6:71.

Priesthood was to deal with servants. The new Priesthood is to deal with Sons. The old Priesthood has the Ten Commandments called 'the Law of Death.' The New Covenant has but one commandment, 'The Law of Life.' John 13:34-35, 'A new commandment give I unto you that ye love one another even as I have loved you.'"[57]

The gospel of the New Covenant is so simple. Men may struggle in prayer, pleading with God to unseat cosmic powers, ever seeking to attain, because they do not really understand; but this is not the relationship of a son with the Father. As John Bunyan writes:

. . . you have some people, it is true, they will go to prayer, in appearance very fervently, and will plead very hard with God that he would grant them their desires, pleading their want, and the abundance thereof; they will also plead with God his great mercy, and also his free promises . . . in thus doing they do not appear before the Lord no otherwise than in an old-covenant spirit; for they go to God only as a merciful Creator, and they themselves as his creatures; not as he is, their Father in the Son, and they his children by regeneration through the Lord Jesus.[58]

But the true child comes to His heavenly Father as a son and heir (Gal. 4:7), seeking only to do the Father's will, confident in the fact that "old things are passed away; behold, all things are become new. And all things are of God" (2 Cor. 5:17-18). Such an one has come to the place of eternal security of which the writer to the Hebrews speaks: "There remaineth therefore a rest to the people of God. For he that is entered into his rest, he also hath ceased from his own works, as God *did* from his" (Heb. 4:9-10). Here is one who, in the words of Richard Baxter, "lives upon God alone; his faith is divine; his love, obedience, and confidence, are divine; his chief converse is divine; his hopes and comforts are divine."[59] God is the source of his life, God is the source of his calling, God is the source of his witness: "For of him, and through him, and to him, *are* all things: to whom *be* glory for ever. Amen" (Rom. 11:36). He who understands this glorious truth gives no place to the devil (Eph. 4:27), but rests in the victory that Christ has already won and it is that victory which he proclaims to the world.

[57]Kenyon, *New Creation Realities*, 133.

[58]Bunyan, "The Doctrine of the Law and Grace Unfolded," in *The Works*, 1:557.

[59]Richard Baxter, "Character of a Confirmed Christian," in *The Select Practical Works of Richard Baxter* (Glasgow: Blackie & Son, 1840), 716-17.

God's Remedy: The Preaching of the Gospel

The conclusions resulting from this research project have far-reaching implications for ministry as a whole, in terms of the advancement of the kingdom of God. SLSW methodology is but representative of a whole range of erroneous teachings, which threaten the people of God by undermining their faith in the Father who, by sovereign grace, has made every provision for their rebirth and victorious life in Christ. SLSW focuses on the devil and his work in supposedly impeding the progress of the gospel. Thus sin and the responsibility of the individual become a side issue and the ultimate reason for man's continued separation from God is directly attributable to the interference of Satan and his demonic host. Such dualism is characteristic of SLSW. It is not, however, validated by the scriptures.

From the time of the Fall, the point at issue between God and man has always and only been one of sin. Man was alienated from God because he chose his own will and way; thus, the real problem was not the power of the devil, but man's unwillingness to be subject to the Creator.[60] Disobedience was, and still is, the key issue (Rom. 5:19); man was led astray only because he had abandoned the truth and accepted the lie. As Billy Graham observes, "The deepest problems of the human race are spiritual in nature. They are rooted in man's refusal to seek God's way for his life. The problem is the human heart which God alone can change."[61] So Jesus came to "save His people from their sins" (Matt. 1:21); He came to "put away sin by the sacrifice of himself" (Heb. 9:26). "This shall be his great business in the world: the great errand on which he is come, viz. to make an atonement for, and to destroy, sin: deliverance from all the power,

---

[60]"To sum up all in a word: nothing hath separated us from God but our own will, or rather our own will is our separation from God. All the disorder, and corruption, and malady of our nature, lies in a certain fixedness of our own will, imagination, and desires, wherein we live to ourselves, our own center and circumference, act wholly from ourselves, according to our own will, imagination and desires. There is not the smallest degree of evil in us, but what arises from this selfishness, because we are thus, all in all to ourselves." William Law, *The Grounds and Reasons of Christian Regeneration or, The New Birth* (London: W. Innys, R. Manby and S. Cox, 1750), 96.

[61]Billy Graham, *God's Ambassador: A Lifelong Mission of Giving Hope to the World* (Minneapolis, MN: Billy Graham Evangelistic Association, 1999), 219.

guilt and pollution of sin, is the privilege of every believer in Christ Jesus. Less than this is not spoken of in the Gospel; and less than this would be unbecoming to the Gospel. The perfection of the Gospel system is not that it makes allowances for sin, but that it makes atonement for it: not that it tolerates sin, but that it destroys it."[62] Thus, the angels who announced the birth of the child in a manger, came with a message of good news, with a proclamation of peace and good will from God to man (Luke 2:10-14). The time of alienation was at an end, and there was one simple reason: "For God so loved the world, that he gave his only begotten Son, that whosoever believeth in him should not perish, but have everlasting life" (John 3:16). This is the essence of the gospel, which Clarke defines as, "The whole doctrine of Jesus Christ, comprised in the history of his incarnation, preaching, miracles, sufferings, death, resurrection, ascension, and the mission of the Holy Spirit, by which salvation was procured for a lost world."[63]

It is God's gospel, it speaks His heart, it represents His power, "the power of God unto salvation to every one that believeth" (Rom. 1:16). In respect to this particular scripture, Barnes states: "It is the efficacious or mighty plan, by which power goes forth to save, and by which all the obstacles of man's redemption are taken away. This expression implies, (1) That it is God's plan, or his appointment. It is not the devices of man. (2) It is adapted to the end. It is suited to overcome the obstacles in the way. It is not merely the instrument by which God exerts his power, but it has an inherent adaptedness to the end, it is suited to accomplish salvation to man so that it may be denominated power."[64] Hodge also comments that "the gospel is that in which God works, which he renders efficacious . . . *unto salvation*."[65]

The reality of the quickening power of the gospel has been recognised by men of God throughout the ages. In 1795, at the formation of the first interdenominational missionary society of

---

[62]Adam Clarke, *Matthew-Luke*, vol. 5A, *Clarke's Commentary on the New Testament*, in *QuickVerse* ver. 7 [CD-ROM] (Omaha, NE: Parsons Technology, 1997).

[63]Ibid.

[64]Albert Barnes, *Romans*, vol. 4 of 8, *A Popular Family Commentary on the New Testament* (London: Blackie and Son Ltd, n.d.), 33.

[65]Charles Hodge, *Commentary on the Epistle to the Romans* (Edinburgh: The Banner of Truth Trust, 1975), 28.

modern times, Rowland Hill spoke of the glorious revivals of the past and said, "What has been done, shall be done. God will ever stand by his own truth, and if he be for us, who can be against us? Preaching the Gospel of the kingdom does all the work."[66]

William Law also had a divine revelation of the life-transforming power of the gospel. He writes these beautiful words: "The Son of God by a love, greater than that which created the world, became man and gave his own blood and life into the fallen soul, that it might through his life in it, be raised, quickened and born again into its first state of inward peace and delight, glory and perfection, never to be lost anymore . . . Can the world resist such love as this? Or can any man doubt, whether he should open all that is within him, to receive such a salvation?"[67]

Similarly, John Wesley gives testimony to the mighty power of God unto salvation in the hearts of men who were ". . . profligate, abandoned sinners, now entirely changed, truly fearing God and working righteousness. . . . inwardly and outwardly changed; loving God and their neighbour; living in the uniform practice of justice, mercy, and truth . . . easy and happy in their lives, and triumphant in their death."[68] He writes, "It is only the Gospel of Jesus Christ which is the power of God unto salvation. Human wisdom, as human laws, may restrain from outward sin; but they cannot avail to the saving of the soul. If God gives this blessing to what is preached, it is a sufficient 'proof of His approbation.'"[69]

Spurgeon proclaims the same conviction when he declares: "To this hour, the voice of God is power. This gospel, which utters and reveals his word, is the power of God unto salvation to everyone that believeth. Our voices are fitly called to praise him whose voice spoke

---

[66]Rowland Hill, *Sermons Preached in London at the Formation of the Missionary Society* (n.p., 1795), 109; quoted in Iain H. Murray, *The Puritan Hope: Revival and the Interpretation of Prophecy* (Edinburgh: The Banner of Truth Trust, 1971), 127-28.

[67]Law, 46-47.

[68]John Wesley, "Sermon 66: The Signs of the Times," *Sermons on Several Occasions*, in vol. 6 of 14, *The Works of the Rev. John Wesley, A.M.*, with the last corrections of the author (London: Wesleyan Conference Office, 1865), 292-93.

[69]John Wesley, "Letter 43: To Mr John Smith," *Letters from the Reverend John Wesley to Various Persons*, in vol. 12 of 14, *The Works of the Rev. John Wesley, A.M.*, 11th ed., with the last corrections of the author (London: John Mason, 1856), 94.

us into being, and gives the effectual grace which secures our well-being."[70] "Oh! Spirit of God, bring back thy Church to a belief in the gospel! Bring back her ministers to preach it once again with the Holy Ghost, and not striving after wit and learning. Then shall we see thine arm made bare, O God, in the eyes of all the people, and the myriads shall be brought to rally round the throne of God and the Lamb. The Gospel must succeed; it shall succeed; it cannot be prevented from succeeding; a multitude that no man can number must be saved."[71]

In the twentieth century, the evangelist Billy Graham was to write of the identical truth, "I have had the privilege of preaching this Gospel on every continent in most of the countries of the world. And I have found that when I present the simple message of the Gospel of Jesus Christ, with authority, quoting the very Word of God--He takes that message and drives it supernaturally into the human heart."[72] "I am just a spectator watching what God is doing."[73]

Oral Roberts has a similar understanding: "Instead of giving personal opinions and the current events, our main thrust is to preach the gospel--the good news that Jesus brought in the new covenant, fulfilling the old by shedding His blood and becoming the eternal sacrifice. God confirmed it by raising Him from the dead, making Him unique forever, one of a kind, our Savior--the one who delivers us from the body of sin, from its guilt and terror and from the wages of sin that lead to death. It is all-important that the Word of God be preached."[74]

The preaching of this gospel is the God-ordained way to bring the unbeliever into the reality of a full and free salvation, for "Faith

---

[70]Charles H. Spurgeon, *Psalms 53-78*, vol. 3 of 7, *The Treasury of David: An Expository and Devotional Commentary on the Psalms* (Grand Rapids, MI: Baker Book House, 1983), 226.

[71]Charles H. Spurgeon, *Sermons Preached by C. H. Spurgeon, Revised and Published During the Year 1914*, vol. 60 of 63, The Metropolitan Tabernacle Pulpit, (Pasadena, TX: Pilgrim Publications, 1979), 198.

[72]Graham, 109.

[73]Ibid., 110.

[74]Oral Roberts, *Acts-Philemon*, vol. 2 of 3, *The New Testament Comes Alive: A Personal New Testament Commentary* (Tulsa, OK: Oral Roberts, 1984), 201.

cometh by hearing, and hearing by the word of God" (Rom. 10:17). Ezekiel 37 records the account of the prophet in the valley of dry bones. As he surveyed the desolation and hopelessness around him God gave him an instruction, "Prophesy upon these bones, and say unto them, O ye dry bones, hear the word of the Lord" (Ezek. 37: 4). That is man's role in evangelism, to faithfully proclaim the gospel of Jesus Christ. The re-creative work is God's, and He promises, "Behold, I will cause breath to enter into you, and ye shall live: And I will lay sinews upon you, and will bring up flesh upon you, and cover you with skin, and put breath in you, and ye shall know that I *am* the Lord" (Ezek. 37:5-6). When God's word is proclaimed in the mighty power of His Spirit, that power silences the voice of the enemy and quickens faith in the heart of the hearer unto salvation. Men preach--the Spirit breathes--and dry bones live. That is God's method of evangelism and it is far removed from what is currently propagated within the context of SLSW. In truth, the church has been commissioned to preach, to teach and to heal, manifesting the love of God in the power of the Holy Ghost. Such commissioning has nothing to do with socio-economic reformation but rather with the glories of new birth and living in the victory of a Spirit-filled life. In Acts chapter 1, Jesus speaks of the coming Holy Spirit who would revolutionise the understanding of the waiting disciples, transforming and empowering them to be living witnesses to their victorious, risen Lord.

However, that which is presented as the gospel in much of Christendom today is an impoverished imitation of what God has provided. It is very often a gospel of excuses and compromise, which fears to present the mighty truths that throughout the ages have set men free and birthed them into the glorious liberty of life in Christ Jesus. It is a gospel which attempts to give people what they want to hear; it is a gospel which has been ensnared by the lies of the enemy. Lloyd-Jones saw the same problem in his day. He writes: "We have been afraid of offending. We have been superficial. We have been so interested in getting visible results that we have kept back certain vital aspects of the truth. It must be the whole counsel, the full gospel . . . We must show that no man is saved by the deeds of the law, by his own goodness or righteousness, or church membership, or anything else, but solely, utterly, entirely by the free gift of God in Jesus Christ His Son."[75]

It is precisely because this glorious gospel has been obstructed and rashly denied that so many Christians are constantly in search of the latest remedy, the latest fad, the latest understanding or experience that will transform their puny faith and make them effective witnesses to the life of God. "Our want of faith has done more mischief to us than all the devils in hell, and all the heretics on earth. Some cry out against the Pope, and others against agnostics; but it is our own unbelief which is our worst enemy."[76]

The author is saddened to see that sections of the church seem to be following the world's insatiable demand for sensationalism. SLSW has diverted much of Christendom to wage an imaginary war on an equally imaginary battlefield. As E. W. Kenyon points out, "Satan knows he is defeated. All heaven knows he is defeated. And yet the Church looks upon him as a Master."[77] Judson Cornwall recounts a significant story in this context, drawn from his own experience as a pastor in Eugene, Oregon. For a period of time, demonic activity had been supposedly interfering with church services and so at the outset of each service Dr. Cornwall would address the spirits commanding them to leave. Then God showed him that in this public context "addressing [demons] as present, calling them by name, and telling them what to do (flee), and when to do it (right now) was considered worship in the demonic realm." When the focus of the service became Christ-centred rather than demon-centred, the interference stopped.[78] The enemy is power-hungry; his ego feeds on attention, especially when it is the attention of the people of God. Thus, while believers are striving and

---

[75]Lloyd-Jones, 218.

[76]Charles H. Spurgeon, *Sermons Preached and Revised by C. H. Spurgeon, During the Year 1890*, vol. 36 of 63, *Metropolitan Tabernacle Pulpit*, (Pasadena, TX: Pilgrim Publications, 1974), 378; quoted in Iain H. Murray, *The Puritan Hope*, 231.

[77]E. W. Kenyon, *In His Presence: The Secret of Prayer* (Lynnwood, WA: Kenyon's Gospel Publishing Society, 1999), 66.

[78]Judson Cornwall and Michael Reid, *Whose War Is It Anyway?* (Brentwood, England: Sharon Publication, 1993), 49-50. However, the author does believe in the reality of demonic possession and that Jesus has empowered His followers to cast out demons in His name (Matt. 10:1, 8; Mark 6:7; Luke 9:1; 10:17).

struggling, in the attempt to unseat mythical territorial powers, the real battle is left abandoned and the devil advances his kingdom of lies and deceit. This is a kingdom where Satan projects the fiction of a power equal to that of God Himself, a kingdom where his purpose is to take away the glorious hope of the gospel of Jesus Christ. But God intends His children to abide in truth. To quote the words of John Osteen: "Jesus said that through the Holy Ghost, WE WOULD BRING A DEMONSTRATION TO THE WORLD THAT SATAN IS ALREADY A DEFEATED FOE! It is not up to us to defeat Satan--Jesus has done all of that! We are to demonstrate that the work is ALREADY done and that every believer can live a victorious life!"[79] The right and privilege of each and every believer is to be a living witness to the power and supremacy of Jesus Christ, who has redeemed His people from the bondage of sin, conquering all principalities and powers both in this world and the world to come.

Sadly, as a result of SLSW teaching, many sincere Christians have lost touch with the reality and simplicity of the gospel, and they appear too insecure to question what they have been taught. Yet the remedy is so simple. It just involves a return to the old, old story of redemption; the story of a God of love who sent His Son; the story of a Saviour who bled and died to open the way back to fellowship with the Father; the story of the Holy Spirit who came to quicken and make alive those who were dead in trespasses and sins; the story of a mighty Christ and an eternally defeated foe. God has set His seal upon the gospel; it is the vehicle of His transforming power.

There also needs to be a return to fearless gospel preaching, without any regard for the opinions or theories of men. Surely, in these early days of the twenty-first century, this is again the cry of the Spirit--and the answer is assured. God will never abandon His gospel. He has a sovereign plan of redemption; He has a people, still held in bondage to the lies of the devil, but awaiting the sovereign word of release.

It is time for the church of Jesus Christ to rise up in His power and authority, confident in the mighty victory that He has already

---

[79]John Osteen, *How To Demonstrate Satan's Defeat* (Houston, TX: A John Osteen Publication, 1978), 24 (original emphasis).

secured over the world, the flesh and the devil. Proclamation of God's message of full redemption will sweep away the superstition and fear that has shrouded too many Christians for too long in the death of unbelief and unbiblical practice. As Charles Price writes:

> Did not Jesus come and tell us that He was the Light of the world and if we would follow Him we would not walk in darkness but should have the Light of life! . . . It was the Light of truth, the glorious sunshine of understanding; the dayspring of immortality. It was the abolition of the darkness of superstition and of fear. It was the breaking of the chains and the smashing of the shackles. He came to liberate those that sat in the valley of the shadow of death and to make it possible for us to live our life here and now by the faith which is the faith of the Son of God.[80]

The cornerstone of this work is the author's conviction that God is sovereign.

In His unsearchable grace and love, He has given the church His Word and His Spirit in order that "ye might be filled with the knowledge of his will in all wisdom and spiritual understanding . . . Strengthened with all might, according to his glorious power" (Col. 1:9,11). That is God's purpose for His people. Yet proponents of SLSW have sought for wisdom outside of the word; they have sought to uproot the ancient landmarks by adducing the inadmissible evidence of anecdote, experience and extra-biblical teaching in support of their arguments. *Sola Scriptura* has become a forgotten cry within the SLSW movement, but it is the author's prayer that it will be heard again throughout all Christendom; that once again the glorious gospel of God's redemption may be proclaimed in the power and anointing of the Holy Spirit.

In conclusion, the author makes no apology for referring once more to the words of Charles Spurgeon, who discerned the errors which threatened the church of his generation, but with faith and confidence turned men towards the truth:

> The day is not far distant when the old, old gospel shall again command the scholarship of the age, and shall direct the thoughts of men. . . . The fight is not over yet; the brunt of the battle is yet to come. They dreamed that the old gospel was dead more than a hundred years ago, but they digged its grave too soon. . . . A new era dawned. Two schools of Methodists with fiery energy proclaimed

---

[80]Price, 48.

the living word. All England was aroused. A new springtide arrived: the time of the singing of birds had come; life rejoiced where once death withered all things. It will be so again. The Lord liveth, and the gospel liveth too.[81]

[81]Charles H. Spurgeon, *Sermons Preached and Revised by C. H. Spurgeon, During the Year 1886*, The Metropolitan Tabernacle Pulpit. (Pasadena, TX: Pilgrim Publications, 1974), 32:429-31; quoted in Iain H. Murray, *The Puritan Hope*, 264-65.

APPENDICES

APPENDIX A

The Fall of Satan

The main source of reference used by many to garner information about the fall of Satan is Ezekiel 28:1-19 and it is therefore necessary to look at this passage in some detail. The prophet Ezekiel is directed to give a message to the ruler of Tyre (v.2). The word for ruler is *nagid*, a term which Samuel used for Saul, in preference to the word *melek* which is translated "king". The title of "king" is used for this ruler in verse 11. The human king of Tyre (v.11) is synonymous with the ruler of Tyre (v.2). He was proud and believed himself to be divine but is clearly informed that he is a man and not a god. This reinforces the idea that the king is the human ruler of the city of Tyre in Ezekiel's day.

The description given of this king in verses 12-19 needs to be explained because of its rather strange terminology and allusions to Canaanite religion and culture. The king is said to be full of wisdom and perfect in beauty (v.12), ideas expressed previously in the passage (v.2-5). "He was also 'the model of perfection' or, more literally, 'the one sealing a plan'. As Tyre's king and the mastermind of the city's commercial sea traffic, it is certainly easy to understand how he would be known as the one who established and approved the function of affixing a seal – a plan that enabled the city to become the maritime leader of its day."[1]

The king was also "in Eden the garden of God" (v.13). The word "God" may mean either the God of Israel or a pagan god. In verse 2, the ruler says, "I am a god; I sit on the throne of a god...." The concept of "the garden of God" was used as a simile in Genesis 13:10 to indicate the fertility of the Jordan Valley. Ezekiel also uses this phrase (chap.31:8, 9) to refer to the king of Assyria as a cedar tree that had no rival, "the envy of all the trees of Eden in the garden of God." The references do not relate to the original Garden of Eden but rather they are used to convey the idea of fertility and splendour. The ancient temples in the Near East often had a large garden around

---

[1]Ralph H. Alexander, "Ezekiel," in *The Expositor's Bible Commentary*, ed. Frank E. Gaebelein, vol. 6 of 12 (Grand Rapids, MI: Zondervan Publishing, 1986), 882.

them. If the phrase is read "in Eden, a garden of a god," then perhaps this "was an expression used metaphorically to describe the splendor of the temple complex of Melkart, the 'king of the city' (which was the meaning of the god's name), with whom Tyre's human king was seeking identity."[2] This interpretation is conjectural, but it is plausible and fits the context without doing violence to it.

Another concept that is usually used to read Satan into the text is the description of Tyre's king as a cherub. In the Near East, a cherub was a composite creature with an animal body (usually a bull or lion), wings, and either a human or animal head. The vision that Ezekiel had earlier (chap.1:5-10), included four living creatures in the form as a man, with four faces and four wings. These are later identified by him (chap.10:20) as the creatures he had seen by the Kebar River, and he realised that they were cherubim, whose normal function is to guard the throne of God. The king of Tyre is the guarding cherub for the temple of Melkart.

Another interesting archaeological point is that the Phoenician male-sphinx (or cherub) was normally bejewelled and sometimes had the head of the priest-king.[3] Alexander makes the following comment, "the sphinx was considered to be all-wise. Such a description fits well the verses under discussion, for the king is called a guarding cherub (sphinx) and the many jewels listed in v.13 as his covering befit the many jewels that adorned the Phoenician sphinx (cherub)."[4]

The phrase "on the day you were created" means the day on which the king came to the throne. To assume that the stones were a garment worn by Satan in the Garden of Eden, and that Satan was a guarding cherub of Eden is purely speculation without any exegetical foundation elsewhere in Scripture. To call him a cherub would mean that he was not in the category of angel, for neither Michael nor Gabriel are ever called cherubim, and he was considered to be on their same level before his fall. Additionally, according to Hebrews 9:5, there were always two cherubim guarding the throne; the Ezekiel passage has only one.

---

[2]Ibid., 883.

[3]R. D. Barnett, *Ezekiel and Tyre, Eretz-Israel*, vol. 9 (Jerusalem: Israel Exploration Society, 1969).

[4]Ibid.

The "holy mount of God" (chap.28:14) was used in Canaanite mythology to indicate where the gods resided in the north. The king of Tyre considered himself to be in the domain of the pagan deities since he thought of himself as a god, and was probably the guardian cherub of the god Melkart. Connecting the mount to the Phoenician area also fits in well with the phrase "walked among the fiery stones." A bowl from Sidon portrays the ritual of burning a god. Melkart's resurrection was celebrated by a "burning in effigy," from which he would then be revitalized through the fire and the smelling of the burnt offering. "Again, in keeping with the Phoenician religious-cultural background with which the passage is so closely tied by the king's claim to deity, perhaps the explanation of walking among the fiery stones is a reference to the king's self-exaltation of himself even as the god Melkart--even to the extent of his claiming resurrection after burning by fire."[5]

Other phrases could be considered, but sufficient has been said to establish the context as that of the king of Tyre. H. L. Ellison has stated the situation well: "For many vv.11-19 are primarily a picture of Satan, before his fall in a pre-Adamic Eden, looking forward to the Antichrist. Those who implicitly hold this view have generally little idea of how unknown it is in wider Christian circles, or of how little basis there is for it in fact."[6]

He then goes on to say, "But this does not mean that there is no truth in the view. All men who go the way of Satan mirror him and his sin in some measure. There is a real parallel between the fall of proud man and proud tempter, but Scripture does not give a picture of the fall of Satan mirroring the fall of men, but the fall of men mirroring the yet greater fall of the evil one."[7]

Given that there is little academic basis to interpret the kings of Tyre and Sidon as representations of Satan, many of the characteristics which are attributed to him on the basis of the above two passages, must also be called into question. In Ezekiel, reference is made to the king's great wisdom and understanding, his perfect beauty, and his privileged position. In Isaiah, the king is clearly one to

---

[5] Alexander, 884.

[6] H. L. Ellison, *Ezekiel: the Man and his Message* (London: Paternoster Press, 1956), 108.

[7] Ibid., 109.

be feared. He is described as, "the man that made the earth to tremble, that did shake kingdoms; That made the world as a wilderness, and destroyed the cities thereof; that opened not the house of his prisoners" (Isa. 14:16-17). Without the backing of these passages, Satan is reduced to his true stature, a fallen angel, a created being who has chosen to disobey God. There is no biblical foundation for ascribing to him such superior intelligence and power as to be almost equal to those of God Himself.

APPENDIX B

Seminar Curriculum Outline

Curriculum Outline

Course Description

The purpose of the course is to evaluate the current teaching on Strategic Level Spiritual Warfare ("SLSW") in the light of biblical truth and church history.

Specific Course Goals

1. A factual analysis of SLSW, in terms of the following:

   a) Its emergence and leaders;

   b) The teaching and doctrinal distinctives (including worldview, territorial spirits, prophecy, prayer, and experiential faith);

   c) The practices and strategies (including, discerning and naming spirits, identificational repentance, warfare prayer, prayer marches, strategic-level intercession, prolonged fasting, identificational repentance); and

   d) The empirical evidence.

2. A biblical analysis of SLSW; this will be based on Old and New Testament teaching and include the following:

   a) An evaluation of territorial spirits and warfare prayer;

   b) Satan; his character, kingdom, deceptions and destiny;

   c) The believer's position in Christ and defence against Satan;

   d) The true context of spiritual warfare;

   e) The true fast of God;

   f) The biblical basis for prayer and evangelism; and

   g) The biblical basis for prophetic revelation and scriptural confirmation.

3. <u>An historical examination of SLSW concepts</u>, based on:

Intertestamental literature, Pauline doctrine, the Church Fathers, Medieval theology, Reformation theology, Quaker and Puritan revival, John Wesley and the Methodists, the development of Pentecostal and Charismatic thought.

Course Objectives

After successfully completing the course, the student should have:

1. A sound biblical basis for understanding spiritual warfare which will enable him/her to discern truth and error in this context;

2. A greater understanding of the victory that Jesus Christ has made available to every believer by His death, resurrection and ascension.

3. An overview of the lessons of church history as they relate to spiritual warfare.

Course Textbooks and other Resources

1. Chuck Lowe, *Territorial Spirits and World Evangelisation? A Biblical, Historical and Missiological Critique of Strategic-Level Spiritual Warfare* (Fearn, Kent: Mentor, OMF, 1998).

2. T. L. Osborn, *The Message That Works*, (Tulsa, OK: OSFO Foundation, 1999).

3. C. Peter Wagner, *Confronting the Powers: How the New Testament Church Experienced the Power of Strategic-Level Spiritual Warfare* (Ventura, CA: Regal, 1996).

4. Michael Reid & Judson Cornwall, *Whose Mind Is It Anyway?* (Loughton, England: Sharon Publications Ltd, 1993).

5. Gene Edward Veith, *Postmodern Times: A Christian Guide to Contemporary Thought and Culture* (Wheaton, IL: Crossway Books, 1994).

6. Sydney H. T. Page, *Powers of Evil: A Biblical Study of Satan and Demons* (Grand Rapids, MI: Baker Books, 1995).

7. *Transformations: A Documentary*, prod. Global Net Productions, 58 min., The Sentinel Group, 1999, videocassette.

8. *Java Harvest*, prod. OSFO International World Missionary Church: docu-miracle film, 1990, videocassette.

APPENDIX C

The Peniel Model
Biblical, Theological and Historical Bases

The Old Testament demonstrates that the battlefield is in the mind and the only issue for a Christian is obedience to the King of Kings. There is no foundation for the practice of engaging demonic forces in a spiritual conflict, nor any indication that the devil has any intrinsic power or authority over believers. Satan's only weapon is deception and his only sphere of influence that which God permits for His own eternal purposes.

The New Testament shows how Jesus dealt with spirit powers in the Gospels, how the Apostles dealt with spirit powers in the Book of Acts, and the teaching of Paul in the Epistles showed a similar picture; there is no evidence to suggest that Christians are called to engage in an on-going conflict with spiritual forces in the cosmic realm. The Scripture is quite clear in its teaching that Christ defeated Satan completely at Calvary and that Christians have been freed from his power. He is a conquered enemy, he is bound, he is already judged, and he is to be cast out of this world and into the lake of fire. He is not a rival of equivalent power to God; rather, he is totally subordinate.

In terms of evangelism, revival in the early church is always directly connected with the Word of God, spoken and applied to hearts in the power of the Spirit of God. There is very little space given to discussing demonic activity in the Pauline epistles; the primary focus, in respect to both evangelism and the growth in maturity of individual Christians, is on the choices and actions taken by people themselves. In his opposition to this process, the operation of the devil is to blind the minds of men. It is, therefore, the great fight of faith, in which the Christian's only weapon is the sword of the Spirit, which is the word of God. Its purpose is "casting down imaginations and every high thing that exalteth itself against the knowledge of God, and bringing into captivity every thought to the obedience of Christ" (2 Cor. 10:5). Prayer, however, is not a spiritual weapon, nor is it an accompaniment to spiritual warfare; it is an expression of the Christian's intimate relationship with the Father.

History demonstrates that Christian doctrine and experience must be firmly grounded in the word of Truth. It could be argued that the church entered its darkest age when it abandoned the supremacy of the authority of scripture, thus allowing the entrance of superstition and witchcraft. Unfortunately, the weakness of the recent Pentecostal-Charismatic tradition has been the paucity of associated biblical exegesis and doctrinal understanding. Increasingly, experience-based analysis rather than truth has become the touchstone of the Charismatic world, and Christendom today is in danger of slipping once more into the spiritual dark ages.

Review of the Contemporary Teaching Associated with SLSW

The practice of SLSW concerns strategies for unseating or "pulling down" territorial spirits as a pre-requisite to the successful advancement of the gospel. Supposed biblical validation for the concept of territoriality and the various techniques which are advocated to depose them (including naming the spirits, spiritual mapping, identificational repentance and warfare prayer/intercession) are given by various authors. On the basis of a systematic appraisal of the relevant literature, the rationale for SLSW stands on extremely shaky biblical and theological foundations. Where scriptural authority is claimed, this tends to be on the basis of proof texts which are manipulated to support the various hypotheses, and scripture itself is viewed through the subjective lens of experience. Most of the validation for SLSW is drawn from extra-biblical sources and empirical evidence which is largely unconfirmed.

The main influences which undergird SLSW methodology are hermeneutical approach, worldview and personal observation and experience. Although its proponents would claim it to be a new methodology, it is but a recurring phenomenon. For example, study Frank W. Sandford, who in the early 1900s purchased ships to sail around the seven continents engaging in intercessory prayer to break the stranglehold of Satan's power over the nations. Today, Wagner has published a 6-book "Prayer Warrior" series and, together with Ted Haggard, he is the co-director of the World Prayer Center in Colorado which holds a 24-hour prayer vigil. Ambulatory prayer has resulted in planes being chartered to engage in warfare prayer as they fly above supposed territorial spirits, to bind and pull them down. All this is strikingly similar to Sandford's activities, including the restoration of apostles to the Church.

Christians have actually been translated from the authority of Satan and birthed into the very family of God. Christ's finished work at Calvary provided us with redemption. The new creation is a reality; this includes righteousness in Christ, the indwelling Christ making the believer a conqueror in every situation, and fellowship with the Father.

APPENDIX D

Testimony

By Reverend Peter Russell (2001)

In the years before I was married, I had committed my life to Christ, and was attending an Evangelical church, but felt that the church fell short of the New Testament pattern. There was no real power or presence of God in the meetings.

Then came the early charismatic days, and I experienced the Baptism in the Holy Spirit. There was a sense of excitement with tongues, visions, and prophecies, which stood out in contrast to the deadness, ritual, and weariness of the Evangelical church. New choruses were scripture songs with a lively rhythm. Early charismatic worship was alive, praising and rejoicing, with dancing and instruments. Gifts of the Spirit were operating giving a sense of anticipation, and sometimes the highlight would be a prophecy one could apply personally. The fellowship was warm and loving, in contrast to the cold formality of the traditional church.

Promises abounded that revival was just round the corner – but it never came. 'New moves of God' came but they never resulted in revival. I read old books on past revivals, and miracle ministries like Kathryn Kuhlman and Smith Wigglesworth. Increasingly I became aware that the charismatic move had not delivered its promises. I also came into contact with deliverance ministry for Christians. I did not discount it as it was practised by well-respected 'men of God.' This led me to the next 'move of God', which was strategic level spiritual warfare (SLSW). By this time I was married, and pastoring my own church. The church was growing steadily, but I was always conscious that something was missing. A revival team led by a well-known 'prophetic' leader came to town, and many of the local churches, including mine, were involved. Much of the teaching was based on Old Testament prophets. The church in this country, we were told, was not experiencing revival, or seeing God's blessing because we were under his judgment due to various sins. The only place God was moving was in third world countries because they did not have the sin of materialism. The church must repent and pray. Only then would God turn and 'heal our land.' At the end of the week, the team, as a last gesture, 'dumped' on the churches a list of spirits which were supposed to be controlling the town and were stopping us from seeing revival. The only answer was to pray, intercede, and bind those spirits. Only when the whole list was dealt with, would we see results (this was many years ago, and nothing changed, in spite of all the 'spiritual' action). Feverish prayer meetings were started in the town. All churches involved had their programmes. Some of the warfare activities we experienced were:-

- All churches prayer celebrations.

- Pastor's monthly prayer gatherings.

- Prayer cells (church split up into twos or threes to pray each week).

- Half nights of prayer with long sessions of tongues.

- Early morning prayer meetings.

- Fasting

- Prayer walks

- March for Jesus.

- Attending 'deliverance and warfare' seminars.

- Beginnings of information coming through about 'high places', and spiritual mapping.

A church in Kent had produced a video of Christians partaking in these activities. We visited a 'high place' in Colchester (the water tower), purchased by Christians to pray over the city. The climb was a good fitness exercise, the grubby and cramped prayer room an anti climax, but the view was fantastic!

Some of the results of this strategic level spiritual warfare activity were:-

- Self-importance of the church – for some reason God had chosen to be unable to help as much as He would like, because He was waiting for His church to rise up and co-operate with Him. This was aided by such (heretical) expressions as 'God's hands are tied unless the church prays'.

- The rise of prayer warriors and intercessors – some of whose favourite expressions were 'The Lord told me' or 'I feel in my spirit.' They often lived in total unreality, sometimes with disastrous consequences.

- Over-consciousness of demonic forces.

- An even greater longing and searching for something real that worked.

In 1990 my wife's brother, to whom we were quite close, died relatively young and in rather tragic circumstances. I was desperate for some answers. At this time I was invited by a pastor to preach in Ghana. I went mainly because it was an opportunity to see God at work in a third world country. I was desperate for some reality, and instinctively knew it would not be found in the madness of SLSW. In Ghana I met Bishop Reid, the pastor of Peniel Church, who challenged me on many issues, including my involvement in SLSW. On returning to this country I visited Peniel and was amazed to see miracles. People were coming to faith in Christ as he touched their bodies with miracle power. It was refreshing to hear the gospel preached, and to see the power of God at work in the church – and all this without any identifying of spirits over the town, or binding them. The heresy of SLSW became very obvious, and it was with a sense of relief that I left it behind. I grasped hold at last of the great truth of Christ's complete victory at Calvary. I began to see the tragedy of so many Christians who focus on demonic spirits, ascribe to them power they don't have, and lose the wonder of all that Jesus accomplished on the cross. I began to see again the truth of Paul's glorious words in Romans 1:16, "For I am not ashamed of the gospel of Christ: for it is the power of God unto salvation to every one that believeth." When I gave up the unbiblical nonsense of SLSW, I found again that the simple preaching of the gospel, which has always been God's instrument to bring the message of salvation to a sin-sick world, is still the same power of God unto salvation today.

BIBLIOGRAPHY
Books

Abram, Victor P. Foreword to *The Golden Light upon the Two Americas* by Frank W. Sandford. Amherst, NH: The Kingdom Press, 1974.

Alexander, Ralph H. "Ezekiel." In *The Expositor's Bible Commentary*. Edited by Frank E. Gaebelein. Vol. 6 of 12. Grand Rapids, MI: Zondervan Publishing, 1986.

Allen, Leslie C. *Ezekiel 1-19*. Vol. 28, *Word Biblical Commentary*. Edited by David A. Hubbard and Glenn W. Barker. Dallas, TX: Word Books, 1994.

Anderson, A. A. *Psalms 72-150*. London: Marshall, Morgan & Scott, 1974, 82. Quoted in Chuck Lowe, *Territorial Spirits and World Evangelisation?: A Biblical, Historical and Missiological Critique of Strategic Level Spiritual Warfare*, 37. Fearn and Kent: OMF and Mentor, 1998.

Anderson, Leith. *A Church for the Twenty-First Century*. Minneapolis, MN: Bethany House, 1992, 20. Quoted in Veith, Gene Edward Jr., *Postmodern Times: A Christian Guide to Contemporary Thought and Culture*, 211. Wheaton, IL: Crossway Books, 1994.

Anderson, Sir Robert. *The Gospel and Its Ministry: A Handbook of Evangelical Truth*. 13th edition. London: Pickering and Inglis, 1969.

Aquinas, Thomas. *Summa Theologica*. First Part. In vol. 19 of 60, *Great Books of the Western World*. Edited by Robert Maynard Hutchins. Chicago, IL: Encyclopaedia Britannica, 1952.

Arnold, Clinton E. *Power and Magic: The Concept of Power in Ephesians*. Grand Rapids, MI: Baker Books, 1997.

Arnold, Clinton E.. *Powers of Darkness: A Thoughtful, Biblical Look at an Urgent Challenge Facing the Church*. Leicester: InterVarsity Press, 1992.

Arnold, Clinton E. *Spiritual Warfare: What Does The Bible Really Teach?* London: Marshall Pickering, 1997.

Athanasius, St. *De Incarnatione*. Notions 30, 47, 48 and 50. In *Contra Gentes and De Incarnatione*. Translated and edited by Robert W. Thompson. Oxford: Clarendon Press, 1971.

Athanasius, St. *Life of St. Anthony*. In vol. 10 of *Ancient Christian Writers: The Works of the Fathers in Translation*. Edited by Johannes Quasten and Joseph C. Plumpe. Translated by Robert T. Mayer. Westminster, MD: The Newman Press, 1950.

Augustine, St. *Enchiridion or Manual to Laurentius Concerning Faith, Hope and Charity*. Translated by Ernest Evans. London: SPCK, 1953.

Augustine, St. *The City of God*. Translated by John Healey. London: J. M. Dent and Son, 1931.

Bainton, Roland. *Here I Stand*. Oxford: Lion Publishing, 1990.

Barbour, Hugh and Arthur Roberts, eds. *Early Quaker Writings*. Grand Rapids, MI: William B. Eerdmans Publishing Company, 1973.

Barclay, Robert. *An Apology for the True Christian Divinity*. London: T. Sowle Raylton and Luke Hinde, 1736.

Barnabas, *Epistle of Barnabas*. Chap. 18. In *The Apostolic Fathers*. In vol. 1 of 23, *Ante-Nicene Christian Library: Translation of the Writings of the Fathers, Down to A.D. 325*. Edited by Rev. Alexander Roberts and James Donaldson. Edinburgh: T. and T. Clark, 1867.

Barnes, Albert. *Romans*. Vol. 4 of 8, *A Popular Family Commentary on the New Testament*. London: Blackie and Son Ltd, n.d.

Barnett, R. D. *Ezekiel and Tyre, Eretz-Israel*. Vol. 9. Jerusalem: Israel Exploration Society, 1969.

Baxter, Richard. "Character of a Confirmed Christian." In *The Select Practical Works of Richard Baxter*. Glasgow: Blackie & Son, 1840.

Baxter, Richard. *The Christian Directory*. Vol. 1 of 4, *The Practical Works of the Late Reverend and Pious Mr Richard Baxter*. London: T. Parkhurst, I. Robinson, and L. Lawrence, 1707.

Beasley-Murray, George R. *John*. 2d edition. Vol. 36, *Word Biblical Commentary*. Edited by Bruce M. Metzger, David A. Hubbard and Glenn W. Barker Nashville, TN: Thomas Nelson Publishers, 1999.

Berkhof, Louis. *Systematic Theology*. Edinburgh: The Banner of Truth Trust, 2000.

Bernal, Dick. *Storming Hell's Brazen Gates*. San Jose, CA: Jubilee Christian Center, 1988.

Boston, Thomas. *Human Nature in its Fourfold State*. London: The Religious Tract Society, 1837.

Bruce, Alexander Balmain. *The Training of the Twelve*. New Canaan, CT: Keats Publishing, 1979.

Bunyan, John. "The Doctrine of the Law and Grace Unfolded." Vol. 1 of 3, *The Works of John Bunyan*. Edinburgh: The Banner of Truth Trust, 1991.

Bunyan, John. "The New Birth." In vol. 2 of 3, *The Works of John Bunyan*. Edited by George Offor. Edinburgh: The Banner of Truth Trust, 1991.

Calvin, John. *Commentaries on the Epistles of Paul to the Galatians and Ephesians*. In vol. 21 of 22, *Calvin's Commentaries*. Grand Rapids, MI: Baker Book House, 1979.

Calvin, John. *Institutes of the Christian Religion*. Bk. 1, chap. 14, par. 4 Grand Rapids, MI: Wm. B. Eerdmans Publishing Company, 2001, 144. Quoted in Chuck Lowe, *Territorial Spirits and World Evangelisation?: A Biblical, Historical and Missiological Critique of Strategic Level Spiritual Warfare*, 97. Fearn and Kent: OMF and Mentor, 1998.

Calvin, John. *Institutes of the Christian Religion*. Grand Rapids, MI: Wm. B. Eerdmans Publishing Company, 2001.

The Catholic Encyclopedia. Edited by Roberts C. Broderick. Nashville, TN: Thomas Nelson Publishers, 1986.

Charnock, Stephen. *The Existence and Attributes of God*. Vol. 2 of 2. Grand Rapids, MI: Baker Book House, 1979.

Christenson, Evelyn. *Battling the Prince of Darkness*. Amersham-On-The-Hill, England: Scripture Press, 1993.

Clement of Alexandria. *Exhortation to the Heathen*. Chap. 1. In vol. 1 of *Clement of Alexandria*. In vol. 4 of 23, *Ante-Nicene Christian Library: Translation of the Writings of the Fathers, Down to A.D. 325*. Edited by Rev Alexander Roberts and James Donaldson. Edinburgh: T. and T. Clark, 1867.

Clement of Rome. *Epistle to the Corinthians.* Chap. 45. In vol. 1 of 23, *Ante-Nicene Christian Library: Translation of the Writings of the Fathers, Down to A.D. 325.* Edited by Rev. Alexander Roberts, and James Donaldson. Edinburgh: T. and T. Clark, 1867.

Conner, W. T. *The Work of the Holy Spirit.* Nashville, TN: Broadman Press, 1949.

Cornwall, Judson and Michael Reid. *Whose War Is It Anyway?* Brentwood, England: Sharon Publication, 1993.

Cox, Harvey. *Fire From Heaven: Pentecostalism, Spirituality and the Reshaping of Religion in the Twenty-First Century.* New York: Addison-Wesley, 1994, 281. Quoted in Martyn Percy, *Power and the Church: Ecclesiology in and Age of Transition,* 188. London: Cassell, 1998.

Dallimore, Arnold. *Spurgeon: A New Biography.* Edinburgh: The Banner of Truth Trust, 1999.

Dawson, John. *Taking our Cities for God: How to Break Spiritual Strongholds.* Lake Mary, FL: Creation House, 1989, 156. Quoted in Mike R. Taylor, *Do Demons Rule Your Town?: An Examination of the 'Territorial Spirits' Theory,* 45. London: Grace Publications Trust, 1993.

Denton, Michael. *Evolution: A Theory in Crisis.* Bethesda, MD: Adler and Adler, 1986.

Dray, Stephen. Foreword to *Do Demons Rule Your Town?: An Examination of the 'Territorial Spirits' Theory,* by Mike R. Taylor. London: Grace Publications Trust, 1993.

Drummond, Lewis A. *The Word of the Cross: A Contemporary Theology of Evangelism.* Nashville, TN: Broadman & Holman Publishers, 1999.

Duff, Alexander. *The British and Foreign Evangelical Review* 30 (1881): 73. Quoted in Iain H. Murray, *The Puritan Hope: Revival and the Interpretation of Prophecy.* Edinburgh: The Banner of Truth Trust, 1971.

Dunn, James D. G. *Romans 9-16.* Vol. 38B, *Word Biblical Commentary.* Edited by Bruce M. Metzger, David A. Hubbard, and Glenn W. Barker. Dallas, TX: Word Books, 1988.

Edwards, Jonathan. *The Works of Jonathan Edwards.* Vol. 1 of 2. Revised and corrected by Edward Hickman. Edinburgh: The Banner of Truth Trust, 1974.

Ellison, H. L. *Ezekiel: The Man and His Message.* London: Paternoster Press, 1956.

Encyclopaedia of Religion and Ethics. Edited by James Hastings. Vol. 4 of 13. Edinburgh: T. and T. Clark, 1981.

Encyclopedia of Religion. Edited by Vergilius Ferm. S.v. "naturalism." New York: The Philosophical Library, 1945, 518. Quoted in Edward F. Murphy, *Handbook for Spiritual Warfare,* 4. Nashville, TN: Thomas Nelson Publishers, 1996.

Entwistle, Noel. *Styles of Learning and Teaching: An Integrated Outline of Educational Psychology.* Pt. 2. New York: John Wiley & Sons, 1981.

Ervin, Howard M. *Spirit Baptism: A Biblical Investigation.* Peabody, MA: Hendrickson Publishers, 1987.

Faupel, D. William. *The Everlasting Gospel: The Significance of Eschatology in the Development of Pentecostal Thought.* Sheffield: Sheffield Academic Press, 1996.

Fee, Gordon D. *Gospel and Spirit: Issues in New Testament Hermeneutics.* Peabody, MA: Hendrickson Publishers, 1991.

Fee, Gordon D. *Paul, the Spirit and the People of God.* Peabody, MA: Hendrickson Publishers, 1996.

Flavel, John. *The Works of John Flavel.* Vol. 1 of 6. Edinburgh: The Banner of Truth Trust, 1968.

Flavel, John. *The Works of John Flavel.* Vol. 2 of 6. Edinburgh: The Banner of Truth Trust, 1968.

Fox, George. *Gospel-Truth.* London: T. Sowle, 1706.

Fox, George. *A Journal of George Fox.* 3d ed. With an introduction by William Penn. London: W. Richardson and S. Clark, 1765.

Friedrich, Gerhard, ed. *Theological Dictionary of the New Testament.* Vol 8 of 10. Grand Rapids, MI: Wm. B. Eerdmans Publishing Company, 1974.

Garlock, Ruthanne. *Fire in his Bones: The Story of Benson Idahosa.* Tulsa, OK: Praise Books, 1981.

Garrett, Duane A. *Angels and the New Spirituality.* Nashville, TN: Broadman & Holman, 1995.

Gordon, S. D. *Quiet Talks on Prayer.* New York: Fleming H. Revell Company, 1904, 120. Quoted in C. Peter Wagner, *Warfare Prayer: Strategies for Combating the Rulers of Darkness*, 106. Crowborough, England: Monarch Publications, 1997.

Graham, Billy. *God's Ambassador: A Lifelong Mission of Giving Hope to the World.* Minneapolis, MN: Billy Graham Evangelistic Association, 1999.

Green, Michael. *I Believe in Satan's Downfall.* Grand Rapids, MI: William B. Eerdmans Publishing Company, 1981.

Grudem, Wayne. *Systematic Theology: An Introduction to Biblical Doctrine.* Leicester: InterVarsity Press, 1994.

Gurnall, William. *The Christian in Complete Armour.* Vol. 2 of 3. Edinburgh: The Banner of Truth Trust, 1995.

Hagin, Kenneth E. *The Triumphant Church: Dominion Over All The Powers of Darkness.* Tulsa, OK: Faith Library Publications, 1993.

Hagin, Kenneth E. *Understanding How to Fight the Good Fight of Faith.* Tulsa, OK: Faith Library Publications, 1996.

Hagner, Donald A. *Matthew 1-13.* Vol. 33A, *Word Biblical Commentary.* Edited by Bruce Metzger, David A. Hubbard, and Glenn W. Barker. Dallas, TX: Word Books, 1993.

Haldane, Robert. *A Commentary on the Epistle to the Romans.* London: The Banner of Truth Trust, 1960.

Harper, Michael. *I Believe in Satan's Downfall.* Grand Rapids, MI: William B. Eerdmans Publishing Co., 1981, 26-27. Quoted in C. Peter Wagner, *Confronting the Powers: How the New Testament Church Experienced the Power of Strategic-Level Spiritual Warfare*, 122. Ventura, CA: Regal Books, 1996.

Hayford, Jack W. *Grounds for Living: Sound Teaching for Sure Footing in Growth & Grace.* Kent: Sovereign World, 2001.

Hayford, Jack W. *Prayer is Invading the Impossible.* Revised edition. South Plainfield, NJ: Logos International, 1977, 92. Quoted in Dutch Sheets, *Intercessory Prayer: How God Can Use Your Prayers to Move Heaven and Earth*, 33. Ventura, CA: Regal Books, 1996.

Hermas, Pastor of. Introductory Note; Book Second. In *The Apostolic Fathers.* In vol. 1 of 23, *Ante-Nicene Christian Library: Translation of the Writings of the Fathers, Down to A.D. 325.* Edited by Rev. Alexander Roberts and James Donaldson. Edinburgh: T. and T. Clark, 1867.

Hesselgrave, David. *Scripture and Strategy: The Use of the Bible in Postmodern Church and Mission.* Evangelical Missiological Society Series, no. 1. Pasadena, CA: William Carey Library, 1994.

Hilary of Poitiers. *Homilies on the Psalms.* In vol. 1 of 3, *The Faith of the Early Fathers,* 387. Edited by William A. Jurgens. Collegeville, MN: Liturgical Press, 1970. Quoted in Chuck Lowe, *Territorial Spirits and World Evangelisation?: A Biblical, Historical and Missiological Critique of Strategic Level Spiritual Warfare,* 87. Fearn and Kent: OMF and Mentor, 1998.

Hill, Rowland. *Sermons Preached in London at the Formation of the Missionary Society.* N.p., 1795, 109. Quoted in Iain H. Murray, *The Puritan Hope: Revival and the Interpretation of Prophecy,* 127-28. Edinburgh: The Banner of Truth Trust, 1971.

Hillerbrand, H. J. *The Reformation in its Own Words.* London: SCM Press, 1964.

Hodge, Charles. *Commentary on the Epistle to the Romans.* Edinburgh: The Banner of Truth Trust, 1975.

Hodge, Charles. *Systematic Theology.* Vol. 1 of 3. Grand Rapids, MI: Wm. B. Eerdmans Publishing Co., 1981.

Honey, Peter and Alan Mumford. *The Manual of Learning Styles.* Berkshire: Peter Honey, 1982.

Houghton, Frank. *Amy Carmichael of Dohnavur.* London: SPCK, 1954.

Howard, Roland. *Charismania: When Christian Fundamentalism Goes Wrong.* London: Mowbray, 1997.

Hunt, Dave and T. A. McMahon. *The Seduction of Christianity: Spiritual Discernment in the Last Days.* Eugene, OR: Harvest House Publishers, 1985.

Ignatius. *The Epistle to the Philadelphians.* Chapters 2. In *The Apostolic Fathers.* In vol. 1 of 23, *Ante-Nicene Christian Library: Translation of the Writings of the Fathers, Down to A.D. 325.* Edited by Rev. Alexander Roberts, D.D., and James Donaldson. Edinburgh: T. and T. Clark, 1867.

Ignatius. *The Epistle to Polycarp.* Chapters 1-3; 6. In *The Apostolic Fathers. In vol. 1 of 23, Ante-Nicene Christian Library: Translation of the Writings of the Fathers, Down to A.D. 325.* Edited by Rev. Alexander Roberts and James Donaldson. Edinburgh: T. and T. Clark, 1867.

Ignatius. *The Epistle to the Trallians.* Chapters 2-4; 10-11. In *The Apostolic Fathers. In vol. 1 of 23, Ante-Nicene Christian Library: Translation of the Writings of the Fathers, Down to A.D. 325.* Edited by Rev. Alexander Roberts and James Donaldson. Edinburgh: T. and T. Clark, 1867.

Ignatius, *The Martyrdom* of. Chapters 2; 7. *In The Apostolic Fathers. In vol. 1 of 23, Ante-Nicene Christian Library: Translation of the Writings of the Fathers, Down to A.D. 325.* Edited by Rev. Alexander Roberts and James Donaldson. Edinburgh: T. and T. Clark, 1867.

The Illustrated Bible Dictionary. Leicester: InterVarsity Press, 1980.

Irenaeus. *Against Heresies.* Preface to Bk. 1; Bk. 2, Chap. 6 and 11; Bk. 3, Chapters 12 and 23. In vol. 1 of *The Writings of Irenaeus. In vol. 5 of 23, Ante-Nicene Christian Library: Translation of the Writings of the Fathers, Down to A.D. 325.* Edited by Rev. Alexander Roberts and James Donaldson. Edinburgh: T. and T. Clark, 1868.

Jackson, John Paul. *Needless Casualties of War.* Eastbourne: Kingsway Publications, 1999.

Jacobs, Cindy. *Possessing the Gates of the Enemy: An Intercessionary Prayer Manual.* London: Marshall Pickering, 1993.

Johnson, Alan F. and Robert E. Webber. *What Christians Believe: A Biblical and Historical Summary.* Grand Rapids, MI: Zondervan Publishing House, 1989.

Johnstone, Patrick. *Biblical Intercession: Spiritual Power to Change our World.* Evangelical Missiological Society Series no. 3. Pasadena, CA: William Carey Library, 1995.

Jonathan Edwards. "Some Thoughts on Revival Concerning the Present Revival of Religion in New England and the Way in Which It Ought to be Acknowledged and Promoted; Humbly Offered to the Public, in a Treatise on that Subject." In vol. 1 of 2, *The Works of Jonathan Edwards.* Revised and corrected by Edward Hickman. Edinburgh: The Banner of Truth Trust, 1974.

Josephus, Flavius. *The Antiquities of the Jews.* Bk. 8, chap. 2, par. 5. In *Josephus: Complete Works.* Translated by William Whiston. London: Pickering & Inglis, 1960.

Justin Martyr. *Dialogue with Trypho, a Jew.* Chapters 30; 39; 69; 116. In *Justin Martyr and Athenagoras.* In vol. 2 of 23, *Ante-Nicene Christian Library: Translation of the Writings of the Fathers, Down to A.D. 325.* Edited by Rev. Alexander Roberts and James Donaldson. Edinburgh: T. and T. Clark, 1867.

Justin Martyr. *The First Apology.* Chap. 64. In *Justin Martyr and Athenagoras.* In vol. 2 of 23, *Ante-Nicene Christian Library: Translation of the Writings of the Fathers, Down to A.D. 325.* Edited by Rev. Alexander Roberts and James Donaldson. Edinburgh: T. and T. Clark, 1867.

Justin Martyr. *The Second Apology of Justin.* Chapters 6; 13. In *Justin Martyr and Athenagoras.* In vol. 2 of 23, *Ante-Nicene Christian Library: Translation of the Writings of the Fathers, Down to A.D. 325.* Edited by Rev. Alexander Roberts and James Donaldson. Edinburgh: T. and T. Clark, 1867.

Kallas, James. *The Satanward View: A Study in Pauline Theology.* Philadelphia, PA: The Westminster Press, 1966.

Karff, Samuel E. *Religions of the World.* New York: St. Martin's Press, 1993.

Keil, C. F. *Pentateuch.* In vol. 1, *Commentary on the Old Testament* by C. F. Keil and Franz Delitzsch. Peabody, MA: Hendrickson Publishers, 1996.

Kenyon, E. W. *In His Presence: The Secret of Prayer.* Lynnwood, WA: Kenyon's Gospel Publishing Society, 1999.

Kenyon, E. W. *New Creation Realities: A Revelation of Redemption.* Lynnwood, WA: Kenyon's Gospel Publishing Society, 2000.

The King James Study Bible. Nashville, TN: Thomas Nelson Publishers, 1988.

Kinnaman, Gary D. *How to Overcome the Darkness: Personal Strategies for Spiritual Warfare.* Grand Rapids, MI: Baker Book House, 1999.

Kittel, Gerhard, ed. *Theological Dictionary of the New Testament.* Vol. 2 of 10. Grand Rapids, MI: Wm. B. Eerdmans Publishing Company, 1964.

Kittel, Gerhard, *Theological Dictionary of the New Testament.* Vol. 4 of 10. Grand Rapids, MI: Wm. B. Eerdmans Publishing Company, 1967.

Kraft, Charles H. "Christian Animism or God-Given Authority," In Edward Rommen, editor, *Spiritual Power and Missions: Raising the Issues*. Evangelical Missiological Society Series no. 3. Pasadena, CA: William Carey Library, 1995.

Kraft, Charles H. *Christianity with Power: Your Worldview and Your Experience of the Supernatural*. Ann Arbor, MI: Servant Books, 1989.

Kydd, Ronald. *Healing Through The Centuries: Models for Understanding*. Peabody, MA: Hendrickson Publishers, 1998.

Latourette, Kenneth Scott. *Beginnings to 1500*. Vol. 1 of 2, *A History of Christianity*. New York: Harper & Row, 1975.

Latourette, Kenneth Scott. *Reformation to the Present*. Vol. 2 of 2, *A History of Christianity*. San Francisco, CA: Harper Collins, 1975.

Law, Terry. *The Truth about Angels*. Lake Mary, FL: Charisma House, 1994.

Law, William. *An Humble, Earnest, and Affectionate Address to the Clergy*. In Vol. 9 of 9, *The Works of William Law*. Canterbury: G. Moreton, 1893.

Law, William. *The Grounds and Reasons of Christian Regeneration or, The New Birth*. London: W. Innys R., Manby and S. Cox, 1750.

Lawson, Steven. "Defeating Territorial Spirits." In C. Peter Wagner, editor, *Territorial Spirits:Insights on Strategic-Level Spiritual Warfare*. Chichester, England: Sovereign World, 1991.

Lea, Larry. *Could You Not Tarry One Hour?: Learning the Joy of Prayer*. Altamonte Springs, FL: Creation House, 1987.

Liardon, Roberts, ed. *Maria Woodworth-Etter: The Complete Collection of Her Life Teachings*. Tulsa, OK: Albury Publishing, 2000.

Lincoln, Andrew T. *Ephesians*. Vol. 42, *Word Biblical Commentary*. Edited by Bruce M. Metzger, David A. Hubbard, and Glenn W. Barker. Dallas, TX: Word Books, 1990.

Lloyd-Jones, D. Martyn. *The Christian Soldier: An Exposition of Ephesians 6:10 to 20*. Edinburgh: The Banner of Truth Trust, 1977.

Lloyd-Jones, D. Martyn. *The Christian Warfare: An Exposition of Ephesians 6:10 to 13*. Edinburgh: The Banner of Truth Trust, 1976.

Lloyd-Jones, D. Martyn. *Knowing The Times: Addresses Delivered on Various Occasions 1942-1977*. Edinburgh: The Banner of Truth Trust, 1989.

Lloyd-Jones, D. Martyn. *Romans: The Final Perseverance of the Saints, An Exposition of Chapter 8:17-39*. Edinburgh: The Banner of Truth Trust, 1975.

Lockyer, Herbert. *All the Promises of the Bible: A Unique Compilation and Exposition of Divine Promises in Scripture*. Grand Rapids, MI: Zondervan Publishing House, 1962.

Lowe, Chuck. *Territorial Spirits and World Evangelisation?: A Biblical, Historical and Missiological Critique of Strategic Level Spiritual Warfare*. Fearn and Kent: OMF and Mentor, 1998.

Luther, Martin. *Table Talk*. In vol. 54 of 54, *Luther's Works*. Philadelphia, PA: Fortress Press, 1977.

Luther, Martin. *Watchwords for the Warfare of Life*. Translated by The Author of Chronicles of the Schönberg-Cotta Family. London: T. Nelson and Sons, Paternoster Row, 1869.

Luther, Martin. *Word and Sacrament II*. In vol. 36 of 54, *Luther's Works*. Philadelphia, PA: Fortress Press, 1975.

Machen, J. Gresham. *The New Testament: An Introduction to its Literature and History.* Edinburgh: The Banner of Truth Trust, 1976.

MacLean, Donald. "Scottish Calvinism and Foreign Missions." In vol. 6, pt. 1. *Records of the Scottish Church History Society.* N.p, 1936, 12. Quoted in Iain H. Murray, *The Puritan Hope: Revival and the Interpretation of Prophecy*, 233. Edinburgh: The Banner of Truth Trust, 1971.

Peter Martyr. *Common Places.* Pt. 3. N.p., 1583, 386. Quoted in Iain H. Murray. *The Puritan Hope: Revival and the Interpretation of Prophecy.* Edinburgh: The Banner of Truth Trust, 1971, 86.

McCallum, Dennis. *The Death of Truth: Responding to Multiculturalism, the Rejection of Reason and the New Postmodern Diversity.* Minneapolis, MN: Bethany House Publishers, 1996.

McKnight, Edgar V. *Postmodern Use of the Bible: The Emergence of Reader-Oriented Criticism.* Nashville, TN: Abingdon Press, 1988, 16, 176. Quoted in Dennis McCallum, *The Death of Truth: Responding to Multiculturalism, the Rejection of Reason and the new Postmodern Diversity*, 255-56. Minneapolis, MN: Bethany House Publishers, 1996.

Miller, Donald. *Reinventing American Protestantism.* Berkeley, CA: University of California Press, 1997, 1. Quoted in C. Peter Wagner, *Churchquake,* 18. Ventura, CA: Regal Books, 1999.

Miller, Jane. *Statistics for Advanced Level.* Cambridge: Cambridge University Press, 1989.

Miller, Stephen R. *Daniel.* Vol. 18, *The New American Commentary.* Nashville, TN: Broadman and Holman, 1994, 284-85. Quoted in Clinton E. Arnold, *Spiritual Warfare: What Does the Bible Really Teach*, 246. London: Marshall Pickering, 1997.

Milman, Henry H. *History of Christianity from the Birth of Christ to the Abolition of Paganism in the Roman Empire.* London: John Murray, 1840.

Moreau, A. Scott. *Essentials of Spiritual Warfare: Equipped to Win the Battle.* Wheaton, IL: Harold Shaw Publishers, 1997.

Murphy, Edward F. *The Handbook for Spiritual Warfare.* Nashville, TN: Thomas Nelson Publishers, 1996.

Murray, Andrew. *With Christ in the School of Prayer.* North Brunswick, NJ: Bridge-Logos Publishers, 1999.

Murray, F. S. *The Sublimity of Faith: The Life and Work of Frank W. Sandford. Amherst, NH:* The Kingdom Press, 1981, 74. Quoted in D. William Faupel, *The Everlasting Gospel: The Significance of Eschatology in the Development of Pentecostal Thought*, 115. Sheffield: Sheffield Academic Press, 1996.

Murray, Iain, H. *The Fight of Faith 1939-1981.* Vol. 2 of 2, *D. Martyn Lloyd-Jones.* Edinburgh: The Banner of Truth Trust, 1990.

Murray, Iain, H. *The Forgotten Spurgeon.* 2d ed. Edinburgh: The Banner of Truth Trust, 1998.

Murray, Iain, H. *Pentecost - Today?: The Biblical Basis for Understanding Revival.* Edinburgh: The Banner of Truth Trust, 1998.

Murray, Iain, H. *The Puritan Hope: Revival and the Interpretation of Prophecy.* Edinburgh: The Banner of Truth Trust, 1971.

Murray, Iain, H. *Revival and Revivalism: The Making and Marring of American Evangelicalism.* Edinburgh: The Banner of Truth Trust, 1996.

Murray, Iain, *H. Spurgeon v. Hyper-Calvinism: The Battle for Gospel Preaching.* Edinburgh: The Banner of Truth Trust, 2000.

Murray, John. *Studies in Theology.* Vol. 4 of 4, *Collected Writings of John Murray.* Edinburgh: The Banner of Truth Trust, 1982.

Murray, John. *Systematic Theology.* Vol. 2 of 4, *Collected Writings of John Murray.* Edinburgh: The Banner of Truth Trust, 2001.

Nielsen, Niels C. Jr., et al.. *Religions of the World.* 3d ed. Edited by Robert K. C. Forman. New York, St. Martin's Press, 1993.

Nolland, John. *Luke 9:21-18:34.* Vol. 35B, *Word Biblical Commentary.* Edited by David A. Hubbard and Glenn W. Barker. Dallas, TX: Word Books, 1993.

Origen, *De Principiis.* Books 1-3. In vol. 1 of *The Writings of Origen.* In vol. 10 of 23, *Ante-Nicene Christian Library: Translations of the Writings of the Fathers; Down to A.D. 325.* Edited by Rev. Alexander Roberts and James Donaldson. Edinburgh: T. and T. Clark, 1869.

Oropeza, B. J. *Answers to Questions about Angels, Demons and Spiritual Warfare.* Eastbourne: InterVarsity Press, 1997.

Osborn, T. L. and Daisy Osborn. *Faith Library in 23 Volumes.* Tulsa, OK: OSFO International, n.d.

Osborn, T. L. *Healing the Sick: A Living Classic.* Tulsa, OK: Harrison House, 1992.

Osborn, T. L. *The Message That Works.* Tulsa, OK: OSFO Publishers, 1997.

Osteen, John. *How To Demonstrate Satan's Defeat.* Houston, TX: A John Osteen Publication, 1978.

Osteen, John. *The Truth Shall Set You Free.* Houston, TX: A John Osteen Publication, 1978.

Otis, George Jr. *Informed Intercession: Transforming Your Community Through Spiritual Mapping and Strategic Prayer.* Ventura, CA: Renew Books, 1999.

Otis, George Jr *The Last of the Giants: Lifting the Veil on Islam and the End Times.* Grand Rapids, MI: Chosen Books, 1991.

Packer, J. I. Introduction to *The Death of Death in the Death of Christ,* by John Owen. Edinburgh: The Banner of Truth Trust, 1983.

Page, Sydney H. T. *Powers of Evil: A Biblical Study of Satan and Demons.* Grand Rapids, MI: Baker Books, 1995.

Page, Sydney H. T. *Powers of Evil: A Biblical Study of Satan and Demons.* Grand Rapids, MI: Baker Books, 1995, 65. Quoted in Clinton E. Arnold, *Spiritual Warfare,* 246. London: Marshall Pickering, 1997.

Palau, Luis, and David Sanford. *God is Relevant: Finding Strength and Peace in Today's World.* New York: Doubleday, 1997.

Penn, William. Introduction to *The Journal of George Fox,* by George Fox. 3d ed. London: W. Richardson and S. Clark, 1765.

Percy, Martyn. *Power and the Church: Ecclesiology in an Age of Transition.* London: Cassell, 1998.

Peretti, Frank. *This Present Darkness.* Westchester, IL: Crossway, 1986.

Perkins, William. *The Combat Between Christ and the Divell Displayed. 2d ed.* London: Melchisedech Bradwood, 1606, 19. Quoted in Bryan G. Zacharias, *The Embattled Christian: William Gurnall and the Puritan View of Spiritual Warfare,* 101. Edinburgh: The Banner of Truth Trust, 1995.

Peskett, Howard. "God's Missionary Railway According to Stott and Wagner." *Evangelical Missions Quarterly* 32 (1996): 480-84. Quoted in Chuck Lowe, *Territorial Spirits for World Evangelisation?: A Biblical, Historical and Missiological Critique of Strategic-Level Spiritual Warfare, 145.* Fearn and Kent: OMF and Mentor, 1997.

Peter Martyr. *Common Places.* Pt. 3. N.p., 1583, 386. Quoted in Iain H. Murray, *The Puritan Hope: Revival and the Interpretation of Prophecy,* 86. Edinburgh: The Banner of Truth Trust, 1998.

Phillips, W. Gary and William E. Brown. *Making Sense of Your World.* Chicago, IL: Moody Press, 1991.

Polycarp, *The Epistle to the Philippians.* Chap. 7. In *The Apostolic Fathers. vol. 1 of 23, Ante-Nicene Christian Library: Translation of the Writings of the Fathers, Down to A.D. 325.* Edited by Rev. Alexander Roberts and James Donaldson. Edinburgh: T. and T. Clark, 1867.

Price, Charles S. *Made Alive.* Plainfield, NJ: Logos International, 1945.

Priest, Robert J., Thomas Campbell, and Bradford A. Mullen. "Missiological Syncretism: The New Animistic Paradigm," In Edward Rommen, editor, *Spiritual Power and Missions: Raising the Issues.* Evangelical Missiological Society Series. No. 3. Pasadena, CA: William Carey Library, 1995.

Psuedo-Dionysius. *The Heavenly Hierarchy and The Ecclesiastical Hierarchy.* Caputs 6; 9. In pt. 2, *The Works of Dionysius the Areopagite.* Translated by Rev. John Parker. London: James Parker and Co., 1899.

Reid, Michael S. B. *Faith: It's God Given.* Brentwood, England: Alive UK, 2000.

Reid, Michael and Judson Cornwall. *Whose Mind Is It Anyway?* Loughton, England: Sharon Publications Ltd, 1993.

Renner, Rick. *Dressed to Kill: A Biblical Approach to Spiritual Warfare and Armor.* Tulsa, OK: Pillar Books and Publishing, 1991.

Robb, John D. *Strategic Praying for Frontier Missions: Perspectives on the World Christian Movement, Study Guide.* Pasadena, CA: William Carey Library, 1997.

Roberts, Oral. *Acts-Philemon.* Vol. 2 of 3. *The New Testament Comes Alive:A Personal New Testament Commentary.* Tulsa, OK: Oral Roberts., 1984.

Roberts, Oral. *Expect a Miracle: My Life and Ministry.* Milton Keynes, England: Nelson Word, 1995.

Roberts, Richard. *The Unlimited Power Within You.* Tulsa, OK: n.p., 1986.

Rodman, William J. *Renewal Theology: Systematic Theology from a Charismatic Perspective.* Grand Rapids, MI: Zondervan Publishing House, 1996.

Rommen, Edward. Introduction to *Spiritual Power and Missions: Raising the Issues,* edited by Edward Rommen. Evangelical Missiological Society Series, no. 3. Pasadena, CA: William Carey Library, 1995.

Rowling, J. K. *Harry Potter and the Chamber of Secrets.* New York: Arthur A. Levine Books, 1998.

Rowling, J. K. *Harry Potter and the Goblet of Fire.* New York: Arthur A. Levine Books, 2000.

Rowling, J. K. *Harry Potter and the Philosopher's Stone.* New York: Arthur A. Levine Books, 1997.

Rowling, J. K. *Harry Potter and the Prisoner of Azakaban.* New York: Arthur A. Levine Books, 1999.

Russell, Jeffrey Burton. *The Devil: Perceptions of Evil from Antiquity to Primitive Christianity*. Ithaca, NY: Cornell University Press, 1977.

Russell, Jeffrey Burton. *Satan: The Early Christian Tradition*. Ithaca, NY: Cornell University Press, 1981.

Sandford, Frank W. *The Art of War for the Christian Soldier*. Amherst, NH: The Kingdom Press, 1966.

Sandford, Frank W. Inside front cover to *The Golden Light upon the Two Americas*. Amherst, NH: The Kingdom Press, 1974.

Sandford, Frank W. *Seven Years with God*. Mount Vernon, NH: The Kingdom Press, 1957.

Schurer, Emil. *The History of the Jewish People in the Age of Jesus Christ: 175 B.C. – A.D. 135, Part 2*. Vol. 3. Rev. English edition. Edited by Geza Vermes, Fergus Millar, and Martin Goodman. Edinburgh: T. and T. Clark, 1987.

Scotland, Nigel. *Charismatics and the New Millennium: The Impact of Charismatic Christianity from 1960 into the New Millennium*. Guildford, England: Eagle, 2000.

Sheets, Dutch. *Intercessory Prayer: How God Can Use Your Prayers to Move Heaven and Earth*. Ventura, CA: Regal Books, 1996.

The Shorter Oxford English Dictionary. Vol. 2 of 2. London: Guild Publishing, 1983.

Silvoso, Edgardo. "Argentina: Battleground of the Spirit." *World Christian*, Oct. 1989, 16. Quoted in C. Peter Wagner, *Warfare Prayer: Strategies for Combating the Rulers of Darkness*, 27. Crowborough, England: Monarch Publications, 1997.

Sire, James W. *The Universe Next Door: A Basic Worldview Catalog*, 3d edition. Downers Grove, IL: InterVarsity Press, 1997.

Spurgeon, Charles H. *An All-Round Ministry: Addresses to Ministers and Students*. Edinburgh: The Banner of Truth Trust, 2000.

Spurgeon, Charles H. Address on "Beaten Oil for the Light." *Sword and Trowel*. Edited by Charles H. Spurgeon. London: Passmore and Alabaster, 1892, 687. Quoted in Iain H. Murray, *Spurgeon v. Hyper-Calvinism*, 12-13. Edinburgh: The Banner of Truth Trust, 2000.

Spurgeon, Charles H. *The Greatest Fight in the World*. Belfast, Northern Ireland: Ambassador Publications, 1999.

Spurgeon, Charles H. Letter to the editor of *Messiah's Herald*, 1874. Quoted in Iain H. Murray, *The Puritan Hope: Revival and the Interpretation of Prophecy*, 263. Edinburgh: The Banner of Truth Trust, 1971.

Spurgeon, Charles H. *Power Over Satan*. New Kensington, PA: Whitaker House, 1997.

Spurgeon, Charles H. *Psalms 53-78. Vol. 3 of 7, The Treasury of David: An Expository and Devotional Commentary on the Psalms*. Grand Rapids, MI: Baker Book House, 1983.

Spurgeon, Charles H. *Psalms 111-150, Vol. 6 of 7, The Treasury of David: An Expository and Devotional Commentary on the Psalms*. Grand Rapids, MI: Baker Book House, 1983.

Spurgeon, Charles H. *2200 Quotations from the Writings of Charles H. Spurgeon*. Edited by Tom Carter. Grand Rapids, MI: Baker Books, 1988.

Spurgeon, Charles H. *Sermons Preached and Revised by C. H. Spurgeon, During the Year 1883*. Vol. 29 of 63, The Metropolitan Tabernacle Pulpit. Pasadena, TX: Pilgrim Publications, 1973.

Spurgeon, Charles H. *Sermons Preached and Revised by C. H. Spurgeon, During the Year 1885*. Vol. 31 of 63, The Metropolitan Tabernacle Pulpit. Pasadena, TX: Pilgrim Publications, 1973.

Spurgeon, Charles H. *Sermons Preached and Revised by C. H. Spurgeon, During the Year 1886*. Vol. 32 of 63, The Metropolitan Tabernacle Pulpit. Pasadena, TX: Pilgrim Publications, 1974, 429-31. Quoted in Iain H. Murray, *The Puritan Hope: Revival and the Interpretation of Prophecy*, 264-65. Edinburgh: The Banner of Truth Trust, 1971,

Spurgeon, Charles H. *Sermons Preached and Revised by C. H. Spurgeon, During the Year 1890*. Vol. 36 of 63, The Metropolitan Tabernacle Pulpit. Pasadena, TX: Pilgrim Publications, 1974, 378. Quoted in Iain H. Murray, *The Puritan Hope: Revival and the Interpretation of Prophecy*, 231. Edinburgh: The Banner of Truth Trust, 1971.

Spurgeon, Charles H. *Sermons Preached and Revised by C. H. Spurgeon, During the Year 1891*. Vol. 37 of 63, The Metropolitan Tabernacle Pulpit. Pasadena, TX: Pilgrim Publications, 1975.

Spurgeon, Charles H. *Sermons Preached and Revised by C. H. Spurgeon, During the Year 1897*. Vol. 43 of 63, The Metropolitan Tabernacle Pulpit. Pasadena, TX: Pilgrim Publications, 1976.

Spurgeon, Charles H. Sermons *Preached by C. H. Spurgeon. Revised and Published During the Year 1908*. Vol. 54 of 63, The Metropolitan Tabernacle Pulpit. Pasadena, TX: Pilgrim Publications, 1978.

Spurgeon, Charles H. *Sermons Preached by C. H. Spurgeon. Revised and Published During the Year 1914*. Vol. 60 of 63, The Metropolitan Tabernacle Pulpit. Pasadena, TX: Pilgrim Publications, 1979.

Spurgeon, Charles H. *Spurgeon's Expository Encyclopedia*. Vol. 12 of 15. Grand Rapids, MI: Baker Book House, 1978.

Spurgeon, Charles H. *Spurgeon on Prayer and Spiritual Warfare*. New Kensington, PA: Whitaker House, 1998.

"Statement on Spiritual Warfare: The Intercession Working Group Report, Lausanne Committee on World Evangelization," *Urban Mission* 13, no. 2 (1995): 52. Quoted in Clinton E. Arnold, *Spiritual Warfare: What Does the Bible Really Teach*, 182. London: Marshall Pickering, 1997.

Sterk, Vernon J. "Territorial Spirits and Evangelization in Hostile Environments," unpublished research paper written for Fuller School of World Mission, Pasadena, CA, 1989. Quoted in C. Peter Wagner, editor, *Territorial Spirits: Insights on Strategic-Level Spiritual Warfare from Nineteen Christian Leaders*. Chichester, England: Sovereign World, 1991, 153-54. Quoted in Mike R. Taylor, *Do Demons Rule Your Town?: An Examination of the 'Territorial Spirits' Theory*, 59. London: Grace Publications Trust, 1993.

Strong, James H. *Strong's Exhaustive Concordance*. Grand Rapids, MI: Baker Book House, 1987.

Sproul, R. C. A press release about *God is Relevant: Finding Strength and Peace in Today's World*, by Luis Palau and David Sanford. New York: Doubleday, 1997. Quoted in Elmer Towns and Warren Bird, *Into The Future: Turning Today's Church Trends into Tomorrow's Opportunities*, 65. Grand Rapids, MI: Fleming H. Revell, 2000.

Synan, Vinson. *The Century of the Holy Spirit: 100 Years of Pentecostal and Charismatic Renewal.* Nashville, TN: Thomas Nelson Publishers, 2001.

Tavard, George H. *Holy Writ or Holy Church: The Crisis of the Protestant Reformation.* New York: Harper and Row, 1959, 16. Quoted in Alan F. Johnson and Robert E. Webber, *What Christians Believe: A Biblical and Historical Summary*, 96. Grand Rapids, MI: Zondervan Publishing House, 1989.

Taylor, Mike R. *Do Demons Rule Your Town?: An Examination of the 'Territorial Spirits' Theory.* London: Grace Publications Trust, 1993.

Tertullian. *Contra Marcion.* Bk. 2, chap. 10. In vol. 1, *The Writings of Tertullian.* In vol. 11 of 23, *Ante-Nicene Christian Library: Translations of the Writings of the Fathers; Down to A.D. 325.* Edited by Rev. Alexander Roberts and James Donaldson. Edinburgh: T. and T. Clark, 1869.

Tertullian. *Apologeticus.* In vol. 1, *The Writings of Tertullian.* In vol. 11 of 23, *Ante-Nicene Christian Library: Translations of the Writings of the Fathers, Down to A.D. 325.* Edited by Rev. Alexander Roberts and James Donaldson. Edinburgh: T. and T. Clark, 1869.

Thiselton, Anthony. *Interpreting God and the Postmodern Self: On Meaning, Manipulation and Promise.* Edinburgh: T. and T. Clark, 1995, 81-85. Quoted in Martyn Percy, *Power and the Church: Ecclesiology in an Age of Transition*, 184. London: Cassell, 1998.

Towns, Elmer and Warren Bird. *Into The Future: Turning Today's Church Trends into Tomorrow's Opportunities.* Grand Rapids, MI: Fleming H. Revell, 2000.

Tozer, A. W. *Born After Midnight.* Camp Hill, PA: Christian Publications, 1989.

Unger, Merrill F. *Biblical Demonology.* Wheaton, IL: Scripture Press, 1952.

Unger, Merrill F. *Unger's Bible Dictionary.* Chicago, IL: Moody Press, 1960.

Veith, Gene Edward Jr. *Postmodern Times: A Christian Guide to Contemporary Thought and Culture.* Wheaton, IL: Crossway Books, 1994.

Wagner, C. Peter. *Churchquake.* Ventura, CA: Regal Books, 1999.

Wagner, C. Peter. *Confronting the Powers: How the New Testament Church Experienced the Power of Strategic-Level Spiritual Warfare.* Ventura, CA: Regal Books, 1996.

Wagner, C. Peter. *Engaging the Enemy: How to Fight and Defeat Territorial Spirits.* Ventura, CA: Regal Books, 1991.

Wagner, C. Peter. "MC510: Genesis of a Concept." In C. Peter Wagner, editor, *Signs and Wonders Today.* Altamonte Springs, FL: Creation House, 1987.

Wagner, C. Peter. *On the Cutting Edge of Mission Strategy: Perspectives on the World Christian Movement, A Reader.* Rev. ed. Pasadena, CA: William Carey Library, 1992.

Wagner, C. Peter. "The Philosophy of Prayer for World Evangelization Adopted by the A. D. 2000 United Prayer Track." In C. Peter Wagner, *Confronting the Powers: How the New Testament Church Experienced the Power of Strategic-Level Spiritual Warfare*, 254. Ventura, CA: Regal Books, 1996.

Wagner, C. Peter. *Praying with Power: How to Pray Effectively and Hear Clearly from God.* Ventura, CA: Regal Books, 1997.

Wagner, C. Peter. "Territorial Spirits." In C. Peter Wagner and F. Douglas Pennoyer, editors, *Wrestling with Dark Angels: Toward a Deeper Understanding of the Supernatural Forces in Spiritual Warfare*, 49-72. Ventura, CA: Regal Books, 1990.

Wagner, C. Peter. *The Third Wave of the Holy Spirit: Encountering the Power of Signs and Wonders.* Ann Arbor, MI: Vine Books, 1988.

Wagner, C. Peter. *Warfare Prayer: Strategies for Combating the Rulers of Darkness.* Crowborough, England: Monarch Publications, 1997.

Wagner, C. Peter, ed. *Breaking Strongholds in Your City: How to Use Spiritual Mapping to Make Your Prayers More Strategic, Effective and Targeted.* Ventura, CA: Regal Books, 1993.

Wagner, C. Peter, and F. Douglas Pennoyer, eds. *Wrestling with Dark Angels: Toward a Deeper Understanding of the Supernatural Forces in Spiritual Warfare,* 49-72. Ventura, CA: Regal Books, 1990.

Watson, Thomas. *The Golden Treasury of Puritan Quotations.* Chicago, IL: Moody Press, 1975.

Watts, John D. W. *Isaiah 1-33.* Vol. 24, *Word Biblical Commentary.* Edited by David A. Hubbard and Glenn W. Barker. Waco, TX: Word Books, 1985.

Wesley, John. "Letter 43: To Mr John Smith." In *Letters from the Reverend John Wesley to Various Persons.* In vol. 12 of 14, *The Works of the Rev. John Wesley, A.M.* 11th edition, with the last corrections of the author. London: John Mason, 1856.

Wesley, John. "Sermon 45: The New Birth." In *Sermons on Several Occasions.* In vol. 6 of 14, *The Works of John Wesley.* With the last corrections of the author. London: Methodist Publishing House, 1865.

Wesley, John. "Sermon 66: The Signs of the Times." *Sermons on Several Occasions.* In vol. 6 of 14, *The Works of John Wesley.* With the last corrections of the author. London: Wesleyan Conference Office, 1865.

White, Thomas B. *The Believer's Guide to Spiritual Warfare.* Ann Arbor, MI: Vine Books, 1990.

Wigglesworth, Smith. *Smith Wigglesworth on Healing.* New Kensington, PA: Whitaker House, 1999.

Williams, William. *Charles Haddon Spurgeon: Personal Reminiscences.* London: The Religious Tract Society, 1895, 138. Quoted by Iain H. Murray, Introduction to *An All-Round Ministry: Addresses to Ministers and Students* by Charles H. Spurgeon. Edinburgh: Banner of Truth Trust, 2000.

Wimber, John. *Power Evangelism.* San Francisco, CA: Harper and Row, 1986.

Wimber, John and Kevin Springer. *The Dynamics of Spiritual Growth.* London: Hodder and Stoughton, 1990.

Wink, Walter. *Unmasking the Powers: The Invisible Forces that Determine Human Existence.* Philadelphia, PA.: Fortress Press, 1986, 88. Quoted in C. Peter Wagner, *Warfare Prayer: Strategies for Combating the Rulers of Darkness,* 95. Crowborough, England. Monarch Publications, 1997.

Woodworth-Etter, Maria, B. *Signs and Wonders God Wrought in the Ministry for Forty Years.* Indianapolis, IN: The Author, 1916, 534-35. Quoted in D. William Faupel, *The Everlasting Gospel: The Significance of Eschatology in the Development of Pentecostal Thought,* 39. Sheffield: Sheffield Academic Press, 1996.

Zacharias, Bryan G. *The Embattled Christian: William Gurnall and the Puritan View of Spiritual Warfare.* Edinburgh: The Banner of Truth Trust, 1995.

Periodicals

"Complete League Tables of GCSE and A-Level Results for England." *The Times School Report* (London, 22 Nov. 2001), p. 11.

Butcher, Catherine and Mark Stibbe. "Harry Potter: Friend or Foe?" *Christianity and Renewal*, Dec. 2001, 19-22.

Garvey, Jon. "Manhattan and the Book of Revelation." *Prophecy Today*, Dec. 2001, 10-11.

Hartman, V. F. "Teaching and Learning Style Preferences: Transitions Through Technology." *VCAA Journal* 9, no. 2 (1995): 18-20.

Hiebert, Paul G. "The Flaw of the Excluded Middle." *Missiology: An International Review* 10, no. 1 (Jan. 1982).

Hill, Clifford. "Moses Is Dead!" Editorial to *Prophecy Today*, Dec. 2001, 4-7.

O'Donnell, John. "Theology of the Holy Spirit, I: Jesus and the Spirit." *The Way* 23 (1983): 48.

Reynolds, Robert. "Is There Spiritual War?" *Moody*, July/Aug. 1997, 15-17.

Smith, Scott. "Middle Earth." *Reader's Digest*, Dec. 2001, 94-96.

Online Sources

"Archiv fur Literatur und Kirchengeschichte des Mittelalters," Berlin, Germany: H. Denifle, 1886. Quoted in *Catholic Encyclopedia*, s.v. "Mysticism." Online posting. http://www.newadvent.org/cathen/10663b.htm. Accessed 7 May 2001.

Boyd, Greg. "Spiritual Warfare: Free Will and the Legacy of Augustine." Online posting. http://www.eternalwarriors.com/lesson1.html. Accessed 22 Aug. 2001.

Butcher, Andy. "Strange Encounters With Another World." *Charisma*, Apr. 2001, 52. Online posting. http://www.alienresistance.org/ce4casefiles.htm. Accessed 7 Jan. 2002.

Calvin, John. "On Prayer." Online posting. http://www.ccel.org/pager.cgi?file=c/calvin/prayer/prayer1.0.html&from=RTFTo/prayer.htm. Accessed 14 Feb. 2001.

The Catholic Encyclopedia, s.v. "Demonology," by W. H. Kent. Online posting. http://newadvent.org/cathen/04713a.htm. Accessed 5 June 2001.

The Catholic Encyclopedia S.v. "Exorcism," by P. J. Toner. Online posting. http://www.newadvent.org/cathen/05809a.htm. Accessed 17 July 2001.

Chambers, Sandra. "Storming the Capital with Prayer." *Charisma*, May 2001. http://www.charismamag.com/online/articledisplay.pl?ArticleID=1038. Accessed 21 Aug. 2001.

Clark, Jonas. "Spiritual Warfare." *The Ambassador Journal Cyber Newsletter*. Online posting. http://catchlife.org/spiritual_warfare.html. Accessed 16 Dec. 2001.

Dager, Albert James. "The World Christian Movement: Evangelism vs Evangelization." *Media Spotlight: A Biblical Analysis of Religious and Secular Media* 22, no. 1 (April 1999): 16. Online posting. http://www.banner.org.uk/globalism/WCM1.html. Accessed 3 Oct. 2001.

"Defeating Territorial Spirits: Battles Against Evil Spiritual Forces Controlling Our Cities Can Be Waged and Won." *Charisma*, Apr. 1990. Quoted in Valley Bible Church, *Spiritual Warfare*. Online posting. http://www.valleybible.net/resources/PositionPapers/SpiritualWarfare.shtml. Accessed 7 Jan. 2002.

Deussen, Paul. "Jakob Böhme:Über sein Leben und seine Philosophie." Kiel,Germany, 1897. Quoted in *Catholic Encyclopedia*, s.v. "Mysticism," by George M. Sauvage. Online posting. http://www.newadvent.org/cathen /10663b.htm. Accessed 7 May 2001.

Dooley, Tara. "Battle of Good and Evil." Online posting. http://www.star-telegram.com/news/doc/1047/1:RELIGION13/1:RELIGION130320100.html. Accessed 20 May 2001.

Ellerbe, Helen. "The Witch Hunts: The End of Magic and Miracles 1450-1750 C. E." Online posting. http://www.positiveatheism.org/hist/ellerbe1.htm. Accessed 17 July 2001.

Flynn, James. Review of *Anthropology for Christian Witness*, by Charles Kraft. Maryknoll, New York: Orbis. 1997. Online posting. http://www.amazon.com/exec/obidos/ASIN/1570750858/ref=ase_.../102-5213116-639852. Accessed 9 May 2001.

Garrett, Tim. "Faith and Reason: Friends or Foes?" Online posting. http://www.probe.org/docs/faithrea.html. Accessed 27 Oct. 2001.

Global Harvest Ministries. "The 40/70 Window Prayer Initiative." Online posting. http://www.globalharvestministries.org/home.qry?ID=204. Accessed 27 Sept. 01.

Global Prayer Covering. "Prayerwatch." Online posting. http://www.prayerwatch. org/penetrating.html. Accessed 17 Dec. 2001.

Hart, John F. "The Gospel and Spiritual Warfare: A review of Peter Wagner's Confronting the Powers." *Journal of the Grace Evangelical Society* 10, no. 18 (Spring 1997). Online posting. http://www.faithalone.org/journal/1997i/Hart.html. Accessed 11 Oct. 2001.

Hiebert, Paul G. "Spiritual Warfare and Worldviews." Online posting. http://www.missiology.org/ems/bulletins/hiebert.html. Accessed 9 May 2001.

Hiebert, Paul G. *De-theologizing Missiology: A Response*." *Trinity World Forum* 19 (Fall 1993): 4. Quoted in Gailyn Van Rheenen. "The Theological Foundations of Missiology." *Monthly Missiological Reflection* 20 (Aug. 2001). Online posting. http://www.missiology.org/MMR/mmr20.htm. Accessed 14 Nov. 2001.

Ilnisky, Esther and Mary Tome. "Esther Network International Children's Global Prayer." May 2000. Online posting. http://www.ad2000.org/re01205.htm. Accessed 15 Oct. 2001.

John G. Lake Ministries. "Statement of Faith: The Ministry Mandate of the International Apostolic Council." Online posting. http://www.jglm.org/statement_of_faith.htm. Accessed 17 Dec. 2001.

"The Kolb Learning Cycle." The College of St. Scholastica, Duluth, Minnesota. Online posting. http://www.css.edu/users/dswenson/web/PAGEMILL/Kolb.htm. Accessed 1 Mar. 2002.

Kraft, Marguerite. "Spiritual Conflict and the Mission of the Church: Contextualisation." Paper presented at Lausanne Committee for World Evangelization: "Deliver Us from Evil" Consultation, 21 August 2000, Nairobi, Kenya. Online posting. http://www.gospelcom.net/lcwe/dufe/index.html. Accessed 20 May 2001.

"Lausanne 1993 Statement on Spiritual Warfare." Online posting. http://www.gospelcom.net/lcwe/statements/spwar.html. Accessed 31 July 2001.

Lowe, Chuck. "Do Demons Have Zip Codes?" *Christianity Today,* July 1998, 57. Online posting, http://www.christianitytoday.com/ct/8t8/8t8057.html. Accessed 21 Aug. 2001.

MacArthur, John F., Jr. "What is True Spirituality?" Pt. 11, *Charismatic Chaos.* Online posting. http://www.biblebb.com/files/MAC/CHAOS11.HTM. Accessed 14 Dec. 2001.

Moore, Art. "Spiritual Mapping Gains Credibility Among Leaders." *Christianity Today,* Jan. 1998, 55. Online posting. http://www.christianitytoday.com/ct/8t1/8t1/055.html. Accessed 21 Aug. 2001.

Moreau, A. Scott. "Gaining Perspective on Territorial Spirits" from the Lausanne Committee for World Evangelization. Online posting. http://www.gospelcom.net/lcwe/dufe/Papers/terspir.htm. Accessed 29 June 2001

Murray, Iain H. Quoted in Stephen Sizer, "The 'Toronto Blessing': A Theological Examination of the Roots, Teaching and Manifestations, and Connection Between the Faith Movement and the Vineyard Church." Online posting. http://www.gospelcom. net/apologeticsindex/sva-tb01.html. Accessed 21 May 2001.

National Council of the Churches of Christ in the U.S.A. "NCCCUSA Hails Courage of Pavle's July 4 Call for Repentance." Online posting. http://www.ncccusa.org/news/99news77.html. Accessed 20 Nov. 2001.

Neff, David. "The Future of Missions?" *Christianity Today.* 1 Nov. 1999. Online posting. http://www.christianitytoday.com/ct/1999/144/12.0.html. Accessed 21 Aug. 2001.

The Observatory. Global Harvest Ministries. "How to Submit Spiritual Mapping Data." Online posting. http://www.globalharvestministries.org/home.qry?ID=446. Accessed 27 Sept. 2001.

Pink, Arthur W. "Another Gospel." Online posting. http://users,aol.com/libcfl/another.htm. Accessed 18 Dec. 2001.

Pray Twin Cities. "How to be a Lighthouse of Prayer." Online posting. http://www.praytwincities.org/howtobea.htm. Accessed 21 Nov. 2001.

"Seven Principles of Good Practice in Undergraduate Education." Online posting. http://www.byu.edu/fc/pages/tchlrnpages/7princip.htm. Accessed 1 Mar. 2002.

Ted Olsen, ed. "Battle Brews Over Warfare Language (Or: Mission Minded Groups Attempt to Heal Each Others' Vocabularies)." *Colorado Springs Gazette.* 19 Aug. 2000. Online posting. http://www.christianitytoday.com/ct/2000/138/42.0.html. Accessed 21 Aug. 2001.

The News and Observer Publishing Co. "Hiroshima mayor to give Japan war apology." Online posting. http://archive.nandotimes.com/newsroom/nt/805abomb8.html. Accessed 11 Oct. 2001.

Tillin, Tricia. "The Lighthouse Movement." Online posting. http://www.banner.org.uk /res/theglory9.html. Accessed 23 Aug. 2001.

Veith, Gene Edward Jr. "Whatever happened to Christian publishing?" Online posting. http://www.worldmag.com/world/issue/07-12-97/cover_1.asp. Accessed 21 Aug. 2001.

Wagner, C. Peter. *On the Cutting Edge of Mission Strategy: Perspectives on the World Christian Movement, A Reader.* Rev. edition. Pasadena, CA: William Carey Library, 1992), 45-46. Quoted in Albert James Dager, "The World Christian Movement:

Evangelism vs Evangelization," *Media Spotlight: A Biblical Analysis of Religious and Secular Media* 22, no. 1 (April 1999): 16. Online posting. http://www.banner.org.uk/globalism/WCM1.html. Accessed 3 Oct. 2001.

Wagner, C. Peter. "The Power to Heal the Past." Online posting. http://www.pastornet.net.au/renewal/journal8/8d-wagnr.html. Accessed 11 Oct. 2001.

Wagner, C. Peter. "The 40/70 Window Prayer Initiative: A New Directive of Prayer." Online posting. http://www.globalharvestministries.org/home.qry?ID=204. Accessed 27 Sept. 2001.

Wakely, Mike. "A Critical Look at a New 'Key' to Evangelisation." *Evangelical Missions Quarterly* 31, no. 2 (Apr. 1995): 152. Online posting. http://www.wheaton.edu/bgc/EMIS/1995/newkey.htm. Accessed 9 Sept. 2001.

White, Thomas B. *Breaking Strongholds: How Spiritual Warfare Sets Captives Free*. Ann Arbor, MI: Vine Books, 1992, 141-42. Quoted in A. Scott Moreau, "Gaining Perspective on Territorial Spirits." Paper presented at Lausanne Committee for World Evangelization, "Deliver Us From Evil" Consultation, Nairobi, Kenya, 22 Aug. 2000. Online posting. http://www.gospelcom.net/lcwe/dufe/Papers/terspir.htm. Accessed 21 Sept. 2001.

Wigglesworth, Smith. "God's Word: Antidote to Evil." Cry of the Spirit: Unpublished Sermons of Smith Wigglesworth. Edited by Roberts Liardon. Online posting. http://bornagain.port5.com/wigglesworth3.htm. Accessed 17 July 2001.

Wilkerson, David. "The Towers Have Fallen, But We Missed the Message." Online posting. http://www.worldchallenge.org/first.htm. Accessed 3 Jan. 2002.

"Winning the Battle for Your Neighbourhood: How You Can Drive Away the Demon Forces Now Dominating the Streets Where You Live," *Charisma*, Apr. 1990. Quoted in Valley Bible Church, *Spiritual Warfare*. Online posting. http://www.valleybible.net/resources/PositionPapers/SpiritualWarfare.shtml. Accessed 7 Jan. 2002.

Yung, Hwa. "Some Issues in a Systematic Theology that Takes Seriously the Demonic." Paper presented at Lausanne Committee for World Evangelization: "Deliver Us from Evil" Consultation, 17 Aug. 2000, Nairobi, Kenya. Online posting. http://www.gospelcom.net/lcwe/dufe/Papers/HYung.htm. Accessed 29 June 2001.

Other Sources

Allison, Lonnie J. Director, Billy Graham Center. Open discussion. The Inaugural Billy Graham Evangelism Roundtable, Wheaton College, Chicago, Illinois, 19 Jan. 2001.

Brierley, Peter. "Peniel Pentecostal Church Congregational Attitudes and Beliefs Survey." *Christian Research Report*. N.p., Nov. 2001.

Clarke, Adam. *Adam Clarke's Commentary*. In *PC Study Bible: Complete Reference Library* Ver. 3.0 [CD ROM]. Seattle, WA: Biblesoft 1992-1999.

Clarke, Adam. *Matthew-Luke*. Vol. 5A, *Clarke's Commentary on the New Testament*. In *Quick Verse*. Ver. 7. Disk 2 [CD-ROM] (Omaha, NE: Parsons Technology, 1997).

Deakin, Ruth. "Christian Perspectives and Values in the Classroom, Session One." Class lecture notes, M.A. in Christian Education, Cheltenham College of Higher Education, Cheltenham, England. Feb. 1998.

Floyd, W. E. G. *Clement of Alexandria's Treatment of the Problem of Evil.* London: Oxford University Press, 1971, 99. Quoted in Conrad E. Smith, "Spiritual Warfare: An Analysis of Modern Trends Based on Historical Research and Biblical Exegesis," 23. M.A. diss. Capital Bible Seminary, Lanham, Maryland, 1994.

Garrard, David, J. "Contemporary Issues in Mission." Class lecture notes, M.A. in Missiology, Mattersey Hall, England, Spring 2001.

Global Gospel Fellowship Handbook (n.p., 2001), 5.

Gokey, Francis X. *The Terminology for the Devil and Evil Spirits in the Apostolic Fathers.* Washington, DC: The Catholic University Press, 1961, 19. Quoted in Conrad E. Smith, "Spiritual Warfare: An Analysis of Modern Trends Based on Historical Research and Biblical Exegesis," 15. M.A. diss., Capital Bible Seminary, Lanham, Maryland, 1994.

Hiss, William C. "Shiloh: Frank W. Sandford and the Kingdom 1893-1948." Ph.D. diss., Tufts University, Boston, Massachusetts, Apr. 1978.

The International Standard Bible Encylopaedia (ISBE). In *PC Study Bible: Complete Reference Library* Ver. 3.0 [CD ROM]. Seattle, WA: Biblesoft 1992-1999.

Irenaeus. *Against Heresies.* Introductory Note. In *The Master Christian Library* Ver. 7.0. Disk 2. [CD-ROM] Rio, WI: Age Software Inc., 1999.

Lawless, Charles E. "A Response to Dr. Charles Lowe Regarding 'Prayer, Evangelization and Spiritual Warfare.'" Paper presented at the Inaugural Billy Graham Center Evangelism Round Table, Billy Graham Center, Wheaton College, Wheaton, Illinois, 19 Jan. 2001.

Lowe, Chuck. "Defeating Demons: A Critique of Strategic-Level Spiritual Warfare." TMs (diskette). N.p: n.d.

Lowe, Chuck. Interview by author. Documented by personal notes. Wheaton College, Wheaton, Illinois, 19 Jan. 2001.

Lowe, Chuck. "Prayer, Evangelization and Spiritual Warfare." Paper presented at the Inaugural Billy Graham Center Evangelism Round Table, Billy Graham Center, Wheaton College, Wheaton, Illinois, 19 Jan. 2001.

MacArthur, John, Jr. *2 Timothy.* In *MacArthur's New Testament Commentary.* Chicago, IL: Moody Bible Institute, 1995. In *QuickVerse* Ver. 7 [CD-ROM] Omaha, NE: Parsons Technology, 1997.

MacArthur, John, Jr. *Colossians and Philemon.* In *MacArthur's New Testament Commentary.* Chicago, IL: Moody Bible Institute, 1995. In *QuickVerse* Ver. 7 [CD-ROM] Omaha, NE: Parsons Technology, 1997.

Matthews, Steve "Building Upon 'Missiological Syncretism: A New Animistic Paradigm.' An Empirical Study of the 'Spiritual Warfare Movement.'" M.A. diss., Columbia Biblical Seminary and Graduate School of Missions, Columbia, South Carolina, 1999.

Nelson's Bible Dictionary. In *PC Study Bible: Complete Reference Library* Ver. 3.0 [CD ROM]. Seattle, WA: Biblesoft 1992-1999.

New Unger's Bible Dictionary. In PC *Study Bible: Complete Reference Library* Ver. 3.0 [CD ROM]. Seattle, WA: Biblesoft 1992-1999.

Osborn, T. L. and Daisy Osborn. *Java Harvest: A Docu-Miracle Film*. Produced by OSFO International World Missionary Church, 1990. Videocassette.

Otis, George Jr. *Transformations: A Documentary*. Produced by Global Net Productions. 58 min. The Sentinel Group, 1999. Videocassette.

Pink, Arthur W. "The Divine Inspiration of the Bible." In *Books for the Ages*. Ver. 1 [CD-ROM] Albany, OR: Ages Software, 1997.

Russell, Jeffrey Burton. *The Devil: Perceptions of Evil from Antiquity to Primitive Christianity*. Ithaca: Cornell University Press, 1977, 185. Quoted in Conrad E, Smith. "Spiritual Warfare: An Analysis of Modern Trends Based on Historical Research and Biblical Exegesis," 8. M.A. diss. Capital Bible Seminary, Lanham, Maryland, 1994.

Schurer, Emil. *The History of the Jewish People in the Time of Jesus Christ*. Div. 2, vol. 2, p. 28. Quoted in *New Unger's Bible Dictionary*. In *PC Study Bible: Complete Reference Library* Ver. 3.0 [CD ROM]. Seattle, WA: Biblesoft 1992-1999.

Smith, Conrad E. "Spiritual Warfare: An Analysis of Modern Trends Based on Historical Research and Biblical Exegesis." M.A. diss., Capital Bible Seminary, Lanham, Maryland, 1994.

Sullivan, Glenn. "The Development of a Learning Style Measure for the Drake P3 Assessment System." TMs (photocopy), p. 3. Pacific Graduate School of Psychology, Palo Alto, California, n.d.

Wagner, C. Peter. "Practical Holiness." A sermon presented at Oral Roberts University Students' Chapel, Tulsa, Oklahoma, 16 Jan. 2001.

INDEX

Names

Scripture

Subject

A Visit That Will Change Your Life

Peniel Church - A Church where healing and miracles happen today. Come and see what God can do for you!

Regular Meetings:

Every Tuesday & Friday at 7.30pm, Sundays at 10.00am where Bishop Michael Reid ministers and prays for the sick

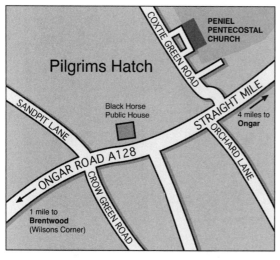

M25: Exit 28. Take A1023 to Brentwood. Continue along High St to double roundabout (Wilson's Corner). Turn left, then follow map

A12: Leave at M25 junction. Then as above.

A127: Leave at A128 junction. Take A128 to Brentwood. Continue to double roundabout (Wilson's Corner). Go straight on, then follow map.

A13: Take A128 to Brentwood, then as above.

Peniel Church, 49 Coxtie Green Road, Pilgrims Hatch, Brentwood, Essex, CM14 5PS, England

Tel: +44 (0)1277 372996 Fax +44 (0)1277 375046

www.peniel.org

The Global Gospel Fellowship

The Global Gospel Fellowship reaches out to every continent and nation to create a forum for leaders of Christian churches and fellowships to share teaching and ongoing education; receive the wisdom of fathers in the faith; obtain encouragement from fellow ministers; achieve ordination and fulfil the challenge of spreading the Gospel of Jesus Christ to all people throughout the world.

"Fostering Christian Fellowship Worldwide"

For more information regarding membership and annual conference details, please contact:

+44(0)1277 376246

or visit our website :

www.tggf.org

Peniel College Of Higher Education

Peniel College of Higher Education was founded as a result of a unique affiliation agreement with Oral Roberts University, making it the only campus in the United Kingdom authorised by ORU and the North Central Accrediting Association to offer ORU degree courses.

At PCHE we believe that practical Biblical study will equip and prepare you for ministry and mission, but more importantly for life. Our courses are therefore open to people from all walks of life who share the common purpose of impacting their individual worlds with the dynamic message of the gospel.

Students at PCHE study in a Christian atmosphere. Our resident faculty are mature Christian scholars who have proved the miracle power of Christ in every aspect of their lives. They will share their expertise in ministry, education and professional life.

We challenge students to reach their full potential in the areas of spirit, mind and body. We encourage success in their careers, their communities and their family life, founded on the Holy Spirit and sustained by a steadfast reliance on Christian principles.

A graduate from Peniel College of Higher Education will not only be equipped with academic qualifications but with a clear work ethic, a sense of responsibility and purpose and an unwavering adherence to Christian truths in all areas of life.

If you have been thinking of studying for a really worthwhile degree, either to prepare for some form of Christian ministry or as an individual Christian interested in developing yourself academically and spiritually, this is the College for you.

Fully accredited degree courses are available on a full or part-time basis.

For a free brochure or more information about PCHE courses:

Call:	+44 (0)1277 372996
Fax:	+44 (0)1277 375332
Email:	pche@peniel.org
Website:	www.pche.ac.uk

Faith It's God Given

This book, packed with Dynamic Illustrations and Truths of Scripture, is written for those who are sick of the false "faith emphasis that condemns and sixcourages, and will realign your thinking to the true Biblical faith in Christ, which is but one, *"Jesus the author and finisher of our faith,"*(Heb 12;2).

The ispired Simplicity of Bishop Reid's message brings a new hope and understanding as he urges his readers to abandon their understanding and accept that **GOD ALONE CAN DO IT**

AUTHOR'S BACKGROUND

Michael Stafford Baynes Reid was born on 15 May 1943 in Beckenham, Kent, England, the second son of John and Ann Reid. He began his education at Canterbury House Primary School in Westgate-on-Sea, Kent, but following his father's death in 1951 was sent to board at the Royal Masonic School in Bushey, Hertfordshire, where he remained until he finished his schooling at eighteen years of age.

Michael's first job was in local government, studying for the Royal Institute of Chartered Surveyor's examinations in estate management. He then moved to a more challenging career with the Metropolitan Police College at Hendon, London, where he "passed out" top of his class. It was in 1965, as a policeman stationed in Mayfair and Soho (the West End of London), that he was led to the Lord and the baptism of the Holy Spirit through Demos Shakarian of the Full Gospel Businessmen's Fellowship International (FGBFI). Michael was subsequently to become Secretary to the Chapter of the FGBFI in England.

After his conversion, he left the police force to work in a centre for drug addicts and alcoholics in Chigwell, Essex, then spent one year studying English and Youth Leadership at C. F. Mott Teacher's Training College, Prescott, Lancashire. He later took up a career in sales, during which time he became a Fellow and Life Member of the Life Insurance Association. Even today he remains a member of the Institute of Sales and Marketing Management.

In 1970, Michael married Barbara (Ruth) Macartney, daughter of an Anglican vicar who ministered in Uganda over a period of thirty-four years. They have three children, Rachel, Matthew and Sarah, and two grandchildren.

In 1976, the couple founded Peniel Church (then Ongar Christian Fellowship) and Peniel Academy, a day school for church members' children, from crèche age to eighteen years, was opened in 1982.

A deep friendship with Archbishop Benson Idahosa (Church of God International, Benin, Nigeria) was formed in 1986 and they travelled extensively and ministered in many countries together until the Archbishop's death in 1998. During this time, Michael was appointed as Director of Idahosa World Outreach for Europe and awarded an Honorary Doctorate for his work in worldwide evangelism by All Nations for Christ Bible Institute. It was Archbishop Idahosa who introduced Michael to Oral Roberts University, where he earned a Master of Arts in Practical Theology in 1998 and a Doctorate of Ministry in 2002. The year 1998 also saw the affiliation of Peniel College of Higher Education with Oral Roberts University.

In 2000, through the inspiration and encouragement of his friend, Dr. T. L. Osborn, Michael founded the Global Gospel Fellowship, a network of international miracle ministries drawn from the contacts that had been established from his ministry in over thirty nations.

His many ministerial positions also include: Associate Regent of Oral Roberts University, Trustee of International Charismatic Bible Ministries, President of Global Gospel Fellowship, and Bishop of the College of Bishops, International Communion of Charismatic Churches. He is the author of six books.